VIRTUAL MURDOCH

This book is to b

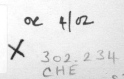

VIRTUAL MURDOCH

Reality Wars on the Information Highway

Neil Chenoweth

Secker & Warburg
London

000637912 90010

Published by Secker & Warburg 2001

2 4 6 8 10 9 7 5 3 1

First published in Great Britain in 2001 by
Secker & Warburg
Random House, 20 Vauxhall Bridge Road,
London SW1V 2SA

Random House Australia (Pty) Limited
20 Alfred Street, Milsons Point, Sydney,
New South Wales 2061, Australia

Random House New Zealand Limited
18 Poland Road, Glenfield,
Auckland 10, New Zealand

Random House South Africa (Pty) Limited
Endulini, 5A Jubilee Road, Parktown 2193, South Africa

The Random House Group Limited Reg. No. 954009
www.randomhouse.co.uk

A CIP catalogue record for this book is available from the British Library

ISBN 0 436 23389 4

Papers used by Random House are natural,
recyclable products made from wood grown in sustainable forests;
the manufacturing processes conform to the environmental
regulations of the country of origin

Typeset by SX Composing DTP, Rayleigh, Essex
Printed and bound in Great Britain by
Clays Ltd, St Ives PLC

For Joe . . . slayer of dragons, part-time visionary,
fairest of travelling companions

ACKNOWLEDGEMENTS

I am deeply indebted to my New York agent, John F. Thornton, who trudged through four years of turgid correspondence from me while retaining his sense of humour, as the structure of *Virtual Murdoch* evolved through a range of implausible gymnastic positions to reach its present form. I'm also indebted to his partner, Joe Spieler; to my London agent, Abner Stein, and his staff; my publisher, Geoffrey Mulligan; and copy editor Louise Thurtell.

This book could not have been written without the generous support and encouragement of my Editor at the *Australian Financial Review*, Colleen Ryan, and publisher, Michael Gill. I am particularly grateful for assistance from my colleague Dimity Torbett, from Associate Professor Deirdre Coleman, Richard Coleman, Ali Cromie, John Davidson, Alan Deans, Valentina Hazell, Sylvia Howarth, Deborah Light, Karen Maley and Trevor Sykes.

Virtual Murdoch draws heavily from my published work for the *Australian Financial Review* over the last eight years. However the forensic process is a wide one. By its nature, it builds upon the previous efforts of many other journalists and writers, not all of whose contributions can be acknowledged. To those writers whose work, whether for reasons of space, time or my own lapses, I have not been able to properly recognise, please accept my apologies. The failure is entirely mine.

For time out of mind while this book has spluttered into existence, Joëlle Chenoweth has argued with me, laughed with me, and most often covered for me. Despite all this, she still seems to like me.

CONTENTS

INTRODUCTION

March 2001

When a major corporate merger is about to go down, it's critical not just that the deal is done, but that it be seen to be done. So in early 2001, when Jack Smith and Rupert Murdoch were in the final approach glide on a deal that would change the future of world media, the big question was how it would appear. The result was a marvel of the spin doctors' art. For months, each twist in the negotiations between Jack Smith, the chief executive of General Motors, and Rupert Murdoch's media empire, the News Corporation – the times and dates of meetings, the changing cast of characters, who was present and what they said – had been carefully leaked to approved journalists around the world. The spinners' work was a line of small, perfectly formed stories across three continents, a trail of eye candy designed to assure investors, bankers and analysts that everything in this perfect deal was on track. In Rupert Murdoch's universe, all was as it should be.

This was Murdoch's $110 billion moment, his shot at becoming the world's leading media player, the man who rewrote the road map for the information highway. It was that big . . . and that elusive. If he failed, Murdoch was an old man playing out his career in the minor leagues. The highway road crews would labour on, but for all intents and purposes, he would not be a serious journeyman. It was all or nothing.

General Motors didn't like this marriage of convenience. News Corporation was not the type of show that played well in Detroit. For more than a year, Smith had been trying to find some way out of his financial woes that meant he did not have to deal with Murdoch. General Motors had $38 billion in unfunded pension schemes weighing down its balance sheet. Unless Smith could raise a mountain of money, the credit ratings agencies were about to impose a disastrous credit downgrade on the group's $135 billion of borrowings. Murdoch might not be the ideal suitor, but the reality was, by January 2001 General Motors had run out of time and options. The reality was, Murdoch had General Motors cold.

On Tuesday 6 February 2001, Murdoch addressed the General Motors board, to draw the broad outlines of an offer they could not refuse. Murdoch's goal had been clear from the start. General Motors, through its technology arm, Hughes Electronics, owned the biggest satellite broad-caster in the United States. Seven years after selling its first satellite dish, DirecTV had 9.5 million subscribers. Murdoch wanted DirecTV, but he didn't want to buy it. In the $70 billion deal he set out, Murdoch wanted Hughes Electronics to buy *him*.

The biggest gamble that Rupert Murdoch had ever taken was being played out in tortuous negotiations across the world. Since January 2000, Murdoch had been racing to float his own worldwide network of satellite and pay-television platforms as a new company called Sky Global Networks. He had tried desperately to have the float signed off before Wall Street's high-tech stock boom fell apart, but he had not succeeded. Murdoch soldiered on with dogged intensity, trying to fill the holes in his worldwide net.

In Britain, he had considered and rejected then reconsidered making a full takeover bid for BSkyB. In America, Murdoch kept searching for some form of deal that would overcome Jack Smith's reluctance to sell him DirecTV. As a fallback, Murdoch was talking to his one-time ally, Charlie Ergen, who ran America's second largest satellite broadcaster, Echostar, out of Denver. On any day in January 2001, half a dozen different schemes swirled in the ether, each as nebulous as the other, as Murdoch struggled to assemble the pieces of this jigsaw, helped by his partner, friend and most dangerous rival, John Malone at Liberty Media.

Murdoch was running out of time. Already investors were growing nervous about whether News Corporation had reached too far and faced liquidity problems. If he failed to bring this juggling act safely to earth, Murdoch's shareholders and bankers would demand a hard accounting. Could he make this all come together? 'It's a dream,' he told shareholders at the BSkyB annual meeting in November 2000. 'I cannot comment. And you can read into that what you will.'

So it was that, after five decades battling media rivals on all continents, Murdoch's future would be determined by a car company. The first step in the $70 billion deal that Murdoch outlined on 6 February was for General Motors to spin off Hughes Electronics as a separate listed company. Step two was for Murdoch to sell his Sky Global Networks to Hughes, in exchange for Hughes shares. John Malone would kick in $1 billion cash to help grease the deal. Bill Gates at Microsoft, his rivalry with Murdoch put aside for the moment, would put in another $4 billion cash for a small stake. At the end of the day, after various asset sales, General Motors would walk away with a large pile of money, and Murdoch would control the new company, Sky-DirecTV, with 35 per cent of its stock.

It was a deal carefully crafted to satisfy all of General Motors' concerns for money, for tax planning and security. So on 6 February the General Motors board had little option but to give preliminary approval for Murdoch's offer and to begin the due diligence procedures and haggling over the fine details.

This was no ordinary media deal. Murdoch would emerge at the head of a global media empire whose many parts were valued at more than $110 billion. Its size and reach would make Murdoch's empire a serious rival – arguably the only serious rival – to AOL-Time Warner. For Murdoch, DirecTV was the final link in his grand slam. When joined to Sky Global, his satellite platforms would stretch seamlessly from North to South America, to Europe, across central Asia, China and Japan, down to Australia. Murdoch would control his own world highway. And he would control what ran on the highway, with a global voice and power that no one in history had ever had.

This was the prize that Murdoch had been inching towards all of his life. After half a century of struggle it was finally within reach. In a matter of weeks – even days – it would be his. There was so little, really, that had to be done. Murdoch and the News Corp executives just needed to sit tight, to focus on the due diligence procedures, and keep massaging their opposite numbers at General Motors and Hughes. Most of all they needed to show what swell partners they were all going to be.

This was where the deal began to unravel. News Corporation has one of the most aggressive corporate cultures in the world. For five decades, Murdoch had run News as a one-man show. In that time he had never had a successful partnership. Where would he begin now? On Tuesday 20 February, exactly two weeks after the General Motors board had approved the deal, the chairman of Hughes Electronics, Michael Smith, walked out of a meeting with Murdoch. Negotiations between News Corp, General Motors and Hughes ground to a halt. Michael Smith was saying that Murdoch's price for Hughes was too low. Smith – who as Jack Smith's brother had a direct line into the chief executive's office at General Motors – wanted to cut News Corp's stake in Sky-DirecTV from 35 per cent to 30 per cent. DirecTV's existing management would remain in control, led by Michael Smith.

Murdoch couldn't believe it. He had paid an enormous price to get this deal up. With his mind fixed on Sky Global, other areas of his empire had been sliding. Murdoch was so driven that when he was diagnosed with prostate cancer the year before, he postponed treatment for weeks. The pressures on his family had seen his daughter Elisabeth leave her job at BSkyB. Most telling of all, as one of the conditions of the DirecTV deal, Murdoch had appeared to jettison his succession strategy. For more than a decade he had schemed and manoeuvred to ensure that one of his children succeeded him at the head of the empire . . . and now he was walking away from that. John Malone and Bill Gates and the General Motors board could be persuaded to let Rupert Murdoch run Sky-DirecTV. Passing the reins to his children was another matter. Lachlan or James Murdoch might succeed Rupert as head of News Corporation, but by then News would be reduced to a media investment company that operated newspapers on the side.

'Lachlan is in a very difficult situation,' said a former News director in March 2001. 'Rupert is going to go on working forever. Lachlan could find himself 45 years of age, then suddenly miss the opportunity to run News.'

Murdoch had shown he was prepared to give up almost anything to make this deal work. And now Michael Smith was telling him that it wasn't *enough*.

There was no question how News Corp would spin this latest setback. It was obscene. This was a naked grab for power by Michael Smith, just to ensure that he didn't lose his job. Was General Motors really prepared to walk away from this deal? Another reading was that News Corp management had gone into a feeding frenzy.

'This is the drawback to the management style at News, those guys tend to play the man and not the ball,' said a former News director. 'It's a real problem. That's what killed the deal with Charlie Ergen in 1997. Murdoch has always underestimated Ergen.'

The News execs had been bagging their opposite numbers at Hughes for weeks. Hughes expected a partnership. What they got was a boarding party. There was nothing personal, it was just the News style – and it spooked Hughes management. By mid-March talks had stopped as Hughes and News Corp resorted to brinkmanship, with both sides talking to new partners. Both GM and News Corp were said to be discussing separate deals with Charlie Ergen at Echostar. More and more, the affair read like a rerun of Murdoch's great American adventure of 1997.

Could Murdoch magically save this deal? The bigger question was, even if a deal was salvaged, could a global satellite operation take on a cable giant like AOL-Time Warner? DirecTV was still losing $550 million a year. Added to the Sky Global losses, Sky-DirecTV would be haemorrhaging $1.2 billion a year. This might be a visionary deal. But in the short term it looked more like two shipwrecked sailors clinging to each other for dear life. How would they survive? Despite months of press leaks, no one had said. But then, when Murdoch was busy conjuring, there were rarely any hard details.

In any account of the information wars at the turn of the millennium, the question is what to make of Rupert Murdoch. On the one hand Murdoch is the archetypal modern media mogul, whose history illustrates the broad changes that have transformed the way the world communicates. Yet Murdoch is also a one-off. He has had a singular impact in the shaping and reshaping of the world's media industries for the last half century. Murdoch is one of the best known and yet most unknowable figures of the modern era. It is impossible to follow him through the media battles of the last two decades without plunging into the bewildering shadowy worlds that comprise the key parts of his global media empire, parts that operate invisibly behind the public face that is Rupert Murdoch Incorporated. Somewhere in this maze of public and private worlds is the real Rupert.

This book is not a conventional biography. It concentrates on Murdoch through his three great campaigns: in the 1980s, when his determination to launch an American television network overturned the media industries of three countries; in 1997, when Murdoch took on every broadcasting group in America; and finally the process of reinventing himself since then. But Rupert Murdoch is more than just a clever dealmaker or financial tactician. The corporate stratagems and ruses, the intuitive leaps and disastrous missteps which have marked Murdoch's career – have all been played out within a society struggling to come to terms with an avalanche of change. Rupert Murdoch described this process as living on a metaphysical rolling log: 'It's what keeps us young. Or at least fit.'

It is easy to forget just how shocking the changes ushered in by the rise of technology have been. What is at stake is how we understand the world. Much of the ideas and the preoccupations and politics of the last decade have represented a continuing battle to come to terms with the rolling crisis triggered by technological advance; where the world's new addiction to change means that many of society's ground lines are on the move; where nothing is as it appears.

In fact, at the turn of the twenty-first century, reality – the scale and measure of the everyday – has become a very strange thing. Once upon a time, reality was like a reasonable man: a member of the boys' club, someone we all felt we knew and could rely upon. Today, courtesy of history, modernity, technology and post-modern Leviathans such as Rupert Murdoch, our experience of reality, and reality itself, has become Medusa-like. It is a fickle, changeable and unknowable woman. Needless to say, once upon a time 'we' were all reasonable men. Today, none of us is quite so sure.

In one generation we have gone from computers that filled a room, to the Palm Pilot; from telex to the Melissa email virus; from Woodstock to MTV to pirated music files on Napster; from extended banking hours to day trading. The waves of scientific innovation that have shaped and reshaped the world in the last three decades have been profoundly unsettling. They have created a deep expectation of impermanence. The basic response to the unknown has switched from 'What's this?' to 'What's next?' We live in the eternal penultimate moment.

Technology, it turns out, fits in very well with the post-modern view of the world. In a society marked by impermanence, the form of things is more significant than the substance. Appearances matter. Where social and technological forms are continually changing, marketing is more important than content. Another way of saying this is that reality is all in the way you tell it – or it is whatever the market believes in. Of course, we always knew that. What made this latest period different was that in the last years of the twentieth century, the wave of technological change intersected with a wave of money. As this wild tide crested, the question was, who would get to ride it?

In the brave new world that technology ushered in, where reality itself became a slippery concept, Rupert Murdoch was a natural. He has always operated like that. Throughout his career, Murdoch has retained a remarkable gift to discern ahead of him a promising if implausible future. Each time, a solid rank of cautioners has insisted that this latest gamble would not work, that this time Murdoch would not make safe harbour. From the early 1950s when he was struggling to expand the little newspaper company that he inherited in South Australia; to the late 1960s when he made his leap to Britain to buy the *News of the World* and the *Sun*; and then his moves across the Atlantic in the 1970s and 80s to buy the *New York Post*

– his critics invariably have said he couldn't do it. He has always had to ride out the waves of scepticism and scorn.

In the process Murdoch has become a master of appearance, a conjurer of realities. He has cajoled, he has persuaded and he has tricked successive generations of investors, analysts and bankers. He has done what he has had to do to secure a suspension of their disbelief: a breathing space, a respite, anything that could buy him a little time to make the magic work. And the magic has indeed worked over time. Half a century of financial legerdemain has built a solid media empire, a lean, hungry machine that continues its inexorable growth, which has had pervasive effects on the societies in which it operates. To follow Rupert Murdoch's career through the growth of the information revolution of the 1980s and 90s – as this book attempts – one must understand that these society-wide changes had their roots at times in the personal idiosyncrasies, enmities and rivalries of those at their heart. Social outcomes were determined by the venal as much as by the banal.

The Murdoch school of management has not been without its problems. Running an international media empire like a magician's act can make day-to-day life very complicated. In any deal that Murdoch does, there is always a second strand running below the public transaction, known only to insiders, and then there is a third strand running under that again which no one ever sees. Murdoch is never where people think he is, or who people think he is: he is never that bad, and he is never quite that good. The danger in all this mystery is that News Corporation is a company that, at any moment, could choke on its own secrets. The hidden side of News Corp – the cash flows through the tax havens of the world, the private investigators, the secret family deals – can threaten to spin out of control.

For Murdoch, as for all the media titans, the last decade has been a bumpy ride. For most of the decade it was widely believed that media executives were the masters of the universe. In the mid-1990s economy they were hailed as The New Establishment. If society was being reshaped by technology and innovation, in 1996 traditional media leaders still represented the leading edge of the change. In October 1998, the Internet stock boom swept up and transformed a handful of struggling start-up companies, and it was clear that media executives had no more idea than anyone else where the future was heading. Six months later these Internet fledglings were worth more than $600 billion. The new media had never made a profit, yet by April 1998 it was worth more than all the old media companies in the world put together. A whole value system had been turned on its head. Almost overnight the masters of the universe became dinosaurs, staggering under the shock of a catastrophic change in climate. This book deals with the struggle by the great media companies to refashion their future, to come to terms with the dire threat that technology posed for them; to reinvent not only themselves but broad sections of their society. The story is framed as the odyssey of one man.

PART ONE

ATLANTIC CROSSING

CHAPTER ONE

VOLTAIRE'S UNDERGRADUATE

Si Voltaire n'existait pas, il faudrait le créer.
If Voltaire did not exist, it would be necessary to invent him.

Motto for Voltaire Society, Oxford

Cruden Farm, Victoria, 1999

Dame Elisabeth Murdoch will face her interrogators in the front sitting room. She has been fielding the same questions for half a century now, so the procedure is familiar. Her visitors enter through the ramshackle front gates of Cruden Farm, 30 miles south of Melbourne. From there, they follow an avenue lined on each side with rows of lemon-scented gum trees. The driveway of crushed stone eventually sweeps around to circle in front of a house set in one of the major private gardens in Australia. Around and beyond it are glimpses of the walled garden, the picking garden, the terraces, the lake and the little bridge.

A major media foray – and only a major media foray gets this far past Rupert Murdoch's vetting procedures – requires a team of at least four people. There must be a camera operator, a soundman, the producer, and the presenter or on-air talent. This is the bare minimum. Less Spartan outfits will include a lighting technician, a researcher, a second camera operator, the various personal staff required to support the tender sensibilities of the on-air talent, and any number of general gofers, all named Bozo. The expedition has become a convoy. As they drive through the gates for the first time the camera crew is already planning the tracking shot that will highlight the arcade of gum trees. The on-air talent looks at the picking garden and decides to do their piece-to-camera *there*, beside the delphiniums. Faced with a feast of colour, the producer wonders uneasily

3

how much foliage and flowers they can decently run without turning the interview into a segment from *House and Garden*.

The clapboard house is half of an antebellum southern mansion. The 90-acre farm was a gift to Dame Elisabeth from her husband, Sir Keith Murdoch, when they married in 1928. At the time, she was 19, he was 43 and editor of the Melbourne *Herald* newspaper. Six months later he was appointed managing director of the Herald and Weekly Times (HWT) group, the largest newspaper chain in Australia. To celebrate this appointment, the Murdochs headed off on a world tour several months after the birth of their first child, Helen, in 1929. An architect was commissioned to remodel their weekend cottage at Cruden while they were gone.

Seeing the Virginian columns on their return was the couple's first indication that the architect had a somewhat grander vision than they had anticipated. There followed an appalled silence as the Murdochs realised that, like Scarlett O'Hara, they had come back to Tara.

The sitting room is reached down a minor hallway from the front door. It is a large room, warm with the afternoon light that drifts through the leadlight windows. The furniture is oak, the floor is polished wood, the heavy beams on the ceiling hand adzed. Armchairs are grouped around a large stone fireplace, with a grand piano in the corner and a Georgian dresser. The walls feature early Australian painters – a large canvas by painter Rupert Bunney, several small William Dobells, a painting of a very young Rupert and his elder sister Helen. This is a quiet, composed room that speaks of order and permanence. It is a fitting stage for the formidable charms of Dame Elisabeth herself.

'It's amazing looking around this,' she says comfortably, with her assured upper-class Australian voice. 'I was just thinking, I've known this room and loved it for over 70 years. And I suppose it's the happiness that's been experienced in this house, to live with the same surroundings for most of your life, I think that's very *strengthening*.'

Dame Elisabeth was born in 1909. In her nineties she retains tremendous screen presence. Age has softened the edges, but the face remains strong, the mind sharp. Her manner is a beguiling mixture of playful warmth and sternness, of generosity and frugality, of kindliness and duty. There will be no nonsense. She has picked up the habit of italicising one word in a paragraph, usually the last, an effect which makes her pronouncements always charming and authoritative.

'Of course my life's been so full. I think that's been fortunate, but that's something to do with one's nature. I don't waste time. I think that's nothing to be highly praised for. But I think it does allow you to fill your life absolutely to the *brim*.'

Her audience loves her. 'Her son is one of the most controversial men in the world. Yet she is one of those rare individuals of whom no one it seems speaks badly,' began a recent television special on the Dame. The late Paul Eddington, the British actor who played the hapless Cabinet Minister Jim Hackett in the BBC satire, *Yes Minister*, was similarly charmed by this 'delightful woman, tirelessly engaged in a round of good works'.

'I once said to a journalist friend that it was hard to believe that such an obviously wonderful woman could have bred the monster so many people believed him (Rupert Murdoch) to be,' Eddington wrote in his auto-biography, *So Far So Good*. His friend agreed, and added, 'But she did.'

This is the conundrum that has drawn writers, journalists and the professionally curious to Cruden Farm for half a century. Dame Elisabeth has entertained them all in her front sitting room, answering their questions about her family with varying degrees of composure. The result is a montage, a crude form of time-lapse photography, as we watch this winsome, commanding personality with her back to the window explain the childhood of her son, again and again . . . and again.

'There's really a lot of extraordinary things said about how Rupert always wants to have my approval, that sort of thing. Well basically I think he does. He's a very dutiful and loving son. I never think much about the material success. His qualities as a human being are what matter to me.'

It is the same conversation that keeps being repeated over 50 years. As in any repeated sequence or picture series, what draws the eye first are the elements in the frame that remain the same. As familiarity grows, however, what come to seem significant are the elements in the picture that change.

The most obvious constant is the curtains. They are always in the interview. For decade after decade they appear as minor footnotes in the published reports. They date back to the days when the Murdochs bought Heathfield, one of the biggest and most prestigious houses in Melbourne. 'Now look darling,' Elisabeth told her husband, 'if you really want (Heathfield) I'll run it, provided we can afford to do it properly. I couldn't face it if we were going to be understaffed and it smelt of stale cabbage and dust like some old houses I have visited.' The Murdochs had ten staff at Heathfield. The four retainers at Cruden Farm were a skeleton staff in comparison. When the Murdochs sold Heathfield in 1947, Dame Elisabeth took the curtains. They have hung in the sitting room at Cruden ever since, a quirky watermark of opulence and austerity. By 1981, visitors were remarking that the drapes had become threadbare. Dame Elisabeth, one of

Australia's wealthiest women, said: 'These curtains will have to see me through until I'm dead.' Two decades later the drapes are still there, framing an unlikely Mrs Haversham. Dame Elisabeth sits indomitably in a room that grows each year more and more tatty.

A recurrent theme is the importance of bloodlines. 'I have a strong feeling that our path in life is destined by what we are made up of. I'm very strong on the strength of genetic strain,' she says. Then there is the cult of the father. 'From time to time people write absolute nonsense about Rupert not having had a loving, happy family life,' says Dame Elisabeth. 'And sometimes that he didn't have a good relationship with his father. Nothing could be further from the truth. They were very, very close indeed. And Rupert reveres his father's memory.'

This is familiar territory, part of the Murdoch legend of the golden childhood. The Murdochs are indeed an extraordinarily close family, tied together by deep bonds of affection. They have weathered the sorts of intense pressures that would split most families.

What makes this family unusual is the way it handles money. For forty years, Rupert's sisters received very little from their inheritance, despite the hundreds of millions of dollars that the shares bequeathed to them by their father had earned. When money did start to flow through the family company, Cruden Investments, in the form of News Corporation dividends in the 1980s, Dame Elisabeth gave much of it away to charity. Rupert Murdoch was exasperated. Here was the odd situation of one of the most powerful media moguls in the world, famous for holding on to all his company earnings, keeping the money in News Corporation and paying pitifully small dividends to stockholders. It is not just that he needs to keep building up News Corporation's capital base. He is also driven by the need to remain one step ahead of his mother's philanthropy. He pays his stockholders next to nothing because otherwise his mother would give the money away.

Rupert's sisters have no complaints. When in the 1990s Rupert finally bought them out for $500 million – less than a quarter of what their shares were worth – the sisters were remarkably ambivalent about their new wealth. 'It's not that we *mind* Rupert giving us all this money,' said his sister Anne doubtfully, when questioned by Australian journalist Ali Cromie, a comment that suggests precisely the reverse of what she is saying.

'The sisters are slavishly devoted to Rupert,' complained one nephew. By any accounting, this is extraordinary behaviour. In the 1990s, this family culture of determined self denial will be critical to determining who controls the global media reach of News Corporation into the twenty-first century.

The family legend was not always quite so seamless. The gaps appear only in the earlier accounts, back more than a third of a century ago, when the Murdochs were less savvy at public relations, less polished at using the media to speak to each other. This is where one needs to look.

Cruden Farm, Victoria, 1966

I suppose I am a fairly average person, a fairly average, extroverted person, I think perhaps with a little bit more than the average share of ambition. Which may be attractive or unattractive to people, I don't know.

Rupert Murdoch, 1966

The face is younger, the picture is showing signs of age. It is black and white, and some of the greys have leached out of the 16-millimetre film over the last 30 years since it was shot in 1965. And here is Dame Elisabeth Murdoch, major Australian public figure: widow of Sir Keith Murdoch, the man credited with setting up Australia's largest newspaper group; mother of Rupert, the country's newest media entrepreneur; and a powerful woman in her own right, knighted in 1963 for her work for the Royal Children's Hospital in Melbourne. Rupert Murdoch's international media empire may be only a vague promise, but at 57 years old his mother is in her prime.

The 40-minute program profiling Rupert Murdoch was one of a series by the Australian Broadcasting Commission titled *Six Australians*. Even at the time it was shot, it was a historic moment, being part of the first television portrait of Murdoch. It would be two decades before he co-operated with the portrait-makers again. At the time, Murdoch was still almost entirely an Australian phenomenon. There were grave concerns about his habit of gambling his media company on risky ventures. But he had no British newspapers yet, and despite the photograph on the wall of Murdoch with President Kennedy, any American aspirations were still only a pipedream.

It was also the first time that modern coverage of Rupert acknowledged that he was not the only Murdoch – that he shared control of his media empire with his mother, his older sister, Helen, and younger sisters Anne and Janet, through a private family company, Cruden Investments.

As the film crew set up, the unnamed interviewer probably knew that he had only one shot at Dame Elisabeth. She had been lured out by the opportunity to add to the tributes to her son, and to fend off the muted criticism which she was already aware the program would include. Dame

Elisabeth is natural talent. The commanding presence she still has nearly four decades later shows here at its prime. She does not yet have the confidence of old age, but she has a coquettish charm. She has Princess Diana's unstudied mannerism of bowing her head in deprecatory fashion, then modestly flicking her eyes up to catch the camera. She has the cultured, rounded vowels of upper-class Melbourne matrons of the postwar period. She speaks with the assurance and resolution of her class. She is a lively conversationalist who conveys genuine warmth and affection, a talent she has passed on to her son, mixed with an appealing and steely determination. She is sitting in the heart of Murdoch country, in the front sitting room of Cruden Farm. And she has something she wants to say.

For all that, the interview is ordinary. It is cut to reflect an idyllic upbringing for the four Murdoch children on the farm. Helen was born in 1929. Keith Rupert Murdoch entered the world on the stroke of midnight on 11 March 1931. Anne was born four years later, in 1935, and a fourth child, Janet, in 1939. Dame Elisabeth wanders among mementoes: 'This picture has always been very dear to me, because it was taken at a time when our family life was so full of promise. We had just been three months in England with three very small children; a husband that had a wonderful report from heart specialists. Rupert at the time was like every little boy of between five and six, full of mischief. Very happy. Quite amenable. And I think that my husband had great hopes for him.'

The film fades to rural rhapsodies, lingering over the sweep of lemon-scented gum trees along the drive of Cruden Farm, intercut with old pictures of earnest children fishing, cycling, and riding in the family car. Children frolic at the big townhouse, the weekend farm, the two cattle properties, with the beloved nanny, while the voice-over intones: 'And in surroundings straight from A. A. Milne, four children, including son and heir Rupert, romped blissfully towards adolescence.'

The break, when it comes, is unexpected. Dame Elisabeth launches into a sidetrack. She breaks off the discussion of childhood on the farm to talk about the decision to send Rupert to board at Geelong Grammar, a boarding school that specialised in educating the sons of wealthy land-owners. His mother, a natural athlete, sent him there because she wanted to 'toughen him up a bit' because she feared he was growing up too soft. Suddenly in this interview she is struggling. The marker for her discomfort is a class thing. Australian women of her background flag awkward or uncomfortable conversation subjects with the word 'perhaps'.

'I think perhaps his home was such a happy one. And he did of course adore being with his father. I think perhaps there was a slight feeling of resentment that he'd been sent away to boarding school. Perhaps his Scottish blood was dominant in this respect. My grandparents were shocked that I was so keen on boarding school. And I'm not *certain* really that my husband was so very keen about it. And I was very young, rather determined, and perhaps I wasn't always very wise. But . . .'

In the course of the speech Dame Elisabeth has progressively lost contact with the camera and the interviewer. She has lost composure. The film cuts to bridging shots of Geelong Grammar. Watching it half a lifetime later, in that moment of discomfort, the mind wanders. If you allow it, as Dame Elisabeth speaks on the old, grainy film, shot a third of a century ago, her words conjure up in the mind a much earlier picture, circa 1940, 26 years before. The picture is wholly imaginary, of course. It is shot in black and white, no colour at all, and moves with the stiffness and irregularity of pre-war home movies, dark and bordering on the unrecognisable. The picture is of a boy who has not yet turned ten, dressed in cap and knickerbockers, walking alone into school as the camera pulls back. The film lingers there for a time, then runs out.

Dame Elisabeth is made of sterner stuff. She rallies: 'But I think Rupert perhaps wasn't a conventional schoolboy, insofar as he didn't excel or wish to excel at sport . . . But on the whole I think that he was very happy.'

The editor breaks this sentence up with a sound bite from Rupert saying that he hated sport, and that he doesn't know whether he was happy or not, but he didn't think so at the time.

Dame Elisabeth is surer on the later history: 'I was very keen that Rupert should go to Oxford. I think that he gained a good deal. I believed then that it was important to go to the other side of the world. I'm sure that it taught Rupert a lot of the facts of life, when it came to hard thinking, and in fact he learnt probably to work at Oxford, better than he ever had before. And he had to – he knew that he jolly well had to put the shoulder to the plough, or he – or he wouldn't get his degree. And I think he learnt to appreciate that this was *pretty* important.'

On Sir Keith's death in 1952 Dame Elisabeth says: 'Of course it was the keenest sorrow to me. And I was burdened with anxiety for Rupert. He was so very young. And I did wonder so much how to help him. But of course I've always believed a mother's role, especially to a young adult, is one of kindliness, affection, and courage, and perhaps one hopes to inspire them to rise to the best that is in themselves. And I did long to be able to help Rupert prove worthy of his father in the newspaper world.'

Dame Elisabeth concludes: 'He's only 35 years of age and, as I say, no doubt he's made his mistakes. But on the whole I say again, and I believe that he has justified his father's faith. I'm very thankful that on the way up, he hasn't made more mistakes.'

Proving worthy of the father is a refrain to which the family will return again and again in interviews in the following decades. What the family does not say is that there is more than just sentiment to this movement. They see it also in the legal terms of Sir Keith's will. It is the knot that ties the family tightly together.

There is much more on the nascent media mogul in the film from Murdoch's colleagues and employees. The voice-over concludes opaquely: 'In most outward ways, Rupert Murdoch is disarmingly ordinary. And yet of course this can't be true.' And then the obligatory note of warning: will the empire builder still be around in ten years time?

The Murdochs hated the film. For a family that has profited so much from exposing the frail secrets of others, it has always been remarkably reticent about baring its own. Back in 1966 the film made waves as the first major piece on Murdoch, and the exclusive inside picture of the rising star. Today, more than thirty years later, it remains memorable for its glimpses of Murdoch family relations.

Dame Elisabeth's comments are part of the long-running internal conversation that the family has conducted about itself over the years. In all these exchanges, the 1966 interview is the only time that Dame Elisabeth has revealed any direct suggestion of concern with the decisions that shaped Rupert Murdoch's childhood. The force of that concern is in the careful understatement. This is not a family that values self-awareness. The public statement is a reflection of private conversations, of wider regrets that range beyond any simple decision on schooling. All this has been frozen into an icon, a single frame, an emblem of the childhood of a man, Rupert Murdoch, whose pursuit of the future has been so relentless that it begs the question as to what it is that he is leaving behind in his past.

The interview is notable for another feature. It lies hidden in the image which Dame Elisabeth's words have painted of the nine-year-old at the school door, standing there in that moment of realisation that even the most golden of childhoods one day comes to an end. It is an indistinct image, which only partly resolves when you ask – what is the figure doing?

In the 60 years since then, it is the only picture where Rupert Murdoch is looking back. Rosebud?

For half a century the Murdochs have treated the outside world to passing glimpses of the family almost as a private running joke. And what peculiar stories they tell about each other. There is the way the older sisters, Helen and Anne, would catch and skin rabbits and collect manure which their brother Rupert would sell, pocketing the money. There is the hut outside the house where Dame Elisabeth allegedly had Rupert sleep, once again 'to toughen him up a bit'.

'I was looked on as rather a disciplinarian,' she says. 'I had to be, because my husband wasn't. If Rupert wants to tease me, you know, he says, 'Of course, my mother used to beat me.' I think there were two occasions when I used the slipper.'

'My mother is a strong character who has influenced me greatly,' Murdoch wrote in 1990. 'But I wish she wouldn't indulge her taste for practical jokes at my biographers' expense – she's responsible for several Murdoch myths.'

There is Murdoch's own story about how his mother taught him to swim on a ship back from England to Australia when he was five – in a pool that was itself moving up and down as the ship pitched: 'I clearly recall my mother throwing me in the ship's pool – the deep end – and not letting anyone rescue me. I had to dog paddle to the side and I was screaming. That was the way to teach you to swim in those days.'

And there is Helen's story of how difficult it was to follow in the footsteps of her young mother, still the golden girl who shone at sports, who regularly won the diving competition in the swimming carnivals held near Cruden Farm at Davies Bay – unlike her shy daughter. As a teenager, Helen was so desperate to avoid the need to compete in this swimming competition which her mother always dominated that she burned herself with an iron. 'I suppose I wanted to shine for them, but I didn't,' she said later.

Every family has its stories, which are repeated over and over again through the years, until they lose most of any meaning that they originally had. They come to be held with affection. This appears to be the case with these Murdoch stories, each of which is recounted by Dame Elisabeth's four children in chapters they wrote themselves in her biography, *Two Lives*. The affection they hold for their mother and their familiarity with the stories obscures for the Murdochs the fact that the most common themes are power and denial.

Dame Elisabeth looms in her children's accounts as a commanding figure, with a deep sense of duty and frugality – perhaps a reaction to Rupert Greene, her adored father and an inveterate gambler. While the need to prove worthy of the father, Sir Keith, may be the family litany, the cult of the father is one administered by their mother. Her power in the family is no less because she is a person of exceptional charm and genuine personal warmth, ready to give visitors a hug, an unexpected gift or donation.

By contrast, Sir Keith Murdoch was indulgent but distant, reluctant to praise, much more willing to be annoyed by his son's efforts to win his attention ('disobedient, wild, sullen boy'). At work he had a reputation as a great shouter. 'Rupert was afraid of his father, he was always trying to please Sir Keith but to no avail,' a contemporary told Thomas Kiernan, the Murdoch biographer who was closest to the family. 'I don't think Rupert was born with the traits that have sullied his reputation as a grown-up. He developed them out of his desperation to encourage his father's approval.'

The Murdochs are intensely patriarchal. Yet each Murdoch male heir in living memory has rejected the legacy of his father and carved out a new life in a completely different direction. Rupert Murdoch's great-grandfather James, rather than take on his father's prosperous merchant business in Sterling, Scotland, became a fire and brimstone preacher at Rosehearty, a fishing village on the north coast of Aberdeenshire. The preacher's role was not, he said, to waken his congregation – 'these slumberers, these twice dead' – by talking of God's grace and forgiveness. 'We have need rather to meditate terror . . . It is demanded of us to expose and warn these barren fig-trees – these wells without water – to cause these sinners in Zion to be afraid and to surprise these hypocrites with fearfulness.'

Family health problems led James to migrate to Melbourne in 1884, where he died three weeks after arriving. His grown son, Patrick, who accompanied him, was also a preacher, originally at Cruden in Scotland. But unlike his father he became an upwardly mobile part of the institutional church, going on to head the Presbyterian Church in Australia. Besides books of sermons he also wrote children's books, full of useful advice to boys and girls in the Scottish tradition:

> Never do anything with your hands or look at anything with your eyes that you would be ashamed to tell your mother about. Turn away at once from any picture that you feel to be filthy or indecent. Put away any book, however interesting, that makes you think filthy thoughts. You should get out of bed in the morning as soon as you awake, and if possible have a cold bath.
>
> Making money by betting is an unjust way of getting other people's property, and that is really stealing . . . You would never take a sixpenny out of another boy's or girl's pocket, for that would be stealing; but how about stealing his good name? If you tell people that

someone is a thief or a liar or a cheat, you make them think ill of him. That is stealing his good name, and is quite as bad as stealing his purse.

Patrick's son, Keith Murdoch, eschewed a career in the church and chose to become a penny-a-line journalist instead. He transformed his fortunes when he filed a controversial and highly critical report about the conduct of British generals during the First World War fighting against the Turks at Gallipoli in the Dardanelles. Britain's great newspaper baron, Alfred Harmsworth, later Lord Northcliffe, seized on the report to force the champion of the Dardanelles expedition, Winston Churchill, out of the British Cabinet. Overnight Murdoch, as Northcliffe's protégé, became a confidant of British and Australian cabinet ministers. More than that, as a journalist he became in many ways the very inverse of his father's ideal.

Whichever way you read it, this was not an easy family to live up to. Rupert Murdoch's eight years at Geelong Grammar were not happy ones. 'As a boy he was rough as guts, he wasn't very subtle or gentle,' said one of his schoolmates at Geelong. 'He was known alternatively as Bullo Murdoch – being a bullshit artist or something – and Commo Murdoch, because he pretended to be a communist. He was rebelling against a capitalist father, I suppose.' Rupert Murdoch was on the opposite side of the world before he found himself for the first time free of his family's expectations.

Oxford 1950–53

In between being thrown into the lake for lack of patriotism, buying a bust of Lenin to annoy his father and being banned from politics for voting irregularities, Rupert Murdoch's lasting contribution to Oxford was the founding of an entirely bogus philosophical society.

Midway through 1950 Rupert's parents flew to Europe with him to see their son settled into England before he started Oxford. They broke their journey in Rome for an audience with the Pope. 'I was quite over-whelmed,' says Dame Elisabeth. 'Rupert said he was unimpressed, particularly with the little silver medals the Pope gave him.'

Once in Britain, the Murdochs drove in a Rolls Royce to a boarding house in Birmingham. Sir Keith had arranged through his friend Pat Gibson (later Lord Gibson), the head of Westminster Press Group, for Rupert to fill the three months before the start of term at Oxford, working as a trainee for the *Birmingham Gazette*.

Sir Keith left Rupert with £60 for 'necessary crockery and establishment costs . . . caution money and entrance fee'. For the crockery, Sir Keith advised, 'You want the proper things but plain and sound and good.'

Throughout Rupert's time in England, Sir Keith, who was alternately exasperated and extraordinarily solicitous with his son, continued to write letters full of useful advice about everything from newspaper design to how many people were needed to run their cattle properties. 'Rupert, give a few half hours to letter writing,' he advised early in the piece, before giving a long list of aunts, uncles and others to contact. 'Whatever you do, never let a week go by without a letter to your Mother.'

'I do hope dear boy that you are not doing too much but using your time usefully and in good shape and heart. We are expecting that you will be refreshed for Oxford after a good holiday and will start quietly. You will, I am sure, make a proper exit from Birmingham and say the grateful good-byes to your colleagues, your bosses and your friends.'

Things did not end at Birmingham quite as happily as his father had hoped. Before leaving the *Birmingham Gazette*, Rupert contacted Pat Gibson and advised him (unsuccessfully) to sack the esteemed Birmingham editor, Charles Fenby. Murdoch arrived at Worcester College in October for the start of Michaelmas term. A short, stocky figure, thickly built but not fat, he soon settled in to the life of a well-upholstered leftist, achieving a level of opulence that most Oxford undergraduates only lusted after. At Worcester College he established himself in the Thomas de Quincey room, named after a nineteenth-century beneficiary who learned to smoke opium there. The oak-panelled rooms were among the most spacious and luxurious in the college. He owned a car, a beige Austin A-40. 'It was like having a private aeroplane or a Rolls Royce in terms of being noticed by your contemporaries,' one of his Oxford friends, film-maker Michael Weigall, said later.

Several of Murdoch's contemporaries from Geelong Grammar were also at Oxford, including John Piper, later a senior Australian diplomat. Piper was at Brasenose College, and through him Murdoch became a regular feature of the group of undergraduates around Brasenose. The group was composed of hopeful young men who went on to become politicians, academics, journalists and spies. By the end of the century they had become influential and powerful figures across Britain and North America.

'He spent most of his time in the junior common room at Brasenose and the beer cellar,' said one of the group, James Mitchell, later director of the National Consumer Council. He was '. . . a quiet individual who made very little impression at the time. All I have is a visual image of Rupert

Murdoch with a group of people drinking beer and never actually saying anything.'

Patrick Seale, who went on to become the *Observer*'s Middle East correspondent and the author of controversial biographies of Syrian president Hafez Assad and Palestinian terrorist Abu Nidal, remembers Murdoch as very bluff, boisterous and charming. Years later, he said:

He had a raw animal energy. Great shrewdness but not a great intellectual, with a bulldozing approach to human relations which I suppose is something one associates with people from Australia. But it certainly cuts corners . . . He's the sort of chap who goes straight to the point, tells you exactly what he wants, no beating about the bush. Obviously too, a strong streak of ruthlessness but that wasn't so apparent at that time; there was more a tremendous kindliness.

Not everyone at Brasenose perceived the kindliness Seale mentioned. 'He was a spoilt overbearing man – what other impression could he make? He was agreeable, he had a certain amount of charm but behind it I think was the money,' said one former contemporary.

'He was a bumptious, opinionated young man from the colonies who had more money than was good for him,' said another fellow undergraduate. 'He was overbearing in his views and aggressively self-confident on political topics.'

While reactions to Murdoch were many and varied, what the group at Brasenose agree on is that Rupert Murdoch was extraordinarily close to Robin Farquharson, an exuberant, erratic South African undergraduate whose brilliance overshadowed the group. What they could not work out was why.

'It's very hard to say what the basis of that friendship was, because they were really very, very different,' said James Mitchell. 'Robin would talk 60 to the dozen on any subject and had wild intellectual and political fantasies which he would build up as he was talking. And Rupert never said anything about anything.'

Farquharson was 'an extraordinarily eccentric chap, and had only his brilliance to commend him,' said Frank Cioffi, later professor of philosophy at the University of Essex, and one of the great critics of psychoanalysis. 'If Rupert cultivated him it shows there must have been an unworldly side to Rupert.'

In his first year Farquharson was already being described by dons as the most brilliant undergraduate they had ever come across. 'Farquharson was exceptionally brilliant, extremely intelligent, a very quick man,' said

Professor Robert Shackleton. Farquharson's doctoral thesis would win the 1961 Monograph Prize of the American Academy of Arts and Sciences in the field of social sciences. It was published in 1969 by Yale University Press as *Theory of Voting*, and described as the mathematics of the process politicians use to vote tactically. More simply, it was about the science of rigging a democracy.

'Farquharson was a brilliant conversationalist,' according to Michael Weigall. 'He would tie up professional brilliant conversationalists . . . I've seen Robin Farquharson, by the sheer brilliance of his argumentative processes, just tying these chaps in absolute knots and then giggling hysterically like a schoolgirl at how clever he had been.'

The press loved big Robin Farquharson when they discovered him several decades later. He was a tall, compelling figure with a tufted beard. With the lithium injections he needed to control his manic depressiveness he bulked up over 225 pounds after university. In 1971, in one of his more celebrated performances he summonsed journalists to a press conference to announce the start of the first term of his Anti-University of London, a novel institution he had founded which boasted some 30 students. The fees were £1 a term – but if you didn't have the money, you didn't have to pay. Farquharson was in fine form at the press conference expounding on courses like Logic (non-standard analysis and intuitionism), Poetry and 'Communication and Anti-Social Work'. Students got a free copy of Farquharson's book, *Drop Out!* which explained, as one reviewer put it, 'how to live on nothing a week in London'.

'I am a manic depressive,' Farquharson wrote in *Drop Out!* 'When I'm up I have no judgment at all, but fantastic drive. When I'm down, I have judgment, but no drive at all. In between, I can pass for normal well enough.' It had been a long-term problem. 'Intermittent psychosis, mania, cyclothymia, manic highs (have) dogged my life since 1955,' he wrote. That was the year when, as a promising candidate for a Fellowship at All Souls in Oxford, he destroyed his chances by a telephone call to the Warden. Farquharson called him away from his High Table to tell him that he had a message for the Warden from God. By the 1960s, Farquharson's struggles with his illness had put any conventional form of occupation out of the question. In the mid-1960s Farquharson had embraced the squatter movement, living in derelict houses, occasionally descending without notice on old friends, before disappearing back into the streets.

But in 1951, Farquharson's bi-polar condition was still quiescent. His father was head of a firm of solicitors in Pretoria. Robin himself lost his South African passport for anti-apartheid protests. He shared a flat with

American John Searle, who went on to become professor of philosophy at Berkeley; and later with Nigel Lawson, who went on to become Chancellor of the Exchequer.

They made an unconventional pairing, Murdoch and Farquharson, the two wild colonial boys. Along with his brilliance, Farquharson had an exuberance, a zest for life that was tremendously appealing, together with an eccentricity and absentmindedness that could see him dress for formal evenings in a tuxedo without remembering to put socks on before his shoes. He was hugely larger than life. His energy and creativity cast even Murdoch in the shade. Murdoch and Farquharson began bobbing up together. One of their first ventures was the Voltaire Society.

Murdoch spent the European summer of 1951 driving to Istanbul with another Australian student, George Masterman, and two History Fellows at Worcester, Harry Pitt and Asa Briggs. Sir Keith had engaged Briggs to offer his son some extra tuition in his Politics, Philosophy and Economics (PPE) courses. Rupert's economics tutor, Professor J. R. Sargent of Worcester, said his student had 'not much interest' in the subject:

It was pretty clear he was interested in the world of politics and journalism and not much else. He is said to have scraped through with Briggs' help . . . Under the Oxford system it's not very easy to fail. I mean, the statistical percentage of those who actually fail is very small. He did get into the lowest class.

By late 1951, the start of Murdoch's second year at Oxford, the group around him had begun to be troubled by uncomfortable thoughts about what they would be doing with the rest of their lives. It was no longer good enough, in order to get a job, merely to say you went to Oxford. You needed to be able to say that you had been 'somebody' at Oxford. An idea began with Michael Weigall, which he later recalled in a series of interviews in 1982.

I personally, and similarly placed friends, all realised halfway through our term at Oxford that we had failed to become anyone. We would never be secretaries of the union, we were not likely to achieve office legitimately in any big society.

The challenge was to find a way to spice up the CV. The answer for Murdoch's coterie was to form their own society. 'The reason the Voltaire Society was founded was that it had more officers proportionate to membership than almost any other university society,' said Michael Weigall. Positions were held only for a term, and circulated among members. As for its aims, the most that could be said was that it was a group that, like Voltaire, was generally opposed to organised religion.

Said Weigall:

> One of the most often quoted statements of Voltaire was that if God did not exist he would have to be invented . . . That's how Voltaire saw it, and the society's motto – Rupert like me was a founder member – was that if Voltaire did not exist, he would have to be invented, which of course rather accurately summed up the circumstances in which the club was founded. It was basically a dining club.

The Voltaire Society's stationery for the Trinity term of 1952 shows eleven elected officials and only fifty regular members. The patron is listed as Bertrand Russell and the senior member as Robert Shackleton, MA. The masthead notes augustly: 'The Society is affiliated to the Voltaire International,' and coyly reminds members that: 'The Society's Library and Iconographical Collection are available for consultation in the Secretary's rooms at 19 St John St on Sunday mornings in term.'

No Voltaire International existed. The 'Iconographical Collection' consisted of one bust of Voltaire and was placed under the care of the official Iconographer, Colin Leys, now a Marxist scholar of Third World development. As a job title, at least, this was better than the previous term, when there had been an official Iconoclast, whose job it was to sneak around pinching busts from other societies. There was also an office of Gardener, says Weigall, because Voltaire was rather keen on horticulture.

Accounts vary as to whether the society library, under the care of the librarian, Michael Smart (president of the Labour Club the year before), comprised two books, or just one. In any case the library and the bust were kept in the rooms of the society's secretary, Robin Farquharson, who was assisted by an officer without portfolio, Rupert Murdoch.

With characteristic gusto, Farquharson leapt at the idea of a bogus society, and promptly cycled to Paris, where he bought a bust of Voltaire from the curiosity shop attached to the Louvre. The bust was unveiled at one of the society's meetings in a private dining room, after Weigall gave an appallingly drunken speech.

> In the stunned silence following what everyone regarded as an inept performance quite out of keeping with the solemnity of the occasion,

the only person who applauded was Rupert. He came and shook me by the hand and said it was the best speech he had ever heard.

In hindsight Weigall suggests that Murdoch could have been shy: 'He as a shy person might have realised . . . it was an absolute nightmare for me to make that speech. It might not have been innocence but compassion that made him be the person to applaud me.'

Voltaire Society members included: John Piper; Patrick Seale; Gerald Kaufman, later a Labour Party luminary and John Brademas, later president emeritus of New York University, congressman and chairman of the President's Committee on the Arts and Humanities. Over time, the society turned to more mundane philosophical pursuits, and the original members dropped off.

As well as the Voltaire Society, Murdoch and Farquharson teamed up again to run the student magazine, *Cherwell*. In the Trinity term of 1952, Murdoch became publicity manager of *Cherwell*, while Robin Farquharson took over as production manager. Patrick Seale was editor, Frank Cioffi sub-editor. Like the Voltaire Society, the *Cherwell* team's aim was to take a snide shot at the world in general. References to Murdoch in the magazine described him variously as 'cataclysmic chauffeur from the outback and prototype of Hollywood's peripatetic publicists', and as 'turbulent, travelled and twenty-one'.

Murdoch's friendship with Farquharson was important for two reasons. First, Farquharson was a mathematician. Oxford in the postwar period was teeming with ideas. One of these was game theory. In 1998, John Von Neumann and Oskar Morgenstern had published their groundbreaking work on the subject, *Theory of Games and Economic Behaviour*. At Princeton in 1951, John F. Nash at 21 years old published the paper for which he would share the Nobel Prize 45 years later. Game theory grew out of the study of poker games and chess. It challenged the classical doctrine that economic outcomes were attributed merely to impersonal forces. Instead it looked at the role of individual people, who it assumed could be mendacious, nasty and often stupid. The tactics it studied were back-stabbing, cheating and mistrust. At one level, game theory seemed to turn everything around, with its implicit suggestion that the successful player in business or politics was the one who ignored convention and social expectations, who cut corners, who broke unwritten rules, who did what no one else in the game was prepared to do. It was what Rupert Murdoch would always do so well.

Today, game theory is best known for the Prisoner's Paradox, a story told about two suspects being questioned by police over a robbery. Each prisoner must decide whether to maintain their innocence, in which case they may be charged with a minor offence; or to inform on their companion in return for immunity. The informant – a sophisticated game player – then walks free at his companion's expense. But if they both inform, then they both receive the maximum sentence. So the question for each prisoner is, how is the other player going to act? This is the difficulty: from an individual's perspective, it is always a better prospect to make the opportunistic choice, to inform on the other players or take advantage of them in some way. But if one player does this, then the long-term result is that everybody else ends up making the same opportunistic choice – either at the start, or at the next time that the same situation comes up. Inevitably, everyone ends up worse off.

John F. Nash is known as the father of game theory. Like Farquharson, he battled for years against mental illness. While one does not have to be mad to understand game theory, it seems to help to be able to think outside of the square. Farquharson meanwhile was developing his own version of the Prisoner's Paradox. It was a sort of Politician's Paradox that he began to develop in 1953 to explain why, when he looked at voting records in the US Senate, so often the end result of legislation was to produce the least desired result for all parties. The end result was the compromise that nobody liked.

The importance of this was that at a time when Murdoch and his contemporaries were taking the mickey out of the Establishment, the brightest star in their intellectual universe was propounding a theory that spelt out the advantages of doing just this. Or rather, of doing this and getting away with it. It was the science of when it was safe to cut corners. There would be a huge financial benefit for Murdoch in doing what no one else would accept, whether it was running topless girls on page three of the *Sun*, as he would do two decades later; or taking on the entrenched British printing unions, as he did in 1986; or exploring the bounds of reality TV, as he did in America in the 1990s with shows such as *When Animals Attack*. British society has always been more regulated by the social contract, the unwritten law, than has North America. This helps explain why Murdoch, the natural game player, has been so much more successful in Britain. In Britain, as he told the *Economist* in 1996, 'all you had to do is just to work hard'. In the US, when it came to being a tough game player, he found he had to take a number.

Farquharson went on to demonstrate that the effect of breaking down the social contract in a system, a rush to the bottom, eventually became a disaster for all parties. It is a basic feature of game theory analysis. Today game theorists talk about game strategies where everybody wins. But Farquharson's friend Rupert never got to this part of the lesson.

The other significance of the closeness between Murdoch and Farquharson was that Farquharson was gay – spectacularly, flamboyantly gay. 'I was the victim, as I saw it then, of a grave and distressing homosexual condition wholly resisting treatment,' he wrote in *Drop Out!*, which is peppered with sexual one-liners. 'Look after the penis and the ponce will look after itself,' he concludes grandiloquently, while describing with great gusto the romance of a 17-year-old boy. 'I lack courage, I know, just as I lack stability and application and patience, qualities I value, and as I also lack consistency and temperance and chastity, qualities I do not value at all.'

What is interesting is that in the course of the next decade, Murdoch came to reject almost every aspect of the life that Oxford represented. It was not only his politics that would become more conservative. His views on other people's sexuality would also change. It would be reflected in his newspapers' growing homophobia, the zeal with which they would 'out' public figures.

All this, however, was still a long way off. The more pressing question was, what was Murdoch to do after Oxford? Says Michael Weigall:

> He didn't seem to be really convinced that following in his father's footsteps was the right thing to do. It was a classic situation. Sir Keith Murdoch had obviously been a very strong, dominating person. His father seemed to be set there for always and was such a powerful man, Rupert said, 'It's not a world for me.' He looked upon himself as a dilettante, he made a joke about it.

Rupert retained his powerful ability to annoy his father. He had bought a bust of Lenin that he installed on his mantelpiece, and continued to refer to Lenin in his letters home as 'The Great Thinker'. In 1952 his father was concerned enough to confide in Hugh Cudlipp of the London *Daily Mirror* group, 'I'm worried about my son Rupert. He's at Oxford and developing the most alarming left-wing views.'

As if to confirm any doubt of Murdoch's left-wing credentials, there was the aquatic excursion of early 1952. This began with an unfortunate misunderstanding over a cocktail party that Murdoch had organised in his rooms. As one of his contemporaries tells it, the problem was that after Murdoch had sent out the invitations, King George VI had the bad grace to die on 6 February. The state funeral was set for the day of Murdoch's party. A less dedicated *bon vivant* might have considered another date, with the whole country, or at least the greater part of Oxford University, in official mourning. But not Murdoch. He got around the ban on private celebrations by sending out new invitations turning his get-together into an interment party. This levity was regarded in some quarters as bad form, and a group of patriotic souls, so the story goes, set out to demonstrate that no man is an island, by turfing Murdoch into the lake. It was 'the best thing that could have happened to him,' one of those present declared happily 30 years later.

Murdoch's view of royalty remains a constant. 'The Queen? Nice little woman, nothing special,' Murdoch would say 40 years later, after a party at Buckingham Palace. He told his British butler, Philip Townsend, 'You know, Philip, it's no big deal when all those Royals get together. Prince Charles was wandering around with no one to talk to. There were nine genuine queens there, and about 50 of the other sort.'

His wife Anna asked somewhat ironically what he meant. 'I mean poofters,' Murdoch said.

'Rupert, you know you're not allowed to use that word,' she replied, referring to a recent ruling by the British Press Council.

'The *Sun*'s not allowed to say it. I can say what I like,' her husband told her.

By mid-1952, Murdoch was under investigation by the Labour Club at Oxford. After he ran for the post of secretary, he was accused, with others, of breaking the prohibition on direct canvassing or electioneering – a practice that was not unknown. Gerald Kaufman, the chairman of the Labour Club in the Trinity term in 1952, later wrote: 'A certain amount of discreet electioneering did take place in the characteristic British way, as could be got along with. K. R. Murdoch decided to blast his way through these effete Pommie evasions.'

Kaufman set up an investigation made up of former chairmen of the club, 'the Bloody Tribbyanal' as the irreverent K. R. Murdoch immediately dubbed it'. Murdoch defended himself before the inquiry, which sat in June, before heading off in his car to Monte Carlo with Seale and Piper.

'I think Murdoch felt it was hard luck that he was one of those who were caught while others were not, and I must say I had some sympathy for him,' said Michael Smart.

Kaufman later wrote that the tribunal found evidence of a pro-Murdoch campaign team that included '. . . one zealous activist (who) was an East European, possibly a Yugoslav . . . whose role at the university . . . had never been established, but who was to be encountered at every meeting.'

Kaufman's trenchant view, expressed decades later, was that 'This was the first stage of Rupert Murdoch's downward path to millionairedom and control of the world's communication media.'

Murdoch's friends at *Cherwell* put a slightly different take in announcing the news of the suspension on 15 October 1952:

> Three prominent members were suspended from the Labour Club, after a tribunal of ex-officers had declared them guilty of canvassing. Here the struggle appeared to be similar to that in the Conservative Club between a group of ex-officers who still had careerist interests in Oxford politics and an apparently outside group. The dominance of this first group appeared to be on the wane until the tribunal dramatically turned the scales. As an illustration of the rivalry it is undoubtedly true that a vital piece of written evidence in the recent dispute was taken from among the private correspondence of the suspended members and handed to the tribunal.

By the time this article appeared Murdoch was beyond caring. He was no longer even in Britain. Eleven days earlier his world had fallen apart.

Melbourne, October 1952

I can't die yet. I've got to see my son established, not leave him like a lamb to be devoured and destroyed by these people, by John Williams.

Sir Keith Murdoch, 1952

Only old journalists could love ancient newspaper buildings. The structures have a dubious charm that may be detected only by the very romantic and people on prescription medication. Newspaper offices absorb part of the histories that flow through them. With the accretions of the years, the atmosphere in their newsrooms comes to reflect the individual styles and practices of the paper. They become comfortable, familiar, down-at-heel, redolent with tradition. They smell.

Every newspaper has its own odour. This is due not so much to the natural aroma associated with large numbers of journalists in a confined space. It is a product of the nocturnal manufacturing process, the muscular, messy business of applying ink to several acres of newsprint each night, cutting the end product up into little bits and putting it into large trucks.

The *New York Post*'s old pressroom mixed the smell of truck fumes, newsprint and decades of grime with other, more exotic, traces. The fanciful could imagine a whiff of the drug deals that went down in the paper's loading bays at various times in its august history. In Australia the pervasive bouquet at Queensland Newspapers, the Brisbane chain that became the Murdoch family's lost birthright, is a product of industrial strength disinfectants, the soap factory next door and the cattle stalls in the showgrounds nearby. When News Corporation's Australian editors met for a conference in the building in early 1999, toilet seats had to be replaced and the more aromatic sections sealed off, to make the effect less over-powering.

Before Lachlan Murdoch's renovations News Corporation's head-quarters in Sydney had a distinctive aroma of old beer and perspiration, an unhappy combination that in large quantities acquires the aromatic qualities of urine. Advertiser Newspapers in Adelaide regularly hosts a more pungent smell when waste trucks pump sewage from the building's grease trap. In Melbourne, the Flinders Street complex built by Rupert Murdoch's father, Sir Keith, for his Herald and Weekly Times newspaper group is more mundane, with the musty feel of old asbestos lining, hot lead from the Linotype machines of two decades before, and ink.

During the week most newspaper smells are hardly noticeable, a grimy undercurrent that lurks in the stairwells. The aromas seep out during the weekend, when the office staff are away and lighting, air conditioning and ventilation are turned down. On Sundays, newspapers run on skeleton staffs. It is a good time for private meetings, for discreet negotiations. The restricted lighting, the unfamiliar quiet and the smells give newspaper buildings a strange feeling of disruption, an air of mystery, of stories not told. Sunday is a time for secrets.

The disruption in the Herald and Weekly Times offices in Flinders Street on Sunday 5 October 1952 was neither quiet nor discreet. This was not a typical newspaper Sunday. The company's chairman, Sir Keith Murdoch had died of a massive heart attack only hours earlier, passing away on Saturday night at Cruden Farm. The family was still in shock, trying to contact Rupert on the other side of the world. Meanwhile Sir Keith's former deputy, Jack Williams, had hired builders to break into Sir Keith's office safe. Williams was a determined man, and, according to later reports, he brought jackhammers into the office for the job. Whatever the means, he had it open by evening.

Sir Keith had fired Williams the day before his death. On Thursday, 2 October he had learned that Williams was plotting a boardroom coup to replace him, and had the board numbers to do it. Instead Sir Keith stared the board down on the Friday, and forced Williams out. For Williams, Sir Keith's death the next day miraculously resurrected his career. The rattled board hastily reversed the decision to fire Williams and anointed him as Sir Keith's successor. In the meantime, Williams made a beeline for Sir Keith's office safe. He was after the papers that documented the stock transfers and secret transactions that had built up the Murdoch private empire alongside the public company that Sir Keith headed. And the mystery on this Sunday, the million-dollar question which would determine Rupert Murdoch's future, was – what was the blind urgency driving Williams? Exactly what was it in that safe that Williams was so determined and so anxious to see?

Death is a formative moment in any dynasty. When the patriarch dies, the circumstances of the departure and the handing on of power can freeze family relationships, emotions and perceptions as unfinished business for decades. It can also freeze finances. Sir Keith Murdoch was the most successful and powerful journalist Australia had seen. The sheer scale of his rise, from his start as an impoverished, penny-a-line reporter leaping from nowhere on to the international stage, a kingmaker and confidant of political leaders in Britain and Australia – all this meant that in the eyes of his family and his colleagues, he was one of a kind. His death at the peak of his power ensured that for some, nothing the son achieved could ever match the brilliance of the father. That Rupert would never outrun his father's shadow. Remnants of that family judgment remain today.

In the family's view, Williams' Sunday raid on the office safe was all of a piece, as the Herald and Weekly Times (HWT) group jackhammered through the inheritance that Sir Keith had built. Despite his role in building up the Herald group, Sir Keith owned almost none of the shares. He had a house in Melbourne, plus Cruden Farm, two cattle properties, and half shares in two newspaper groups, Queensland Newspapers in Brisbane and News Limited in Adelaide. All Sir Keith's assets were held in a recently formed family company called Cruden Investments. There was a lot of debt. Together with death duties, it made the inheritance far more modest than the family had bargained on.

Harry Giddy, the executor of Sir Keith Murdoch's will, was also the chairman of the Herald and Weekly Times group. He sold the country properties, convinced Dame Elisabeth to sell the half share in Queensland Newspapers to the Herald and Weekly Times Group, and almost persuaded her to sell the News shares as well. The terms were not generous – the Herald doubled its valuation of the Queensland Newspapers investment when it floated the company three years later in a new holding company, Queensland Press Limited. But Giddy's concern was to see Dame Elisabeth and her three daughters provided for. The son on whom Sir Keith had at times poured such open scorn would be quite capable of making his own way.

The family would come to see Giddy's actions as another betrayal, a theft of the Murdoch inheritance by men who only days before Sir Keith's death had been plotting his downfall. The betrayal was intensely humiliating for his son, Rupert. His father's funeral and cremation had been held as he was still in the air on his way back to Melbourne. Jack Williams had delivered the eulogy. Not only would Rupert have to live up to the legend of his father, he was forced to watch powerless as almost all that his father had built up was dissipated. All that he salvaged was a promise from his mother that she would not sell the News shares if he went back to Oxford to complete his degree.

'I felt very bitter about the destruction of the newspaper group because a lot of hard work went into it,' a close family friend later recalled. 'In my opinion it was stolen. And if I felt like that and I wasn't Sir Keith's son, how do you think Rupert felt? . . . It was an absolutely appalling business.'

There was another view, held just as trenchantly by Sir Keith's critics. His most vitriolic critic was John Hetherington, former editor-in-chief of the *News* in Adelaide, whom Sir Keith replaced.

[Sir Keith] Murdoch was a fascinating study in human dynamism. Physically and mentally massive, he never wavered in his purpose of grasping the best apples on the tree for himself; he often did this with the aid of other men who were somehow hypnotised into believing they would be rewarded with a share of the apples, only to find when the division was made, that Murdoch had all the juiciest and rosiest pieces of fruit, while they – if they were lucky – had the yellowed and rotting windfalls. Murdoch was fond, in expansive moments, of expressing his admiration for what he called the Man with a Mission. He himself was a man with a mission which was the acquisition of money, possessions, position and power.

Williams and others on the Herald board also saw a stolen inheritance, but they saw a different perpetrator. 'Williams said that Murdoch had managed to divert News Limited into his own pocket, had managed to filch the property owned by the Herald while he was head of the company,' Cecil King, former chairman of the London Daily Mirror group and the nephew of Lord Northcliffe, claimed years later, 'Williams regarded it as disgraceful skulduggery, absolute unblushing theft.'

The Murdochs had made their fortune out of the Depression – using the princely salary Sir Keith commanded at the Herald and Weekly Times to buy property at depressed prices. But his salary came nowhere near being able to pay for a newspaper empire, raising the question of where the money had come from? The history of how Sir Keith acquired the Queensland Newspapers stake is inconclusive. But he had been able to do the deal only because of financial assistance he arranged from the Herald and Weekly Times, whose board claimed that in return they had been given an option to buy the stake back on Sir Keith's death.

The situation was more acrimonious with News Limited, the Adelaide newspaper business. The Herald and Weekly Times group was actually a maze of interlocking shareholdings between newspaper companies around Australia that formed a tight takeover defence. In Adelaide, the Herald and Weekly Times controlled Advertiser Newspapers, which in turn owned 48 per cent of a smaller newspaper group, News Limited. At least it did until Sir Keith did a management buyout as slick as anything American entrepreneur Michael Milken did in the 1980s.

In 1947 Sir Keith took the 48 per cent stake in News Limited that Advertiser owned and flicked it to the Herald and Weekly Times, in exchange for Herald and Weekly Times stock. The Herald and Weekly Times subsequently on-sold the News Limited stock that it had just bought to Queensland Newspapers. Ostensibly this was to diversify ownership of the papers. With newsprint in short supply, Sir Keith argued that the government might object to one group producing two newspapers in Adelaide. Sir Keith was the only director to sign the account of the deal in the Herald and Weekly Times directors' report.

In 1949, Queensland Newspapers on-sold its News Limited shares to a new investor – Sir Keith himself – who put them into his family company, Cruden Investments. At the end of the day then, this half share in News Limited had gone from being owned by Advertiser Newspapers, to being owned by Cruden. The problem was, how was Sir Keith or Cruden going to pay for these News shares? News Limited had an undervalued asset – a large stockholding in Advertiser, the company that had originally controlled News. It was part of the takeover defences used throughout the group – which also kept share prices low. Sir Keith had News sell off its Advertiser shares and declare huge dividends to stockholders. As a 48 per cent shareholder, almost half this money went directly to him at Cruden. This paid off most of Sir Keith's purchase price, which meant that he had picked up News for almost nothing. As Williams saw it, the Murdochs had got control of a valuable Herald asset for a fraction of what it was worth. It was a steal. Not just that, by selling the Advertiser shares, Sir Keith had also opened up a dangerous gap in the group's takeover defence. It was a gap that Sir Keith's son would exploit four decades later.

On Sir Keith's death the Herald and Weekly Times board wanted their News shares back. Sir Keith's will had been equivocal:

> I desire that my said son Keith Rupert Murdoch should have the great opportunity of spending a useful, altruistic and full life in newspaper and broadcasting activities and of ultimately occupying a position of high responsibilities on that field with the support of my trustees if they consider him worthy of that support.

A later codicil repeated Sir Keith's caveat: 'If my trustees judge him worthy of such a place in the community.' When Sir Keith was rushed to hospital for his second prostate operation in April 1952, five months before his death, he wrote: 'It could be that Rupert's strong political views will make his career in newspapers impossible.'

His executors shared this scepticism. When Rupert convinced his mother to retain News Limited, the Herald made another buyout offer, this time threatening a circulation war to drive News out of business. The Murdochs eventually emerged with a half share in News valued at around $200,000. In present-day money values this was about $3 million (that was just the stock valuation of the time – today the newspaper company would probably be worth around $50 million).

However, after returning to Oxford to scrape through his finals, then brushing up his newspaper skills at London's *Daily Express*, Rupert did not want to come home. 'I'm staying,' he cabled his mother.

'No you're not!' she cabled back.

'Please?' he cabled.

'It's too late. All arranged for you to go to Adelaide. Everything awaits your return. You wanted it. Now you must do it.'

Of course it is immaterial how the Murdochs won control of News. The really critical issue is how the Murdochs themselves – and Rupert Murdoch in particular – came to see it. Three things became blindingly clear for Rupert in the aftermath of his father's death. The first was the huge gulf that exists between the people that own a company and the paid staff. Henceforth he would always know that it is the stockholders who win the spoils of success in any business, while the paid staff pick up the termination payment.

Secondly, the Murdoch family's belief that they had been wronged had one useful outcome for Rupert. The more the Murdochs' sense of injustice grew, the more need there was to restore family honour. This could only be done if Rupert took up the cudgels for the family, to rebuild the family newspaper empire. All other causes must be secondary to this. The greater the Murdochs' grievance, the more secure Rupert's position became. The family would fall in line behind Rupert, though he did not as yet control the family holding company, Cruden Investments. And so the family inheritance would be locked up in the News shareholding for four decades, controlled by Rupert.

Lastly, after a childhood marked by gestures of resentment and rebellion against his father, Rupert Murdoch had a new range of patriarchal figures to challenge. The bitterness that would mark his struggles suggests that, while for the Murdoch family it may have been a question of restoring family honour, Rupert Murdoch had a more basic driver. He was looking for revenge.

CHAPTER TWO

THE DRUNKEN SAILOR

Newport, September 1977

Down by Newport Harbour, Robert Edward Turner III, otherwise known as Ted Turner, was tired and emotional. He had already fallen over once at the start of the riotous post-race press conference. He would fall down again at its conclusion as he staggered down an alley under unofficial police escort, helped on his way by two of Newport's finest. Not that any of this put him off his stride. Turner may have been having problems with the vertical and horizontal control, but there was nothing wrong with the volume. 'The Australians are the best of the best,' he slurred at the press conference. He almost dropped the microphone, but recovered it with a lunge. 'You hear that? That's important. They are the best of the best. I love 'em.'

Turner had been drinking steadily since he crossed the finish line of the America's Cup course two hours before. He was celebrating one of his lifetime goals, the apex of 12-metre yacht racing, a successful defence of the America's Cup. 'It's the oldest trophy in international sport,' he would say a day later. 'It was won 25 years before baseball was invented.'

Turner on *Courageous* had whipped Alan Bond's challenger *Australia* four races to nothing. Tubby little Alan Bond, who began his career as a sign painter before he made his fortune from precarious property development, was crestfallen. It would be another six years before he wrested the America's Cup from the New York Yacht Club. Five years after that he would be involved in fraudulent schemes to strip $A900 from a public company – schemes for which he would go to prison in the 1990s, for failing to act honestly as a company director. But such unpleasantness was still a decade away. In September 1977 in the air of gloom as *Australia* glided back to its berth after the race Bond rallied and shouted, 'Let's go see *Courageous*.' The Australian crew piled on to a tender and weaved their way past the spectators' boats to the American defender where, with decks awash with champagne and beer, the two crews took turns throwing each other into the water.

Turner, dripping wet, sat swigging rum and aquavit. His mother on the wharf called, 'Teddy!' Turner waved back: 'It's okay, Mommy, I'm just sipping.' Then he set out for the press conference. In doing this he presented the assembled media waiting for him an ethical dilemma. A dishevelled American hero slips under the table on live television. How would the press cover the story? No one has ever accused Ted Turner of having a drinking problem, but he has a legendary ability to party. The Australian reporters, who had just seen their national team humiliated, had no doubts about where their duty lay. 'Mouth of South is drunk as skunk' was a typical headline. In America, *Sixty Minutes* featured it, but print coverage was more restrained. The *New York Post* was the local paper most likely to make mileage from Turner's antics. Yacht racing is a rich man's hobby way outside the normal interest of *Post* readers. However, the unprecedented press fascination with Turner had prompted the *Post* to send veteran reporter Jim Sullivan to write a wrap-up piece on the Americans' clean sweep. In the normal course of events, what the *Post* did with Turner would be decided by its editor. In this case, the final decision lay with the *Post*'s interventionist owner, the brash Australian who had bought the paper from Dorothy Schiff ten months before. It would be Rupert Murdoch who decided what should they do with the drunken sailor.

In fact, Murdoch didn't do anything. This first encounter between the two men was a non-event. Sullivan filed his piece on the Cup without mentioning the choreography at the press conference. Murdoch and Turner would be the most creative business forces in American media for the rest of the century. They would pursue one of the most high-profile feuds of the business world. Yet here Murdoch had Turner as exposed as he would ever be, a head waiting to be kicked, and nothing happened. The two men were barely aware of each other's existence.

By 1977, Murdoch had already lived in America for four years. While Britain would continue to consume much of his attention, remaining the solid cash engine that drove his empire for another two decades, already Murdoch's main game was the United States. From the day he took over News Limited in Adelaide at the end of 1953, the growth had been spectacular. News profits had been dropping for three years before Sir

Keith died. In 1951 News earned just £A24,877 (about $US50,000). Two years under Rupert had seen net assets double. He fought off a rival Sunday newspaper launched by his father's old newspaper chain, went into television in Adelaide, expanded to Perth in Western Australia with a Sunday newspaper, then leapfrogged the continent to Sydney in 1960 to revive the *Daily Mirror*, a faded afternoon paper.

The pattern was already set. For half a century, Murdoch would spend the first years of each decade recovering from his latest great gamble. By the middle of the decade he would have settled the empire down, beaten back the bankers, and embarked on the next growth phase. The deals would grow more and more dizzy until by the end of each decade Murdoch's News empire would look impossibly stretched, his critics declaring that this time, this crisis would be his last.

Murdoch consistently demonstrated a quality of total determination, a complete commitment to do whatever was necessary to win through. In Adelaide, after fending off a circulation challenge from his father's old group, he launched a cheeky, unsuccessful takeover bid for its local arm, Advertiser Newspapers. In Sydney, a dispute over an office building with a printing press culminated in one of the local press barons, Sir Frank Packer, sending his two sons, Clyde and Kerry, with four other heavies to seize the building by force. Murdoch, in turn, hired a group of bouncers who broke in through a window and expelled the Packer boys and their heavies in a huge brawl. Kerry Packer, today the richest man in Australia, departed with a large red dart sticking out of his shoulder.

In 1964 Murdoch launched a national quality newspaper, *The Australian*, in the national capital, Canberra. The paper's first editor, Maxwell Newton recalled the first night:

> A new newspaper is very exciting. They were still putting machines in. But all the staff were there, freezing cold, Murdoch among them, sending everybody running with immense amounts of energy. And then he asked me to go round with him to his house.
>
> And we had a couple of drinks and he got to talking, and I had this strange feeling that through me knowing his father he was – he was trying to justify something. Even a sort of guilt if you like. Because he said to me – he said, 'Well I've got where I am by some pretty tough and pretty larrikin methods . . . but I've got there.'
>
> 'And now,' he said, 'what I want to do – I want to be able to produce a newspaper that my father would have been proud of.'

In October 1968 Murdoch flew to London as a white knight to rescue the beleaguered Carr family, who were trying to fend off a hostile takeover bid from Robert Maxwell. Maxwell, an ambitious Czech-born media entrepreneur with a talent for corporate theft, had made a share raid on the Carrs' News of the World organisation. The company's major asset was the *News of the World*, a down-market Sunday newspaper with a circulation of six million. Murdoch ended up with control of the paper for a minimal cash outlay. He convinced the chairman, Sir William Carr, to issue voting shares to News in exchange for various News subsidiaries that were earning £1.1 million a year before tax. After other cash purchases Murdoch emerged with 49 per cent of the voting stock of *News of the World*, and six months later, despite a promise to retain Sir William, had forced him to step down as chairman.

In November 1969 Murdoch took over a struggling British afternoon newspaper, the *Sun*, which was in such dire financial straits that the initial purchase price was only £50,000, the first of a series of annual instalments. The total payment was to be £500,000, but only if the paper survived long enough. Two years later, the *Sun* was earning this much every month. The mix of cheeky headlines, sensational news and scandal, cash promotions and pictures of topless women on page three prompted *Private Eye*, the British satirical magazine, to christen Murdoch 'the Dirty Digger'. But sales had taken off. When Murdoch took over the *Sun*, its circulation was one million. It hit two million in 1971, and three million in 1973.

By then Murdoch had left Britain. In October 1973 he paid $19 million for two Texas newspapers, the *San Antonio Express* and its afternoon stablemate, the *News*. Under Murdoch the papers became more profitable as they became more racy, with headlines like, 'Armies of Insects Marching on SA', and 'Killer Bees Move North'. For the next two decades San Antonio would be one of the few parts of Murdoch's American empire that made any money, chugging out a steady $7 million a year profit through the 1980s. Murdoch meanwhile settled his family in New York. While he would go on to become the most powerful media baron in Britain, it is remarkable that after Oxford Murdoch lived in Britain less than five years. From 1973, while Murdoch spent much of his time running his newspapers in Britain, he lived in America. To qualify to own Australian television stations he listed his home address as a cattle property near Canberra.

These had been hard years, particularly the early ones in Adelaide. In 1956 Murdoch had married an airline hostess, Patricia Booker. They had a daughter, Prudence, in 1959. However, the marriage became increasingly unhappy and ended in 1966, after divorce proceedings so acrimonious that, according to one account, Murdoch ordered that the name of his wife's lawyer should never appear in any of the News publications. In April 1966, Murdoch married again. He was 36 years old. His bride, Anna Marie Torv, was a 22-year-old reporter. According to News Corporation press statements, 1967 was also the year that the woman who would be Murdoch's third wife, Wendi Deng, was born in a dirt-poor province in China.

Anna Torv grew up in difficult circumstances. Her father was a war refugee from Estonia who married the daughter of a family with a dry-cleaning business in Scotland, where Anna was born on 30 June 1944. When she was ten, her parents emigrated to Australia, where they ended up running a snack bar in a Sydney caravan park. But the snack bar sent them bankrupt, and her mother later walked out, leaving Anna as eldest with much of the child-rearing responsibilities for her sister and two brothers. Anna left school at the Sisters of Mercy convent when she was sixteen and, after a succession of jobs, ended up with a position as a cadet journalist at the Sydney *Mirror* in 1962. She was 18, bright, serious, very attractive, with great hopes for a writing career, when she interviewed her boss for the in-house paper, and ended up dating him.

It was a fitful romance. When Murdoch launched the *Australian* in 1964, Anna went to Canberra as part of the sales promotion team. Later, when Anna worked as a reporter, she and Rupert lived in an apartment at Blues Point Tower. Initially, Patricia had won custody of Prudence. However, as Patricia went from one disastrous romantic entanglement to another, Prudence asked her father if she could live with him instead. Prudence came to live with Rupert and Anna in Sydney about the time that Anna's first child Elisabeth was born, in August 1968. Overnight, Anna had a new baby to look after as well as a nine-year-old stepdaughter. Two months later the Carr family sent their distress call for help with *News of the World*, and Anna lost her home. Rupert telephoned her from Melbourne and told her to meet him at Sydney airport, on the way to London.

Anna found establishing herself in English society difficult. The attacks on her husband and on herself she found dismaying. There was also the tragedy of a bungled kidnapping. At Christmas 1969, two brothers, Arthur and Nizam Hosein kidnapped and killed Muriel McKay, the wife of News International executive Alick McKay. It was a case of mistaken identity, after they saw Muriel McKay driving the Murdochs' Rolls Royce. Further tragedy followed. Anna was the driver of a car that knocked down and killed an old woman crossing the street. The coroner found Anna had had no time to react.

Both the Murdoch sons were born in Britain – Lachlan on 8 September

1971 and James 15 months later on 15 December 1972 – but Anna never seemed to enjoy living in England. When the family moved to America in 1974, she clearly found life in New York more convivial.

The business struggles in Murdoch's early years as a media proprietor stripped the idealism from him. The loosely held political convictions from Oxford bleached away. By the mid-1970s they had disappeared completely. He had cut his ties with the world he'd embraced at Oxford. When Anthony Blond, a Brasenose alumnus who had helped Robin Farquharson publish his book *Drop Out!*, went to see Murdoch to ask him to help his old friend, Murdoch turned him down. 'He said, 'No, no one can help him.'' Blond recalled. In March 1973, firemen carried Farquharson's badly burned body out of a derelict terrace house in Camden Town he'd been sharing with other squatters. He died ten days later, on 1 April.

Farquharson's death was, his friends and former colleagues agreed at the inquest, a tragic story. Only a handful of people made it to the funeral. A notable absentee was Rupert Murdoch. Murdoch had left Farquharson behind him long before, along with everything else from his time at Oxford, from a past that was now closed to him, a world that no longer offered any possibilities for him. Over half a century the course of Murdoch's odyssey would be marked regularly by the painful moments when he jettisoned cargo: people and ideas and places that he had outgrown. His direction was always forward. Later, when explaining the latest in the long list of executives that he had dumped at News, Murdoch would say, 'I learned when running a public company not to grow too close to people.'

In 1974 Murdoch launched the *National Star* in the US as an unsuccessful rival to the *National Enquirer*. Two years later it was relaunched as the *Star*, a women's magazine with a circulation of three million. In November 1976 Murdoch finally established a beachhead in New York when he persuaded the long-time owner of the *New York Post*, Dorothy Schiff, to sell the then loss-making paper to him for $30 million. Murdoch then moved on New York Magazine Company, founded and run by Clay Felker, who had befriended Rupert and Anna Murdoch, introducing them to New York society. Despite a spectacular fight with the outraged Felker, Murdoch bought the company for $26 million and picked up *New York* magazine and *Village Voice*. *Time* magazine ran a cover showing Murdoch as King Kong standing on top of the Empire State Building, with a strap line, 'Extra!!! Aussie Press Lord Terrifies New York.'

For all the sound and fury, in 1977 Murdoch was barely a blip on American media's radar scope. Ted Turner, by contrast, had come to loom very large indeed. He had inherited one of the country's largest billboard companies, and had done well with a couple of television stations. But real fame came thanks to a lawyer called Gerald Levin. On 30 September 1975, Levin, who headed a tiny pay-television operation called Home Box Office that was an obscure part of the Time Inc empire, triggered a huge change in the US television industry. He did it by renting satellite time to carry the Muhammad Ali-Joe Frazier fight, the so-called Thrilla in Manilla, to cable customers in New York, Mississippi and Florida.

This was a breakthrough, because for the first time a cable program could be shown simultaneously across the country. Up until then, the cable networks that had sprung up across America could only show videotapes, and programming that cable operators received via expensive microwave links. What it meant was that, while their cables could carry a lot of channels, all that the cable operators had to offer their customers was rebroadcasting nearby free-to-air television stations. What Levin had shown was that, if cable companies bought an earth station, they could receive all sorts of programming via satellite, that they could then put on to their cable nets. Suddenly they could offer their paying customers dozens of channel choices. For the first time cable offered not just clearer pictures, but a clearly better product than local free-to-air television. The huge growth this would produce in cable viewing would change the balance of power in America media. But some of the biggest opportunities lay in providing the new programming.

Within months of Levin's historic broadcast, Turner had moved to set up an uplink station that would broadcast his Atlanta television station, WTCG, to an RCA satellite. Any cable operator with an earth station could pull the signal down and rebroadcast Turner's super station as a cable channel all over America. And they did. That single move would eventually make Turner a multi-billionaire.

In 1977 the differences between Murdoch and Turner were easier to spot than any similarities. Turner had inherited a billboard company in the American South. Murdoch's heritage was newspapers. Turner was seven years younger than Murdoch. Their temperaments were worlds apart. Turner with his bipolar disorder was closer in personality style to Robin Farquharson. However, the two moguls-in-waiting did have some points in common. One was an intuitive feel for where media was heading. This would lead them to make remarkably similar gambles on the future of US media in the 1980s. They were both superb game players. As well, they both liked sailing and they both liked winning, though not necessarily in that order.

The sailing is important, because it would be a key factor in the relationship between Murdoch and Turner. It would determine the chemistry between the two fierce competitors for two decades. That chemistry would be an underlying driver in the fight between Murdoch and the cable companies in 1997. But well before that, the events that it would trigger in 1985 would do much to shape the future of media in the 1980s.

Stories about Ted Turner and sailing boats have become collector's items. Like the time he was at the back of the fleet in an ocean race from Nassau to Jamaica. He wanted to catch up an hour by cutting between two islands. But there was a reef in the passage. What was the chance of getting through, he asked his navigator. 'About ten per cent, skipper,' the navigator told him.

'That's good enough for me, let's go for it,' Turner said. They duly ran hard aground.

'Sonofabitch!' shouted Turner, along with other nautical terms that old sailors bring out on heavy weather days. It took two hours to get the boat refloated, and back to where they started.

Meanwhile the tide had risen. What was the chance of getting through now, he asked again. 'About ten per cent, skipper,' the navigator said.

'That's good enough for me, navigator,' said Turner. Which is how they ended up back on the sandbank.

While he sailed as a child, Rupert Murdoch's major interest dates back to 1960, when he moved to Sydney to revamp the *Daily Mirror*. He bought an old 59-foot ketch, *Ilina*, to sail around Sydney Harbour. But the real lure was the Sydney to Hobart, one of the world's top three offshore races. It begins on 26 December each year, and offers sailors a 1000 kilometre adrenaline rush, surfing down the east coast of Australia across Bass Strait to Tasmania, rounding Tasman Island, then beating back north across Storm Bay and up the Derwent River into Hobart. In a good year the trip is gruelling. In a bad year, with a southerly buster blowing up from the Southern Ocean, it is terrifying. Seven sailors drowned in abysmal conditions in the 1998 race. Larry Ellison, the owner of software giant, Oracle, won that race on his boat *Sayonara*, with Lachlan Murdoch on board as a crew member. Ellison said that at one point, facing 60-foot waves and winds touching 100 miles per hour, he was sure he was going to die. His immediate response was that he was never going to sail the race again; but six months later he was talking about racing again – maybe with Ted Turner. 'The Sydney to Hobart is a little like childbirth,' said Ellison. 'It takes a while to suppress the pain, and then you're ready to do it again.'

In the 1960s Murdoch hired the *Mirror*'s wily yachting correspondent, Boy Messenger, as sailing master, and became a race regular. While it is a handicap event, inevitably most attention goes to the first yacht across the finish line. *Ilina* came eighth before handicap in 1961, and twenty-first in 1962. Murdoch missed a year, then in 1964 he almost won, in an episode with uncanny similarities to Turner's adventures on the sandbank. Three and a half days into the race, with just the final beat across Storm Bay to come before reaching the Derwent River, *Ilina* had clawed its way into the lead, when Murdoch's sailing master told him he had to reduce sail.

'I ordered the crew to put three reefs in the main and hoist a number three yankee and staysail,' Messenger said later.

'We were going round Tasman Island in a howling nor'-wester and I knew it was going to be worse once we got around the corner,' Messenger said.

Murdoch looked over his shoulder at the yachts behind and refused to slow down.

Messenger was an old salt who had been sailing the event since 1945, and was also the race bookie. 'So I told him, in very plain language, what lay ahead and why we had to reduce sail to survive it. I told him that, as soon as we got around the corner, we were going to get the hell belted out of us.'

Instead Murdoch ordered more sail. The two men stood glaring at each other across the heaving cockpit. 'And then something snapped,' said Messenger. 'I told him that, as of that moment, I was resigning. And I also told him where he could put his boat.'

Five minutes later Murdoch backed down as the yacht hit 20-foot waves. 'Of course, I was right about the weather,' Messenger said. 'As we headed across Storm Bay I got the message to take charge again.'

The steel sloop behind them was dismasted, but a larger yacht further inshore crept past to take line honours. *Ilina* was second. Murdoch said he was giving up racing. Despite this he made one last attempt the following year. *Ilina* came fourteenth.

Turner has also been a regular sailor in the Sydney to Hobart, though more successfully than Murdoch. In 1968 he crewed on *Ondine II*, which won line honours. In 1971 he came second in his *American Eagle* then won line and handicap honours in the same boat the following year. After his America's Cup defence in 1977 Turner went on to win the Fastnet race in Britain two years later, despite atrocious conditions in which 15 sailors drowned and Turner himself was mistakenly reported lost. In 1980 came the débâcle of the America's Cup defence, when Turner's yacht

Courageous was beaten badly by both of the other American contenders. Still fulminating against the New York Yacht Club, Turner announced his retirement from racing. Henceforth he would pursue land-based sports.

In all these years Murdoch and Turner had never sailed against each other. Now it looked as if they never would. So really it was just bad luck that brought them together again in a race in 1983. And it was really very bad luck indeed that Murdoch's yacht ended up running Turner aground, sparking nearly two decades of passionate blood feud.

New York/Hobart, New Year 1983–84

It began and ended as a grudge match. In the early 1980s Marvin Greene, the head of a New York television production group called Reeves Communications, built one of the most luxurious – and fastest – maxi yachts afloat. He then set off on a two-year campaign racing the boat, the 81-footer *Nirvana*, around the world. In race after race Greene kept running up against a British insurance executive called Bob Bell, whose 80-foot *Condor* kept challenging *Nirvana* for supremacy. By December 1983, when both yachts were scheduled to race in the Sydney to Hobart, feelings between the crews were heated, and Bell and Greene made a 'moderate wager' on who would get to Hobart first. Greene hired a top New Zealand navigator. Then Bell pulled out a trump card by convincing Ted Turner, the last great amateur sailor, to fly in to Sydney to skipper *Condor*.

Two months before, Alan Bond had finally taken the America's Cup away from the New York Yacht Club (NYYC) – who were not Ted Turner's favourite people. And Greene, as it happened, was entered in the Sydney to Hobart in the name of the New York Yacht Club. For Turner this meant the race would be a private rerun of the America's Cup. Beating Greene would be a minor way to redress some of the indignities that the stuffed shirts at the New York Yacht Club had inflicted upon Turner over the years. For Greene's part, earnings were down at Reeves Communications, and running a $5 million yacht with a crew of 28 is not a painless business. He had sought some backers. His Australian wife knew the Murdochs, and Rupert Murdoch reportedly had become a sponsor, in pursuit of that Holy Grail, victory in the Sydney to Hobart.

Not that Murdoch was really thinking much about yacht races. That summer Stanley S. Shuman, Murdoch's investment banker since 1976, had introduced him to Steve Ross, the chairman and chief executive of

Warner Communications Inc. On 1 December 1983 News Corporation announced that it had bought 6.7 per cent of Warner. Ross told Murdoch to back off.

From the time the starter's gun set the fleet off in Sydney Harbour on 26 December, it was clear that this was just a two-boat race. The two big maxis shadowed each other down the coast, Turner leading. There was never more than a mile and a half between the two boats as they hammered through the choppy seas, two giant yachts each the size of a small building, flying along at up to 30 miles an hour. Then as they turned into the Derwent River on the final stretch on 29 December, the wind eased. Turner on *Condor* sailed into a wind hole, and *Nirvana* crept inshore and tacked past. But Turner found wind, and suddenly his bow was in front again. The two huge maxis edged closer and closer together, the 28-person crew on each crowding the decks.

Six miles from the Hobart finish line, the land snakes out on one side to a point called White Rock Head. As the waterway narrowed and Turner began to run out of sea room, he shouted to *Nirvana* to give him space to clear the point. He had right of way as the skipper with an overlap, on a boat that was moving faster *Nirvana* kept its course. Turner shouted again, and then the boats touched briefly. Booms clashed, *Condor* ran aground and then the big blue hull of *Nirvana* was sailing on alone.

'He wiped out our antenna pretty good,' Greene said later. Turner had a bit of experience getting boats off sandbanks. Within four minutes *Condor* was sailing again. Turner made up two and a half minutes in the last six miles, but he was still 200 yards behind when Greene reached the finish line. A protest jury disqualified *Nirvana* the next day and awarded the race to *Condor*. A tearful Ted Turner said he didn't want it to end that way: 'We're good sports on both boats and there are no hard feelings.'

One of the lesser-known post-race features of the Sydney to Hobart is an institution known as the Quiet Little Drink, a title that the Cruising Yacht Club spokesman that year called 'the greatest misnomer of all times'. Indeed, the previous year a local newspaper had run an editorial that began by saying, 'Go home, foul-mouthed drunken bum yachties.' That was before the editorial-writer *really* got snippy.

The Quiet Little Drink lasts anything from one to four days and it includes a competition where crews attempt to beat the standing record for the number of jugs of rum and coke (a 60/40 mix) that a crew can consume in 12 hours. In 1983 the existing record was 134 jugs, set two years before. The *Condor* boys began with a handicap, as the winning crew traditionally begins proceedings by downing 20 jugs of a cocktail mix made from two liqueurs and milk.

Another race tradition, that on occasion blurs boundaries with the Quiet Little Drink, is a more formal affair, the post-race dinner. A number of speeches are made, including one traditionally made by the skipper of the winning boat. Which is how Ted Turner came to be getting to his feet to deliver a long and rambling speech in which he made it clear that on reflection he was feeling not quite so chipper about being forced to run aground. In fact he was definitely peeved with everyone remotely connected with *Nirvana*. This included particularly its sponsor, Rupert Murdoch. Australians were no longer the best of the best. Or rather, this Australian wasn't the best of the best. Quite the reverse, in fact. Once Turner started on Rupert he went on and on and on. By the time he sat down again, he had delivered unpardonable offence. In Turner's mind at least, from this point on Murdoch was an enemy.

Rupert Murdoch had not the faintest clue of what was going on. It had been his habit to spend Christmas at his Cavan cattle property in Australia with the family. He was there this year, but his mind was firmly focused on the other side of the world. On 29 December New York time, several hours after *Condor* ran aground, Steve Ross had ambushed Murdoch by pulling off a cute little exchange of stock with his friend Herbert J. Siegel. Siegel's Chris-Craft Industries would pick up a 19 per cent stake in Warner Communications, in exchange for Warner taking a 42.5 per cent stake in the Chris-Craft group's string of television stations. Warner now had a major new shareholder to fend off Murdoch. But more importantly, it meant that now Warner controlled American television stations. As a television investor Warner had the protection of Section 310 of the Communications Act of 1934, which decreed that alien companies, like the Australian-owned News Corporation, could not hold more than 25 per cent of its stock. Warner had been Murdoch-proofed.

Rupert Murdoch's response was pure rage. The bitterness over Sir Keith's inheritance, the fierce struggles in Adelaide and Sydney against rivals with political muscle and greater resources, his rejection by London society and the torrid newspaper wars in New York: all stoked a deep wellspring of anger which he carried within him. It was an anger looking for a target. 'It's a tone he adopts – he feels the world is out to get him,' Clay Felker once said. The rage still lurks beneath the surface today, despite the polish that half a century of winning has given Murdoch. It is easier to see this in earlier, less scripted productions, as when Murdoch tore into his competitors while testifying before the Australian Broadcasting Tribunal in a television licence hearing in July 1979.

'They are the monolithic companies in this country. My life has been spent fighting them, starting with a very small newspaper, standing up to attempts to push me out of business at the age of 23 in Adelaide. But I kept it alive through my own skill and effort . . . The same in Sydney . . . I am now accused of not being an Australian. Who in this room can say that I am not a good Australian or a patriotic one? Who else chooses to be battered and bruised ten months of the year in being an Australian when it would be a lot easier not to be one . . . Who else has risked his every penny, his reputation and his career in fighting for what he believes is right for this country?'

The only other person in the American media business who can produce quite this much moral indignation and spontaneous outrage is Ted Turner. Murdoch now directed his rage towards Steve Ross. He called his hardball New York lawyers, Squadron, Ellenoff, Plesent and Lehrer. The senior partner, Howard M. Squadron, had been a key part of Murdoch's US deals since he'd bought the San Antonio papers in 1983. But recently much of the work had been done by the head of corporate at Squadron Ellenoff, Arthur Siskind.

Over the New Year, Squadron and Siskind launched a legal blitzkrieg against Warner Communications in state and federal courts, challenging the Chris–Craft deal. They accused Ross and the rest of the Warner Communications board of racketeering.

The civil cases that followed were remarkable only for the extraordinary legal invective that Murdoch's lawyers spun off – one judge called it a corporate form of feudal warfare. The cases were duly thrown out, but the ferocity of the Squadron Ellenoff legal onslaught eventually induced Steve Ross to buy back Murdoch's Warner stock. Murdoch took a $41.5 million profit, plus $3 million for his interest bill and $5 million to cover Squadron Ellenoff's legal expenses.

As coincidence would have it, at the same time that these events were unfolding, one of Squadron Ellenoff's other major clients was taking a more proactive interest in racketeering. While News Corporation had become the firm's biggest source of fees, its second largest client was a rapidly growing defence contractor in the Bronx called Wedtech. While it was not immediately apparent, Wedtech had a simple corporate strategy. Essentially this was to attempt to bribe every politician, regulator or government official who came within range of its pocketbook. On its way to becoming one of the major corporate and political scandals of the 1980s, Wedtech gained $500 million of US Defense Department business by claiming that US minorities – in this case Puerto Ricans – held the majority of the company's stocks. At the time of Wedtech's initial public offering in

1983, it became clear that this was not true. Wedtech had engaged a new set of lawyers, Squadron Ellenoff, who were instructed to research various ways to change the ownership structure 'for a limited period of time' that would satisfy the minorities requirement of its defence contracts. However the stock would revert to the original owners several years later.

In November 1983, lawyers in Squadron Ellenoff's corporate section, headed by Arthur Siskind, came up with five separate strategies to change Wedtech's ownership, none of which were acceptable to the government. Wedtech management then decided on a simple sale of their stock to the company's Puerto Rican founder, Tony Mariotta. Mariotta would not pay for the stock for two years, and it would be held in escrow. The escrow agreement was signed on 27 December, as Ted Turner tacked down the Australian coast. Siskind was on vacation out of town. What made this sale contract illegal was a side agreement that Moreno would never complete the deal, and the Wedtech stock would end up back with the original owners. The side agreement made the whole sale document a sham. The Squadron Ellenoff lawyers testified that they knew nothing of the side agreement, and would not have worked for Wedtech if they had known.

'Mr Guariglia (the Wedtech president) asked me whether or not he could have a side agreement with Mr Mariotta where Mr Mariotta would agree to default,' Siskind later testified. 'I told him that he absolutely could not, that it was improper, that this was a proposal to be made, this was the proposal everybody had to live up to.'

An aggressive young US Attorney for New York, Rudy Giuliani, later brought racketeering charges against Wedtech executives, senior government officials and politicians, based in part on the side agreement. In court proceedings, Giuliani's office would describe Siskind as an 'unindicted co-conspirator' in the racketeering case. Siskind said later that this was merely a tactical move which allowed prosecutors to table a Squadron Ellenoff memo which otherwise would have legal privilege. At one point the Securities and Exchange Commission advised Squadron Ellenoff that there could be a conflict of interest in the firm continuing to represent Wedtech. 'At no time did anybody indicate to me that they were considering having me indicted,' Siskind testified in 1988. 'I never believed I would be indicted in this matter.'

This would be merely a matter of ancient history but for the fact that 13 years later, these disparate elements – the feud with Ted Turner, the bad blood with Warner, and the memories of Wedtech – would come together again in October 1996 when Time Warner refused to carry Murdoch's Fox News on its cable systems in New York. The rush to the courts that followed saw Rudy Giuliani, now the mayor of New York, line up shoulder to shoulder with his old sparring partners at Squadron Ellenoff, to fight Murdoch's old enemies, Ted Turner and Time Warner.

Back in 1983, while Rupert Murdoch had more on his mind to worry about than a boat race on the other side of the world, he was angry and ready to join cause against anyone who criticised him. In 1997, Turner's biographer, Porter Bibb, told Paul Farhi of the *Washington Post* that it was the Sydney to Hobart race that had sparked the bad feeling between Murdoch and Turner. Over a decade and a half some of the details had blurred. Bibb's sources in the Turner camp told him the race was in 1979, and that it was Murdoch's boat that ran aground. What they were clear on was the depth of the feeling that now ran between the two men.

Looking back, it's hard to avoid the conclusion that this wasn't really about a boat race, that the speech Turner gave afterwards actually gave form to an underlying grievance. Ted Turner was already annoyed with Rupert Murdoch in 1983 because Murdoch had gone after something that was the pride and joy of Turner's heart, the very thing that would spark the Time Warner cable fight in New York in 1996. Murdoch wanted a piece of CNN.

By the early 1980s, Murdoch's corporate empire had assumed much of its contemporary structure. The original company that Sir Keith Murdoch had controlled, News Limited, was now only the operating company for the News group's Australian interests. News International was the British equivalent, as the operating company for Murdoch's Fleet Street newspapers. The American subsidiaries, like News America Holdings, had parent companies in the Cayman Islands or the Bahamas, which in turn were owned jointly by News International and News Limited. This shared holding meant that they did not come under the sole control of British or Australian banks or tax authorities. The umbrella holding company that ultimately controlled and owned all of the other News companies, no matter how indirectly, was an Australian public company, The News Corporation Limited.

Murdoch was now the best-known newspaper publisher in the world. In America, besides the *Post* and the San Antonio papers he owned *Village Voice*, *New York* magazine, the *Boston Herald* (bought in December 1982 for $1 million plus up to $7 million in future profits), and the *Chicago Sun-Times* (acquired in November 1983 for $90 million). In Britain he had bought the *Times* and *Sunday Times* in 1981, and now produced 30 per cent of the national newspapers. He had subsided for a year or two in the early 1980s for his customary beginning-of-the-decade financial crisis. But his interest was turning. In Europe he had bought a majority stake in Satellite Television Plc, which ran a desultory European satellite service called Sky. In America he had bought control of Inter-American Satellite Television Network, which would become Skyband Inc. Neither of these ventures would work, but in early 1983 he was looking at programming for a satellite television service. In mid-year he had tried to bid for Showtime, but the second biggest cable channel was snapped up by a venture led by Warner. Murdoch's thoughts turned to television news, and this led him to Ted Turner.

In January 1984 Ted Turner confirmed to Australian journalist Glenda Korporaal he had been talking to Murdoch. 'He sat in that very chair a year ago,' Turner said. 'He was talking to me about Cable Network News. He likes it very much.' With the *New York Post*, with Clay Felker's *New York Magazine*, and with Showtime and Warner Communications, the difference between Murdoch liking something and trying to buy it was just a matter of timing. Turner and Murdoch talked about CNN providing raw footage for a European news channel that Murdoch wanted to produce. The message was clear. This was an area Murdoch coveted. Turner didn't like it.

If anything further was needed to cement the dislike between the two men, there was the bitter legacy of 1985. In a three-month period the two men set out on almost identical quests to revolutionise American media. The events that they triggered changed the media business on three continents. Both of them faced certain disaster. Only one of them emerged unscathed. The question has always been how Rupert Murdoch survived.

Hollywood, Feb to May 1985

By 1985 Ted Turner and Rupert Murdoch had come to remarkably similar conclusions about the future of the media industry. Other than the minor encroachments achieved so far by cable companies, the decline of afternoon newspapers, and the reshuffling of media owners, the media business in the US had run pretty well unchanged since the 1940s. There had been no new television networks since ABC was launched in 1948, and even that had not made any money until the 1970s. The major players had little idea of the wholesale changes that were about to overtake the industry, initially through the huge advances forged by cable operators. But whatever changes the new world of media would usher in, the ground rules would remain the same: media is about content, and about a distribution system to deliver that content to consumers.

The future that both Rupert Murdoch and Ted Turner saw in 1985 lay in the big Hollywood studios, and the free-to-air television networks. The studios' film libraries and production facilities offered huge programming content for the media revolution that was unfolding. The television networks provided the biggest distribution platform in the world for new programming. What no one had tried yet was to put these two elements together.

Turner and Murdoch would each make combining content and distribution systems their grand play. Events in 1985 unfolded at furious pace. In late March, News Corporation announced it was buying half of the Twentieth Century Fox movie studio from oilman Marvin Davis for $250 million, a price that included some working capital for the cash-strapped studio. This was a big swallow for News Corporation. Just two months before, Murdoch had closed a $350 million deal to buy 13 trade magazines from the Ziff Davis group. The cash drain would grow even bigger later that year, when Murdoch was forced to buy the other half of the Fox Studio for yet another $325 million. The three transactions would cost a dizzy $925 million. Yet Murdoch remained in buying mode.

The initial purchase of half of Twentieth Century Fox was announced on Monday 21 March. Murdoch spent the rest of that week in Los Angeles at Michael Milken's high-yield conference for clients of junk bond issuer Drexel Burnham Lambert, the so-called Predator's Ball. That week at a cocktail party associated with the conference, Murdoch spoke with the head of Fox, Barry Diller, and with John Kluge. Kluge was an old friend of Murdoch's who had a chain of television stations called Metromedia and a little debt problem. Within days Murdoch had decided he wanted to buy some television stations as well.

As it happened, Ted Turner had been thinking along similar lines to Murdoch. On 13 March, a week before the Fox deal, Warren Buffet and the Capital Cities group had bid for the ABC network. Ted Turner had been working for months to put together a deal to move on CBS or ABC. He couldn't match the Capital Cities bid for ABC, but on 18 April, four weeks after Murdoch had announced his deal to buy half a movie studio, Turner stood on the stage of the grand ballroom of New York's Plaza Hotel to announce Turner Broadcasting System was bidding for CBS. The counter-attack that CBS mounted was long and torrid, and culminated in a crippling $1 billion stock buyback announced on 3 July. Fighting off Turner would leave CBS crippled, and vulnerable to another corporate raider, Laurence Tisch. Turner fought on through July with his bid for CBS, but his enthusiasm for the fight was waning.

Murdoch's and Turner's paths continued to cross. On 2 May, a fortnight after Turner went public with his CBS bid, Twentieth Century Fox announced it was buying Metromedia from John Kluge. After an already contracted sale of Kluge's Boston television station went through, Fox would be paying a net $1.55 billion for Metromedia's six remaining stations. While Turner learned of the nasty surprises CBS had planned for him with its stock buyback on 3 July, Murdoch had received some bad news of his own the week before. Marvin Davis wanted out of the Metromedia deal, and out of Twentieth Century Fox. For Murdoch, going alone without a partner meant that the cost of the exercise had just doubled. He told his own journalists straightfaced that he was 'absolutely delighted' at the prospect.

In the last week of July, News finally announced what had been an open secret for months – that it planned to use the Metromedia television stations to launch a new television network, Fox. The news almost coincided with a CNN report on 29 July that Ted Turner had given up on his CBS aspirations, and was meeting with executives at Kirk Kerkorian's MGM/ UA studio. Turner signed a deal to buy the MGM studio on 7 August for $1.6 billion.

Murdoch and Turner finally had their hands on what they had been looking for. Each had a movie studio. Murdoch had the basis to launch a new network. Turner had a secure source of films for his super station. And neither man had enough money to hold on to their prize. They had done enough to break both of their companies.

The problem with being ahead of your time is that the bankers and investors who can make corporate dreams a reality are usually looking backwards, judging loan prospects by what has happened in the past. The junk bonds that Michael Milken had made famous were the obvious – the only – source of funds for Turner and for Murdoch in 1985. But even Milken would struggle with these two transactions. They weren't really 1980s sorts of deals. For years Milken had told his Savings & Loans customers, who provided the funds for his money machine, that junk bonds were like any other form of lending, only more profitable. He had exhaustive research going back to the 1950s that studied the borrowing records of second-rank companies that didn't have a blue-chip credit rating. The research showed that, while such loans were more risky for the lender, despite the occasional failures the higher interest rates charged meant such lending was more profitable than cheaper loans to blue-chip companies.

While this may have been the rationale, the deals that Milken put together in the 1980s were quite different from the sort of lending his studies portrayed. At heart, Michael Milken's junk bond deals were bridging loans, expensive money for a takeover or a management buyout. Once the deal was done, the borrower needed to replace the junk debt by selling off parts of the business, injecting new capital through a stock offering, or tapping new lines of credit in the target company. Corporate raiders used junk to make a quick profit. It was an effective way to break out the under-used wealth hidden away in large companies. Junk bonds weren't effective if, like Murdoch and Turner in 1985, the companies you were buying didn't have undervalued assets that could be stripped off, and instead you were making a strategic investment that could take five years or more to pay off.

Such was Milken's ironclad reputation for raising money that by 1985 his firm Drexel Burnham Lambert had taken to issuing letters to prospective borrowers stating that they were 'highly confident' of raising funds for them. Milken had to issue two 'highly confident' letters before he got Turner's MGM deal away. On 26 March 1986 the deal finally closed, with Milken raising $1.2 billion in junk bonds after various asset sales. Kirk Kerkorian the vendor had agreed to accept $220 million in preference shares as part of the price.

This deal contained a bomb with a delayed fuse. Under the conditions for the preference shares, Kerkorian had to be paid dividends in Turner Broadcasting System (TBS) stock, rather than in cash. What was worse, the moment that the TBS stock price fell below $15, Kerkorian would be issued more TBS stock to compensate. If Turner's stock price continued to fall, Kerkorian would pick up a swag of TBS stock, and it was just a question of time before Kerkorian ended up controlling Ted Turner's company. By early 1987 Turner's stock price was spiralling down.

It ended in tears. By March 1987, Turner was desperate to raise money to renegotiate the remaining junk bonds, and to pay out Kerkorian. John Malone at TCI organised a summit of cable company leaders, who agreed to invest $550 million in Turner's company. One of the reasons the cable guys were ready to save Ted Turner was the fear that otherwise CNN might fall into the hands of Rupert Murdoch.

'I had three choices, oddly enough, for investors,' Turner told the National Press Club in 1994. 'One was Rupert Murdoch, and I appreciated his offer very much. And the other was General Electric and the other was from the cable operators. Well, it wasn't hard to decide who I wanted to go with.'

The rescue package the cable operators put together solved Turner's problem, but it came at a price. He was now a partner with the cable companies, who built in safeguards that gave them veto power over any decision by Turner. If he wanted to spend more than $2 million on anything, even on his beloved Atlanta Braves baseball team, he needed to get their approval. Years later, Turner said:

> The cable companies wanted some restrictions on me because they were investing in my company and they thought I was, you know, a little loony because I had just started CNN a little before and almost went bankrupt there and I nearly went bankrupt when my father died and I nearly went bankrupt when I bought MGM. Of course, subsequent time showed all of the deals I made were excellent deals. So anyway, they told me they had to have financial controls over me, so I wouldn't make a mistake and imperil the company – like I wanted to imperil the company. Remember, every move I've made, not one of them turned out to be a wrong move. I mean, I'm not talking about how I ran the Braves for ten years. That was a disaster.

While Turner continued to hatch new schemes for the next decade, besides picking up a couple of independent film studios, none of the schemes came to anything. His cable partners blocked them all, to Turner's chagrin. Turner's role as *enfant terrible* of the American media was on ice.

The question is, how did Rupert Murdoch escape falling over the same precipice? Survival stories are the inverse of whodunnits. At the top of a deadly 1,000-foot drop the victim is found mysteriously alive and unharmed. The question that the detective has to solve is, did the victim not fall, or wasn't he pushed? Murdoch faced a much more daunting challenge than Turner's. At least Turner started off with the right nationality. Murdoch was an Australian buying US television stations, raising twice as much debt, and with huge other problems in his media group. Getting out of the Metromedia deal unscathed would be an escape act worthy of Houdini.

So Murdoch's great American run began not in March when he swooped to buy the first half of Twentieth Century Fox in Los Angeles, but six weeks earlier in New York, in his penthouse apartment on Fifth Avenue. On Sunday 10 February, Murdoch flew his British executives to New York for the weekend for secret talks about moving his British newspapers – the *Sun*, the *News of the World*, the *Times* and the *Sunday Times* – from his hugely overstaffed and highly unionised printing presses on Fleet Street to a new facility he was building at Wapping, in the London Docklands. Instead of printers from the Society of Graphical and Allied Trades (SOGAT) he planned to employ members of the less militant electricians' union, the EETPU. He would need a lot less of them. News already ran some of the most profitable newspapers in the world. The wages Murdoch would save at Wapping would be worth another $150 million a year in profits to him – a saving that would pay the interest bill on a huge amount of new debt.

The downside was that this was a blatant challenge to the power of British trade unions. If Murdoch lost this fight he could wave goodbye to Britain and the profit machine that his British subsidiary, News International, had become. He would be forced out of the UK, and News Corporation would almost certainly go broke. There was no halfway mark here. It was either huge success or momentous failure. It all depended on the tightest secrecy, and Murdoch and his British execs discussed how to maintain security and create smokescreens to draw attention elsewhere.

In any big corporate deal, or series of deals, there is an event horizon. This is the line of no return, where the huge black hole of debt in the deal has become inescapable, overwhelming; there are no exits and the deal maker must make this mess work and emerge from it on the far side, or perish in the attempt. Turner, for example, had a string of opportunities to back out of his MGM deal with Kerkorian, but he ignored them. It is entirely in keeping with Murdoch's penchant for gambling and for secrecy that he passed the event horizon in February 1985 at least a month before anyone even knew there was a deal going down.

By late February, Murdoch had signed a contract with Atex, the Boston electronics firm that would supply the Wapping computer terminals for the journalists, and he had met Eric Hammond of the EETPU, to draw up plans to hire staff secretly. From this point Murdoch was committed. So as he turned to launch his assault upon America in Los Angeles three weeks later, Murdoch had absolutely nothing to lose. But no one knew of this. Murdoch was like a gambler who keeps buying more chips, while nobody at the casino realises that he has run out of credit. What does a smart gambler do when he has nothing to lose? He doubles his bets. Wapping and the doomsday deadline was Murdoch's warm little secret as he turned his attentions to Hollywood.

Of course, the commitment worked the other way as well. The more that Murdoch was forced to pay for Twentieth Century Fox and then Metromedia and then to launch the new Fox network, the more committed he was to making his move to Wapping. Murdoch was prepared –

and by now he was required – to push through with a change at Wapping that would overturn the British industrial relations system, simply to finance a new American television network. He was committed to over-turning the social system in one country to pay for a commercial venture in another. By any standard, this was game play of the highest level. And it didn't stop there.

The common thread in all of Murdoch's deals in 1985 was that each move he made – buying Twentieth Century Fox and Metromedia and building the Wapping plant – had the effect of getting an inordinate number of people around the world seriously upset with him. The list of the discomfited, beginning in Washington and moving east, ran like this: Murdoch needed to take American citizenship and convince the Reagan administration to give him some slack on foreign ownership laws. Then he had to show the Federal Communications Commission that both he and the company which would control the Metromedia stations were American. Unfortunately, while *he* could change nationalities, it was a little harder for News Corp to do the same thing. Murdoch also had to convince the Federal Communications Commission that he should be given a waiver to the US cross-media laws to allow him to continue to own the *New York Post* and the *Boston Herald*, in addition to the local television stations he was buying. Then Murdoch needed to placate his existing bankers, while at the same time raising the net $2.7 billion he needed for Twentieth Century, Metromedia, Wapping and the $350 million deal for Ziff Davis magazines he had settled in January 1985. Murdoch's bank covenants had been designed specifically to prevent precisely this sort of deal.

In London, Murdoch needed assurance that the British Prime Minister Margaret Thatcher would back him in his battle at Wapping with the immensely powerful printing unions that had dominated the British newspaper industry for so long. By late 1985 Thatcher was already facing challenges to her leadership over her move to sell the Westmoreland helicopter company to an American defence group, of which Murdoch was a director. In the process Thatcher had ditched her own government policy and defence minister Michael Heseltine. The question by January 1986 as Wapping opened was not just whether Thatcher owed Murdoch any favours, but because of the Heseltine factor how long she would be around to give favours. Murdoch has never liked Heseltine. At the height of the Westmoreland fight, the *Sun* ran an anti-Heseltine front page headed 'You Liar' over a letter Heseltine wrote. An unconfirmed account by one former News executive suggests that part of the reason for the antipathy was that in the 1980s Heseltine sat on the board of one of the Queen's charities, which complained to the *Sun* or *News of the World* about a story. The matter was settled, but during the negotiations Murdoch came to the view that Heseltine fought his corner a little too hard, that the greatest of these should not necessarily be charity.

In Australia, for light relief, Murdoch needed to placate Prime Minister Bob Hawke, whose nose was out of joint because he had given Murdoch privileged status as an Australian in his local media deals. There was also the Australian Broadcasting Tribunal, which had allowed Murdoch to hold two Australian television licences because he told them he lived in Australia and would remain Australian. Murdoch was changing nationality, but he fully intended holding on to his Australian television stations. At least the US move would help clear up Murdoch's position with the Australian Tax Office, which had queried Murdoch over his personal income tax returns over an eight-year period from 1975. In July 1979, Murdoch had testified before the Australian Broadcasting Tribunal that although he held a US green card on the basis that he was a resident alien living in New York, he still qualified as an Australian resident for the purposes of the Australian Broadcasting Act, and had obtained absentee postal votes by signing declarations that his "real place of living" was his Cavan property in New South Wales. The issue with the Australian Tax Office was whether Murdoch also fitted the definition of an Australian resident in the Tax Act, and whether the source of his income was in Australia or elsewhere. His personal income tax returns had sought partial relief from Australian tax on the grounds that he lived principally in New York. Despite reports that Murdoch was planning a Supreme Court appeal against new assessments issued by the Tax Office based on his ABT testimony, the matter never hit the courts, and appears to have been resolved between the two parties.

The bottom line? Murdoch had a political problem, he had a financial problem, and he had a legal problem. This wasn't a percentage game. He could win most of these battles and still go down. He needed to win virtually all of the battles. The difficulty was that what he was proposing to do was politically impossible and it looked like financial suicide. And to boot it was probably illegal.

'I am very proud and grateful to be sworn in as an American citizen,' Murdoch said at his swearing in ceremony on 3 September 1985. His wife Anna and their three children would be naturalised quietly several years later. Despite this, a decade later the Federal Communications Commission would find that News Corp had probably breached the alien ownership provisions in the way it bought the Metromedia television stations, but no sanctions were imposed.

In 1985 what Murdoch needed was for everyone to get off his back for long enough to let him make these deals work. Like any conjurer he needed a suspension of disbelief. If, realistically, there was no way that the deals were viable, he needed to fashion his own realities. What News Corp was doing, who Rupert Murdoch was, would depend on to whom he was talking. He would practise his own version of virtual politics, where he could convince Ronald Reagan and Margaret Thatcher of his deeply right-wing affiliations, while assuring the Australian Labor Prime Minister, Bob Hawke, of his special support. There was the virtual nationality – since 1986 Murdoch has described himself as an American or 'at heart' an Australian, as the occasion demanded. To help Americanise News Corp in 1985, Murdoch bought more stock to lift his stake in News Corp to 50.1 per cent. Within weeks of receiving Federal Communications Commission approval for the deal Murdoch sold the extra stock again, to win an entirely different tax argument with the Internal Revenue Service.

Murdoch's lawyers would pioneer a form of virtual law, which allowed Murdoch to assure the Federal Communications Commission in 1985 and every year since then that the Metromedia television stations were American-owned because he and Barry Diller owned 75 per cent of the voting stock of Twentieth Holdings Corporation, the holding company for the stations, and thus he and Diller controlled the stations. At the same time, the News lawyers would tell the US Securities and Exchange Commission that News Corp, a foreign company, controlled Twentieth Holdings. (It held 99.9 per cent of the company as non-voting stock, and could force Diller and Murdoch to sell the voting stock back to it at any time.)

Then there were the virtual finances that Murdoch used to convince his bankers that they should keep lending. By this time, News Corporation had developed the corporate equivalent of multiple personality disorder. The really critical part to working with virtual realities is to keep them apart. The separate worlds must never collide.

While Murdoch's change of nationality, his relationships with politicians and the battle that saw him finally lose the *New York Post*, all provoked storms of media coverage, the controversy that all these issues stirred up obscured one basic fact. The key element of this deal was not the politics, the patriotism or the legalities – it was survival. This deal in 1985 was the most important in Rupert Murdoch's life – a decade later, the businesses it would spin off would be worth $40 billion. The issue that would make or break Murdoch was always going to be finding the money to make this deal work . . . and to allow News Corp to stay solvent.

Major money-raising exercises are a little like watching a carnival shell game. The speed of the movement and the dazzling sleight of hand obscures the pattern of strategic advances and retreats. In the end all one knows is that a large amount of money seems to be disappearing rapidly down a small hole. What made this shell game particularly engrossing was the way that the master players, Michael Milken and Rupert Murdoch, for all their marvellous dexterity, managed to expose News Corp to a potential loss of $3.6 billion. How they did it still seems a matter of mystery. It is hard for anyone to rack up a potential loss of such magnitude, though in recent years several entrepreneurs have given the task a solid try. How could Michael Milken and Rupert Murdoch miscalculate so badly? The difficulty began because when Milken came through with the money for Murdoch's Metromedia deal, as with Turner he put a provision in the borrowing agreement for the junk bond package that turned out to be a time bomb.

To appreciate Murdoch's predicament, you need to understand two things. First, Murdoch's existing bankers had loaned him large amounts of money with one condition: at 30 June every year, News Corp's total debt could never be more than 110 per cent of its assets. This is called a gearing limit. The banks imposed this limit because of the natural preference that bankers all around the world have for ensuring that when a loan goes bad, it is someone else who loses money. There are two parts to any company: there is the bit that the shareholders own, and there is the bit that the banks and creditors own. A balance sheet lists all of a company's assets. If you take away the debt and liabilities from the total assets, what you have left is the part that the shareholders own. Essentially this is what the company is worth. It is called the net assets, or shareholders' equity. Most of this is held by the shareholders in the form of shares or stock, though other sorts of securities are sometimes lumped in to be counted as part of shareholders' equity.

The more equity or net assets that a company has, the easier it is for its bankers to sleep at night. If the company hits the wall and goes into bankruptcy, the banks get paid first, and the shareholders get paid last. So it is much more agreeable for bankers that shareholders have a lot of money to lose, and a lot more pain to suffer, before the banks themselves are affected. Not all debt is created equal. There is senior debt, and junior debt and subordinated debt, all of which have different rankings and priorities when it comes to getting money back out of a mortally wounded company. Bankruptcies can descend into internecine squabbles between banks as to which one gets the money from selling a particular part of the company. It can be very messy. The banks' view is that it really is much better for almost everyone if it is the shareholders who carry all of the loss. For one thing, shareholders are much less likely to take the banks to court. So banks like to make sure shareholders have a hefty lot of equity in a company that they can lose before the banks themselves feel any pain. In the case of News Corporation, the banks' gearing limit meant that on 30 June each year, for every $100 million of assets on the News Corp group's balance sheet, debt could never be more than $53 million. The other $47 million had to be equity of some kind. What the banks didn't realise was the large number of things that Rupert Murdoch could include in his measure of equity.

In 1985, under US accounting standards News Corp had net assets of $166 million, which suggested Murdoch could only borrow about $175 million. He was raising new debt of $2.7 billion, fifteen times more than the banks' lending limits allowed him. It was enough to induce cardiac failure in even his most hardened bankers. The only way that Murdoch could borrow more money was to increase his net assets, or shareholders' equity. The easiest way to do this was to raise capital by issuing stock, as Turner eventually did with the cable companies. But it cost Turner control of his company. Murdoch was never going to allow this to happen.

Murdoch had two ways of getting around this bothersome lending restriction. First, his finance director Richard Sarazen argued that News Corp's newspapers were worth far more than the modest value assigned to them in the group's balance sheet. And to prove his point, he kept revaluing them. While US accounting rules do not allow assets to be revalued upwards, Australian accounting rules have no such scruples. Between 1984 and 1987, Sarazen wrote up the mastheads of the group's newspapers by $1.5 billion. The increase meant News Corp's net assets jumped by that amount, which meant that Murdoch was allowed to borrow another $1.6 billion.

The revaluations solved half the debt-raising problem. Arthur Siskind and the legal team at Squadron Ellenoff solved the other half of the problem. Murdoch needed to raise $1.15 billion in junk money from Michael Milken to buy Metromedia. It was, as Siskind later told *American Lawyer*, 'an extraordinarily complicated and very unusual financing'. Siskind's twist was that instead of treating the loan as junk bonds, News would call it preferred stock. While in essence this would be a $1.15 billion loan, it would appear in the News Corp balance sheet as a stock issue. Because it was called a stock issue, it would be treated like an asset.

'Under Australian [accounting principles], a preferred stock, even though it is designed to have all the attributes of debt, would be treated for accounting purposes as equity,' said Siskind. 'I always referred to it as a 'junk preferred'.'

Because the junk preference debt was treated as virtual equity, it appeared as an asset in the News Corp balance sheet rather than a liability. This meant not only that News Corp could borrow $1.15 billion through Michael Milken. It meant that after the increase in assets from this slick piece of bookkeeping, News could go out and raise *another* $1.2 billion in bank debt.

It was really very clever, and the lawyers at Squadron Ellenoff were pretty chuffed about the whole deal. But the honeymoon was short, because in early 1986 the Milken junk issue turned out to be a complete disaster. It began with an industrial revolution at Wapping that proved a little too successful.

CHAPTER THREE

WAPPING'S CASUALTIES

London, January 1986

In the rolling revolution of the Thatcher years, a decade that transformed the social and economic landscape of Britain, two events stand out. The first was Murdoch's acquisition of *The Times* and the *Sunday Times*. After weeks of negotiations with the Thomson organisation, Murdoch settled the deal some time after midnight on the night of 21 January 1981. When he jubilantly called his wife Anna, she promptly burst into tears. Anna was in Australia remodelling their Cavan farm, under the mistaken notion that they had both decided to move back to Australia. When asked to nominate which country they would be living in now, Murdoch narrowed it down to the northern hemisphere. At least for most of the time.

Working out a price for *The Times* and *Sunday Times* was the easiest part of the acquisition. The deal only became commercial reality six days later when John Biffen, Britain's Secretary of State for Trade, announced that in view of promises Murdoch had made to guarantee editorial independence, the government would not refer the deal to the Monopolies Commission. The way was clear for Murdoch to become the largest newspaper proprietor in Britain.

The picture of Murdoch the next day, holding a copy of *The Times* in front of him with Biffen's decision as the front page lead, became the hallmark image of Murdoch in Britain. It shows a slight man in a dark suit looking directly at the camera. His face is gaunt and shows deepening wrinkles, his hairline is marching inexorably northwards above dark, hooded eyebrows which are God's gift to cartoonists and those who would seek to demonise him. The two striking aspects as he stands there, his arms outstretched, are the intensity of this man regarding you so intently; and at the moment of his triumph how indistinct this figure is. There are few hard edges or textures to lift the shape beyond the nondescript. He is defined by his surroundings: the corridor behind him, and the newspaper he is holding but not reading. He is a powerfully ordinary figure.

At the time the photo was taken, Murdoch was six weeks away from turning fifty. He had just secured the biggest win of his career to date, in seizing the flagship of Establishment Britain. He had done something for which he could not be ignored, and for which he would never be forgiven. Remarkably, after three decades of empire building, the most important gambles of his life were still ahead of him.

Some of the charges that would be laid against Murdoch were: that he did not honour his commitment to editorial independence; that *The Times* takeover spelt an end to an era in British journalism, to a tradition of crusading, investigative journalism pioneered by the *Sunday Times* Insight team under journalists such as Philip Knightley and Bruce Page. The low point would come in 1983 when the *Sunday Times* ran the forged Hitler Diaries – a journalistic embarrassment which Murdoch defended as a commercial success.

The Times and *Sunday Times* represented different styles of journalism. By appointing *Sunday Times* editor Harold Evans as editor of *The Times* and sacking him a year later, Murdoch split the ranks of his critics, who would argue for a decade whether Evans had been a good or bad editor for *The Times*. This mixed response was characteristic of the deep ambivalence that the changes of the Thatcher years brought to Britain. Murdoch would inspire similar ambivalence with the second standout event of the Thatcher years, his move to Wapping.

In any grand strategy, the difference between success and failure often comes down to who is telling the story. In January 1986, Rupert Murdoch embarked upon an industrial campaign which would transform the finances of his media empire. It revolutionised the newspaper industry in Britain, and arguably broke the back of the British trade union movement. Its influence would reverberate in workplace relations across Europe and leave a deep scar on British domestic politics. Yet for Murdoch the results were equivocal. This masterstroke which was his financial salvation also did more than anything else to commit Murdoch to years of financial crisis.

At 7.30 p.m. on Friday, 24 January 1986, the 5,500 print workers who produced Murdoch's British newspapers – the *Sun*, *The Times*, the *Sunday Times*, and *News of the World* – voted to strike, over plans by News

International to move its papers to a new plant at Wapping. As they filed out, each printer was handed a notice of dismissal. By striking they had given up the right to negotiate a conventional retrenchment package which could cost News more than £120 million.

Wapping was an archetypal technology war. From the early 1970s the newspaper business was buffeted by technological advances, witnessing the disappearance of the setting of each line in hot lead using linotype machines, rows of page galleys in the compositing room, the mysterious and terrifyingly noisy vacuum tubes that sucked containers filled with editorial copy from the newsroom to the stone. Instead, a computer type-setter produced a photographic bromide of text which was cut up and glued to a page for photographic reproduction. Soon this would be replaced by computer pagination, in which a journalist could assemble an entire page on a computer screen.

The casualties of this technological change would not just be old equipment and newspaper mystique. The trade of newspaper compositing – one of the oldest in industrial society – would disappear. Several hundred thousand people would discover that their chosen career path had no future. The process was inescapable, inasmuch that no one has ever found a way to resist technological change indefinitely, to remain in business when someone else is doing your job faster, better, cheaper. All that remained to be decided were the conditions and timing under which the change would be made, how smoothly it would come, and the comfort that employers would offer to a large workforce that would walk away without a livelihood.

The British printing unions were not an easy group to like. They had used their industrial muscle to ensure that they remained in charge of the entire production process, insisting that any editorial typed in by journalists must be keyed in again by a printer, negating much of the advantage of a computerised typesetting system. They had also created corrupt work-places, which were overstaffed, sometimes by fictitious employees, where slowdowns, wildcat strikes and even sabotage had become commonplace. However, changing this system presented huge problems.

When Rupert Murdoch decided to move his newspapers from their separate locations in Bouverie Street and Grays Inn Road to Wapping, a site that he had bought in 1978 and rebuilt in 1984, the biggest hurdle was that his plan would involve journalists. The difficulty here lay not in any uncertainty about whether News editorial staff would accept the picket lines, the 12-foot walls and rolls of razor wire which would grace their new working environment. News International never showed any serious doubts on this quarter. The problem was that a lot of journalists would need to keep a secret. Traditionally, journalists have been far more proficient at extracting confidences than holding them. After Rupert Murdoch briefed his London editors in New York on 10 February 1985 on his Wapping plan, it took only a month for the news to get out. On 10 March, even before Murdoch had signed a contract for Atex computer terminals for the new plant or finalised a deal to use staff from the electricians' union to run the presses, the *Daily Telegraph* reported that News International was moving to Wapping to launch a new title.

News International told the print unions that in view of their opposition to Wapping, for the time being it had shelved plans to move its existing newspapers there. Instead it would use the new plant to launch a paper called the *London Post*. This wasn't what News was saying to the TNT transport group. News wanted TNT to distribute all of its titles from Wapping. News executives later testified that this agreement was merely a prudent safeguard, to ensure News was in a position to print all its titles at Wapping should the printers try to block production of the *Post*.

In legal actions the following year, lawyers for the printing unions would argue that the *London Post* was a complete sham, 'a smokescreen behind which (News International) carried out a plan, already conceived, to transfer the existing titles to Wapping without the unions and to sack their existing labour force at minimum cost to themselves,' as Justice Stuart-Smith put it. After testimony by two News executives, Stuart-Smith found that the serious allegation could not be sustained, and counsel for the printers 'very properly withdrew it'. This had a somewhat terminal effect on the printers' argument that News came to the court with 'unclean hands'.

These were confusing times. Andrew Neil, the then editor of the *Sunday Times*, later wrote that 'the *Post* was a ruse: it was never meant to happen,' that 'the pretence of the *Post* had to be maintained' and that it was 'a ruse thought up by Rupert himself'. Elsewhere in the book, however, Neil is more ambivalent about whether a full-scale move to Wapping was always planned. Refreshingly, not everyone needed a cover story. According to Neil, the peculiar view of the world at the *Sunday Times* ensured that when James Adams, one of its senior editorial executives, began disappearing for large periods of time to prepare for the move to Wapping, some journalists assumed he had been doing his bit for flag and country by freelancing for MI5. It was not every newspaper where the security services would seem the obvious alternative vocation.

By September 1985, with presses installed at Wapping and members of the electricians union ready to run them, Murdoch had hardened his stand, setting a three-month deadline for a new agreement with the printing unions. The unions wanted an assurance that their members would not be sacked until retirement age, but they later dropped this with other concessions as they sensed the ground was shifting. At the final meeting between Murdoch and the print unions on Thursday 23 January 1986, the unions appeared to be in a state of panic. While significant concessions were offered for any move from Grays Inn Road to Wapping, Murdoch's view was that it was too little too late. Nothing was printed on the Friday night after the printers walked out, but on Saturday night the *Sunday Times* and *News of the World* went to press at Wapping and went out on trucks from TNT, which was being paid £1 million a week to distribute the papers. Those who were there on the first night at Wapping paint a fearful picture of a raging Murdoch hassling and intimidating subordinates: 'You fuckwit! You bastard! Get this fucking newspaper out!' he railed at James Adams.

Events unfolded with all the gritty immediacy of a major industrial confrontation. There was shouting, semi-riots, assaults, death threats, abuse and harassment, with flares, rocks and missiles thrown at the buildings. On one night protesters knocked down 40 yards of the 12-foot iron railing fence topped with barbed wire that ringed Wapping, but they didn't breach a second defence line of heavy rolls of razor wire. Each day, between 50 and 200 protesters would be outside the Wapping main gate. On Wednesday and Saturday nights the numbers would climb to 700 or more, and on occasion between 6,000 and 7,000. The longer the dispute lasted, the larger the crowds grew. On 24 January 1987, the first anniversary of the beginning of the dispute, more than 10,000 protesters clashed violently with 1,200 police.

The TNT trucks brought in to distribute the newspapers from Wapping were a popular target for protesters. In the first four months, protesters broke 92 windscreens on the TNT delivery trucks, rammed another 16, set fire to two trucks, slashed five sets of tyres and damaged another 84 trucks. Such conflicts had a brutalising effect on everyone involved – not least on the police, who bore the brunt of the dismissed printers' anger in nightly confrontations for more than a year. The toll was chronicled in unhappy little tales that trickled through the British courts.

Today the passions and bitterness that drove the Wapping dispute appear remote. The relics are old courtroom transcripts, statistics of violence, and dry arguments about whether words such as 'Scab, we will get you!' amount to a threat. Geoffrey Richards of Farrer & Co, the News lawyers, had reminded his client, 'Since the very first day I was involved . . . I have advised that, if a moment came when it was necessary to dispense with the workforces at TNL and NGN, the cheapest way of doing so would be to dismiss employees while participating in a strike or industrial action.' Eventually the 5,500 printers, who had worked for News for an average of 15 years, were paid about £50 million, or £620 for each year served, in an agreement worked out in early 1987. Other Fleet Street papers quietly negotiated similar concessions with the printing unions. Wapping's legacy, however, was not so easily settled. Whatever the rights or wrongs of a dispute like Wapping, it left its mark on the national psyche.

Wapping had a lethal effect on Labour Party politics in the UK. Faced with what was arguably Britain's greatest social convulsion of the decade, Labour politicians found themselves in No Man's Land, opposed to the confrontational and opportunistic tactics of News International, yet unable to defend the working record of the printers or the violence of the protesters. Whichever way Labour politicians leaned, their record was marked by the experience. Labour would remain out of power until it appointed a leader who had taken a determined position of non-involvement with Wapping. Tony Blair would know better than anyone the danger that a conflict like Wapping carried.

The importance of Wapping in Britain and its contribution to the Labour Party's woes were incidental to Rupert Murdoch. What was more apparent to him was that his success at Wapping had created a financial problem. For Murdoch, Wapping was only a by-play in his attempts to raise the money to buy the Metromedia television stations and launch his Fox network in the US. It all depended upon Michael Milken at Drexel Burnham Lambert getting away Murdoch's issue of $1.12 billion of junk prefs.

As with the Turner MGM deal, Milken found raising funds for Murdoch difficult. In November 1984, Milken had raised $1.2 billion in junk bonds to refinance John Kluge at Metromedia. The junk package was so outrageous, and the prospects of Milken's lenders ever getting their money back were so remote, that the case became a *cause célèbre*, an example of the wild excesses generated by Drexel's junk bond lending binge. The critics had their own name for the Metromedia bonds. They called them toxic waste.

Six months later, Murdoch had come along and offered Kluge a price for Metromedia that was in effect $800 million more than Kluge himself had paid. So when it came to going back to Milken's lenders to borrow more money for this new extravagance, the reception was a little cool. The old lenders just wanted their money back and new lenders proved hard to attract. The $1.15 billion issue had a closing date of 20 February 1986. That had to be pushed back to 27 February, then back again to 28 March. However, a sudden rush allowed the issue to close early, on 6 March, three weeks before Ted Turner's MGM junk bond issue closed. (According to News Corp executives, the delays had more to do with allowing Drexel Burnham Lambert to charge another $50 million in fees, but whatever the circumstances this cannot have been an easy sell.)

Murdoch had to treat the junk bonds as preference stock to slip it past the banks' debt-equity rule. A conventional debt raising would not help him here – he needed equity, or something dressed up to look like equity. Call it virtual equity. To make the package more attractive to his lenders, and to make it look more like real equity, Milken put a nasty provision into the deal. The debt would remain the same for three years. But after that, how much the lenders were paid back would begin to depend on the News Corp share price.

It worked like this: on the day that Milken's junk pref issue closed, News Corp stock was trading just above $8.50. The $1.15 billion that Murdoch was raising was equivalent in value to about 150 million News Corp ordinary shares. For three years, the Milken package behaved just like straight debt. It could be repaid at any time by paying back the $1.15 billion. But after 6 March 1989, a growing portion of the debt repayment would be based upon whatever 150 million News Corp ordinary shares were worth at the time. The payout would never be less than the original $1.15 billion, but if, for example, the News Corp share price rose to $9.50 (or $1 more than the day when the junk prefs were issued) Murdoch would need to pay out $1.15 billion plus another $150 million. The arrangement took several years to take full effect. But the bottom line was that the higher that the News Corp share price went, the higher the Milken junk debt payout would be; and the more that Murdoch would have to repay. This arrangement must have seemed like a good idea at the time – as long as News Corp didn't do anything to make its share price spike up. It turned out to be a spectacularly effective way to tear up money.

As journalists at Wapping agonised over whether or not to cross the picket lines, the new presses continued to crank out Murdoch's newspapers. By February 1986, investors had begun to realise just how much money Murdoch was going to make from the move. After all, this was the point of Wapping. The outcome from the riots, the nightly confrontations and abuse would help propel News International's operating income from £38.4 million in 1985 to £150.2 million in 1987. The News Corp share price drifted up over $6 in January 1986. When Michael Milken's junk pref issue closed on 6 March – the date that fixed the base price for paying back the preferred stock – News Corp ordinary stock was hovering above $8.50.

Two months later News Corp stock hit $16. It was a disaster – because just as the stock price had doubled, eventually the price of paying out the Milken junk prefs would also double.

Wapping had turned back to bite Murdoch. The news kept getting worse. By March 1987, a year after the Milken junk issue, News Corp stock, after allowing for a share split, had hit $35. Unless Murdoch could find a way to refinance, Michael Milken's little poison pill would eventually raise the debt to $4.7 billion. It looked like the most expensive company loan in history. Wapping had turned Milken's conversion clause into a $3.6 billion nightmare. What was most galling was that the huge loss facing Murdoch was a self-inflicted wound. The more that his business gambles succeeded, the more he faced having to pay the holders of the junk prefs.

As a desperate alternative, if Murdoch could not find the cash to pay off the junk debt, he could pay off the junk holders with News Corp ordinary shares. But this would dilute his own stockholding down to 9 per cent, and he would lose control of his company – a result that would make Ted Turner's cable bailout look like a masterstroke. Murdoch had to get out of this deal. He couldn't just raise a bank loan to pay Milken out. The junk prefs were supposed to be equity. To stay within his banks' gearing limits he had to replace the prefs with some other kind of virtual equity.

Murdoch would spend the rest of 1986 bedding down his new studio and television stations and launching the Fox network. He would keep his nerve steady and his pocketbook out as he kept spending. Fortune would continue to smile upon him, as he became on paper one of the richest men in the world. To get some perspective on this: in June 1982, Murdoch's entire stockholding in News Corp was worth $52 million. By March 1985, that had climbed to $300 million. Two and a half years later, the Murdoch shares were worth $3 billion. And while that was paper money – the stock market had discovered virtual wealth long before anyone else – the political power that went along with it was quite real.

But eating at Murdoch throughout 1986 was the knowledge that Milken's time bomb was ticking. Murdoch had left an indelible mark on two countries. He had overturned the media business in America by starting a new network, and in Britain by revolutionising newspaper manning levels and breaking the power of trade unions. The after effects of those two changes would reverberate through both countries for years. And the troubling thing was, it still wasn't enough. All that pain had not ensured that Rupert Murdoch's media group would survive. If, by March 1989, he hadn't found some way to refinance the Milken prefs then you could forget the stock price, and the paper wealth. The game would be over.

The Lost Inheritance

By the end of 1986 Rupert Murdoch had realised how to solve his debt problem. He needed to spend a lot more money. He needed a Major Acquisition. On 3 December 1986 Murdoch took advantage of changes in Australian media law announced the week before to bid $A1.8 billion for his father's old business, the Herald and Weekly Times group. It had been more than three decades coming, but Murdoch was about to have his revenge on the company that he believed had treated his family so shabbily after his father's death. At least, that is what it looked like. But while sentiment and revenge were a major part of this deal, the money trail suggested something quite different.

To understand what Murdoch was really doing, it is useful to think of a master magician working the crowd, ostentatiously handing out shiny coins to members of the audience. When he returns to the stage he gestures theatrically before opening his cloak to reveal that all of the coins are mysteriously back in his pocket. By sleight of hand he has ended up with all the money. Rather than money, Murdoch was handing out shares which would end up back under his cloak.

The key lay in the way the bid was pitched, and where the shares would end up. About a third of the Herald and Weekly Times shareholders would take a cash payment. The rest would elect instead to take News Corp shares or convertible notes in exchange for their stock. Three associated companies – Queensland Press Limited in Brisbane, Advertiser Newspapers in Adelaide, and Davies Brothers in Hobart – owned 36 per cent of the Herald and Weekly Times. In turn, the Herald and Weekly Times owned 46 per cent or more of each of them, so whoever controlled the Herald and Weekly Times controlled the associates as well. This arrangement was the relic of the takeover defence that Murdoch's father had built into the group a generation before. All three associates elected to take the News Corp convertible notes offer rather than cash. So when Murdoch took over the Herald and Weekly Times, after allowing for the shareholders that took cash, more than half the stock he issued for the takeover ended up in three companies which he now controlled.

This was the perfect deal. Murdoch could pay for a Major Acquisition with a huge issue of News Corp stock without diluting his own control of News. In fact, he would end up controlling more of News after the takeover than he did before. It was a neat system. The new equity meant he no longer needed Michael Milken's junk prefs to artificially boost his gearing levels for the banks. He could pay Milken out and replace the prefs with cheaper bank loans. Murdoch would end up with 70 per cent of Australia's newspapers, but the thing to remember is that this was not a media play. It was the Murdochs' grand revenge on Sir Keith's company. But even more than this, the financial heart of the deal was a debt restructuring exercise. Murdoch had taken over a country's media industry to help his gearing level.

Murdoch had already overturned the American media industry to start up his new Fox television network. He had needed to move to Wapping and overturn the British newspaper industry to pay for his American adventure. Now, to help Murdoch with the debt blow out produced by Wapping, it was Australia's turn. National boundaries had ceased to matter for him. Murdoch would do a deal wherever it took him in the world, creating social shock waves in as many countries as he needed, in order to survive. Unfortunately once again it all went horribly wrong.

Within days of Murdoch's announcement of his Herald and Weekly Times bid on 3 December, the Sydney-based Fairfax newspaper group and then South African entrepreneur Robert Holmes à Court launched a disastrous bidding war that added $500 million to Herald and Weekly Times' price. What was worse, Holmes à Court began a flanking move by bidding directly for Queensland Press, which owned 24 per cent of the Herald and Weekly Times. Whoever won Queensland Press would win the battle for the Herald and Weekly Times. There was no easy counter to this. Murdoch realised that to ward off Holmes à Court he would need to bid for Queensland Press as well. And for Advertiser. And for Davies Brothers. The total cost had doubled to $A3.6 billion.

Things had taken a truly disastrous turn. The neat system Murdoch had devised no longer worked. A subsidiary company cannot hold shares in its parent. If Murdoch took over *all* of Queensland Press, Advertiser and Davies Brothers (rather than owning just under 50 per cent of them) they would not be able to keep their News Corp shares. They would have to sell them. Murdoch would have to let go of these precious parcels of stock upon which he was depending to keep control of News.

And yet Murdoch couldn't walk away. The spectre of Sir Keith Murdoch hovered like Hamlet's father. For decades Murdoch had dreamed of avenging his father's memory with the Herald and Weekly Times. Now, with the goal almost within his grasp, it was about to be snatched away again. No matter how successful he had been around the world, back in Australia once again he would be rebuffed, and on a matter which had so much emotional significance for his family.

Murdoch was trapped. He was damned if he went forward, and damned if he retreated. So Murdoch came up with his most desperate plan yet. He would find someone else to buy Queensland Press and control that critical block of News stock that Queensland Press owned. The Murdochs would do it themselves. After all, Queensland Press was the business that Sir Keith had left them. The family company, Cruden Investments, would bid $A600 million for the 56 per cent of Queensland Press that was in public hands (the other 44 per cent would continue to be owned by the Herald and Weekly Times and its new parent, News Corp). It was a close run thing. The outcome was still in the balance when the MD of Queensland Press, Keith McDonald, decided to support Murdoch's bid rather than arguably higher offers from Holmes a Court. His support was unchanged even when Holmes a Court launched legal action, accusing him of not acting in the interests of all shareholders. McDonald backed Murdoch because he was a newspaperman. He was a true believer who saw media in straightforward if uncritical terms:

> Newspapers are the products of human minds and brains and hands, and decent, wholesome men of integrity will produce decent, whole-some newspapers . . . Anybody who knows [Murdoch] or listens to him knows that he hasn't picked up much from the US. They can have him as a citizen because their fool laws are like ours: you can't own more than this or that – it's a marriage of convenience if you like . . . Whatever else Rupert is – and he is a great many things – he is a good newspaperman.

Cruden's takeover provided a sense of closure to the trauma of Sir Keith's death; his ghost could finally be laid to rest. The only problem was that Cruden didn't have any money. On paper, it was a very rich company. In January 1987 its 116 million News Corp shares were worth $1.5 billion and rising steadily. But it had no cash, and its only income was $8 million a year in News Corp dividends. Cruden had to raise $4 million debt to pay for Queensland Press, and the interest payments were $60 million a year. How was it going to pay its bankers? By the middle of 1987, as Cruden's interest bill kept piling up, it wasn't just a risky investment. It had become a debt problem waiting to happen. Murdoch had swapped the Milken debt bomb in News Corp, the public company, for an even more threatening debt bomb in Cruden, his private family company. The Milken debt was a virus that had just switched hosts. Nevertheless it looked like Murdoch had scraped through. The only way that he could run into problems in late 1987 was if share prices crashed.

CHAPTER FOUR
***

THE PARTY LINE

London, 6–7 December 1990

In the last hours of Thursday 6 December 1990, Rupert Murdoch almost went broke. Such defining moments are rare in modern finance. Major corporate failures are usually well telegraphed and tend to be more prolonged affairs. The warning signs are a lingering decline, a slow downward spiral. There is rarely a determinative moment that marks the difference between survival and bankruptcy. In general, huge corporations do not live or die on the outcome of a single telephone call.

But 6 December was Rupert Murdoch's moment, as he sat in the offices of Clifford Chance, the London lawyers for Citibank, preparing to make a phone call. Within hours, News Corporation was due to be placed in liquidation. It would be the end of the empire: the end of 37 years of struggle and fighting, of endlessly recreating himself and his company, of juggling realities and possibilities, of forging a media group that reached around the world. And Rupert Murdoch could save it all, it seemed. He could turn the crisis around with just one telephone call to the president of a bank in Pittsburgh. Once the call was placed, everything would depend on Murdoch's powers of persuasion. If he could convince the Pittsburgh banker to hold off, to give him a little time to solve his financial problems, Murdoch and News Corporation would march on. If Murdoch's charm failed, the empire faced fragmentation and dissolution. Those next to him said later that Murdoch's hands were shaking as the connection was made. However, the voice on the other end of the line was only a secretary. The banker in Pittsburgh was refusing to take his call.

Murdoch was in London because his media empire had run out of other people's money. This wasn't a huge problem. It had run out of other people's money before. News Corporation was due to repay a $A1 billion loan it had taken out three years earlier. It was falling due on the other side of the world from London, on what was already Friday 7 December. News Corp didn't have the money to repay it and wanted to roll the debt over. When the Australian loan was syndicated, by chance a small piece of the loan had ended up across the Pacific with Pittsburgh National Bank. Pittsburgh National had taken on one per cent of the debt, a modest $A10 million. A rollover is a smooth procedure for professional bankers. All concerned charge a hefty fee and the money goes through without even touching the sides. That is, it does unless one of the lenders begins to worry about getting their money back. Then the whole rollover process clogs up, it all starts to stick. Pittsburgh National wanted its $A10 million back. They gave Murdoch a sticky roll.

Murdoch and his key senior legal and financial executives, together with a crisis team from Citibank, had spent the whole day wrestling over the loan with bankers around the world. Murdoch had begun the day in Zurich talking to Credit Suisse, before flying to Heathrow. Australian banks had put up most of the resistance to the rollover falling due that day. Then the Japanese banks had dug their heels in and refused to extend the loan. After a titanic struggle Murdoch's advisors at Citibank and British merchant bank Samuel Montague had talked the Australian and Japanese hardheads around. They would roll. The battle was won. The fates which guide banking destinies had decreed that today was not the day that Murdoch's media empire crashed and burned. That wouldn't happen for at least another week and a half. Today the fight was over. If only Pittsburgh knew that.

David DeVoe, News Corporation's new chief financial officer, had called the chief loan officer at Pittsburgh National from Murdoch's London flat that afternoon. It should have been a formality. Instead, the Pittsburgh loan officer had refused point blank to roll the loan. He didn't want DeVoe's assurances, he just wanted News to pay him his money. Murdoch later described the moment to his biographer, William Shawcross: 'We said, "We can't. You know what that means. We'd go out of business," Murdoch said. The loan officer said, "That's right." We said, "You're telling us to liquidate our company?" And he said, "Yes." '

Murdoch's last option that evening was to try an end run around the chief loan officer, calling his boss, the president of Pittsburgh National. When he called from the Clifford Chance offices the bank president's secretary put him back to the chief loan officer.

For nearly three millennia, one of the cornerstones of Western and Greek narrative has been a belief in the day of reckoning. No matter how high Icarus flies, there comes a moment when he falls to earth; when Achilles meets Hector; when Oedipus meets the old man on the road. Macbeth's vaulting ambition o'erleaps itself, and falls on the other. History catches up with us all. Hubris must be called to account, the grand vision inevitably collides with reality. There are no exceptions, our doom is inescapable. It is an entirely post-modern notion that a protagonist may confront their moment with destiny and walk away; that they may endure their worlds colliding, their past rising up to bury them, and yet not perish. So what is one to make of the fact that Rupert Murdoch survived the certain disaster that threatened him on 6 December? For the post-modern hero there is no date with destiny, there is only a weary endurance through the latest in an endless series of crises that stretch out of sight behind and before him.

For News Corporation, life had become a mesmerising sequence of near-death experiences. The group had been in crisis since 4 October, the day that David DeVoe sat down nervously with seven of News Corp's chief bankers in the News International boardroom at Wapping in London. DeVoe had been chief financial officer at News for all of one month. News Corp's legendary finance director Richard Sarazen had been moved out of the job in early September and given the title of senior executive vice president. He was still a member of the chief executive's office, but he had no more direct input into News Corp finances.

In January 1990, DeVoe had been appointed deputy chief financial officer, just as News Corp's lines of credit began to dry up. A $750 million bridging loan on 1 January 1990 was News Corp's last before a global credit squeeze took hold. It fell due for repayment on 30 June. News paid back $250 million, and received a three-month extension on the balance to 30 September. Just before the deadline, DeVoe as the newly appointed chief financial officer had asked for a one-month extension. The meeting at Docklands the following Thursday 4 October was called by a group of angry senior News Corp bankers who wanted an explanation and some serious reassurances that the sun was still shining in the News Corp universe.

DeVoe is an unostentatious man. While the typical career history that News Corporation published on each of its directors could fill two pages, DeVoe's biography ran to four lines. As he cleared his throat at the Docklands meeting, the bankers before him knew already that he was not the showman Sarazen had been. What they were not expecting was that this quiet unassuming man would diffidently tell them a horror story.

DeVoe said that News Corp had a temporary cash problem. News had more than $7 billion in unsecured bank debt. On top of that it had another $3 billion of trade creditors. News was due to repay $2.6 billion by next June – and DeVoe's first news was that News Corp wouldn't be able to make those payments. In fact, the mountain of money that News Corp had already borrowed would not even ensure the group survived the year. News Corp needed another $600 million just to keep going. Would this be a problem? At some point in the mass of figures and schedules that poured forth, it became apparent that News Corp would only have a future if the bankers in that room could organise a rescue party.

By Friday the shouting had dropped a few decibels, and the bankers had agreed on a rescue plan, to be co-ordinated by Citibank and Samuel Montague. News needed to reschedule $7.6 billion of debt held by 146 institutions around the world. The bankers' chief problem was that the group's international structure had been set up specifically to stop any takeover by the banks. The group's debt was unsecured, and flowed through a series of offshore News Corp companies, whose convoluted ownership structure would make bank efforts to secure assets horribly complicated. In a liquidation, the banks faced years of expensive court actions in exotic parts of the world to sort out which assets belonged to which banks. The rescue plan that the banks settled on instead was a Debt Override Agreement which gave News the extra $US600 million in working capital that it needed, and three years to pay back its entire debt. Not one bank was to be allowed to withdraw, to get its money back, until everyone did.

The important thing to remember in any bank rescue operation is just who is being rescued. In a bank rescue, the chief object of compassion and worthy recipient of any succour is not the hapless borrower. It is an aid exercise directed at the banks; and inasmuch as the rescue is organised by the leading bank, the most worthy recipient of all is the leading bank itself. The rescue operation mounted by *les miserables* in the pinstripe suits would cost News Corp $150 million as a flat fee. The banks would get all of their money back by 1993, and in the three years to then, News would pay the banks $2.3 billion in interest payments. The chief difficulty was that those banks and institutions that had the least money at risk tended to feel the least urgency for the rescue, and to suspect quite correctly that those with the most to gain were the senior banks. They wanted the seniors to pay them out. The senior banks were playing hardball, insisting that if even one little bank was paid out early, it would trigger a stampede for the exits that would hurt everybody.

In the three months it took for the Debt Override plan to be adopted, News kept running into repayment deadlines as different sets of loans matured, giving any of the banks in that loan the capacity to put the entire group into liquidation. The domino effect of even one tiny default – and some of the banks that held out were owed as little as $2.5 million – would trigger cross defaults which would overwhelm the group. Murdoch almost went broke on 31 October, when the original one-month rollover fell due. There was a lynching party in Sydney on 15 November, when a bunch of ornery Australian bankers went into a meeting with Murdoch and other News Corp executives determined to take a serious bite out of Rupert Murdoch. They were candy. Once in the charm zone, they proved as diffident about challenging the Murdoch vision of the future as four decades of bankers before them.

A fortnight later on 30 November Murdoch almost went broke again. There was the crisis on 3 December, then it was plain sailing until 6 December, and Pittsburgh. Of course at the end of that terrifying afternoon and evening Pittsburgh folded. After the loan officer at Pittsburgh National told DeVoe he wanted to put News into liquidation, John Reed, the chairman of Citibank, called the Pittsburgh National chairman to warn him of the dangers to the entire banking system and western civilization if News Corporation crashed. When Murdoch called Pittsburgh, before he could speak the loan officer was assuring him that he had thought about his conversation with David DeVoe and 'we don't want to be difficult'. He would roll. End of the Pittsburgh problem.

For Murdoch and News Corp it was on to other battles, other cities, other bankers to cajole. These scenes would haunt Murdoch for years. During November he called his elder son, Lachlan, and pulled him out of Princeton to be with him in London as he did the endless rounds of bankers. As Lachlan, then 19 years old, walked home with his father down Fleet Street at 1 a.m. one night after a long haggling session he wondered why his father seemed so stressed and dispirited. 'I wanted to put my arms around him and hold him up,' he told the *New York Times* later.

The crises continued. There was some smart work in New York on 21 December, then Murdoch nearly went broke again the night before Christmas. There was another date with almost-insolvency on New Year's Eve, a pause for a brief respite, then in the early days of January 1991 Murdoch was back to almost going broke again.

By then he was getting used to it. It lasted 116 days. And then at 2.15 a.m. on the morning of 1 February 1991 the ordeal was over. The whole series of rolling crises which made up Murdoch's great debt crisis was finished. The banks had all signed up on the rescue package, the Debt Override Agreement was secured, News Corporation had its three-year breathing space, and Murdoch had survived.

Strangely, when News Corp executives and bankers felt free to talk about their four-month ordeal, they talked about Pittsburgh. They told *Institutional Investor*, and then the *Financial Times* in London, about the fears of that night. Murdoch talked with his biographer, William Shawcross, about how the Pittsburgh president had refused to take his call, about his need for a stiff drink afterwards. It was a classic tale, with a moral that could be varied according to whoever was telling the story. The Pittsburgh affair was an example of how a mighty international empire could be brought to its knees by a minor mistake or incident, the One Fatal Flaw. Alternatively it underlined the Frightening, Inescapable Power that even the smallest banks could hold over huge multinational companies. Most of all it was a story that showcased Rupert Murdoch's phenomenal capacity to survive, his ability to face his date with destiny and walk away.

The most remarkable aspect of the Pittsburgh incident was its timeless quality. There was no past and no future to this story. For all News Corp's willingness to recount the affair as an anecdote, as a colourful *episode* in the rich tapestry of unravelling disaster that was the debt crisis, the same News Corp executives proved far more reticent when it came to giving details about the history of the Pittsburgh loan. For example, how was the money raised in the first place, what was the original loan used for? For all intents and purposes the track of the Pittsburgh money was lost in the crisscrossing web of hundreds of inter-company loans that form the way that News Corporation conducts its business on any day at hundreds of points around the globe. End of story.

At the time, the only suggestion that there was more to the Pittsburgh affair came in an odd series of conversations on the other side of the world. The *Sydney Morning Herald*'s banking writer, Karen Maley, had been covering the News debt crisis for two months. Her adroit courting of Australian bankers involved in the Debt Override operation had given her a steady flow of inside information about how different banks were responding – particularly the unhappy minor banks. On Sunday 2 December she spoke to several bank executives who for the first time raised their concern that not all of the money covered in the Debt Override was for News Corporation. According to the Dolphin Memorandum, which was the blueprint for the rescue plan, $450 million of private debt owed by the Murdoch family was being mixed in with News Corporation's corporate debt in the Debt Override Aagreement. The senior lenders were keen to do this, as they previously had loaned money to both News and the Murdochs. The smaller lenders who had no exposure to the Murdochs didn't see why the two sets of loans should be mixed up. Maley's sources were concerned that money that belonged to News Corporation's shareholders (or more to the point, to News Corporation's bankers) might be used to pay off Rupert Murdoch's personal debts.

On Thursday afternoon, the same bankers alerted Maley to a problem with a large loan that was falling due for repayment the next day. The lenders were particularly reluctant to let the debt be rolled over. The unhappy borrower was an Australian arm of the Murdoch empire called Queensland Press Limited, based in Brisbane. This was an intriguing twist to the debt crisis, but it needed confirmation. Then Maley got lucky. Late on Thursday afternoon she put in a call to Keith McDonald, the chief executive officer of Queensland Press. 'I couldn't believe it when he picked up the phone,' she said later. McDonald confirmed Queensland Press had a loan falling due the next day, and that there had been discussions about it with the banks, but he dismissed any suggestion of a serious problem.

Allowing for different time zones, it seems fair to assume that the Pittsburgh crisis on 6 December London time and the Queensland Press rollover on 7 December were the same deal – McDonald did not realise how much his future would soon depend upon an unknown bank executive in Pennsylvania. McDonald, who also sat on the main News Corp board, was supremely confident when he spoke to Maley. There was no suggestion that he was going to lose any sleep over the loan that night, or indeed that he or anyone else would need a stiff drink afterwards.

What made this so unusual was that although News Corporation owned 44 per cent of Queensland Press, it was not part of the News Corporation group. The Murdoch family had bought 56 per cent of Queensland Press as part of the 1986–87 battle for the Herald and Weekly Times Group. The desperation in London over whether Pittsburgh would put News Corporation into liquidation had been triggered by a dispute about debt in the Murdoch family's private companies. This was not quite the story that News Corp told *Institutional Investor* and the *Financial Times*.

Then there was Citicorp's insistence that the whole basis of the Debt Override was that none of Murdoch's banks could be paid out. 'We are where we are,' and 'Nobody gets out,' were the two rules that the Citicorp team had hammered down the throats of bankers around the world. This wasn't strictly accurate. In Australia, according to minor lenders, the Commonwealth Bank had drawn up a list of minor lenders in its syndicates, particularly its Queensland Press syndicate, and quietly taken out any bank owed less than $A10 million. An account manager with one of these minor lenders recalls a meeting with a Commonwealth Bank loan manager where he expected to be told firmly that he wouldn't be seeing any of his money in the Murdoch debt. Instead the Commonwealth Bank man handed him a cheque to pay out the loan. Pittsburgh National's $A10 million loan was just above the pay-out point. Not surprisingly, Pittsburgh wasn't happy.

News Corp was just as reticent about what happened next.

In late March 1991, the chief legal officer in Queensland for the Australian Securities Commission, Robin Chapman, walked down the short corridor at the ASC's Brisbane office to see her boss, Queensland Commissioner Barrie Adams. The ASC (since renamed the Australian Securities & Investments Commission) had been in existence for just three months as Australia's new corporate watchdog.

Chapman had been looking at a 1987–88 deal in which Queensland Press bought a parcel of News Corporation shares from the Murdoch family company, Cruden Investments. In 1989 Chapman had helped to rewrite the Australian laws that restrict a company from buying its own stock, or from lending money or giving financial assistance to another party to buy its stock. From the scanty details on file, Chapman told Adams she suspected that Queensland Press had financed its own takeover by Cruden, as part of the Herald and Weekly Times takeover back in early 1987.

At a hastily called briefing session, Chapman explained the complex legal issues and corporate structures to Adams and a team of investigators. Eventually he shifted in his seat a little, and asked the billion-dollar question: 'If we took the view that News Corporation shareholders were disadvantaged by the deal, what would be the effect if we forced them to reverse the transaction?'

The room went silent. This was just weeks after the debt crisis. Murdoch was still hanging on to his empire by his fingertips. Reversing the deal could trigger a financial crisis for Cruden and put the News Corp Debt Override Agreement into default. To raise money, Murdoch would have little option but to sell most of his News Corp shares. Such a forced sale would depress the News Corp share price even further. The likely result was not just that Murdoch would lose control of News Corp, but that he would also go broke. And News Corp itself would hit the wall.

'We can live with that,' Adams said easily. 'If that is what we find is appropriate, we're comfortable with that.'

Of course it wasn't that simple. What the ASC would decide to do at the end of its inquiry was one thing. The more immediate problem was what the market would *expect* the ASC to do, if investors knew about the inquiry. In the following two years, Murdoch would raise $7 billion in new debt and capital raisings to pay out the Debt Override Agreement. To raise that much money, he needed to convince investors and bankers that their money was safe. It wasn't just that News Corp was profitable, but also there were no lurking problems in the closet that could threaten the group's future . . . problems like the ASC inquiry.

Markets work on appearances. Any suggestion that the ASC was considering, no matter how remotely, legal action that could cost Murdoch control of News Corp and destabilise the News share price, could undermine the financing deals that Murdoch was negotiating to reforge his empire. This would be true even if eventually the ASC gave the Queensland Press deal a clean bill of health. By then the damage would be done. So during the two years that Murdoch was refinancing his empire, on any day what the ASC investigators suspected about News Corp's past had become critical to News Corp's future.

The ASC inquiry focused on a turbulent week in October 1987. It was a week barely comprehensible to those who did not live through it, who did not experience those momentous days when the financial world tottered on its bearings. For the world's stock markets, it was the week of the near miss, when for a moment catastrophe beckoned, then withdrew. It was also Rupert Murdoch's first debt crisis, the one no one knew about, when he saved his empire by going to a party.

Manhattan, 18–23 October 1987

On 18 October 1987, New York was enjoying the last hours of a lazy Sunday afternoon in late autumn. The first snowstorm had hit the northeast two weeks before, but no trace of that remained. New York was back up to 71 degrees and bathed in sunshine. The leaves were in full colour along the Connecticut shore for the benefit of day-trippers. Otherwise October 18 was a slow news day. For the media, Sunday is a nothing day, really.

The lack of excitement in New York was in contrast to – even in spite of – the intense concentration that was being poured on the city from around the globe. On the other side of the world it was already Monday morning. From New Zealand to Australia, to Tokyo, Hong Kong and Singapore, brokers, portfolio managers and major investors were hunkered down in briefing sessions before the financial markets opened. On the previous Friday, after the Asian markets closed, Wall Street had suffered the biggest points drop in its history. The Dow Jones index of industrial stocks had dropped 108 points, more than half of it in the last hour of trade. It had followed another disastrous day on Wednesday, when the Dow had dropped 95 points. It was down 9.5 per cent in three days. So, in the early hours of what was for them Monday morning, the brightest and best analysts in Asia and the Pacific were concentrating on just what was going through the minds of New York brokers and funds managers, in their homes in Westchester and western Connecticut, as they enjoyed the last of the warm Sunday. When Wall Street opened fifteen hours later, which way would they jump? Was the correction over? Was anyone feeling lucky? Was it safe? Monday was always going to be a bad day for the Asian markets. The Asian analysts had to intuit whether this was just medium bad, or doomsday. They chose poorly.

One of the mysteries on that quiet Sunday afternoon, in the lull before the storm, was what Rupert Murdoch was doing in New York. By rights he should have been in Australia. On the Friday two days before, News Corporation had held its annual meeting in Adelaide. For once, the chief executive was a no-show. Richard Searby, Murdoch's long-time friend and the News Corp chairman, presided over the annual meeting on Friday 16 October, but it was a lacklustre affair.

In the normal course of events, Murdoch would have ripped through the News Corp meeting – a perfunctory annual ritual that on a slow year stretches as long as 15 minutes – had a cup of tea with shareholders, then flown to Sydney for a road show with Australian analysts to boost his stock. Murdoch would then spend the weekend at his Cavan property west of Sydney with Australian execs and family, before heading back to the US late on the Monday. This was what Murdoch did every year when the News Corp annual meeting came around. He would usually drag some of his senior lieutenants along with him, on the general principle that into every life a little South Australia must fall. So in the normal course of events, on Monday night Murdoch would have been trapped on a plane in the middle of the Pacific when his world fell apart, unable to do anything to stave off the initial paralysing panic that seized his bankers when the world's stock markets went into free fall.

For some reason Murdoch broke with his pattern of 34 years. Because he didn't go to Adelaide he also didn't go to Sydney, or to Cavan. Instead Murdoch was in New York, with his family in their penthouse on the corner of Fifth Avenue and East 88th Street. In the next four days, his decision not to go to Australia that year would save Rupert Murdoch's empire from imploding. It was one of the luckiest decisions he would ever make. It would allow him time to make one of the worst and the best deals of his career. But what had kept him here?

A range of possible reasons could have kept Murdoch in New York. He might have stayed to meet with Peter Kalikow, the real estate developer who was talking about buying the *New York Post*; or with Pearson executives, who were agitated that he had just snatched 15 per cent of the UK media group. But it's unlikely. One clue to Murdoch's movements was his position as a rising star on the horizon of the rich and famous. There may have been other secret Murdoch machinations; but whatever else was happening, one piece of business was very clear. Like any good New Yorker, Rupert Murdoch had stayed in town to party.

The press previews for the *Forbes* 400 list for 1987 hit the newsstands the week of 12 October. Each year *Forbes* magazine publishes its list of the 400 richest people in the world. The list has become one of the major markers of personal and corporate power. At the head of the list, Sam Walton, officially America's richest human with $8.5 billion from his holding in Wal-Mart Stores, was not happy. 'I could kick your butt for ever running that list,' he said testily.[7] Others in the ranks of the rich and powerful were not so averse to a little public adulation. John Kluge was listed in second place with 'at least' $3 billion – in large part due to his fortuitous sale of Metromedia to his friend Rupert Murdoch.

Rupert Murdoch had just joined the billionaires' club. Forbes valued him at $2.1 billion, the eighth richest person in America. He ranked equally with Warren Buffet. Murdoch was the star performer among the 23 new billionaires. The list of newly mega-rich also included a young software developer and Harvard drop-out called Bill Gates, trailing Murdoch at $1.1 billion.

Unhappily, by the time *Forbes* hit the streets later in the week of 18 October, Murdoch would no longer be a billionaire. The News Corp stock price that is the basis of his wealth was about to fall into a deep dark hole. He himself would stave off bankruptcy by the barest of margins, hanging on to his worldwide media empire by his fingernails. But even when misfortune beckoned, there was still this hour in the sun.

New York likes a party the way Hollywood loves a secret. On the Tuesday night, 13 October, Malcolm Forbes held a cocktail party. Strictly speaking it was a book launch. Forbes, David Mahoney and Shirley Lord had joined together in the Forbes building to help their friend David Brown, the film producer and husband of *Cosmopolitan* editor Helen Gurley Brown, to launch his new book, *Brown's Guide to Growing Gray*. They did it in gratitude for the way Brown had encouraged each of his hosts to write books. When it came to dialling up the corporate A-list to get the party off on the right note, Malcolm Forbes knew exactly who to call. The guest list featured a string of the big hitters who were about to feature in the *Forbes* 400 list.

John Kluge was there. So were Laurence Tisch, Donald Trump and Ronald Perelman. And so was Rupert Murdoch. There, in the winners' circle, was the man who hates parties, graciously consenting to make an appearance. The absurd $3 billion that Murdoch paid for Triangle Publications the following year would show that Murdoch was as susceptible as anyone to being included in the inner circles of the American Establishment. Forbes' party was Murdoch's triumph. After all the mud that had been thrown at him over the years, he had finally arrived.

Going to the book launch meant that Murdoch could not fly out of New York for the News Corp annual meeting until Wednesday morning, 14 October. Wednesday morning in New York would already be early Thursday in Australia. Murdoch had little more than 24 hours to fly half-way around the world to Sydney, change planes and then fly on to Adelaide to make the annual meeting on Friday morning. For a man with a private jet and his own airline it was probably just possible. But any hold up would leave him hours away in the air as the shareholders got restless. Murdoch didn't take the risk. He stayed in New York after the party.

Tokyo was steadiest on that Monday, down 2 per cent. New Zealand fell 4.2 per cent. Hong Kong was off 9.8 per cent. The Australian market on the Monday suffered its biggest points fall on record. The All Ordinaries index dropped 80 points, a fall of 3.7 per cent, and most brokers went home stunned, but still relieved that the worst of the bad news was behind them. It was bad but they had survived. The fall had been contained. Unfortunately the action was a long way from being over on 19 October.

London dropped 10 per cent after opening and kept sliding. But it was not until Wall Street opened, just before midnight Australian time, that Australian brokers realised how badly they had got it wrong. Pandemonium reigned. In wild scenes the Dow Jones index dropped 516 points. When the Australian markets opened on the Tuesday morning, the index dropped 500 points – some 22 per cent – in minutes. It was a bloodbath that would destroy nearly all of the Australian entrepreneurs of the 1980s.

'I hope someone else is paying, I've just lost a billion dollars,' Murdoch quipped at dinner that night in New York. News Corp had been one of the worst hit. The share price had touched $A24.50 earlier that month. On Tuesday 20 March it opened in Australia at $A11. It rallied to close at $A13, but by the following Tuesday panic selling had slammed the price down to

$A8.50. And $US1.7 billion of Rupert Murdoch's personal fortune had disappeared. Just like that.

The week that never happened

As far as the popular history of News Corp and Rupert Murdoch goes, the week of 19 October was a week like any other. News Corporation's finances spread across so many countries that at any time only a handful of people have any real understanding of the group's money trails. The only insights for the outside observer come from timing and the documentary record.

Nine months before, the Murdoch family company, Cruden Investments, had borrowed $A600 million to finance its takeover of Queensland Press. Cruden had nowhere near enough income to service the loan, and by late September 1987, the correspondence between Cruden and the Commonwealth Bank suggests the bank was getting twitchy. There seemed no major grounds for concern. The News Corp stock held in Cruden and in Rupert Murdoch's own private company Kayarem was worth $A3 billion. In addition, Queensland Press held News Corp convertible notes from the Herald and Weekly Times takeover worth another $A750 million. The Cruden debt, which with interest payments was now close to $A670 million, didn't seem so bad.

That was before 20 October. When News Corp shares crashed to $A11 in the first minutes of trading in Australia, Murdoch had dropped $A2 billion. When the share price hit $A8.50 in the following days, the Murdoch shares in Cruden were worth just $978 million and falling. Queensland Press was down another $A450 million on its News Corp notes. The Commonwealth Bank was suddenly stuck with a loan of $A670 million ($US475 million) with insufficient cashflow to cover the interest bill, secured by shares that kept dropping in value.

The bank had been twitchy when it had $A3 billion of security. Watching that margin of safety drop overnight to $A300 million is the sort of thing that can put a loan manager into spasm. While the safety margin still seemed a large number, any forced sale of shares by the Murdoch family to meet the debt could send the News Corp stock price down through the floor, the bank would shoot into losses, and it would be all over for Murdoch.

It was all in the timing. The Australian share market opened at 10 a.m. on Tuesday morning and the News Corp share price had self-immolated by 10.05am. Any time from then, Rupert Murdoch was toast. But shock waves took time to move out from the market. In New York it was just after six o'clock on Monday evening when the News Corp share price plunged. It is unlikely that alarm bells were ringing for any Australian corporate loan managers until later on the Tuesday. By that time it was after midnight in New York. Red flags would now be attached to Murdoch's personal debt position. But it is unlikely that anyone from the Commonwealth Bank's New York offices in Lexington Avenue would have spoken to Murdoch before Tuesday 20 October local time. Probably a meaningful conversation could not have taken place before Tuesday evening in New York time – which was early Wednesday morning at the Commonwealth Bank's head office in Sydney.

Some conversation must have taken place, because just after midday on Wednesday in New York, the Commonwealth Bank took a lien over the Murdochs' penthouse on East 88th street. The only official record of this move is a grubby, fading docket in the city register of New York County. The docket is signed by Keith Rupert Murdoch and Anna Maria Murdoch, and stamped 12.23 p.m., Wednesday 21 October.

There is no indication why, two days after the Crash, Murdoch's bank was taking security over his home. The timing of the New York mortgage suggests the bank was making a margin call on Murdoch, slapping security on any personal assets that were handy. What Murdoch needed – and because he was in New York he was able to provide – was something to stall the bank with. Just over 24 hours later, something happened on the other side of the world that solved Cruden's debt problems.

By this time it was Friday morning in eastern Australia. In Brisbane, Keith McDonald, the chief executive officer of Queensland Press Ltd, was preparing for a board meeting. Since the takeover by Cruden, Queensland Press had run operationally as part of the News group, with its board dominated by News Corp execs. Early on the morning of 23 October, a senior News executive called McDonald. Rupert Murdoch later said:

In late 1987, [Queensland Press] was given the opportunity to acquire approximately 42 million News Corporation shares from Cruden Investments . . . The board took up the opportunity . . . No member of the Cruden Investments board or member of the Murdoch family participated in the QPL board's decision, or was present when it was made.

The deal put to McDonald on Friday 23 October, three days after the

Crash, was that Queensland Press could buy 42 million News Corporation shares from its parent, Cruden, for $A671.5 million ($475 million). When added to the News Corp notes that Queensland Press already owned, the company would hold 21 per cent of News Corp's stock, ranking just after Cruden Investments itself as the largest shareholder in News. Most of the Queensland Press directors heard of the deal for the first time when the board meeting convened later that morning. By the time it broke for lunch, the board had decided to buy the News Corp stock at $16 a share. There had been some discussion with McDonald, and during the meeting itself, about Queensland Press taking a put option, which would allow the company to sell the shares back to Cruden in six months time for $16.75. The option plan was later dropped, which suggests Friday's board decision had some flexibility.

Later that day in New York, Rupert and Anna Murdoch signed over further personal security to the Commonwealth Bank. News Corp raised a new $A1 billion loan facility with the Commonwealth Bank, of which half went to Queensland Press to cover its deal with Cruden, which settled in Sydney on the night of 8 December 1987. Cruden's debt problem had been solved. Black Monday had been a nasty fright for Murdoch, but now it was back to operations as normal. 'I dropped two bills – but it's only paper,' he told News executives airily several weeks later.

Three queries remain over the Queensland Press deal. First, did the board make an independent decision? John D'Arcy, the chief executive of the Herald and Weekly Times, who sat on the Queensland Press Limited (QPL) board, raised concerns about the price during the board discussion. 'The deal was basically to benefit Rupert Murdoch,' he said later, though he believed the transaction was quite legal. The directors were not aware of Murdoch's dealings with the Commonwealth Bank in New York the previous day.

In January 1993 the Australian Securities Commission wrote a highly critical draft report on its two-year investigation of the deal which concluded: 'It appears from the books that the deal was a *fait accompli* and . . . Mr McDonald and the other QPL directors simply accepted . . . the decision without carrying out a full investigation . . . The interest problem made it apparent to the QPL directors that the deal may not be in the interests of QPL as a whole. As a result, the QPL directors sought legal advice as to the consequences of their actions.'

The concern here was that, in return for dividend payments of less than $A3 million, Queensland Press would face interest payments of $A110 million a year. This was more than Queensland Press had ever earned, so there was quite a lively possibility that the interest bill would send the company broke. However, despite the ASC criticism in the draft report, no action was ever taken.

The second query is: at $16, did Queensland Press pay too much for the shares? The ASC investigators, who never learned of the penthouse mortgage that Murdoch signed in New York on 22 October, and presumably did not connect the share deal with the market crash three days before, made no findings about the sale price. News shares opened on the Friday morning, 23 October, at $A13.80. They closed that afternoon at $A12.80 and by the following Tuesday, when Queensland Press engaged lawyers to prepare sale documents, the price had hit $A8.50. Even at its best moments on Friday 23 October, Queensland Press was paying $A93 million more than the market price. By the Tuesday, Queensland Press was paying 90 per cent more than the market price. That is to say, it was paying $A671.5 million for shares that had a market value of just $A356 million. On Tuesday's closing price, Cruden was receiving a $A315 million premium. As News owned 44 per cent of Queensland Press, it can be argued that the premium given to Cruden cost News Corp shareholders $A138 million.

The sale price seems all the more remarkable because it looks like Cruden was a forced seller. It had rising debt, no cashflow and falling security. Selling the shares to any other buyer but Queensland Press would have cost Murdoch control of his empire. However it is important to note that while Murdoch would have known this background, the Queensland Press directors and their advisors didn't. Their point of view was that this was a unique opportunity.

The third query is: was the deal legal? Section 129(1)(a) of the Queensland Companies Code prohibited a company from providing financial assistance to another party to buy its own shares. The bank's term sheet referred to a proposal to 'assist QPL with acquisition from Cruden Investments of sufficient . . . News Corporation . . . shares to enable full clearance of Cruden's indebtedness to CBA and Citibank.' If Queensland Press was buying the News shares to get Cruden out of its debt hole, which had been produced by buying Queensland Press itself, then it was technically financing its own takeover, albeit several months later.

News has always been at pains to stress that helping Cruden out was not the major factor in the minds of the Queensland Press directors, that despite what the Commonwealth Bank may have thought, the directors' sole motivation was to make a profitable and strategic investment in 'probably the most dynamic media enterprise on planet earth'.

Brisbane commercial lawyer John Humphrey later commented, 'Section 129(1)(a) would have been breached by QPL (Queensland Press Ltd) if a substantive purpose of the acquisition of the News Corp shares was to provide Cruden with financial assistance in connection with its earlier acquisition of QPL shares.' The problem, he noted, was the difficulty in determining what the 'substantive purpose' of the deal was. What were the Queensland Press directors thinking when they agreed to the deal? Corporate law in this instance depended on your state of mind. An action was only wrong if you meant it to be wrong.

'The books also indicate that the QPL directors were aware that the sole purpose of the transaction was to enable QPL's majority shareholder (Cruden) . . . to repay their (sic) debt incurred to acquire the QPL shares and notes,' the Securities Commission 1993 draft report found.

The report concluded: 'Such conduct by a company director of course falls short of that expected and required by the law and would constitute a contravention of Section 232 of the Corporations Law.'

John Atanaskovic, the Sydney lawyer who represented Queensland Press directors in the ASC inquiry, paints a very different picture of the deal. He bitterly attacked the ASC draft report, which, he wrote,

> . . . creates an impression of a finding of wrong-doing and illegality on the part of our clients where no such impression or finding is justified. Although the investment was a large one, it did not necessarily require long and tortured examination by the board . . . [The directors] were, we were instructed, not motivated by a desire to assist [Cruden] or any other person. Rather they were motivated solely by their desire to advance the interests of [the Queensland Press group] through the making of a profitable and strategic investment in the interests of those companies.

Atanaskovic stresses that October 1987 was an unusual time: 'It is now acknowledged that stock exchange prices were influenced by a relatively short term hysteria.' Within a few months, this had become plain to most people. To their credit, the Queensland Press directors had the presence of mind not to be unnerved by the 'then current hysteria affecting stock exchange trading'. As this was a substantial off-market transaction, the current market trading price was not particularly relevant – and even if it was, the discount on the Friday morning when the board decision was taken was not so far out of line with the market price. In any case, buying that many shares on the market would have driven up the price. Instead, the Queensland Press directors based their views on a report on the value of News shares prepared earlier that year by their financial advisor, Wardley Australia, during the Herald and Weekly Times takeover. The Wardley report reflected considerations 'of a longer term and more considered nature than daily share price variations'.

Through the Herald and Weekly Times takeover, in February 1987 Queensland Press had acquired 28.4 million News Corp convertible notes at $18.75 a share, at a total value of $532.1 million. In this light, $A16 appeared to be a favourable price for a similar sized parcel of News shares eight months later. Once the decision to buy the shares had been made on 23 October, says Atanaskovic, the subsequent share price fluctuations were irrelevant – and in any case, by 1993, the rise in the News Corp share price had made the deal a spectacularly good investment for Queensland Press. Today the investment is worth $A3.7 billion. 'Where is the detriment for any shareholder?' says Atanaskovic.

It was also natural, given the litigation launched against Queensland Press by Robert Holmes a Court in early 1987, that directors would take advice as to their legal position, says Atanaskovic. Keith McDonald was advised that the deal would have been wrong if it was to benefit just one shareholder but was quite legitimate if it was taken as an investment opportunity. His handwritten notes stated, 'Both shareholders keen – OK'.

If a deal is a good one and in the interests of shareholders generally, it is irrelevant that one shareholder may derive additional benefits from the deal, Atanaskovic says. The Queensland Press directors were not bound to inquire why Cruden was selling. The suggestion that Cruden was a forced seller is 'merely speculation', he says.

How much were News Corp shares worth in late October 1987? Before the Crash, the shares had traded as high as $A24.70. After Black Tuesday they slipped as low as $A8.50. The Queensland Press view was that post-crash market prices did not reflect the underlying value. The 'relatively short term hysteria' to which Atanaskovic refers actually lasted six years. News Corp's share price stayed low, and it was 1993 before the Queensland Press investment moved out of the red. The Wardley report was made in relation to the Cruden takeover offer for Queensland Press. The Wardley valuation reflected current market prices, at a time when the market was moving sharply upwards. As the tech wreck has since shown on world markets, in a share market crash there is nothing so out of date as a buy recommendation made during the boom.

At the same time that Queensland Press was buying News shares, News Corp was making a takeover bid for minority shareholders in Advertiser

Newspapers. The independent report on the bid by merchant bank Lloyds International valued the parcel of News Corp convertible notes held by Advertiser in November 1987 at \$A11.18 – a figure calculated from the average closing price over 15 trading days in November. Significantly, both the Wardley report and the Lloyds International report came up with valuations for News Corp stock that were close to current trading levels.

Entry price is critical in any investment. If you pay \$300 million too much to buy in, no matter how profitable the investment eventually turns out, the return will always be \$300 million less than it could have been. Atanaskovic's view is there is no detriment because the shares today are worth \$A3.7 billion. But one might also argue that if Queensland Press had negotiated a lower sale price per share, this would have forced Cruden to sell more News shares to Queensland Press to pay out its debt. These extra shares today might be worth another billion dollars.

Both these views are the product of hindsight. At the end of the day, it is hard to be too critical of the Queensland Press directors, or their advisors. In a turbulent market following the Crash, any investment decision would have been difficult – and this decision eventually ended happily. Other investors also paid too much for media stock that month – most notably Warwick Fairfax's disastrous decision to proceed with a takeover bid for the Fairfax newspaper group. When Keith McDonald sought legal advice, his notes stressed that the investment was a commercial decision. Evidence of that lay in the support for the investment from both of his shareholders, Cruden and News Corporation. If the deal had not been in News Corporation's interests, McDonald rightly expected that News Corp would tell him so. He and the Queensland Press board were not aware of the correspondence between Cruden and the Commonwealth Bank, or of the mortgage taken on Murdoch's penthouse the day before. Only Murdoch himself knew that. And if, as the managing director of News Corporation, Rupert Murdoch had reason to believe that Queensland Press was buying shares from his family company for more than their current value, or that the deal could have been bettered, it was up to him to say so. If there was a problem with this deal – and as Atanaskovic notes, any conclusions about Cruden being forced to sell remain speculative – only Murdoch was in a position to realise this. Unfortunately he has never commented on it.

The easiest way to establish that this was an arms length transaction would have been to announce it publicly. Instead, News Corp investors only learned of the deal from an *Australian Financial Review* report in 1990 by Martin Peers, who discovered it in an obscure corporate filing by

Queensland Press the year before. But as no date was given for the deal in 1987–88, investors had no reason to query the $A16 sale price.

News Corp continued to prop up Murdoch's control of the empire. In addition to the 21 per cent of News Corp held by Queensland Press, Murdoch also managed to keep hold of another 4 per cent block of stock, the News Corp notes that had been issued to Advertiser Newspapers in the Herald and Weekly Times takeover, by selling them to an off-balance-sheet company called Dexenne Pty Ltd. By the middle of 1988, News Corp had $1.2 billion secretly committed to propping up Murdoch's control of the empire.

The Commonwealth Bank syndicated parts of the Queensland Press loan among Australian and Japanese banks. A little piece of it even ended up with an American bank that had just opened an office in Brisbane. It was called Pittsburgh First National. By 1990, Pittsburgh had had its fill of Australian bad loans and had closed its Australian office.

To recap: Murdoch had never been able to afford his great move in 1985–86 to buy Twentieth Century Fox, the Metromedia television stations and to launch the Fox network. To pay for it, he moved his British newspapers to Wapping and triggered a year of violent industrial confrontation. The Wapping success produced a new debt problem that he tried to solve by taking over the Australian newspaper industry. When that plan went wrong he had been forced into a deal that left a crippling debt in his family company. Then, in the deals after Black Monday 1987, Murdoch flipped the problem back to News Corp. Cruden's loan problem was now once again News Corporation's lurking debt crisis. And nobody knew. News Corporation shareholders had no idea how closely their company's future was now tied to the problems of Murdoch's private world.

Perhaps the most damaging part of this arrangement was that it all came so easily. Rupert Murdoch had had the scare of his life. He ignored the warning. In 1988 the Great Acquirer embarked upon his biggest spending spree yet. In June 1988 Murdoch announced he would be setting up a hugely expensive new satellite television service for Britain called Sky Television, challenging the government-approved British Satellite Broadcasting. On 31 October 1988 News Corp announced it was buying Triangle Publications from Walter Annenberg for $3 billion. Triangle published *TV Guide* and *Seventeen* magazines. The same month, Murdoch ordered 39 giant MAN Roland presses for his newspapers in Britain and Australia for $450 million. A month later he spent another $350 million mopping up the rest of William Collins Plc, which he later folded into the US publisher Harper & Row to form HarperCollins, together with US educational publisher Scott, Foresman and Company, which he bought for $455 million.

Murdoch would spend 1989 and 1990 fending off his looming financial problems, as News Corp spiralled down and his bankers lost patience. Eventually it all caught up with him. At the end of 1990 Murdoch got caught in a worldwide credit squeeze. Murdoch should have locked in long-term borrowings the year before when money was still easy.

How much had Murdoch's private financial problems contributed to this? In October 1990, News Corp's immediate problem was that it had $2.6 billion debt falling due that year that it needed to roll over, and it needed $600 million of additional loans. From 1988, News Corp had had $1.2 billion tied up in loans and investments that propped up Murdoch's control of the media group.

In October 1990 when Murdoch's senior banks planned their rescue package for News Corp, the question was what should be done with Murdoch's private borrowings in Queensland Press. The senior banks decided the funds were so intertwined they would wrap them all up together in the Debt Override. Not all banks agreed. That was what the dispute was about in London on December 6. Queensland Press's deal to buy News Corp stock had settled on 8 December 1987. The three-year $A1 billion loan raised for the deal fell due slap bang in the middle of Murdoch's worst nightmare. The dispute with Australian and Japanese banks that day, and the much-maligned Pittsburgh National, was about bailing out the Murdoch family.

The ASC's Queensland Press inquiry slowly petered out. In mid-1991 an ASC staffer described the case as the state's highest-ranking matter after the pursuit of fugitive entrepreneur Christopher Skase. It was later downgraded into a documents-only investigation. 'It's a routine matter,' an ASC spokesperson said in late 1992. 'They [the Murdoch companies] got their knickers into a knot.' The ASC resolved no legal action would be taken. Instead, in January 1993 the ASC wrote a draft report which was sharply critical of the Queensland Press deal. ASC staff hoped to have the final report tabled in the Australian parliament by June. In mid-1993 Chapman postponed a final report and assigned an ASC investigator, Phil Shifton, to follow up reports of further News Corp share deals linked to a related company, Dexenne Pty Ltd. However, by late 1993 the inquiry had been overtaken by events. No final report was written, and the matter lapsed. Thus those involved in the Queensland Press deal were exonerated.

The last word went to John Atanaskovic. He wrote his scathing response to the ASC's draft report on its investigation on 3 March 1993. Atanaskovic declared flatly that the ASC was wrong in its interpretation of law, and had not shown that the sole or dominating purpose of Queensland Press directors in approving the stock deal in 1987 was improper. Further, he said that by failing to call witnesses the ASC was depending on a documentary record that was incomplete when it sought to portray unease among Queensland Press directors about the deal. 'I do not believe that, at the end of its consideration of the matter in 1993, the ASC did in fact consider that Queensland Press might have been providing financial assistance for its own takeover,' says Atanaskovic.

The runaway News Corp stock price took the steam out of the ASC inquiry. By late 1993, when the inquiry was finally closed, News Corp stock (allowing for share splits) had hit $A48. Queensland Press, which bought its stock for $A16, was now sitting on a little gold mine. As News Corp's stock price continued to rise – adjusting for share splits the $A16 shares were worth $A160 in March 2000 – Queensland Press became News Corp's private little bank, Murdoch's lender of last resort. It also had become his golden parachute. If Murdoch ever tired of running the empire, selling the News Corp shares held by Queensland Press offered a spectacular exit.

CHAPTER FIVE

THE FUGITIVE

London/Jerusalem

By 1991, News Corporation's aversion to paying corporate income tax had become legendary. Since 1986 its tax bill had averaged less than seven cents in each dollar it reported in earnings. Murdoch's huge US investments in buying Metromedia and Twentieth Century Fox and launching the Fox network – with debt that was funded by his operations in Britain and to a lesser extent Australia – had allowed him to structure the News empire around holding companies in the Bahamas, the Cayman Islands, the Channel Islands and the British Virgin Islands – in short, almost any offshore destination that shared an enlightened view about the need to pay taxes. This archipelago of tax havens allowed Murdoch to channel the News group's money streams away from high-tax areas like the US, Australia and Britain. As the Citibank rescue team had found, it also made News Corp's corporate structure unbelievably complicated. That complexity had helped save the group, discouraging Murdoch's bankers from wanting to liquidate assets because the ownership was so hard to unravel.

In the months that followed Murdoch's 1991 debt crisis, his empire continued to battle for survival. In a world full of sceptical bankers, disaffected investors and incredulous analysts, the group inched its way back towards solvency and kept its own council. There were dark and far-flung corners in News Corporation that did not need to see the light of day. This included most of the group's dealings in the tax archipelago. While News Corp had always been happy to talk about the low-tax profits that the group made, it had been much more reluctant to talk about how the tax savings were achieved, or about the men and women who ran this secret side of News. The subject was clearly marked private and off-limits, a corporate no-go zone – as indeed it is for most multinationals that use tax havens. The downside to a corporate obsession with confidentiality is that sometimes a company can choke on its own secrets.

For all the ingenuity of the tax lawyers and accountants in New York and London, multinational corporations depend for their smooth running on a relatively small number of middle-management executives running subsidiary companies around the world, as well as the community of expatriate lawyers and accountants who actually live on tax haven islands and administer the offshore subsidiaries as directors and company secretaries. The bigger and more far-flung the corporation, the greater trust and responsibility that executives in the outposts of the empire carry. People entrusted with the routine tasks of moving money from one offshore account to another need to be up to the task. What is best for the company needs to be uppermost in their mind. In 1991, Rupert Murdoch's empire was plunged into crisis when confronted with the spectre of a criminal in the no-go zone. When a middle-level executive set out to defraud the group, it was perhaps inevitable that he would use the tax archipelago to hide his tracks.

The roots of Murdoch's next crisis dated back to 1977. That was when a group of mathematicians in America came up with a better way to keep secrets. In many ways the possibility of secrets – the idea that one can make something appear or disappear, to look other than what it is, that one can hide the real meaning of something from the world at large, while ensuring that under the surface the hidden message is always accessible to the select few – has always been a critical element of social organisation. Knowledge is not something to be dispensed indiscriminately to the profligate.

Codes generally involve a key, usually a number. To encode or decode a signal, you have to find that number.

In 1977, Ronald Rivest, Adi Shamir and Leonard Adleman, all professors at Massachusetts Institute of Technology, developed a new way of making codes with a mathematical formula or algorithm. Their encryption system came to be known as RSA, after their initials. The twist to the RSA system was to have two separate parts to the key or codebook that locked and unlocked the code. One part could be shown to anybody. The other part was the secret bit.

The system was based upon pairs of prime numbers – that is, numbers that are not the product of any other numbers. Under the RSA system, 15 might be the public key for the code. You could tell the number to anyone who wanted to send you a message, and they could encode the message by feeding the number 15 into the RSA formula, or algorithm. However, once the message was encoded, the only way to decode it was to feed in three and five, the original prime numbers that multiplied together to make up your public key of 15. Five and three are the private key, the part that has to be kept secret, known only to the person to whom the message is addressed. It isn't very hard to work out what prime numbers produce 15, so it's not a very good code. But if the public key is a huge number, 110 digits long, the prime numbers that make it up as the private key can be 55 digits long. A computer can eventually work out what those two prime numbers or private keys are, but to do this you need a supercomputer and several decades of spare time. At least that's the theory.

One of the three professors who developed RSA, Adi Shamir, moved to Israel in the early 1980s, where he worked with a Dr Fiat at the Weizmann Institute of Science. Together they developed the encryption process further with the Fiat/Shamir algorithm. The technology that spun off from the Fiat/Shamir algorithm would eventually be worth billions of dollars. By the mid-1980s, the Weizmann Institute and its commercial arm, the Yeda Research and Development Corporation, had begun to look at ways to make some serious money from Shamir's cryptic know-how.

One of Shamir's colleagues at the Weizmann Institute, a scientist called Uzi Sharon, was a world expert in laser technology. Sharon was a knock-about character with a colourful past. In 1980 Sharon became friends with an Australian telecommunications consultant called Bruce Hundertmark, who by the mid-1980s had become Rupert Murdoch's technology adviser in Europe. Sharon and Hundertmark both saw the commercial potential for Shamir's work. They started looking for people who needed to keep secrets.

Hundertmark's big idea was to come up with a new way of applying Shamir's technology, which was arguably more important than the encryption algorithms themselves. The encryption process was based around sets of private and public keys. The thing about a set of keys is that you want to be able to carry them about. Hundertmark suggested embedding the private key to the code in a microchip in a plastic card. A process to do this had just been developed in California by an Indian-born electrical engineer called Bharat Kumar Marya. Known as BK, Marya had produced his first single-chip smart card in 1986. Hundertmark still hadn't figured out how to make money from Shamir's encryption technology, but now he had made it mobile.

Rupert Murdoch was not at all interested in Hundertmark's musings. 'You're interested in fucking smart cards and I'm not!' he told

Hundertmark. But Hundertmark persisted with the idea, and by February 1988 he had persuaded Murdoch to invest $3.6 million in a company in Israel to develop Shamir's encryption process. In the meantime, Uzi Sharon had introduced Hundertmark to Michael Clinger, an American-Israeli with a remarkable marketing background in high-tech business.

The feature of almost every relationship Michael Clinger had ever had was his obvious intelligence and his ability to win people's confidence. There was something about him that inspired trust. Physically he was unimpressive – a stodgy figure, with a wide face and large glasses. He looked like a maths teacher. Perhaps the geeky appearance was part of his charm. And he was certainly charming. It helped that at 36 years old Clinger was already independently wealthy. Clinger's social skills were enhanced by his wife, Niva Von Weisl, who became one of the leading lights of Jerusalem society after the couple moved from New York to Israel in 1987.

Hundertmark and Clinger set up a News Corp venture that traded as News Datacom, in which they held a minority share. From the start of News Datacom, tax was clearly going to be an issue, and the entity that was set up existed somewhere between the legal and tax reaches of Tel Aviv, London and Hong Kong. The business was based on a research company in Israel called News Datacom Research Limited (NDRL), but the holding company, News Datacom Security Products Limited (NDSP), was based in Hong Kong. A News Corporation company in Bermuda, News Publishing Limited, owned 60 per cent of NDSP; Professor Adi Shamir owned 10 per cent; and the Weizmann Institute's commercial arm, Yeda, owned another 10 per cent. The remaining 20 per cent was held by International Development Group NV, a company owned by Clinger and Hundertmark which was based in the Dutch Antilles. Under the shareholding agreement for News Datacom, each shareholder would have pre-emptive rights to buy the other shareholders' stock if they wished to sell out. News Datacom Research Limited was set up with due ceremony in February 1988, in a technology park in Jerusalem near the Weizmann Institute. Despite the fanfare, it was a very modest operation, a great idea looking for an application. That all changed four months later.

In mid-1988, Murdoch's empire was wobbling along in its customary fashion. The Fox television network in America was haemorrhaging money and Richard Sarazen told reporters that if the losses continued News would have to dump the new network. A day later Sarazen was saying he had been misreported. In Britain, Murdoch's tabloids were doing themselves proud. The *News of the World*, in between stories about Captain

Mark Phillips' candle-lit dinners with his Canadian public relations manager, and an orphaned puppy that was being breastfed by a sturdy British housewife, had covered itself with glory with a story about a tribe of perverted cannibals in Papua New Guinea called the Chimbu. The local arm of the News Corp empire duly reprinted this story in Port Moresby, and 40 irate Chimbu tribesmen descended on the British High Commission looking for the name of a good libel lawyer. Meanwhile, Murdoch was busy amalgamating HarperCollins. He was about to spend $3 billion buying *TV Guide* and Triangle Publications, he was spending a fortune on new printing presses. And then, on 8 June, he stunned a dinner in London sponsored by the British Academy of Film and Television Arts by announcing that he was about to launch a satellite television service called Sky. The new service would use a medium-power Luxembourg satellite to launch four unauthorised channels to Britain in eight months time. Up until this moment, the partners in British Satellite Broadcasting, the consortium that in December 1986 had won an exclusive licence from the British government to run a satellite television service, had believed they had the field entirely to themselves. Murdoch's proposed launch date meant that Sky would be operating months before BSB was ready.

'We are seeing the dawn of an age of freedom for viewing and freedom for advertising,' Murdoch announced. This was 'the dawn of television's new age and the most dramatic innovation in broadcasting since the launch of commercial television in Britain more than three decades ago'.

It is difficult to appreciate just how knuckleheaded this decision must have seemed at the time. Murdoch's broadcasting experience had been limited to owning a few television stations in Australia, and launching a new television network in America a year before, a network that continued to bleed his empire. Sky was to be based upon a low-power European satellite operation Murdoch had owned since 1982, which had virtually no viewers, no advertising, and in five years had gracefully lost £30 million. Murdoch had absolutely no experience in pay-television. So his model for the revamped Sky would continue to be free-to-air television, based on advertising revenues. Murdoch planned to beef up Sky's existing general entertainment channel, buy sports programming from a new channel called Eurosport, have a news channel, and form a joint venture with Michael Eisner at Disney to produce a movie channel.

Murdoch believed that people would be pounding at the doors, wanting to shell out £200 for a satellite dish. The business model had disaster written all over it. It would indeed have been a disaster epic, if Hollywood had not rallied to save Murdoch with a solid dose of outraged paranoia. The movie business is built around the issue of copyright, on making sure the only people who get to see the moving pictures are the paying customers. Studios were willing to show their films on free-to-air television stations – after every other possible market had been tapped, from cinema to videos to cable – because TV could be controlled. Beyond a 40-mile radius from the television tower, even *Gone With the Wind* begins to look like the Great Alaskan Snowstorm of 1954. By comparison, a satellite's reach is limited only by the curvature of the earth. The idea of broadcasting movies from a satellite into the void, to be picked up and pirated across the major land mass of Europe by *anyone* with a satellite dish; mixing markets and blurring the distinctions that allowed the studios to extract the maximum dollar of revenue from every territory where their films were shown; all sparked fear and loathing in the sensitive hearts of movie executives. They flatly refused to supply films for Sky as a free-to-air channel. Sky Movies had to be a pay-television channel. This meant that Murdoch had to find a way to scramble the Sky signal, so that only approved customers could see the movies, and the studios would thus have a way of knowing how much to charge Sky. This posed a bit of a problem, because Murdoch had already committed to using the old PAL European television format, and no one had ever encrypted PAL.

This is where the penny dropped for Hundertmark. It was the question he had been nagging at for years: who in the modern world most needs to keep secrets, besides banks and racecourses? Who needs to control flows of information, to make things appear or disappear at will? The answer was obviously media companies. Information and entertainment is a commodity, and like any commodity it must be protected from unauthorised use. Within four months of Murdoch's Sky announcement, Adi Shamir had produced an encryption system for PAL called VideoCrypt, which would control access to satellite television transmissions. Pay channels on Sky would be encrypted, and decoded in the set-top box in each viewer's home. Actually the first efforts barely qualified to be called encryption. VideoCrypt in a fairly rudimentary way scrambled the lines that made up the picture. The really clever part of the system was the smart card which Sky subscribers had to insert into their set-top box. BSB had to put back its launch six months because of teething problems with the DMAC encryption chip in its set-top box. Sky went to air on time knowing that it could fix the holes in VideoCrypt later, not by replacing the whole set-top box but just by issuing a new smart card. Replacing the cards regularly – every three months was the plan – would also thwart hackers who wanted to pirate the Sky signal.

Of all the Herculean tasks undertaken in the frenetic months before and after the Sky launch in February 1989, VideoCrypt was one of the greatest. Developing an encryption program, a set-top box that would use smart cards, programming a smart card chip, setting up a manufacturing supply of set-top boxes and another one for smart cards, and building an administrative and account-keeping structure to make this system work, was an insanely complex procedure. What it all meant was that, once Sky had gone to such elaborate lengths to satisfy Hollywood's concerns for copyright, it was a simple step forward to turn Sky into a pay-television service . . . to create the means eventually to turn Sky into a huge profit earner, although making a profit was still years away.

Hundertmark played a major role in solving the technical problems that Sky posed. 'Without his drive, Murdoch could not have put numerous things together in time,' one of those involved in the launch later commented.

But even before this, back in August 1988, with pressure to solve the Sky encryption problem at its peak, Hundertmark had come across an unhappy secret. He wanted Michael Clinger to go to a conference in the United States. Clinger refused to go. Hundertmark began asking his Israeli contacts about Clinger's US travel phobia.

Michael Cornelius Clinger was born in England in 1952, but by the 1970s he was living in New York working as a credit analyst with the Chase Manhattan Bank. In 1974 he left Chase Manhattan to work for a Swiss medical supply company. Four years later he agreed to become a business partner of a woman called Deborah Rothfield, who wanted to form a company to market surgical lasers, called Advanced Surgical Technologies. Clinger took up the idea, but Rothfield claimed he never gave her the half share they agreed upon. When he sold the company three years later he pocketed the entire $3 million. He then moved on to a new laser distribution company called Endo-Lase Inc. Clinger as chairman and chief executive of Endo-Lase floated the company on Wall Street in January 1984 for $3.5 million. The profits he reported to shareholders were fictitious right from the start. After 16 months the stock had risen from $2 to hit $14, largely on the back of dodgy profit numbers and creative accounting.

The wheels began to fall off several months later, when the US Securities and Exchange Commission queried the Endo-Lase accounts. Clinger jumped ship in June 1986 at the insistence of the company's bankers, and Endo-Lase filed for Chapter 11 bankruptcy protection two months later. In July 1987, the Securities and Exchange Commission charged Clinger and two other Endo-Lase executives with defrauding investors, falsifying accounts and insider trading. The three did not admit or deny the charges, but settled the case by agreeing to pay back $814,194 in illegal profits, of which $810,600 was to come from Clinger, plus an undisclosed amount raised from the company's stock and bonus money. Facing a barrage of class-action suits from Endo-Lase stockholders who had lost their shirts, Clinger decided not to stay around to face the music. 'Mr Clinger left the country and went to Israel,' said the senior counsel of the Securities and Exchange Commission's Division of Enforcement, James Mann.

Clinger was reluctant to visit the US because he knew that the moment he set foot there he would be hit by an avalanche of subpoenas and writs from the Endo-Lase stockholders. Hundertmark was confronted with the knowledge that he was in business with a major-league hustler. After angry confrontations with Clinger, Hundertmark claims that he wrote to a News Corp lawyer detailing Clinger's history. Clinger himself says he discussed his legal problems with a senior News Corp executive, who was unconcerned and referred to legal actions taken against Rupert Murdoch in locations around the world. News Corp categorically denies that any such conversation took place.

There were certainly enough crises elsewhere that needed attention. Murdoch had planned to run the movie channel as a joint venture with Disney. But Michael Eisner pulled out of the venture just before Sky launched, on the grounds that Murdoch's *Sun* newspaper was running topless page 3 girls holding satellite dishes with the Sky and Disney logos. Sky said Eisner had cold feet because the bidding between Sky and BSB for movie rights from other studios had grown too rich for his comfort. Murdoch was furious with Eisner and sued Disney for $1.5 billion. Meanwhile many of the Sky set-top boxes had proved faulty, with fuses that needed to be replaced. The smart cards were put together at Sky's Livingstone site in Scotland by News Gem Smartcard International, a joint venture between News Datacom and French technology group Gem Plus. But many of the cards also had faults. While Sky launched in February 1989, the encryption operation was not up and running until twelve months later. But Sky still solved its problems faster than its rival, BSB Holdings, which because of its delays developing its encryption chip, did not launch until April 1990.

By June 1990, News Corp had written off £235 million in losses on Sky. In the next four months it lost another £48 million. The huge losses were undermining any hope Murdoch had of convincing his banks to fund him out of the debt crisis that was developing at News Corp. The total cost of

Sky had grown to £550 million. If Sky folded, this would be a total loss. On 27 September Murdoch called Peter Davis at Reed International. He had met Davis at Claridges on 24 July where they'd had an inconclusive discussion about merging Sky with BSB. Now Murdoch told Davis he was ready to talk seriously.

After pumping £850 million into the rival venture, the four major BSB shareholders – Reed, Pearson, Granada and Chargeurs – were just as anxious to stop the blood-letting. The BSB shareholders knew Murdoch was in trouble, but they didn't realise how close to the edge he was. On 4 October David DeVoe had his crisis meeting with News Corp's bankers at Wapping. What the BSB shareholders did not know was that from that point the fate of Murdoch's empire hung on the Citibank rescue plan. In the week of 14 October, Murdoch met privately with Ian Irvine, the deputy chief executive of BSB shareholder Reed International, at Cavan, his country property in Australia to discuss a merger. On 21 October, formal talks began in intense secrecy at the Lucknam Park, an obscure Wiltshire hotel near Bath. BSB and News executives booked into the Lucknam Park hotel using false names and said they were executives with a company called Melloward. BSB Holdings needed to keep the talks secret because it had just completed a difficult bank refinancing. If news of the merger talks got out, as Granada legal manager James Tibbitts put it, 'BSB would not be dead in the water, it would be dead underwater.' News faced a different danger. If the BSB partners learned of the dire debt crisis it was facing, they would offer fewer concessions – or they might not do the deal at all, and wait for News and Sky to fall over.

In five days of tough negotiations, the shape of the merger was thrashed out. It would be a fifty-fifty merger between Sky and BSB, which would be run by News.

'No cash has changed hands,' Granada chief executive Derek Lewis said later when the merger was announced.

> What effectively we did was to look at the balance sheets of the two companies, look at the asset values of them before deducting any debt, conclude that they were roughly equal and then just lump those two sets of assets into the new merged company.

Despite BSB's reluctance, the new venture, BSkyB, would stick with Sky's ancient PAL technology, and dump the high-power DMAC signal used by BSB. Britain would be forced back to the old PAL television system for the next decade. The problem with this, as the BSB shareholders had discovered, was that a pay-TV service lives or dies on its encryption system. BSkyB would not own the VideoCrypt technology that was so important to its future. VideoCrypt was supplied by News Datacom Security Products, which was owned by News Corp and the Israelis. What would happen if News Datacom withdrew the technology? The BSB shareholders had already agreed to take only a half share in BSkyB, though they had invested more than Sky. They had conceded that News would run BSkyB. News Datacom offered News yet another way to squeeze the partnership.

The talks continued through the next week. Unbeknownst to the BSB shareholders, News Corp almost went broke on 31 October when the one-month rollover of a $500 million loan fell due. The BSkyB merger was finalised 48 hours later. It was announced at 9 p.m. – even before the BSB board approved the deal. Justice Arden would later find that late on Friday afternoon a BSB board meeting had been called for 8 p.m., but the meeting to approve the merger was not held until 2 a.m. on the Saturday morning – and that meeting was later found to be invalid. Both sides immediately began the delicate task of briefing Downing Street, regulators, media analysts and bankers. The briefings continued through the following week, as the new chief executive of BSkyB, Sam Chisholm, descended like an avenging angel upon the BSB head office.

Chisholm had landed in London to run Sky on 13 September. His style was personal – joking, persuading, shouting, in your face. Despite a serious lung condition he was a heavy smoker. Chisholm was alternately described as abrasive and rude, or charming and a pushover. A former floor-wax salesman, he had gone into television, working his way up to head Australia's National Nine Network, owned by Kerry Packer. Chisholm had transformed Nine into Australia's leading network with a swaggering management style mixing fear, flattery and a talent for the grand gesture. There was a Good Sam and a Bad Sam. The Good Sam had an intensely loyal cadre of executives and on-air talent, and was famous at Nine for lavish spending. 'Winners have parties, losers have meetings,' he told staff. The Bad Sam had a sign on his desk at Nine that said, 'To err is human, to forgive is not my policy.' Some people thought he was kidding.

Chisholm began sacking staff within hours of taking over BSkyB. In the next eight months, estimates of the direct and indirect casualty toll would go as high as 3,000. Two satellite operations with two sets of head offices, uplink centres, satellite transponders, television studios, maintenance and administration staff, all had to be slashed. The need for secrecy remained paramount. News Corp, in the middle of its debt crisis, had decided that it would not be appropriate to tell its investors how much of News Corp's investment was being written off as a loss. News accountants took the Sky/BSkyB investment off the group's balance sheet for five months and treated it as a loan. During that time, BSkyB wrote off £750 million of losses, but News never said a word about this to its shareholders.

Meanwhile, by early 1990 Bruce Hundertmark had developed lung problems and wanted to return to Australia. His high-handed approach to solving problems had not won him friends at Sky. He had fallen out with Murdoch, Clinger was badmouthing him, and in May 1990, News International secretary Peter Stehrenberger, who was also on the News Datacom board, asked Hundertmark to resign. This left Michael Clinger in charge in Israel, running News Datacom Research Limited, the most secret part of the Murdoch empire. As head of the encryption operation, Clinger had become News Corp's official keeper of secrets.

Meanwhile, in New York the Securities and Exchange Commission had not forgotten about Clinger, or about the $810,600 settlement that he had agreed to pay in July 1987. The problem, said the SEC's James Mann, was that 'Clinger never paid the money'. In November 1990, the SEC ran out of patience. On Thursday 8 November 1990, as the frenzied lobbying and briefing sessions over the BSkyB merger continued in London, as Sam Chisholm stepped up his wave of wholesale sackings, and as the Citibank rescue bid for News Corp stepped up another notch, a New York grand jury indicted Clinger on 51 counts of insider trading, fraudulent accounting and obstructing the SEC. A warrant was issued for Clinger's arrest. From this point on, one of the most critical arms of News Corporation was being run by an international fugitive. Michael Clinger didn't feel abashed by this. Nor did he feel any need to share this development with News Corporation management, who in any case were busy with the secret arrangements of the BSkyB takeover and the debt crisis. If anyone could keep a secret, it was Michael Clinger.

In April 1991 Rupert Murdoch made the unpleasant discovery that, after four horrific months battling with banks to refinance News Corporation's debt, he had another banking problem on his hands. After seeing how shaky News Corp's financial position was, BSkyB's bankers were refusing to provide the next round of funding for the struggling business covered by BSB's original loan facility. The banks wanted the BSkyB shareholders to kick in more money themselves. This was a problem for News Corp because of the tight restraints imposed by the debt override agreement. After another heart-stopping crisis, where liquidation seemed again only days away, the BSkyB shareholders stumped up the cash. To meet News

Corp's half share, Murdoch ended up borrowing £22 million through his family holding company, Cruden Investments. Significantly, he raised the money from another Australian bank, Westpac. He had dropped Commonwealth Bank of Australia.

In the course of this restructure, the BSkyB shareholders wrestled out a new shareholders' agreement. One of the biggest issues to resolve was what to do about the ownership of VideoCrypt and the Hong Kong holding company, New Datacom Security Products. A News Corp subsidiary in Bermuda, News Publishing Limited, owned 60 per cent of NDSP. How could BSkyB ensure that it would always retain access to the VideoCrypt technology? And given that News Corp had management and board control of BSkyB, how could the other shareholders be sure that News would not demand extortionate prices for the smart cards? The underlying question for the former BSB shareholders was, how much did they trust Rupert Murdoch? Emotions ran high. 'It's Rupert's technique to use the power of the management,' Frank Barlow of Pearsons told Mathew Horsman later. 'News wanted to run (BSkyB) as a News subsidiary.' The differences degenerated into shouting matches across the board table between Barlow and Arthur Siskind, the News Corp lawyer and BSkyB board member.

'Arthur really couldn't stand Frank, they went at each other all the time,' said one director. Siskind, who had a tendency to be tubby, had lost a lot of weight after a heart attack. At one point Barlow shouted at Siskind, 'Look, my heart can stand it, can yours?'

On 11 May 1991, to settle the concerns over VideoCrypt, News Corp agreed to insert the following three clauses in a wider shareholders' agreement: Clause one: any deals between News Datacom Security Products and BSkyB would be on an arms' length commercial basis. Clause two: if News Corp's stake in BSkyB ever fell below 33.33 per cent, BSkyB could force News to sell its stake in NDSP to BSkyB. Clause three: News International through News Publishing Limited in Bermuda would use its 'best endeavours' to consult with the Israeli shareholders 'as to the possibility' that BSkyB could buy some or all of the News stake in News Datacom Security Products. In short, BSkyB wanted to buy News Datacom Security Products, and News would do its best to make it happen.

The problem was, the 1988 News Datacom Security Products shareholders' agreement meant that any change of ownership required the approval of the other shareholders. So it wasn't clear how News could possibly make the commitment in clause two to sell its stake without the approval of the Israeli shareholders. The Israelis didn't complain because

News never told them about clause two. Actually it looks like News never got around to telling the Israelis about clause three either. 'I have no evidence of News International having so consulted with the minority shareholders in NDSP,' Justice Lindsay found in the Chancery Court in November 1998. This was not a minor omission. Siskind subsequently testified in an affidavit that in late 1991 BSkyB discussed buying News out of NDSP, but 'the discussion never became serious'. In late 1999 News floated NDS Group, the business into which NDSP evolved. In March 2000 the market value of NDS hit $5 billion, before it settled around $3 billion. Back in 1991, NDSP was headed for great things, but who would end up with this windfall, BSkyB or News Corporation? The News group's failure to consult with the Israeli shareholders about a share sale to BSkyB meant the big winner would be News. This omission arguably cost BSkyB several billion dollars.

Meanwhile the News Datacom business in Israel was getting out of control. The Israeli staff had a personal loyalty to Michael Clinger, and regarded News Corp executives as 'merely occasional, uninformed and not always welcome visitors', Justice Lindsay later concluded.

Early on, Clinger had hired an accountant friend of his, Leo Krieger, as finance officer for both News Datacom Research and the holding company NDSP at $48,000 a year. The two were as thick as thieves. Meir Matatyahu was another young Israeli whom Clinger hired in March 1990. He told Clinger in a telephone call,

> You know, it is, how you say . . . shitty company, well, I mean it is not a shitty company but the way that people think, the way that people talk, you can hear it so . . . the standard is so low, it is unbelievable . . . It's such stupid things . . . but this is it, this is what we have.

Clinger responded:

> Yeah, but you know that is one of the reasons we can manipulate it . . . it cuts both ways . . . you know, you have got to keep that in mind . . . we would not be doing what we were doing if they were particularly brilliant . . . It is a headless management with each guy going in his own direction and, you know, it has its upside.

Clinger was spending a lot of time in Paris and had become a little hard to contact. He carried a string of passports under different names. He travelled variously as Michael Clinger, Michael Klinger, Cornelius Clinger and Cornelius Klinger. Life on the run had not restricted his lifestyle, or his role as the official face of News Datacom. In June 1991, for example, he was in Brussels to brief the European Community Research Commissioner, Filippo Maria Pandolfi, who was trying to negotiate a new set of broadcasting rules for the European Common Market.

In London, Clinger had not struck it off with Sam Chisholm. The Israelis were just as uneasy about being minority partners with News as the BSB partners were. In the same way the BSB partners feared that News would exploit its control of BSkyB to its own advantage, the Israeli shareholders feared that News management would channel any profits from the encryption technology towards News Corp rather than News Datacom. In the eyes of the Weizmann Institute and Professor Shamir, Clinger was the only defender of their interests. Clinger complained, with some justi-fication, that BSkyB was buying smart cards at less than cost price (though this was balanced for the moment because BSkyB's minimum orders meant it was paying for more cards than it used). The original contract had been to replace the smart cards every three months. To cut costs, Sky had unilaterally decided to extend the life of the cards – a move which would help Sky but stood to cost NDSP millions of pounds. Clinger, perhaps rightly, saw it as a breach of contract. As the row with Chisholm worsened, Clinger threatened to insert a built-in expiry date into the cards, after which they would not function. The two men had an angry exchange of letters, which ended with Chisholm attacking Clinger's character, refusing to deal with him, and even suggesting he might not be honest. In those desperate months when BSkyB was fighting for its very existence, Chisholm had taken the role of the hard man. He was determined to cut costs on all sides, and to chisel price reductions out of all BSkyB's suppliers – particularly to renegotiate with Hollywood studios the huge fees for movie rights. In this bigger picture, Clinger was just a minor irritant.

Chisholm was right, of course. Clinger was stealing News Corp blind. Initially Sky had manufactured the smart cards at its Livingstone factory in Scotland through News Gem Smartcard International Ltd, a company jointly owned with the Gem Plus group in France. News Gem had quality problems – up to 12 per cent of cards supplied to Sky's customers didn't work. Clinger convinced BSkyB to close News Gem, and have the cards assembled by Bharat Kumar Marya in California. With Clinger's help, BK Marya became the sole supplier of smart cards for BSkyB, through a Jersey company called Phoenix Micro Inc. In return, Clinger took half the profits BK made – though the trail of the money was soon lost in the archipelago of tax havens. At BK's request, the pair began using false names in correspondence. Clinger was Jack Higgins. News remained unaware of Clinger's secret arrangements with BK, but in what followed, it wasn't always clear who was stitching up whom.

The larger question is, when did News Corporation's senior management realise that one of the group's most sensitive subsidiaries was being run by a criminal? When asked in June 1996, a senior News executive initially said that senior News management remained unaware that Clinger was wanted in the US until mid-1992, after he had cut all links with NDSP. Several months later, the date of the discovery was amended to late 1991. What wasn't clear was *which* News executives knew about Clinger. Given News Corp's centralised management style, it seems strange that Rupert Murdoch was not told, though when the affair hit the British courts Murdoch strangely appeared to play no part in the saga. News execs – including presumably Rupert Murdoch – claimed they learned of Clinger's arrest warrant around the time they finalised an agreement to buy the Israelis out of NDSP.

By August 1991, Clinger had become too much trouble for News. Stehrenberger wrote to News Corp's chief operating officer, Gus Fischer, about the need to buy out the 'non-performing and disruptive partner' in NDSP. In the end it would be just a question of price. How much would it cost to get this man out of their hair? News wasn't feeling generous. In May, as part of an unrelated tax restructure of the group, the Hong Kong office of accountants Arthur Andersen had valued News Corp's 60 per cent stake in NDSP between $29 million and $33 million. On that basis, the combined 40 per cent owned by all the Israelis was worth between $19 and $22 million. On 27 September, Siskind met Clinger and offered to buy all the Israeli partners out of NDSP for $6 million, plus some further payments out of future earnings. Clinger turned the offer down. Apparently News learned about Clinger's criminal status some time in the next six weeks, because on 6 November when News lifted its offer to $12 million in staggered payments, it came with a demand that Clinger leave the NDSP offices immediately. Professor Shamir and the Weizmann Institute agreed to the terms. On 8 November, exactly twelve months after the grand jury indictment, Clinger cleared out his desk at the News Datacom offices in Jerusalem and didn't return.

What does a major American broadcasting group do when it discovers it is in a business deal with a US fugitive? In News Corporation's case, the answer apparently was to try to cut a better deal. News management set about screwing back the sale price they had just negotiated. Arthur

Andersen had another look at the NDSP accounts and decided that, while in May 1991 they had valued 60 per cent of NDSP between $28 million and $33 million, on the basis of new information supplied by News executives the accounts now showed that NDSP was losing money on every card it made for BSkyB, its debt was more than its assets, and it was technically insolvent. It was actually worth nothing. News shared this with the Israeli shareholders, and suggested that the $12 million offer it had made was too generous. At a meeting in New York on 21 January (a choice of location which ensured Clinger did not appear but was represented by his lawyer), Fischer told the Israelis that News was cutting the agreed purchase price to $10 million. Clinger's share through his IDG holding company would be $5 million. Clinger hummed and hawed, then on 17 March he told News that the whole deal was off.

The News executives were furious. The other shareholders had accepted the offer, but the whole object of the exercise was to get rid of Michael Clinger. Now, after months of work, it had all come to nothing. A frenzied series of telephone calls, letters and face-to-face meetings followed, between Clinger and half a dozen senior News International executives. News Corporation now found itself in a peculiar situation. News Corp was run and controlled by an American citizen. It regarded itself as an American-owned company and a good corporate citizen. While it had no power to arrest Clinger, its civic duty lay in alerting US authorities to Clinger's location. It wasn't just that senior executives in the News group and their lawyers were meeting with a fugitive or criminal. They were proposing to provide the fugitive with active support, to the extent of paying him $5 million in cash for his shares in NDSP. Actually their challenge was to *persuade* him to accept their $5 million.

The two sides gave different accounts of what was said during the negotiations. Clinger claimed News representatives told him his shares in NDSP were worth very little, that if he didn't sell out BSkyB would dump the technology; alternatively, News would call in its loans and put NDSP in liquidation. The six News executives and lawyers named by Clinger denied making any such threats. Justice Lindsay found that News had no obligation to inform Clinger that two reports by News International development manager Paul Vatistas had concluded that the £3 that BSkyB was paying for smart cards was 'unrealistically low' because the technology was crucial to BSkyB, and the price made no allowance for Israeli research costs. Justice Lindsay accepted the News International view that Vatistas was too young and inexperienced to understand technology.

By 8 May, Clinger had agreed on new sale terms. The sale price stayed at £10 million for the 40 per cent of NDSP, but News would sling Clinger $560,000 in consultancy fees that Professor Shamir and the Weizmann Institute would not see, and further payments based on smart card sales. Clinger signed a sale contract on 14 May with final settlement due for 1 July. The same day, NDSP started negotiations with BSkyB about changing the price for smart cards. Two events had changed the outlook for News Datacom's smart cards. On 9 March BSkyB had broken even for the first time, and was now making profits. So it could afford to pay more. Secondly, on 18 May at the Lancaster Hotel in London, BSkyB had won the television rights for the Premier League. Within weeks, BSkyB had signed up a million people for its Premier League package. They all needed smart cards.

When Clinger, Professor Shamir and the Weizmann Institute settled the sale of their NDSP shares on 1 July, they didn't know that two days before, BSkyB had provisionally approved an increase in the price it paid for smart cards. The price would go from £3 to £4.50 plus a monthly 'maintenance' fee of 45 pence. The price had more than trebled. It amounted to £9.90 in just the first year of the card's life. BSkyB would order more than six million cards each year for the next three years, and pay more than £180 million. Admittedly BSkyB would no longer make minimum purchase commitments to take cards it might not use, but even so, the former BSB partners now in BSkyB were unhappy when told of the deal in July 1992. Justice Lindsay later noted that Steven Brown, the News International finance controller who had also become finance director of NDSP, 'spent some time convincing the BSkyB shareholders who were not in the News group that the price was justifiable'.

The buyout of the Israelis' shares had valued the entire NDSP business at $25 million. Seven days later News sold the business into a new offshore British company called News Datacom Limited, for $43.2 million. Given the resale price, the new sale contracts and the huge price rise for cards, it can be argued that Professor Shamir, the Weizmann Institute and Clinger received less than their shares were worth. Four years later News would be planning to float News Datacom for $750 million. Four years after that the market value of the company's shares would touch $5 billion. It looks like News stitched the Israelis up – though the British High Court would later dismiss any claim of legal impropriety. But the game wasn't over. The object of the whole exercise had been to get rid of Michael Clinger. As the News lawyers completed the formalities of the sale on 1 July, they believed that at last News was rid of this annoying irritant. Michael Clinger would prove a lot harder to shake.

CHAPTER SIX

THE PRETENDERS

Los Angeles, June 1991

In early 1991 the mood among the scores of News Corporation executives flying in to Los Angeles for budget talks was relieved but apprehensive. The relief reflected News Corp's continued existence after the debt crisis. The apprehension amongst division heads was about the big promises they would need to make about what they could deliver in the next year.

Among the News Corp crowd was a stocky 30-year-old called Matt Handbury. Handbury had spent a decade in a string of News Corp posts around the world, culminating in his latest position running Murdoch Magazines, a small unit which published homemaker and women's magazines in Sydney. But after years of hard work he had not been able to shake his nickname as the Man from Uncle. Matt Handbury was Rupert Murdoch's nephew, son of his older sister, Helen.

'I think he has always been a bit suspicious of family members working in the company,' Handbury said later, though over the years Murdoch has had many family members on the payroll.

'I'm a great believer in nepotism,' Murdoch told Bruce Hundertmark in the late 1980s.

Handbury was in Los Angeles to tell Murdoch he wanted out of News. As an exit, he wanted to make a bid for Murdoch Magazines. When he met his uncle he said all this and Murdoch was regretful. He took his time. Eventually Murdoch said, 'Fine.' He paused again, then said, 'You know you could – you could run this. You could head the company up one day if you stuck around.'

For a frozen moment the two looked at each other. In the previous four months Murdoch's face had collapsed. There had been a physical cost to surviving the debt crisis, and Murdoch had paid it. Handbury was the eldest child of the eldest child. At that point, of the Murdoch clan he was the only senior News executive, the only family member who could develop a credible business record by the time Murdoch stepped down. Two years later when he described that moment, Handbury still would not be able to keep the regret from his voice. 'He did say you could run this,' he recalled.

The two men looked at each other, uncle and nephew, and for a moment both knew that this was the truth, that Handbury could indeed one day run the greatest show on earth. He could be the one. He could be king. But they both knew that Murdoch did not really mean it. Handbury would always hit a family ceiling. The succession issue would be decided by stricter blood lines. The reins of the fiery chariot would be passed to another pair of hands. Murdoch's successor was still at school.

'But if you want to do your own thing, I respect that,' Murdoch continued. The moment passed. Neither ever said it. But the knowledge lay between them.

You owe me.

On 21 January 1948 Sir Keith Murdoch signed his last will and testament. He was still in hospital when he dictated the new will, having been operated on to remove a secondary cancer in his bowel. As a historical document, the will doesn't shed much light on the family finances, because of the subsequent codicils and settlement agreements Sir Keith added. It is, however, a guide to the shape of the succession that he had in mind. The trustees would be his wife, Dame Elisabeth; Harry Giddy, head of the National Bank, who succeeded Sir Keith as chairman of the Herald and Weekly Times; and his son Rupert.

Under the provisions of the will the inheritance of his three daughters was to remain locked up in the trust into the next generation, providing income for them and for their children. While that was Sir Keith's broad intention, however, once a daughter turned 21 the trustees could at any point decide to pay out her share of the estate. The trustees also had a wide brief about where the funds in the estate should go. Sir Keith had already given his eldest daughter Helen £10,000 to buy a house when she married Geoff Handbury. In practice this meant that for many years Helen was the only daughter who ended up with any money from her father. Many years later, that would mean her sisters' final payout would be hundreds of millions of dollars higher.

The broad principle was that a major part of the estate's income would go to Dame Elisabeth, the children would receive something like equal shares, but Rupert would have more voting shares to enable him to have 'the great opportunity of spending a useful altruistic and full life in broadcasting activities . . .' In the two years that followed, Sir Keith reorganised his corporate holdings around a new family company called Wyamba, which was later renamed Cruden Investments. Cruden's A shares had ten votes, while its B shares had only one.

In late 1950, the three Murdoch daughters were summoned to Harry Giddy's office at the National Bank. Sir Keith had drawn £50,000 in cash from his account, and in Giddy's office he duly presented gifts of £10,000 to Helen and Ann, £10,000 which was put aside for Rupert in Oxford, and £20,000 to Janet. This was to make up for Helen's earlier wedding gift. The children then gravely passed the money back to their father, who issued them shares in Cruden in exchange, and the money went back to the bank to pay down some of Cruden's huge debts. There were several settlements like this, which by passing assets over early allowed Sir Keith to reduce some of the death duties his estate would face.

When Sir Keith died in October 1952, his eldest child, Helen, was 23. Rupert was 21; Ann was 17 and about to sit for her final school exams; Janet was just 13 years old. Cruden Farm went to Dame Elisabeth. The rest of the estate consisted chiefly of a house in Melbourne, an art collection, two cattle properties and shares in Cruden Investments. Almost everything was sold to repay bank debt and to meet death duties. Rupert had been left with 28 per cent of Cruden's shares, to be held in a separate trust. They were all A shares, which gave him 36 per cent of Cruden's voting rights. Eventually this trust was held in a company named after Rupert's initials, Kayarem. Secondly there were the various settlement trusts that Sir Keith had made before he died, which accounted for 35 per cent of Cruden's capital, and 34 per cent of its voting rights. It appeared that Dame Elisabeth was entitled to receive the bulk of the income from the settlement trusts. Thirdly there was the rest of Sir Keith's estate, held for Helen, Ann and Janet, who also held a small number of shares in their own right.

Rupert did not initially control the News Limited board, nor did he control the Cruden board, nor the trusts which controlled Cruden. Control lay with his mother. The board of Cruden after Sir Keith's death comprised Rupert, Dame Elisabeth, Harry Giddy, and the general manager William Jones. With Giddy counselling caution, and Rupert ever ready to sound the charge, Dame Elisabeth's vote was decisive. Helen said later: 'In those early days after Dad died we would have family conferences around the schoolroom table. There wouldn't be any disagreements with Mum sitting there with her beady eyes . . . We really were the staunchest of families.'

Giddy resigned from Cruden in the late 1950s. To raise capital for News Limited's headlong expansion, Murdoch made a placement of stock in 1966, which diluted Cruden's holding. In 1970 Cruden distributed a small portion of its News Limited shares to family members as a dividend. The total inheritance was now worth $A18 million. Eighteen years after Sir Keith's death, this was the first substantial payout that Rupert's sisters had received. It also paved the way for Rupert's first takeover move on Cruden.

Cruden had borrowed £A1.2 million in the 1960s to buy more News shares, but by the early 1970s its stake in News had fallen to less than 35 per cent. To cement their control of News, the Murdochs needed to buy more shares. Rupert was the only family member who could raise the money needed. Cruden borrowed $A6 million from Commonwealth Bank from 1977 to 1978, and used the money to buy News shares to build its holding up to 43.4 per cent. This coincided with an issue of partly paid shares to Rupert's personal company Kayarem, with a total cost of $A5 million. Each year Kayarem would pay off small instalments on the shares. In effect these payments serviced the interest on Cruden's bank debt.

The new shares lifted Murdoch's Cruden stake to 41 per cent. This was a pretty good deal for Murdoch. For $5 million he had assured himself of future control of Cruden – and he had the best part of a decade to pay up. He was also entitled to some of the shares held in the settlement trusts that his father had set up. It's not clear whether Rupert had always been entitled to these shares or had bought out some of his sisters' entitlements. But added together with the new partly paid shares Cruden had just issued, Murdoch now held 54 per cent of Cruden's capital and its voting stock. However, that didn't mean he actually controlled Cruden. In practice that was still his mother's preserve. This was a matter of some importance, because Cruden was about to start earning a lot of money.

Throughout the 1970s, the $7 million in dividends Cruden received was largely swallowed up by the company's financing needs and its share buying. Even after News Limited was reorganised into News Corporation in 1979, the dividend stream continued to be meagre. However, as Cruden, in line with its shareholding, picked up 44 per cent of the total dividends paid, the payout did not have to be high to make a major difference to Cruden. By 1980 Cruden was earning $A3 million a year in News dividends. In 1985 that went up to $A5.2 million, then $A8.1 million in 1987. From 1980 to 1990, the dividend payments to Cruden totalled

$A61.5 million. One of the puzzling mysteries of the Murdoch dynasty was where that money went.

Most people who come into major money engage accountants, they get a company structure, they start to make investments. They buy new houses or country properties. Murdoch's three sisters showed little sign of this. They lived comfortably but not ostentatiously. There was little in their lifestyles to suggest that they owned what amounted to a fifth of one of the largest media companies in the world, which had reported profits during the 1980s of more than $3 billion.

Dame Elisabeth has a clear view that wealth does not necessarily make for happier lives. She has always been closely involved with the Royal Children's Hospital in Melbourne, but this is just one of the many causes she supports.

'She has always been a great supporter of charities,' one of her nephews said. 'That's where the money went.'

'It drives Rupert crazy,' said a friend of the family.

For whatever reason, little money appears to have flowed from Cruden to the sisters for much of the 1980s. What money there was went in tax, in buying more News Corp shares, to philanthropy, or remained in Cruden. In January 1987, however, the picture changed. In 1987, Cruden's share capital was just 2.9 million $2 shares. As part of the Queensland Press takeover, Cruden made a bonus issue of 1 billion new $2 shares. The shareholdings remained the same, but now the extended family was in no doubt that although they might not be getting any substantial income from it, they were sitting on a $A2 billion fortune. The family had lived with this regime all their lives. But all of Dame Elisabeth's children now had children of their own, many of whom were adults, who did not always see things in the same happy light. Rupert himself had grown restless with his sisters' shareholdings. 'I can't go on making money for all of you forever,' he told his mother. 'I have to think of my children.' The unstable situation that the Cruden share restructure had created would last just three years. While Sir Keith's will had envisaged the family holdings in media being carried into the next generation, it was clear that henceforth the dynasty would continue on more restrictive lines.

On a golden summer afternoon in the Hudson Valley in upstate New York in the late 1970s, Anna Murdoch sat in the garden of the Murdochs' farmhouse in Old Chatham watching the erratic paths of the bees and the yellow-jackets, and mused on the frustrations of sex and motherhood. 'We are reading,' she wrote, my son sitting snug between my thighs, smooth bulwark against any stings, while splashy sounds of other siblings reach us now and then above the hums. Niobe-like, languid and proud, I hold him at the end of summer . . . now squirming to be off; white soles flashing as he races through the meadow to join the others, crushing wild strawberries and clover with his heels. My own Achilles.

Anna had begun part-time studies at Fordham and later at New York University, majoring in Greek mythology. Her studies were the basis for an article that she wrote late one summer entitled 'Motherhood and Mythology: Summer Thoughts on Sex and Creativity' exploring role models for mothers in Greek myths. The outcome of her musings that afternoon would surface over the following decade, in the three novels she would write. Each of the novels deals with a business dynasty, and appears to be shaped by her own experiences and family. But it is in the garden at Old Chatham that she writes most directly about herself and her children. The most recurring theme in her reverie is that in the midst of plenty she is frustrated and unhappy. At that time she feared that any prospect of the writing career she had once dreamed of was over.

By mid-1977 Murdoch had bought the *New York Post* and was filling it with sensational stories of the Son of Sam serial killer, David Berkowitz, of looting and rioting during a power blackout, and endless politics. At the end of 1976 Murdoch's move to take over *New York* magazine had provoked bitter opposition from *New York*'s founder Clay Felker, who with his wife Gail Sheehy had been one of Anna and Rupert's first friends in America. Prudence, who loved London, had chosen to finish her education at an English boarding school. Anna and Prudence have always been polite to each other, without being intimate.

At the time Anna wrote her Greek mythology article, Elisabeth was ten years old, Lachlan six, James five. In the exploration of her relationship to her children in the article, Rupert was entirely absent. She wrote that she had thrown away her productive years for her children and had no time for serious work. Anna described the rich scene before her in terms of emptiness. The raspberry canes were dry, stick-looking: 'We have eaten all the goodness from them.' The leaves were yellow, 'the chlorophyll sucked out by the heat of the August days'. Anna framed her musing around a succession of female figures whom she posed as role models for motherhood. At one point Anna played with the argument that the *uterini*, children of the one mother, sharing the same uterus, are closer than those who share the same father.

Anna's gaze turned to the despair she felt about wanting to write. She quoted Tillie Olsen's book *Silences*, which claimed that no mothers – as almost no part-time, part-self persons – had created enduring literature. Anna wrote: 'Part-person. Parturition. By being whole, have I become less? Has all the creativity I once felt in my pen been confined to that creativity between my legs? A sick joke is woman.'

Anna rejected feminism ('I am afraid. I am afraid of modern-day Athenas. They are seducing us with their torches and their songs,') and asserted that creativity and motherhood were not exclusive: 'God, I wish I could convince myself, lay waste this cold question which won't leave me alone. Have I given up my best work for them? Is that all there is?'

Philip Townsend, who worked as a butler in the Murdochs' London apartment in the late 1980s, painted a chaotic picture of the Murdoch household. In *Just Rupert*, an unpublished account he co-wrote of his Murdoch years, he recounted pouring orange juice into guests' coffee, Murdoch apologising to guests for the menu, and an American chef who was an ex-marine flown to London to cook for an important meal, before flying on to cook on the Murdochs' yacht. When the dog that the Townsends secretly kept in the apartment died while the Murdochs were in residence, in order to escape detection Townsend hid the dog in the large kitchen freezer. What Townsend particularly didn't like about Anna Murdoch was that she asked him and his wife to wear uniforms. Townsend's account was all the more colourful for the fact that shortly after *Punch* published extracts of the manuscript, Townsend went to prison for illegal business practices after he started a company selling vegetables.

It made for a dizzy lifestyle. As a very young child in England Elisabeth recalled being overjoyed to receive a Shetland pony, only to discover that it was to be the prize for the winning reader in a promotion for the *Sun*. A friend of the children who stayed overnight with the Murdochs recalled that Anna woke them at 5 a.m. to dress the children to meet their father, who was returning home from a trip. It was Anna (as she recounted the story to *Time*) who often had to reassure a young James that there was nothing wrong with his father's hearing, he just wasn't listening. James himself, she told *GQ* in 1999, was frustrated that as youngest he was always served last at the dinner table, and continually sought to rearrange the table seating to change the serving order. A former executive recalled James, apparently for similar reasons, hatching complex schemes to persuade his father to let him switch bedrooms.

In the peripatetic global lifestyle that Rupert Murdoch pursued for half a century, Anna Murdoch provided the centre of gravity for the family. Her upbringing had given her a strong sense of the importance of form. With adults this could give an impression of aloofness or class consciousness – an insistence that she and Rupert be treated with a gravity appropriate to their station. In this respect she was quite different from her husband. However, given the degree of uncertainty that attached to much of their lives, an ability to impose structure on domestic life was a saving grace for her children.

Despite a life based almost entirely around their father's travel schedule and telephone calls, the Murdoch children have always been remarkably close to Rupert. 'He is a very good and moral human being, and we are bringing up our children that way,' Anna told the *Washington Post*. 'We know what we are about and time is on our side.'

By the mid-1980s, strains had emerged in the Murdoch family. Elisabeth was expelled from her expensive Connecticut boarding school, reportedly for smuggling in a bottle of rum. One of Murdoch's early biographers, Thomas Kiernan, wrote that Lachlan and James were starting to display behaviour problems of their own, which Rupert blamed on the intense negative publicity that he had been receiving. Anna, said Rupert, 'had buried herself in this novel she's just finished to prove that at least one Murdoch can publish something worthwhile'. Anna pulled her children out of their New York schools and spent a year living in Aspen, where they attended the Aspen Day School.

In the early 1980s Murdoch gained control of the trusts set up by his father in Kayarem. He set up a new structure called the A E Harris Trust (named after Australian businessman Ted Harris, who suggested he and Murdoch swap names for their family trusts, in the interests of anonymity). The trustees of the A E Harris Trust, which would hold almost all of Murdoch's fortune, would be accountants and lawyers. Murdoch's control lay in his power to appoint or sack the trustees. This meant that when it suited him he could say he controlled the trust (as, for example, when he spoke to the Federal Communications Commission in Washington), while at other times he could say he was not the owner of the assets in the trust. This would be useful when dealing with government regulators. It was also a structure that would fortuitously turn out to be rather handy in a divorce.

In mid-1990, Murdoch's lawyers came up with a plan to buy his sisters and their children out of Cruden Investments. The price was worked out on the basis that the News Corp stock that Cruden owned was worth $A20 a share, which would value the sisters' holding around $A1 billion.

Unfortunately, the buyout plan was overtaken by the debt crisis at the end of the year. The debt crisis was as much a surprise to Murdoch's family as it was to him. After subordinating their interest in News for 38 years, suddenly it seemed as if it could all be taken from them.

On 15 January 1991 the News Corp share price touched $A3.19. At this price, Cruden's subsidiary Queensland Press was barely solvent. It appears that Cruden had guaranteed the bank debt in Queensland Press, which was controlled through another subsidiary, Cruden (ACT) Pty Ltd. On 23 January Dame Elisabeth and all three of her daughters were appointed directors of Cruden (ACT). It gave them control of the board, as the family became aware of how perilous their situation was.

'You'd be wrong to say there was concern about people being left with nothing,' said one family member. 'There was always absolute confidence in Rupert.' The move on to the Cruden (ACT) board was not because the sisters said 'we'd better get control of this', the family member said: 'It just didn't happen like that.'

What was going on? In the middle of these dark days the Murdochs held a family council. It was then that Rupert Murdoch put up a business proposition. Struggling desperately with the biggest crisis of his life, the Great Acquirer still found time to set up another deal. According to sources close to the family, Murdoch proposed buying options on his sisters' shares in Cruden. The sources say that the deal Murdoch proposed valued the News shares between $A7 and $A12, considerably higher than the share price at the time, and it would ensure the family emerged with something if News fell over. But it was a long way below the family's original expectations.

While News Corporation was an empire built entirely on Rupert Murdoch's efforts with no input from his sisters, he has always run the empire on the basis that it is the shareholders, the people who own the capital in a company, who are entitled to its rewards, rather than the gifted employees. A year later, Barry Diller would leave News for that very reason. Almost half the capital that Rupert Murdoch had used to create the empire was his sisters'. There are several versions of the discussion that followed after Rupert tabled his buyout offer. Some family friends suggest that parts of the family were unhappy about the price. Others disagree. 'No one was banging on the table,' asserted one family member soon afterwards. 'The sisters have always been slavishly supportive of Rupert.'

At least some family members took up the deal. The 1990 Cruden annual report had shown Helen Handbury's children holding a small number of Cruden shares in their own right. By 30 June 1991, they were no longer the beneficial owners of the shares. When Matt Handbury flew to Los Angeles to tell his uncle he wanted to get out of News Corp with Murdoch Magazines, he was really telling him how he wanted to spend the buyout payment. 'There's been a bit of money that's going around,' Handbury said at the time.

In the summer of 1992, Rupert and Anna and his three sisters and their husbands went on a luxury ocean cruise to Alaska. During the trip the family finally worked out a deal that would leave Rupert's family as the sole owners of Cruden. In addition to the sisters' payouts, Murdoch's nephews and nieces would end up with $A20 million apiece. Murdoch said privately, 'Some will piss it against the wall and some will turn it into $200 million.' The total buyout price was about $A650 million, but it included an escalation clause linked to the News Corporation share price. And finally the empire was all Rupert's . . . at least in name. Once Rupert Murdoch had convinced his family to sign on the dotted line, he was left with the same problem his father had faced more than 40 years before. He had secured his children's inheritance. Now how was he going to pay for it?

PART TWO

AMERICAN JIHAD

CHAPTER SEVEN

HERB ALLEN'S PORCH

Sun Valley, Idaho, 11 July 1996

Among the crop of wild rumours and far-fetched tales that swirled around Rupert Murdoch in the American summer of 1996, the wildest and most far-fetched was the story going round the traps that Murdoch did not really exist. He had died years ago, the yarn went, some time during the 1990 debt crisis. Since then the chief executive's role at News Corporation had been played by half a dozen Murdoch look-alikes. This was the reason for the contradictory strategy moves coming out of News Corporation in the previous 12 months. Indeed watching Murdoch during this time was like watching a contortionist under a strobe light. The strobe throws up a series of disconnected and wildly improbable positions. Flash. Flash. Flash. Which was the real Murdoch?

The answer, on a mild July evening in the mountains of Idaho, was taking the air on the porch, talking quietly and watching the richest man in New York, Ron Perelman, the 53-year-old proprietor of Marvel Comics, Revlon and the New World Entertainment television chain, chomp his way through his cigar. Clearly the figure next to Perelman was the real Rupert Murdoch, because he was talking about spending $2.5 billion.

Murdoch in the summer of 1996 was once again a shining orb in the firmament of the rich and powerful. He had now been a major force in Britain for a quarter of a century. His debt crisis was now five years away. In those five years Murdoch had recreated himself as a corporate entity and American persona. *Time* magazine now rated him as the fourth most powerful person in the United States, just behind the President, the head of the Federal Reserve Bank, and Bill Gates at Microsoft. *Vanity Fair* had

Gates and Murdoch taking turns each year for the top spot in what it called the New Establishment in America, heads of the new power elite and the most powerful private citizens in the world.

Murdoch was long free of the irksome restrictions that his bankers had imposed upon him in the 1991 debt override agreement. Within 28 months he had replaced it all with long-term debt and a little judicious capital raising. Fox was now established as the fourth US television network – and Murdoch had the *New York Post* back again. In Britain his aggressive price cutting had given a costly boost to circulation figures for *The Times* and the *Sun*. BSkyB had been transformed from a ruinous loss-maker into a runaway success. Murdoch was working on clones of BSkyB around the world. One of them, Star TV in Hong Kong, had a satellite footprint that stretched halfway around the globe, from the eastern Mediterranean across India and all of Asia. In Australia the government-owned telephone giant Telstra was paying for a $3 billion fibre-optic cable rollout for Foxtel, a joint-venture cable service with Murdoch. Murdoch had stakes in satellite operations in Mexico and Brazil, he was working on Europe, and three weeks before he'd announced a satellite operation for Japan with Softbank Corporation called JSkyB. In the US, News Corp and telephone company MCI had spent $682.5 million in January 1996 on a satellite broadcast licence. Or rather, MCI spent $682.5 million and News Corp came along for the ride.

For all this furious activity, Murdoch's US rivals seemed to be passing him by. In the second half of the 1990s, the future of mega-media in the US – and the rest of the world – was being shaped by a series of huge mergers. Recent moves by Walt Disney Company, Time Warner and Viacom had been worth $44 billion. Among the big four media companies, when it came to pulling out the pocketbook News Corporation had been positively frugal. Murdoch was about to fix that. In the next twelve months he would commit to deals totalling $10 billion, scattered across the American media landscape, as he bet the empire again. In 1997 these would spark the most brutal, wide-ranging series of turf wars in media history. In the process they would rewrite the future of media in America, and in the world. It began with this uneasy exchange with Ron Perelman at Herb Allen's annual media and business conference.

Each July Herb Allen summons the cream of America's business and media executives and their families to a ski resort near the tiny town of Ketchum, population 1,200, for a five-day mix of business presentations and resort leisure.

The head of investment bank Allen & Co, Allen was America's premier media investment adviser. His family was worth at least a billion dollars in 1996, thanks to the smart media deals he did in the 1970s. The event is aimed at mainstream business as well, but since kicking it off in 1983 Allen has made this annual conference the most significant business ritual for US media in the 1990s. It is a compulsory road station in the titanic struggles shaping the information superhighway. Not that anyone calls it a super-highway. 'The country creates a tidal wave, and some people get to ride it,' Allen told *Vanity Fair*, with appropriate old-money diffidence and the confidence that comes from making your money a decade before anyone else in the room.

'This is where smart people go to talk to each other, not the rest of the world,' said one veteran. Barry Diller, who started up the Fox network for Murdoch and at the 1996 conference was CEO of Silver King Communications and trying to start up another network, called Allen 'the gatherer of circus animals.'

'There are very few places where that many gigantic egos are so fungible,' said Diller. (Fungible is originally a legal term. Its use in media circles reflects how much time media executives spend talking to lawyers.)

'It's a bazaar,' Allen said in 1999. 'And you spell that both ways.'

Running down the guest list at the conference was like looking at the score card for the media industry for the 1990s, a rollcall of survivors in the corporate battles to control the country's content and distribution systems. The media business has always been a contact sport, but in the 1990s the underlying fear of the future had given the battles a ferocious edge. So far not many of the mega deals had worked very well. Whatever the result, everyone came to Sun Valley. The winners and the losers ended up at Herb Allen's retreat sitting together cheek by jowl.

Bill Gates, the founder of Microsoft, had been coming religiously for years, even in the dim distant past before he became a billionaire. John Malone was always there. Highly influential, Malone had remarkable reach. Through Tele-Communications Inc Malone controlled one in every four American cable boxes, and through Flextech more than half the cable boxes in Britain, while through Liberty Media, Malone had interests in 23 per cent of US cable programming. His cavalier attitude with the nation's elected representatives had made him the cable guy politicians loved to hate. In the days when they were still speaking, former presidential candidate Al Gore had described Malone as the Darth Vader of the cable industry. At Sun Valley Malone was spruced up to be user-friendly.

Barry Diller was there in 1996, frostily avoiding Sumner Redstone of Viacom. In late 1993 and early 1994 Diller and Redstone waged a bitter bidding war for Paramount studio, a war that Redstone finally won after lifting his bid close to $10 billion. In one of the strange outcomes that mark modern debt financing, Redstone raised the money in part by spending another $8.4 billion buying the Blockbuster video store group. Paying for Blockbuster with stock meant that Redstone could borrow more money to buy Paramount. In 1996 two things were apparent. First, it didn't look like the Paramount-Blockbuster deal had worked for Viacom; and at 73 Sumner Redstone was as obsessed as ever with outplaying Rupert Murdoch.

Michael Eisner of Walt Disney Company, still on a roll from the $19 billion deal he had stitched up the year before to buy CapCities/ABC, was a surprise absentee. Time Warner chief exec Gerald Levin was at Sun Valley. Either Levin was days away from losing his job, or he was about to pick up a whole new pack of dealing cards – it depended which way you read it. Levin took the helm of Time Warner almost by accident in 1992, after the death of Steve Ross, who was the architect of the 1989 deal to merge Time Inc and Warner Communication. The most notable move in Levin's career was still his groundbreaking decision back in 1975 as head of Home Box Office to use a satellite link to beam coverage of the Ali-Frazier boxing match in Manila down to cable operators across America. With his quiet east-coast manner Levin remained a fierce exponent of the future for interactive cable programming. In effect he had bet Time Warner's future on cable. But the trial of Time Warner's interactive technology in Orlando had recently flopped. Six years after the merger that formed it, Time Warner was still struggling under its huge debt, and business reporters were speculating on how long Levin had before he was dumped by his board. The ace that Levin still held was the deal he worked out with Ted Turner the previous year to merge Turner Broadcasting System into Time Warner. The deal was due to be finalised in September 1996. But then, in 1996 who wanted more cable assets?

The four principals in the new Dream Works SKG studio were at Sun Valley: legendary film-maker, Steven Spielberg; record industry leader, David Geffen; Jeffrey Katzenberg, who was the brilliant head of Disney's core animation business until he fell out with Michael Eisner in September 1994; and Paul Allen, the man who co-founded Microsoft with Gates in 1975. Another familiar face at Sun Valley was Edgar Bronfman Junior, the 41-year-old head of Seagrams who, a year after buying the MCA studio for $5.7 billion also held nearly 15 per cent of Time Warner and a seeming ability to prompt an anxiety attack for Gerry Levin almost at will.

Rupert Murdoch, himself a long-time regular, was back after a break in

1995. He couldn't make it that year because he was busy holding a News Corporation management conference on the other side of the world, at his Hamilton Island resort on Australia's Great Barrier Reef. The 1995 clash of timing with Sun Valley was a product of the schedules which dictated when Murdoch's chief guest, British Labour leader Tony Blair, could get there. The superb speech which Blair gave there was indicative that he believed he needed his friend Rupert as much as Rupert needed him. Murdoch's decision to get up close and personal with Blair would not pay off until two years later when the Labour leader came to power in Britain, heading a party which for almost two decades has demonised Murdoch's media grip on the UK. Blair would be promoted by Murdoch's trans-Atlantic adviser, Irwin Stelzer, as the first Labour leader since the 1970s who could say Murdoch's name without shuddering and making the sign of the cross.

The Sun Valley list went on and on, about 130 executives all up, plus wives and children. Some were there because of the superlative opportunities to network; some for a holiday with the children; some because they were afraid of offending Herb Allen. Everyone was represented: the film studios, the television networks, the cable companies, software companies, microchip manufacturers, the new Direct Broadcast Satellite operators, the agents, the content producers, the investors.

If debt funding had become less fashionable in the 1990s, no one at Sun Valley seemed to be aware of it. The legacy of the super deals that had forged Time Warner, Viacom and the big cable groups had been crippling debt payments. Ironically, among the major players Murdoch was the man with the least debt – and the man bankers still worried most about. So did his peers, for different reasons. As NBC president Bob Wright interjected in 1996 in a Sun Valley debate about the future of communication, 'That's not the question! The questions is, 'Where's Rupert?' '

Malone was the other danger man in this crowd. Together with Bill Gates and Ted Turner, he and Murdoch were the only real builders at the big table. The rest, like Michael Eisner at Disney, Gerry Levin at Time Warner and Sumner Redstone at Viacom, were basing their strategies for the future largely on fitting existing pieces of media together to form bigger blocks, on the synergies of multi-billion-dollar acquisitions. Creating new media assets is a much trickier business. The advance of Bill Gates and Microsoft in all directions had a certain inevitable and predictable quality that in the end looked likely to bury all of them. Ted Turner had the required maverick quality, but his ambitions had been held in check through the 1990s, first by his cable shareholders and then by his imminent merger with Time Warner. Only Murdoch and Malone had the capacity and the resources to think outside the square on a grand scale. Only they had the imagination and recklessness as well as the authority as principals to take the big gamble that could turn an industry around. If anyone could meet the challenge that Microsoft would pose to established media groups in the next decade, it was these two.

For years Murdoch and Malone had performed a delicate and accelerating dance around each other, composed in equal parts of rivalry and co-operation. Vertical integration was really just 'All about trying to catch Rupert,' Malone maintained stoutly.

'John's just saying that to take the attention away from himself,' Murdoch responded. 'I should think we are all responding to John Malone. Dancing to his tunes. I still do sometimes.'

Such was the power of the guest list. The 130 executives in attendance were the major players shaping the future of the world's media. At least that was what the hype around the conference claimed. The prize they were fighting over was the 200-million-plus single-language media market in the US. The pool they play in was so big that whoever won the US mega-media wars of the 1990s would create a juggernaut too big for anyone else in the world to handle. The battles were all about form and content, about distribution and programming, but no one knew just what the successful mix of these two would be. For Herb Allen, bringing these violent rivals together for a house party every year requires the skills of an illusionist, a piece of legerdemain. It is a question of form. The illusion is that these men are not robber barons squabbling, or Mafiosi on a coffee break from the endless turf wars. Rather, this is a fraternity, a gathering of colleagues, an enlightened get-together of the powerful, the far-sighted, and the worldly-wise. Just good ol' boys whoopin' it up.

Herbert Allen doesn't believe any of this himself. While he respects the power of these individuals, 'It's no different from people fighting over rail-roads,' he concedes engagingly. 'People hunting money and power have pretty much the same style.' The remark is an exquisite class marker, the delicate distinction between the zookeeper and the exhibits. This is not to deny the power of the Allen & Co magic. Unlike the in-your-face public style of the 1980s, the underscore here is mellow. It is cosy little meetings, good family fun. The entrepreneurial mood of the 1980s was signalled by Drexel Burnham Lambert's client conferences, the annual shindig for Michael Milken's junk bond clients that became known as the Predator's Ball. Much of the original cast was here, but heavy hitters didn't do that stuff any more. In the 1990s at Sun Valley Idaho it is more like Masters of the Universe Do Brunch. Media moguls at summer camp. Whatever way, it's show time.

The geography of power has been infinitely dispersed; the superhighway has a thousand different trunk routes. And these players are road warriors. Media brush wars flare at a hundred different spots across the continent, at thousands more sites around the world. The players fly in after the advance party, they do the deal, and they are gone. Thus the choice of location is the first of the many forms in Herb Allen's annual illusion. Allen & Co will go to enormous lengths to recreate the informalities and the comforts of home. The first requirement is that this is not happening at home, or at work, but at some in-between space. The confab takes place in Idaho, not Los Angeles or New York. So the pleasures on the mountain must be underlain with the whiff of aviation fuel. The virtual realities these players will create are, of necessity, high-octane dreams.

The transport is just part of the seamless web which Herb Allen spins for his famous week. There are hundreds of little details that are part of good form, from the bright red fleece-lined Allen & Co jackets for everybody, to the private security force to ensure privacy. And delicate questions of protocol. Who will join the private meals at the Allens' house, who will sit on the panels for the sessions, who gets not to sit next to Bill Gates?

The 1,200-odd population of Ketchum alternately ignore or disapprove of 'Herbie and the boys.' After a decade and a half of rubbing shoulders with billionaires in the street each summer, they remain hugely unimpressed. 'They come in all the time, they're just nice folks,' Fonda Peters, a clerk at Main Strip T's in Ketchum, told a journalist kindly in 1999. On reflection, she thought there was something that set them apart from her other customers: 'They're all short.'

This was a low blow. If the media industry agrees on one thing, it is that size does matter. Cutting down short poppies, lopping any upstarts, any threat of competition, is one of the things the American media business has become good at. As Michael Eisner once said of his former lieutenant at Disney, Jeffrey Katzenberg, 'I think I hate the little midget.' There is the story about Ted Turner (which he denies) that when he was unhappy with one of his employees who was on the short side he ordered one of his executives to 'stand him on the desk, look him in the eye and tell him he's fired'.

Annie Liebovitz, the photographer who first shot all the big names at Sun Valley in a 30,000-mile odyssey for *Vanity Fair* in 1994, has a different take on her subjects. She found they were control freaks. They were all *in charge*. 'I felt that (the common theme was) the negotiating factor,' she said later. 'There was a lot of negotiating. And there was also a great sense of control.' Rupert Murdoch agreed to take Liebovitz out with his wife Anna on his 158-foot yacht, *Morning Glory*, which he sailed himself. 'It's funny, he and his wife said that, if they lost everything else, they didn't care, as long as they could just have the boat. The boat was their life.' Murdoch married his third wife, Wendi Deng, on board *Morning Glory* in New York Harbour in June 1999. He sold the boat several months later.

On Wednesday afternoon families can go whitewater rafting down a six-mile course on the Salmon River. The organised social events are not compulsory. One impromptu side trip back in 1990 began with a little mishap over the basic ground rule of the river: the one about how when whitewater rafting, the important thing is to stay in the raft. Even Rupert Murdoch doesn't walk on water. Flailing wildly, the world's only real global media baron made it back above the surface of the Salmon River a hundred yards downstream. While slightly bedraggled, Murdoch apparently was none the worse for wear. Elsewhere at Sun Valley there is a golf course and tournament, there is fly-fishing, horseback riding, hiking, skeet shooting and a tennis clinic. Transport is by chartered buses. Allen & Co's bomb squad tries to be unobtrusive as it checks the undersides of the coaches.

Then there was play time. Friday night is the awards banquet at Herb Allen's big house, with Allen & Co managing director John Schneider master of ceremonies. The roasting he stages with oversize props is all good clean fun. Jeffrey Katzenberg had already set the mood earlier in the day. While speaking as a panellist in a discussion on the state of the entertainment business, he whipped out a Supersoaker water cannon and shot at all and sundry. This would be a light-hearted, spontaneous gesture, except for the care with which Katzenberg had arranged for his aides to conceal the water cannon in place beforehand. In this league, even humour cannot be left to chance. Back at the dinner, Schneider traditionally handed out boxing gloves to conference attendees who were at war with each other. In 1996 he used sandwich boards with pointed messages. Amid the many gags, agent Jeff Berg, head of International Creative Management, was presented with a two-foot vibrator – after Ovitz's move to Disney, Berg was subsequently dubbed 'the biggest prick in Hollywood'. It was all happening with these wild guys, and *Vanity Fair* was graciously allowed in to take photos and write colour on the new masters of the universe.

In this atmosphere of clubby bonhomie it wasn't surprising that in 1993 Jeffrey Katzenberg, then still head of Disney studios, smelt a deal in the air when he spotted Turner Entertainment president Scott Sassa playing tennis with the CEO of Castle Rock Entertainment, Alan Horn. And sure enough Ted Turner later bought Castle Rock (one of the only deals his cable company partners allowed him). And in 1994 while Michael Eisner at Disney was getting his first chest pains which would require emergency heart surgery days later, Paul Allen, the co-founder of Microsoft and a heavy metal fan, got talking to music mogul David Geffen about art. As the friendship prospered, Allen ended up putting $500 million into Dream Works.

And it is entirely appropriate that at the 1995 conference, while Time Warner's Gerald Levin indicated he was moving more towards becoming a content company (he wrapped up a deal to buy Turner Broadcasting five weeks later), Michael Eisner was walking up Wildflower Lane when he chanced upon investor Warren Buffet coming out of Herb Allen's house. It was 1.15 p.m. on Friday, 14 July. Eisner was still fired up after an impressive presentation on Disney's improving divisions. He had been looking for Tom Murphy, the CEO of CapCities/ABC, which he had been trying for years to buy, but was now on the way back to the airstrip to fly home to California ahead of Disneyland's 40th anniversary celebrations. Buffet was the largest shareholder in CapCities/ABC and was about to meet Murphy and Bill Gates for a round of golf. Such was the magic of the moment that in a few minutes' conversation it was apparent that finally both Eisner and Murphy were prepared to be flexible over what they wanted. The merger was announced two weeks later on 31 July. At $19 billion it was the second largest merger in US corporate history, making Disney/ABC a $50 billion colossus.

The question at Sun Valley was what to make of this little summer interlude, this engaging piece of virtual reality that Herb Allen had created in a lonely place in the middle of America. Did it mean anything at all, or was its significance merely as a media construct created by Herb Allen and Graydon Carter, the editor-in-chief of *Vanity Fair*. In 1994, Carter in his efforts to forge a role for *Vanity Fair* as a 'magazine of the world stage' had advanced the line that the leaders of the American media industry were as he put it 'the pioneers that have made America sort of the first superpower of the Information Age.' Their economic and political muscle made this group America's new power elite, the new establishment. Sun Valley was the fraternity clubhouse for this new order, as Carter had portrayed it each year since then. Such was the impact of the *Vanity Fair* coverage that by the end of the 1990s journalists from all over the world were staking out the conference each July, with television anchors making live crosses to Sun Valley several times a day for updates on what was happening. By then Sun

Valley as a media event had become something quite different, perhaps barely recognisable, to the perceptions and memories of those who actually took part.

Time would show that the new establishment at Sun Valley in 1996 had barely a clue about the wave of change that was about to hit them. The bubbling explosion of the dot-com revolution would surprise them more than anyone. The new establishment at Sun Valley was actually old media. Even Bill Gates got it wrong. In the mid-1990s Gates was still committed to developing the Microsoft Network for on-line users, rather than building a browser for this strange new thing called the Internet. In 1996 Herb Allen, the world's premier media adviser had not yet touched a computer. In 1999 he confessed:

> Andy Grove (head of Intel) sat me down in front of a computer for the first time two years ago. He showed me how to turn it on, what to do. It was like seeing electricity for the first time.

Allen went on at some length to stress that he immediately saw all the possibilities of computers and he was now completely on top of the new media.

While the leaders of the new establishment at Sun Valley may not have known where they were going, their power was such that this didn't matter. They controlled the biggest media organisations in history, and when eventually they realised that they had been left behind by new media they would play a mean game of catch-up. Bill Gates could get it wrong about the Internet and yet still win the race to produce the world's dominant Internet browser, though not without some cost to Microsoft. Cable operators could misjudge their markets, promise hundreds of channels that never arrived, squander money on interactive experiments, yet still end the decade with unrivalled reach and power.

The wave of mega media mergers was unleashing huge new forces on the world's information economy. In films, in books, in television, in cable, in sport, in newspapers, magazines and radio, the struggle between the media giants was polarising the entire playing field. No area was too small, no undertaking too minor to escape this competition for influence. There was no single battle for supremacy, no final resolution. In the post-modern world there were only endless turf wars. All of these skirmishes had to be fought. But the strategic picture was often hard to see for those left standing earthbound.

All this was still to come. In 1996, the vision thing was looking a little dim. Michael Ovitz, the new Disney president under Eisner, came to Sun Valley in the hope of sitting down with Katzenberg, Disney's former studio chief. Ovitz wanted to try to work out Katzenberg's differences with Eisner and his huge lawsuit. But somehow the meeting never happened. Instead, the action was on Thursday evening, 11 July, on Herb Allen's porch. Barry Diller later claimed to have brokered the encounter, telling Perelman to buttonhole Murdoch, while advising his former boss on how to handle Perelman. So after dinner and over cigars Rupert Murdoch and Ron Perelman talked. Murdoch had known this moment was coming for more than two years – ever since May 1994 when he paid $500 million for a 20 per cent stake of Perelman's New World Communications group. He had just hoped Perelman would wait a little longer before cashing out.

Ronald Perelman is not Rupert Murdoch's kind of guy. About the only points they have in common are large amounts of money and Michael Milken. Perelman was a long-time Milken client in the 1980s who at one point had a Drexel Burnham Lambert consultant working out of his New York townhouse. Milken's advice and more importantly his money-raising machine had made Perelman the richest man in New York – and perhaps in the entire country. Unlike many of the 1980s entrepreneurs Perelman had proven highly skilled at turning around companies like Revlon and Pantry Pride. In the mid-1990s Perelman's fortune was estimated at $4.2 billion. His corporate style was aggressive. At a personal level a court-appointed psychiatrist would later note that Perelman had been in therapy since 1991 to handle anger. His love for the high life, his fondness for actresses, and the failure of journalists in a decade and a half to detect any evidence of a sense of humour within the Ronald, as he was called, had made him a gossip writer's dream. Perelman's spectacularly acrimonious divorce and support battles through 1996 to 1998 with his third wife, former Democratic fund-raiser Patricia Duff (chronicled gleefully by Murdoch's *New York Post*), and his readiness at one point to hire President Clinton's favourite pizza delivery girl Monica Lewinsky at Revlon, would add lustre to the legend.

In 1996, despite his enormous wealth, life was not going swimmingly for Perelman. In addition to his marital problems, corporate raider Carl Icahn had made a cheeky raid to try to wrest control of Marvel Comics from him. Also, he needed money for casino investments in Las Vegas and Atlantic City. Perelman had known Murdoch only as another rider on the Michael Milken money merry-go-round. In 1984 and 1985 Murdoch had attended the Predator's Ball. It made an unlikely scene, the Australian who hated parties, mingling in the crowd of nouveau super riche. In 1994, while still performing 40 hours a week of community work as a condition of his parole, after a prison sentence for violating US securities laws, Mike Milken had had another big idea for media. Perelman had used a public company he controlled called New World Communications to buy up a string of television stations. New World had 12 stations, ten of which were CBS affiliates. Milken convinced Perelman he could make a lot of money by flipping his television stations' network affiliations. Then Milken reintroduced Perelman to Murdoch.

At the beginning of 1994, Murdoch's Fox Broadcasting Company (FBC) had broken the CBS stranglehold on Sunday afternoon football by offering an outrageous sum for the right to broadcast National Football League games on eighteen Sundays a year. CBS had balked when Murdoch bid $1.58 billion for the four-year contract – CBS was already losing heavily on the existing contract. The deal with Perelman in May 1994 was a bombshell for the big three networks. News invested $500 million for a 20 per cent refundable stake in New World. In return, Perelman flipped his 12 stations to become Fox affiliates. When New World Communications CEO Bill Bevins called Tony Malara, the CBS president for affiliate affairs, to tell him New World was switching affiliations to Fox, a scandalised Malara asked: 'Which market?' It took a little while to sink in that New World was flipping stations in all of its markets.

The big three networks, faced with a flood of defections to Fox by their affiliates who wanted the Fox NFL games, found only one way to retain their reluctant troops: to throw money at them. 'Rupert is driving the other networks crazy,' Ted Turner reported later that year. NBC had been screwing back the payments that the network made to affiliates from $200 million a year to $100 million in recent years. 'Now it's back up to $200 million – and that comes right off the top,' said Turner. 'And he's done the same thing for CBS and to a lesser extent ABC. And God knows where he will strike next.' (Ted Turner might not have known Murdoch's next move, but he had a pretty shrewd idea. If Murdoch was on the prowl with Michael Milken as his adviser, at some point his mind would turn to his old adversary. In mid-1994 Turner quietly put Milken on retainer. If Murdoch or anyone else was going to make a move on Turner Broadcasting, Turner didn't want Milken loading the bullets.)

'When [the NFL deal] was brought to us, I thought we would get a few affiliates as the years went by,' Murdoch told News shareholders a trifle smugly in October 1994. In fact in nine months the Fox network had jumped from 130-odd affiliates to 190. By 1996 it was up to 210 affiliates. 'This has caused a tremendous scramble among the other networks. We are happy to report that they are spending up to $100 million a year for the next 10 years to confirm or to hold on to other stations in their networks to prevent them switching over to [Fox Broadcasting Company]. So, we do have the pleasure not only of having greatly strengthened FBC, but we have caused some little irritation in other areas.' The last line was pure Murdoch. The NFL play had hurt Murdoch's rivals far more than it hurt him. How sweet it was.

The 1994 deal with Perelman was the first, crucial step in Murdoch's campaign to retake America in the 1990s. It made his NFL play look like a masterstroke, and transformed Fox into a fully fledged network. And it had worked while New World wasn't earning any money, recording net losses through 1994 and 1995. But in February 1996, the new Communications Act had been proclaimed by Congress. It lifted the maximum audience reach for a wholly-owned network to 35 per cent, meaning Murdoch could buy more television stations.

Murdoch was going in the opposite direction to the rest of the industry. The smart money was saying that the way to win the future was to buy into programming. But Murdoch knew that this wasn't the real key. Murdoch's whole career in the US had been like a series of Houdini escape acts. Time and again he had wrestled his way out of the handcuffs, achieved the incredible escape, then taken off the mask to discover that at the end of the day he was once again locked outside the city, hammering to get in. More simply, Murdoch had been blocked by the impossibility of getting the distribution he wanted for his programming. So his strategy was simply an extension of his general corporate philosophy. At the turn of the twentieth century, appearance dictated substance, form controlled content, distribution determined programming. So Murdoch was buying television stations before anyone else caught on.

In an ideal world, Murdoch would have liked to keep the New World stake at 20 per cent, and buy other stations which could also be flipped to take Fox programming, and in the process overtake CBS as third largest network. Perelman wasn't having any of that. He had been pressuring Murdoch for a buyout of New World since the start of the year. When talks bogged down in April, Perelman produced a squeeze play, setting up a $1.5 billion deal to merge New World with the King World programming and distribution group. The deal would mean a huge increase in the price when Murdoch finally got around to buying out New World. And if News Corp did not secure New World, eventually it would lose the stations. Despite the ten-year affiliation agreement, in the end New World would flip them, as sure as God made little channel selectors. This would push the Fox network back into the minor leagues. So this meeting at Sun Valley on 11 July 1996 was the last gasp, the final chance to snatch the deal back and make it work. It was a purely defensive move for Murdoch. News Corp would not gain a single viewer for Fox from the deal that Murdoch was about to hammer out with Perelman. Murdoch was about to pay $2.5 billion to buy something – access for the Fox network – which he already had.

'He had me over a barrel,' Murdoch said later. The association had been profitable, but personally Perelman and Murdoch had never been close.

On Herb Allen's porch Perelman was in the charm zone, as he sat down to haggle with the Master of Virtual Reality. Up close and personal, Rupert Murdoch is one of the most persuasive forces on earth. Time and again throughout his career he has wooed and won over the most unlikely foes, convinced the most sceptical and diehard critics to give him their trust, to believe that they are the ones for whom it will be different.

The mannerisms help. Murdoch has a way of letting people into his confidence, into the inner circle, with his gravelly, diffident voice casually dissecting the world. He has a knack of puffing out his cheeks as he gathers for a response. The eyebrows peak, he leans forward and the voice becomes almost a whisper. He lets drop the most devastating information as a casual, bored commonplace. It is always interesting because the mind is always working, shooting out ideas at a hundred miles an hour. And such ideas.

It is more than just the manner. What Murdoch offers – what Murdoch is offering here to you now – is a piece of the future. The man before you has this uncanny ability to make the future happen, in a way that almost no one in the world can. It is a future of ideas and visions that makes Murdoch almost irresistible to anyone with a spark of imagination. It is this quality that gives Murdoch such a devastating effect on politicians, particularly on those to the middle and left of centre, whose rhetoric depends upon imagination. Murdoch's natural home is deep on the right, and Democrat and Labour politicians understand this in their heads. And often it makes no difference. Murdoch in your face at Force Ten still takes your breath away, with his tantalising, attainable view of a possible future. This is Murdoch in full seductive mode.

But Perelman wasn't buying. He had Murdoch's measure because for Perelman there was no mystique about the media, there was no magic to the business which Murdoch could conjure. Perelman rated television stations like property assets. This was all about money, end of story. So the first point which Murdoch made was that he was not actually going to pay Perelman any cash. The deal would have to be made in exchange for News

Corporation's new non-voting preference stock. Perelman would accede to that. But how much would the deal be? Talks between the two had broken down in April over price: Perelman wanted $29 a share for New World and Murdoch was offering $23 a share. On the porch the price was settled at $27 a share. Take it or leave it. Perelman would walk away with $1.15 billion, a $600 million profit, most of it in the form of News Corp prefs. In all, Perelman's tough negotiating had gouged another $366 million from Murdoch. Murdoch would hate that.

And the market would hate the deal. It seemed an outrageous price for a network with limited upside. If Fox executives could perform miracles at New World, over the subsequent five years it might become worth almost as much as Murdoch had paid for it. But that wasn't the point. Murdoch wasn't paying for product or for profits. He was paying $2.5 billion to hold on to an outlet for Fox programming. Behind all the talk of the 1990s about the supremacy of content over form, Murdoch's corporate experience was exactly the opposite. He had content, but not enough distribution. After two decades of trying in America, he was still locked out, still clawing for access.

The Sunday night after Herb Allen's week of entertainment, Murdoch called Perelman from his ranch in Carmel, California. Against the advice of his own executives, he agreed to Perelman's price. And so the deal was done. Just like that. At least that was the public story, graciously eked out to the trade press and later the *New York Times*. That was the big deal, Sun Valley 1996. History records it as the last major deal to come out of Sun Valley in the 1990s. Everything that came after that year would just be hype.

Only with Murdoch it's never that simple. There are two rules for negotiating with Rupert Murdoch. The first is that he is never quite where you think he is. The second is that there is always a deal running underneath the main deal, with another deal running simultaneously underneath that. Ron Perelman would discover the first of these subterranean levels three days later, and it would cost him a lot of money.

Los Angeles, 14–17 July 1996

Hollywood loves a secret. It is *de rigueur*, part of the dress code anywhere north of the Santa Monica Freeway, to be the proud owner of a personal confidence. Or rather, of someone else's personal confidence. There are certain minimum requirements. Like radioactive isotopes, secrets have a high decay rate in northern Los Angeles. Sometimes half lives are measured in hours. And by definition, a Hollywood secret is something that everyone else knows. What other value is there in having a secret?

Rupert Murdoch's particular problem on Sunday evening, 14 July 1996, was that he had a secret that he really couldn't afford to let anyone know about. He only had to hold it for a couple of days – any thought of keeping it under wraps for longer than that was a hopeless pipe dream. But for those 48 hours it had to be that most sentimental of anachronisms, a *secret* secret. One slip-up, one indiscretion, would cost Murdoch a couple of hundred million dollars.

As Murdoch hung up the phone at his Carmel ranch after sealing the deal with Ron Perelman to buy New World Communications, the poker hand was only half played. The deal had been stalled since April over the price issue. Murdoch offered $23 a share, while Perelman hung out for $29. On Sunday evening the deal had been fixed at $27 a share. All up, News would pay $2.48 billion for New World Communications stock. Perelman's tactics had increased the price by $366 million, and his own personal profit by $155 million. In the next two days, Murdoch would try to get all of this back.

Murdoch and Perelman were still stalking each other, still probing for weaknesses, united only in mutual suspicion and the need for speed. It was time to start lawyering up. The legal teams that assembled had 48 hours to close a frighteningly big and complex transaction on assets totalling $3.8 billion.

Part of Ron Perelman's squeeze play on Murdoch had been to set up a deal where he was about to buy King World Productions, a major television distributor for shows including *Oprah Winfrey* and *Wheel of Fortune*. Perelman would go back to talking to King World if Murdoch didn't meet his price. As far as the King World executives knew, the deal was still on the final approach path, due to be sealed later in the week. The moment that King World executives caught a whiff of what was happening – that Perelman was planning to jilt them – they would be out of the picture. If they walked, so did much of Perelman's negotiating leverage over Murdoch. If the Fox deal fell over, it would cost Perelman more money to placate King World, and get the acquisition talks started again. So he needed to keep the deal with Murdoch secret.

King World was both a squeeze play and an insurance policy for Perelman in case the deal with Murdoch soured. So Perelman would continue the merger talks. The New World board would continue its meetings with the King World directors until late Tuesday to finalise an agreement which would never take place. But by Wednesday the jig would be up. So Wednesday was Perelman's deadline for the deal. It had to be done by then. In any case, Perelman was too tough a negotiator to want to give Murdoch any time or room to edge back from this deal. He had a good price, and he needed to keep the pressure on Murdoch to get it all signed up as fast as possible.

But Rupert Murdoch knew something that Ron Perelman didn't. He knew his own stockholders. This was important, because this wasn't a cash transaction. Murdoch was offering Perelman News Corp stock: he was giving him a piece of his paper. Stock transactions are another sort of virtual reality – and just how do you value paper?

The key to any stock transaction is timing. Murdoch had agreed to pay Perelman $27 for each New World share, by giving him (and other New World stockholders) that same value in News Corp limited voting preference stock. (This was a line of stock Murdoch had issued 18 months before that essentially had no voting rights. Unlike the Milken junk preferred stock in the 1980s, this was genuine equity.) The problem with paying someone in stock is that the price of the stock goes up and down. So in drawing up a stock deal, negotiators have to fix a day on which the stock will be valued. Generally this will be either the day the deal is struck, or the day many months later when the deal is settled.

In the US, News Corp stock trades as American Depository Receipts (ADRs). In the New World deal, the value of the News Corp ADR prefs was fixed at $18.62, their closing price on Monday 15 July. This became the benchmark for the entire deal. In the document nutted out by the lawyers, it was agreed that for each New World share, News would issue 1.45 News ADR prefs (which works out to $27.01 for each New World share). The ADR prefs were trading at $20 just two weeks before (which would value the New World offer at $29 a share), so the price looked good for Perelman.

It looked good to Murdoch too, for quite different reasons. What had become painfully clear to Rupert Murdoch in the previous six months was that the Australian institutional funds that still formed the backbone of the News Corp share register didn't like his prefs. In fact a lot of fund managers hated them. Ever since Murdoch had foisted the preferred limited voting stock on his shareholders in a bonus issue in 1994, Australian fund managers had treated them as having all the social appeal of the meningococcal virus. Australian institutions had been bailing out of the prefs since early 1996, partly out of suspicion over what Murdoch was about to do with them.

And fund managers were going to hate this deal. It would confirm all their fears that Murdoch would use the prefs as a form of junk debt, used to pay excessive prices for assets. Because of the small size of the Australian market, Australian institutions tend to take larger stakes in public companies than is usual in the US. This gives them more market clout. So Murdoch knew that after this deal he would have some powerfully unhappy shareholders who would punish him by dumping his stock. Once news of the deal broke, the price of the prefs would drop like a stone. In doing this, the institutions would be sending Murdoch a signal: don't mess with us. So Perelman would end up with News Corp stock that was worth a lot less than the $27 that he thought he was getting. This was an ambush, but it only worked if it remained a surprise. If the deal had not been finalised by the time the news broke and Murdoch's stock started sliding, Perelman would back out of the deal, or at least insist that Murdoch gave him more stock to make up the $27 price. Murdoch would hate that.

Ron Perelman was still in the dark. He might have been expecting a minor price drop in News Corp stock, but not a rout. He did not understand the forms of this virtual transaction. This was the tricky bit. If the deal was signed and watertight before any news leaked out, then when the stock plunged, it would be Ron Perelman's loss rather than Murdoch's, locked into a deal to accept low-price News Corp prefs. It wouldn't cost Murdoch any less in terms of the number of shares he had to issue, but he avoided having to issue millions more to honour the price he had negotiated with Perelman. So secrecy here was absolutely imperative. Perelman had to keep thinking he had a good deal.

The secret broke with a gasp on Tuesday evening. Joe Flint and Jenny Hontz at Hollywood's *Daily Variety* heard a garbled version of the deal and began making calls, seeking confirmation. It was news to the King World board, just out of late meetings with New World execs. Brandon Tartikoff solved the management uncertainty at Fox by resigning on the Tuesday night after hearing the news. He decamped, comforted only by a $1 million a year golden parachute which would keep paying out until 1999, and 1 million New World stock options.

At that point on Tuesday night, with the news out, the New World board still had not signed the Memorandum of Understanding (MOU) that would seal the takeover. But meanwhile two other mega deals were providing cover, diverting investors' attention. On Wednesday the Federal Trade Commission signalled it would approve Time Warner's $7.5 billion purchase of Turner Broadcasting System. Late on Tuesday night Kirk Kerkorian had won the race to snatch the MGM studio, which was being auctioned by French financial group Credit Lyonnaise. Kerkorian had beaten a range of rival bidders including Murdoch for MGM, though Murdoch popped up as a shareholder in Kerkorian's silent partner, Australia's Seven Network. With this much background noise going on, the New World deal slipped through without a problem. The New World board signed the memorandum of understanding early Wednesday, and the deal was announced with appropriate enthusiasm.

'This acquisition continues the momentum towards our goal to become the leading over-the-air free broadcast television network in the United States, and underscores our commitment to play a major role in this industry for decades to come,' Murdoch said in the press release, in a nicely judged comment which avoided the temptation to say anything meaningful.

The line from New World was that it was a negotiating triumph for Perelman over Murdoch. 'The bottom line is, they were arguing over price, they had already agreed on strategy,' commented one of the New World execs. 'For you to come back and get (nearly) the price you were looking for just weeks ago, it's an outstanding chess move.'

Perelman's supporter must have been talking early in the day. Across on Wall Street, the outstanding chess move was looking more like the expensive end of a three-card trick. The News prefs had begun their predictable descent. The deal had been struck at $18.625 on the Monday close. It eased a little on Tuesday, then dived Wednesday to $16.50. At this level, Murdoch's effective price for New World was $23.93 a share. A week later his bid price had dropped even further, down to $22.66. The value for New World shareholders dropped $244 million the day the deal was announced, and another $100 million over the following week. Murdoch had won back all of the extra price that Perelman had wrestled out of him. But no one was pointing that out to reporters, who focused instead on the small drop in News Corp's ordinary stock.

It wasn't all loss for Perelman. He had a little insurance that other New World shareholders did not have, because part of his price was paid in cash. On the Monday Murdoch had agreed to pay for part of Perelman's shares by taking over existing debt in a holding company. In a series of deals Perelman was to receive $1.15 billion, a profit of about $600 million. About $435 million of that was in debt and cash, which did not go down in value with the News share price. But by Thursday three days later, the value of Perelman's shares – and his profit – was still down $130 million.

It would be hard for the senior ranks at News Corp not to have felt some gratification at Perelman's discomfiture. His returns were back down around where they would have been if he had taken cash at $23 a share three months earlier. It was all most satisfactory. The warm glow of a happy outcome was cooled only slightly by the downside. The Ronald was not happy. Up to now, Murdoch's chief shareholders had been a bunch of unhappy fund managers. Now he was sharing the register with a bunch of unhappy fund managers and an 800 pound gorilla. But that would be next year's problem.

This jousting with Ron Perelman would have been just another piece of corporate chicanery or smart footwork, but Rupert Murdoch is never quite so easy to define. There was a twist underneath the New World deal that was produced by his complex family relationships. Ron Perelman wasn't the only one depending on the price of the News Corp preference shares. The stock price had become a critical matter for securing the Murdoch family succession. In July 1996 Murdoch was halfway through a tortuous process to buy the rest of his family out of Cruden Investments. That wasn't Murdoch's only hurdle. Murdoch didn't really have quite enough News Corp shares to ensure his children would control News Corp. Once he had bought his sisters out, Murdoch would need to husband his pennies to buy more News Corp voting stock. Every dollar would count. In March 1996, Murdoch had taken out a \$A373 million bank loan through Westpac Bank in Sydney, to complete the first leg of the family buyout. The only way he could pay off the bank debt was to sell Cruden's News Corp non-voting preference stock some years later. Of course, Murdoch could have sold the stock right away, without raising any bank debt. Paying the family with a bank loan like that meant that Murdoch was gambling that the stock price of the prefs would go up before the repayment fell due – so in the end he would have to sell less of the prefs, which would leave him with more money to buy News Corp voting stock. He was that confident the price would go up. In fact, it was imperative that the prefs' stock price go up. It would certainly be disastrous if it went down . . . as the News stock price had in 1987, the last time Murdoch bet on it. It would be same ingredients . . . debt piling up, secured only by a line of stock that was going down.

    That was the plan. Then along came Ron Perelman. As Murdoch said, the Ronald had him over a barrel. Murdoch had no choice but to buy New World. There was one small window of opportunity. It was always going to be a tough outcome for Perelman, because he needed to raise money for his casino operations quickly, so he wanted to sell the News Corp prefs that he picked up in the deal as soon as possible. By contrast, Murdoch's loan repayment and the final instalment in the family buyout were two or three years away. Murdoch would have known, that Sunday night at his Carmel

Valley ranch when he sealed the deal with Perelman, that this transaction would hit the pref stock price badly. The public story would be that this deal was a great triumph for Ron Perelman. The in-house story at News was how the tables had been turned on Perelman. But the personal story underneath everything else was that, much as Murdoch could enjoy Perelman's discomfiture, the fall in the stock price was hurting Murdoch just as much.

So why did he do it? What is this strange twist beneath the mega-deal? The only thing that Murdoch had going for him was a gambler's belief that, even though the prefs would go down, the price would recover again by the time he needed to pay out his personal bank loan.

'Murdoch's view is that if he is willing to be patient, other shareholders should be patient too,' a News adviser told the *New York Times*. Murdoch was fond of describing his business ventures as times when he bet the company on the big venture of the moment – like buying *News of the World* in 1968, or Metromedia in 1985, or Wapping in 1986, or Sky Television in 1989. But this was not a wager made with Other People's Money. This time, as he had when he bought Queensland Press in 1987, Murdoch had bet the family. It was white-knuckle stuff. Yet knowing all of this, that hot night in Carmel Valley, Murdoch took the gamble without a blink.

CHAPTER EIGHT

THE APPLE FUMBLE

New York, Tuesday 17 September 1996

For more than a century, Hollywood film-makers have known that New York is the centre of the universe. It is one of the truths that the film industry holds to be self-evident. No one knows quite why this should be so. The best theory is that it is the result of some celluloid wrinkle in space-time. Manhattan Island exercises a profound gravitational attraction that most living entities and large inanimate objects find impossible to resist. Giant gorillas, mutated lizards, alien invasion fleets, romantic insomniacs from Seattle and huge meteorites, all realise instinctively (or at least by the third reel) that if they want to make a splash, New York is the only place to go. Hold New York to ransom and you have the world's attention. Hold Cleveland to ransom and you have, well, half of Cleveland's attention.

The latest round in the eternal quest to storm Manhattan began on 17 September 1996 along with a rain front that swept in from Long Island. It had been wet all day, a cold steady rain that turned traffic into a snarling mess. In midtown the downpour caught Gerry Levin as he left the Time Warner building to make the short trip up Sixth Avenue for an uncomfortable interview with Rupert Murdoch.

'Good luck,' Time Warner president Richard Parsons said to Levin as his boss walked out.

It had already been a long day for Levin. He was 22 days away from closing the most important deal of his life. Four years before, after the death of Steve Ross, the legendary head of Warner Communications, Levin had become the head of the biggest media group in the world. Levin had been corporate strategist for Time Inc in the $14 billion merger in 1989 that produced Time Warner, but Ross was the architect of the deal. By and large the merged entity that Levin inherited from Ross had not worked very well. However, in August 1995 Levin had stamped his own mark on the group by persuading Ted Turner to merge his beloved Turner Broadcasting System (TBS) with Time Warner. It had been a $7.5 billion deal at the time, but the sagging Time Warner stock price meant that by September 1996 the Time Warner stock that Turner and his TBS stockholders would receive was worth $1 billion less.

The merger was due to settle on 10 October. While Federal Communications Commission had approved the deal in July, the Federal Trade Commission had hung tough and insisted on some peculiar conditions to the merger, finally giving its approval on Thursday, 12 September. Putting together a big merger is like an excruciating juggling act. Not the least problem for Levin to juggle in the last month had been working out what to do with Ted Turner. Turner was about to become Levin's biggest stockholder – he would end up with 10.6 per cent of Time Warner. For nearly a year Levin had been working on a management restructure for the merged group that would leave Turner vice chairman and the most senior figure at Time Warner after Levin himself, without actually having a job.

Turner had been stung by press reports to this effect. Over the Labor Day weekend at the end of August Levin had flown to Turner's ranch in Montana and discovered that Turner was an unhappy camper. Turner had a long list of grievances and demands – virtually all of which Levin had been forced to meet. The upshot was that on 17 September, Levin threw over his management restructure plans and gave Turner a real job, appointing him to oversee all of Time Warner's cable operations in the newly merged group. Turner was now the head of the most important and most profitable division in Time Warner. Like any major announcement in a group the size of Time Warner, Levin's move had sparked a whole new range of forest fires and consternation in the management ranks that needed to be seen to. So it was late in the day when Levin got to the last item on the agenda, which was to see Rupert Murdoch.

Levin got on well with Murdoch. At least, he didn't get on badly. The two men were polite to each other. Time Warner had cable channels that it wanted to run in Britain on Murdoch's BSkyB satellite service, and Murdoch wanted to run his new Fox News cable channel on Time Warner's cable networks – particularly in New York. At Herb Allen's Sun Valley conference in July, Levin and Murdoch had spoken cordially to each other about their plans, and made a handshake deal, as Murdoch put it, to do what they could to provide access for each other's programming in their various ventures around the world.

Murdoch was too ferocious a competitor for Levin to want to cross, his feeling for media too intuitive to gamble against. Murdoch's abrasive approach to business was almost the complete opposite of Levin's own measured, almost academic responses and buttoned-down style. Murdoch had lusted after Levin's company for more than two decades. When Murdoch first arrived in the US in 1973, he had briefly contemplated a hostile bid for Time Inc. In 1983 he had made a run for Warner Communications. In 1989 he had seriously considered joining the battle for Time Warner. In mid-1995, John Malone at Tele-Communications Inc had tried to talk Murdoch into making a joint bid for Time Warner. Each time the quarry had escaped, and Murdoch had been left scrambling to catch up. Murdoch had no great regard for Time Warner management, which he derided as monolithic and ineffective. However, Levin was not quite as innocuous or as flatfooted as he appeared.

For Levin, there was still the suspicion that Murdoch saw him as a lightweight. These and other reasons saw Levin brave the rain on 17 October to be the one to tell Murdoch in person that he didn't have room to run Fox News on Time Warner's cable systems.

Levin returned to Time Warner on the Tuesday evening thinking his problems were over. 'Actually, Rupert took it very well,' he told Parsons. He described the conversation they'd had as brief and polite. Murdoch even thanked Levin for his consideration in braving the weather. Taken by surprise, Murdoch probably responded almost by remote control, with the upper-class manners of his upbringing. Certainly, there was nothing on the surface to indicate that hours later News Corporation and Time Warner would be locked in one of the most spectacular turf wars of the decade.

Yet what was Gerry Levin trying to manage here? What was he *thinking*? He only had to look at Rupert Murdoch's history to know that he was walking into trouble. In reality, resolving the 'what if' alternatives was simple. Whatever Levin did or said that Tuesday evening, the next day he would still have been facing World War III. The only thing he could have done better was to wear a helmet. Of course that is easy to say in hindsight.

Murdoch had had to sell his beloved *New York Post* in 1988, but he and Anna had continued to live in their Manhattan penthouse. It took the 1990 debt crisis to make Murdoch leave town. In January 1991 as the battle to save News Corp raged, Murdoch quietly put the Fifth Avenue penthouse on the market, saying he was shifting his home base to Los Angeles, which was now the head of his US operations. Moving to the West Coast helped calm his bankers' nerves, the money raised from the sale went to fund the first stage of Murdoch's secret family buyout. But while Anna loved Los Angeles, Murdoch felt marooned on the wrong side of America and hankered to return east. By 1996 Murdoch had fought two battles to do just that. He had won one, and lost one. The important one had been the battle to win back the *New York Post*, a rollicking affair that Murdoch won with the help of Squadron, Ellenoff, Plesent & Lehrer.

In the years after Murdoch sold it in 1988, the *New York Post* had fallen on hard times. In June 1992, Manhattan district attorney Robert Morgenthau told New York courts that the Mafia had controlled the paper's circulation since 1987. Morgenthau charged thirteen *Post* employees and members of the Bonanno crime family with extortion, coercion, larceny, bribery and falsifying business records. The 99-count indictment said the Mob had run loan sharking, extorted money from *Post* employees, and sold guns from the loading docks. Some of those charged were alleged to be part of a heroin ring involving the Genovese and Bonanno families. The *Post*'s owner, real estate developer Peter Kalikow, declared bankruptcy in August 1991; but the *Post* limped along until January 1993 when Kalikow's banker, Bankers Trust, pulled the plug.

The *Post* was losing $300,000 a week. As the money dried up its cheques for its paper suppliers began bouncing. *Post* reporters were unable to travel – for example to cover the Oscars in Hollywood – because its travel agent had stopped giving credit. Photographers bought their own film and paper, reporters paid for their own pens and made notes on the back of press releases because there was no notepaper. In the final indignity, the *Post*'s Washington bureau had its water cooler repossessed. The head of security reported that security guards ostensibly on shift were moonlighting elsewhere, and that the building had become the night-time haunt of drug dealers and prostitutes. This unique New York institution, which *New York Times* editor A.M. Rosenthal had described as 'mean, ugly, violent journalism' under Murdoch, and *Columbia Journalism Review* had called 'a force for evil', seemed to have reached the end of the line.

Back at the *Post*, Sunday 24 January 1993 was the day that Kalikow was to announce the paper's final demise. Instead, New York was shocked to learn that in the previous 24 hours Kalikow had found someone brave enough, wealthy enough and foolish enough to take over the *Post* and its problems. Such an act of civic nobility made the new owner, Steve Hoffenberg, nothing less than a genuine American hero. The man was a monument.

Or at least that was the prevailing sentiment for at least the first five minutes after the announcement. Unfortunately it soon became apparent that the only thing monumental about Steve Hoffenberg would be his eventual prison sentence. Hoffenberg was a major-league hustler. Within a fortnight, the Securities and Exchange Commission had launched a civil suit against him for fraud, in the biggest Ponzi scheme in US history.

The situation went from bad to worse at the *Post*, because with his funds frozen by the Securities Exchange Commission Hoffenberg brought in a friend as a silent partner. Abe Hirschfeld, an eccentric parking lot developer who liked to call himself Honest Abe, would be convicted of conspiring to murder a business partner in August 2000. 'What the hell do I know about publishing? I can't write and I can't type,' Hirschfeld said at the time with a shrug. Hirschfeld fired Hoffenberg's new editor, Peter Hamill, after Hamill refused to print poetry written by Hirschfeld's wife. In scenes that perhaps could only take place in New York, the *Post* staff declared open war. When Hirschfeld held a press conference, *Post* staff interrupted with shouts of 'animal' and 'liar' and called him racist and mentally incompetent. Hamill unilaterally rehired himself and published a paper with the banner headline, 'Who is this nut?' next to a cartoon of the new owner in a straitjacket.

The *Post* filed for bankruptcy protection on 15 March. Hirschfeld now had cold feet over the whole deal. The situation was out of control. No one would seriously consider buying the paper now. Or rather, almost no one. On 25 March, Hirschfeld told the *Post*'s bankruptcy judge that he would not be putting in any more money to keep the paper running over the weekend. The same day, Hoffenberg's lawyers at Squadron Ellenoff put Towers Financial Corporation into Chapter 11 bankruptcy – a move that froze the *Post*'s accounts receivable, the paper's last hope of raising money. And then – marvellously – a new bidder appeared.

'I am not here as some fairy godmother to pour more money into the paper,' Rupert Murdoch assured all and sundry in his downbeat gravelly voice, to universal acclaim. *Post* staff cheered when he visited the newsroom on Monday 29 March and appointed Ken Chandler as the new editor. 'I am assuming that Mr Chandler will produce such a brilliant newspaper that the circulation will rise, but I don't expect or hold out any promise of sudden magic,' Murdoch said breezily.

New York Governor Mario Cuomo and Senator Alfonse D'Amato had been working the phones on both sides of politics to help Murdoch win a permanent waiver from the Federal Communications Commission's cross-media rules to allow him to buy the *Post* and keep WNYW, his New York television station. Cuomo did it with gritted teeth.

It took another six months of gruelling negotiations and brinkmanship. And then it was finished. The *Post* was won. Murdoch was back in the Big Apple. This was his town.

That was the battle that Murdoch won. The fight he staged a year later to put a cable channel into New York he lost.

Under the 'must carry' provisions of the US cable Act, cable companies were obliged to carry all free-to-air stations on their nets in addition to their own programming. In 1992 the government increased the amount of compensation that he free-to-air stations could charge the cable companies for running their programs. Rather than more money, the big networks instead asked for access for their own cable channels. NBC used this access to launch a low-budget news-oriented channel called America's Talking. In 1994 Fox launched its own light entertainment cable channel, called f/X. The channel featured a grab bag of shows, from the obligatory breakfast program to a show about pets. 'It's the best line-up that $100 million and no brains could buy,' scoffed Roger Ailes, the acerbic exec who ran NBC's two cable channels, CNBC and America's Talking.

Fox launched f/X with 18 million subscribers – more than half of them from John Malone's Tele-Communications Inc, who led the way by agreeing to pay an astonishing 25 cents a month for every subscriber. Fox was able to strong-arm other cable companies to take the channel on the same terms, though resentful cablers suspected that it was another one of those special deals that Murdoch and Malone kept hatching, and that Malone would be compensated by Murdoch for his trouble with another deal somewhere else in the world.

The major hold-out from f/X was the second largest cable company, Time Warner, which controlled the country's most important cable market, New York. Time Warner's cable execs complained about the quality of the programming and resolutely refused to carry the channel, even when the *New York Post* ran a campaign encouraging its readers to write in to Time Warner to complain. So while f/X was shown around the country, the 1.4 million cable subscribers in New York City never saw it. Of those 1.4 million subscribers, the only really important ones were the advertising executives on Madison Avenue. They were the people who decided whether to put advertising on a cable channel, and it was hard to convince them to put money into something that they had never seen.

Round two in the battle for New York had been lost. But by 1996 both these episodes were ancient history.

★

In January 1996, Rupert Murdoch announced that in October he would launch Fox News, a 24-hour channel that would stand in opposition to what Murdoch saw as CNN's 'left-wing bias'. Ted Turner had seen off threats to CNN before and said 'I'm looking forward to squishing Rupert like a bug.'

The old chemistry was still sparking between the two men. 'He's ten years older than me, and if the actuarial table are right, he'll be dead ten years before me, and I'll have ten years of peace and quiet after he's gone,' Turner had told the *Financial Times* in 1993. Murdoch replied by sending him a note, 'Dear Ted, Let's have lunch before it's too late. Rupert.'

'I can't hate him,' said Turner when he recounted the story. 'I'd like to, but I can't. It's really good to have good, tough competitors . . . I know he'd like to have CNN, so I have to worry that he'd like to eat me.' Relations between the two men had thawed so much that in April 1994, Murdoch gave the keynote speech at a lunch honouring Turner at the Center for Communications in New York Plaza. But the truce didn't last long.

Murdoch told a Washington press conference in February 1996:

Ted Turner has been particularly energetic in describing what I'm all about, I appreciate his help. Ted last week called me the schlockmeister. To this, I guess, I must plead guilty, if your idea of schlock is the *X-Files* or *The Times* of London or NFL Football, even the *Simpsons*, Sky or Star Broadcasting, Fox Educational Children's Programming, and many other things . . . We do, however, draw the line at professional wrestling and brown-nosing foreign dictators. You'll have to turn to one of Ted's channels for that. I'm reminded of something Disraeli once said to a colleague in Parliament: 'Honourable sir, it's true that I am a low, mean snake. But you, sir, could walk beneath me wearing a top hat.'

News had become one of the core drivers for television programming. It ranked with sport, movies, music and children's programming as one of the basic building blocks for Disney, Time Warner, Viacom and News Corp as they worked to turn their program content into worldwide brands. The 1990s had seen a major change in the economics of the media industry. Hollywood now made more than half its movie earnings from international sales. The satellite and cable pay-television platforms that were being set up around the world promised in the same way to offer big earnings for television content producers. It all came down to distribution – to finding a way to make sure the world could watch your programs. News Corp was well on the way to controlling a worldwide distribution system for its programming, through its satellite and cable operations like BskyB in Britain, Star TV in Asia, Foxtel in Australia and SkyLatin in South America. Yet ironically the economics of program production meant that the only way to create a worldwide brand was to succeed first in the huge US market. It was the only way to achieve economies of scale. So the more that Murdoch expanded around the world, the more he needed to make it in the United States. And here distribution was much more of a problem.

Time Warner's New York cable system carried 77 channels, of which nine were set aside for the city's use as public, educational and government channels (known as PEG channels). Another 11 channels were set aside for leased access, and a further 15 channels carried the local free-to-air television stations, as required under the 'must carry' provisions of the Cable Act. These left Time Warner with 42 channels at its discretion. By the time it had allocated channels for basic programming, premium packages and pay per view, the network was full. Running a new channel, no matter how good, meant bumping off an existing channel, a move which would almost certainly annoy a group of their subscribers. This cablers were reluctant to do.

NBC solved the distribution problem by deciding to run its own news channel, MSNBC, on its existing America's Talking cable channel. This guaranteed MSNBC had 21 million subscribers when it launched on 16 July. Roger Ailes, the disgruntled former head of America's Talking and former campaign adviser to Ronald Reagan and New York mayor Rudy Giuliani, quit NBC. Murdoch promptly hired him to run Fox News. Ailes' Republican credentials made him the perfect choice for the conservative political approach that Murdoch favoured.

Murdoch could have taken the NBC route. He could simply have converted his f/X channel into Fox News. But unlike America's Talking, f/X didn't run in New York and in any case Murdoch had far more ambitious plans. He had committed f/X to his burgeoning sports alliance with John Malone to run Fox Sports. Instead, for the Fox News launch Murdoch would use one of his most daring stratagems yet. 'Money is something you can use to trade to get distribution,' said Ailes. 'Everybody knows it. Anybody who has the nerve can play that game. This is capitalism and one of the things that made this country great.' To this point the most that any new channel had offered cable companies for carriage was Viacom's offer of $1.20 up front fee for every subscriber for its reruns channel, TV Land. In April at the National Cable Convention in Los Angeles Fox changed the cable television landscape by telling cable executives it was prepared to pay them an incredible $11 per subscriber to run Fox News. To be viable, Murdoch had said that Fox News needed at least 25 million subscribers. At $11 each, that meant he was prepared to fork out $275 million just to get Fox News on the channel selector.

Murdoch's offer shocked the industry and badly rattled his rivals at ABC and NBC. In June he announced a deal with Malone. At the launch in October, Tele-Communications Inc would carry Fox News to 10 million of its 14 million subscribers. According to several reports Malone had forced Murdoch to nearly double his price. Murdoch would pay Malone $200 million, or $20 a subscriber, and Malone would take 20 per cent of Fox News.

This was not quite the act of pure philanthropy on Murdoch's part that it appeared – it was a multi-year contract with sliding charges that would eventually see Fox get its money back; but at the latest level Murdoch was prepared to shell out half a billion dollars just to buy a news voice. This was quite apart from the costs of setting up a worldwide news operation, and projected operating losses of $366 million before breaking even in the seventh year.

To get to critical mass, though, Murdoch needed Time Warner to carry his signal for its 11 million subscribers. In particular he needed New York. And so he had sat down with Gerry Levin at Sun Valley in July to reach an understanding. Their rapport did not go unnoticed. On Tuesday 15 July, as News Corp lawyers were feverishly putting the New World deal together with Perelman's lawyers in Los Angeles, NBC chief executive Robert Wright oversaw the launch of MSNBC. He told reporters at the press conference that Levin and Murdoch were about to announce a big distribution deal. This was a major problem for MSNBC because while Time Warner had allowed MSNBC to launch on America's Talking, it had warned that it believed the change was a breach of the original pro-gramming agreement, and it had the right to pull the channel at any time. If Time Warner did a deal with Fox News, MSNBC would be the easiest channel to dump.

In this already tangled scene, Time Warner's lobbyists and lawyers negotiated an arrangement with the Federal Trade Commission that was either a masterstroke or another example of a big corporation shooting itself in the foot. The new Federal Trade Commission chairman, Robert Pitofsky, was a Georgetown law-school professor with a specialist interest in media concentration. He didn't like the Time Warner-TBS merger, but the politics of the Federal Trade Commission board meant there was not a lot that he could do to stop it. What he settled for was a requirement that Time Warner agree to turn another 24-hour news channel to rival CNN, to half of its 11 million subscribers. The requirement was so specific that only Fox News and MSNBC could satisfy this condition. For Time Warner, the appeal of this arrangement was that they were giving Pitofksy something that they were going to do anyway. In fact, Time Warner intended to run both of the new channels. Joe Collins, the then chairman of Time Warner Cable, wanted the $125 million that Murdoch was prepared to pay for running Fox News, and he also wanted to avoid the huge legal fight that would ensue if he dropped MSNBC.

Levin favoured running both news channels in addition to CNN. It was left to Ted Turner, 'the madman from Atlanta', to point out just how crazy it was to assist CNN's rivals, when Levin phoned him at the end of August. Time Warner was now stuck with taking one of the news channels, because of the Federal Trade Commission's demand. But why take two channels?

It was part of a much longer litany of complaint that Turner went through with Levin and Richard Parsons at his ranch in Montana over the Labor Day weekend. Levin was caught. When Levin had sold the merger to Turner, he had promised him an active role running the group, but in the year since he had gradually eased him out of the picture, encouraging him to stay on his ranch in Montana and come into the office only once or twice a month. Levin already had an unhappy Edgar Bronfman Junior on his register after the merger, controlling 9 per cent of Time Warner. John Malone would hold 10 per cent, though for antitrust reasons he was not allowed to vote the stock. Now Ted Turner, who with 11 per cent would be the largest stockholder, was steamed up with him. Turner could still torpedo this whole deal.

Levin ended up conceding on almost every point Turner raised. He agreed not to sell New Line cinema. CNN would be pulled back from the print news division and run with the cable group. The cable channels would be pulled back from the control of Terry Simel and Robert Daley at Warner Brothers, and Turner himself would oversee them. Even the Goodwill Games, Ted Turner's money-losing sporting event, would be given a new lease of life and $25 million promotion. And Fox News? Well, Time Warner has since argued fiercely that the decision to dump Fox News had nothing to do with Turner. In the broader context, this assurance is unconvincing. In any case on 17 September after appointing Turner head of cable, Levin went for his little walk in the rain.

Levin's rebuff stunned Murdoch and News Corp execs. 'They were within a half-hour of signing a contract with us, which Mr Levin assured me was totally on track,' said Murdoch. 'Then they backed away and said they would rather wait until Federal Trade Commission approval came through.'

The realisation sank in slowly for Murdoch and the News Corp executives that, despite already spending $300 million and committing to investing several hundred million dollars more, Fox News would launch in 20 days time with a woeful 11 million subscribers. This was not a viable operation. The Fox News budget projections had predicted the operation would rack up $366 million in losses on top of the start-up costs before breaking even after six years in 2003 – but those numbers had assumed Time Warner would be carrying it.

Levin didn't know it, but he had pressed all of Rupert Murdoch's buttons. Murdoch had been outmanoeuvred, he had been excluded, and he had been publicly humiliated. He rose up in a cold fury the next day to call Levin back. 'What the hell happened?' Levin asked Pressler, who had had a similar angry call from Chase Carey. 'I came back and everything was fine. Then Rupert called and he went crazy on me.'

As news of the setback broke, the Fox execs hit the phones to work the press. Time Warner's move was 'an enormous breach of faith and a personal affront' for Murdoch, Ailes told journalists.

'We were dealt with in a duplicitous manner, and essentially lied to,' said Carey. 'I don't know how Mr Levin is going to conduct himself in doing business with people when that is the manner he deals with people.'

'We are not going to dignify those vituperative comments with a response,' Time Warner spokesman Ed Adler responded.

'We have a contract and we expect them to live up to it,' said Murdoch. 'If we're not carried by Time Warner here, Time Warner's services will not be welcome on our distribution. We're not signing any contracts to carry them in Britain.'

While Murdoch's and his executives' initial response was an attack on Gerry Levin, it didn't take long for Murdoch and News Corp executives to detect other fingerprints on the Time Warner knife. It was Ted Turner who had humiliated Murdoch, they believed, and he had done it in front of an industry audience. Cable executives were on their way to New York for Hell Week, a title that refers more to what cable executives raise than to what they endure. Hell Week was an annual event, a series of industry meetings that would climax in the annual Walter Kaitz dinner on 25 September, where Turner's triumphant accession to the head of Time Warner's cable operations and Murdoch's discomfiture over Fox News would be plain in front of 1,900 industry figures.

On 18 September Murdoch sat down with Arthur Siskind, together with Carey and Ailes to discuss options. The basic question was how wide they were prepared to make this conflict. First, Murdoch could sue Time Warner. The legal remedies were limited – because despite News Corp protestations, at the end of the day there was no contract, only Time Warner assurances.

Judge Jack Weinstein would later conclude in the District Court:

These were not Adam- and Eve-like innocents slipping naked into the cable television and broadcast jungle to negotiate with each other and the serpent. They were hard-bitten executives steeled in such hagglings . . . The cajolery, as well as the blandishments, honeyed phrases and assurances that are to be expected in major negotiations of this sort in the media entertainment field did not constitute fraud.

Siskind ticked off Murdoch's other options for retaliation. News Corp could make trouble for Time Warner at the Federal Trade Commission, and challenge the Turner Broadcasting System merger on antitrust grounds. 'It is quite possible that new evidence could come forward of [Time Warner] practices and how they have been allocating channels,' Murdoch told journalists archly later that week. 'There are many people trying to start channels who might have something to say about not being carried by a major cable operator like Time Warner. We are considering our position on that.'

Alternatively Murdoch could dump Time Warner's programming in Europe and where possible America as well – thought the danger was that Time Warner would retaliate and the whole conflict would escalate. 'We don't want to burn too many bridges,' cautioned Siskind.

In the end News Corp did what superpowers usually do: it decided to fight its battle by proxy. News would call in political favours and twist arms all across town to ensure local politicians took up arms on its behalf against Time Warner. The first step proposed by Ailes was to tap his links to the mayor of New York, Rudy Giuliani. In June, Giuliani had given News Corp a tax break in return for a commitment to create 1,475 new jobs in New York, 513 of which would come from Fox News. Giuliani would show remarkable tenacity defending those 513 Fox News jobs. The mayor held a very powerful lever. The Time Warner/Turner Broadcasting merger meant that the City needed to renew Time Warner's cable franchise over Manhattan. This usually straightforward process was due to take place on 9 October after a public hearing on 7 October. But the mayor could decide the process was not quite so straightforward. If Time Warner didn't come to Murdoch's party, the City could refuse to renew the franchise.

Ailes put the call in to Giuliani. On Friday 20 September Giuliani called deputy mayor Fran Reiter to say Fox had run into a problem with Time Warner that he wanted her to investigate. The situation 'was very serious', he said. On Thursday 26 September, as the Fox press war gathered steam, Reiter and the City's counsel, Paul Crotty, met Fox lawyers, who described the problem as an antitrust issue. At Crotty's suggestion, Siskind spelt this out in a letter to Reiter on Friday, stressing how important the New York market was to Fox News. He urged Reiter to refuse to consent to both the Time Warner/Turner merger and to the renewal of Time Warner's cable franchise agreement in New York.

On Wednesday 25 September, Giuliani and New York Governor George Pataki had attended a Time Warner press conference where Levin and Turner announced that the Goodwill Games would be held in New York in July 1998. Time Warner already employed 11,000 people in New York. The financial fillip the Games would give the city should have earned Levin brownie points with Giuliani and Pataki and made him their favourite employer. But Giuliani and Pataki were listening to other voices.

The *New York Post* was its usual strident self in its coverage. Besides running cartoon caricatures of Levin next to scathing articles about the Time Warner decision, it even dropped the CNN program guide briefly – like Time Warner Cable, the *Post* said it was having capacity problems. The personal attacks got to Turner. On Thursday 26 September after a lunch with journalists and executives to discuss the Time Warner merger, Turner launched into a virulent attack on Murdoch and his yellow journalism. Time Warner, he said, 'Doesn't tell its journalists what to write.' He went on to compare Murdoch to Adolf Hitler – 'Talking to Murdoch is like confronting the late Fuhrer' – and said Murdoch wanted to rule the world. Time Warner, by contrast, just wanted to make money.

'This kind of venal rhetoric has no place in a civilised society,' Siskind replied on Friday. 'Mr Turner's statement, which is one more expression of his personal animosity toward Mr Murdoch, must be viewed as deeply offensive not only to Mr Murdoch and his associates . . . but to all people of goodwill.'

The Anti-Defamation League of B'nai B'rith complained, and Turner was forced to apologise to victims of Nazism. The *Post*'s response was more robust. It suggested Turner had not been taking his medication, and ran a banner headline, 'Is Ted Nuts? You Decide.' (In late October when Jane

Fonda linked the mayor's support for Fox News to Murdoch's political support for Giuliani and his wife Donna Hanover, Giuliani's on-air job at Murdoch's Channel 5, the *Post* ran a huge picture of Fonda visiting Hanoi in 1972, and dismissed her as 'just another scatty-brained Hollywood nude-nik'.

'This is better than the Tyson fight,' said John Malone. 'This is great comedy to me. Ted Turner hasn't felt so young and energetic in years. He loves a good fight. I would waste no tears on either of these guys.'

Believing the whole issue was about Time Warner not having enough room on its channels to run Fox News, Fran Reiter tried to come up with a solution. On Sunday evening she phoned Time Warner's Derek Johnson to say she was 'very concerned' about the Fox News situation and that the City might be able to help Time Warner out by opening up one of the nine PEG channels set aside for the City's use under the franchise agreement with Time Warner. She asked for a meeting with Gerry Levin or Richard Parsons.

Neither Parsons nor Levin made it to the meeting Reiter organised on Tuesday. Instead they sent Dick Aurelio, the head of Manhattan Cable, to talk to the deputy mayor. The politics of the meeting were always going to be a problem. Parsons, besides his history as a Republican aide to Nelson Rockefeller, was a former law partner of Giuliani's and one of the mayor's few high-profile African-American backers. Aurelio, by contrast, was a prominent Democrat. Of the ten people who crowded into Reiter's office, half were lawyers. On Time Warner's side, Aurelio was flanked by Robert Jacobs, general counsel for Time Warner's New York City cable group, and Alan Arffa, Time Warner's outside counsel. On the City's side were: Bruce Regal, assistant corporation counsel, Normal Sinel of Arnold & Porter as outside counsel and Elaine Reiss, general counsel for the city's Department of Information, Technology and Communication, which oversaw cable arrangements.

Reiter proposed that Time Warner run Fox News on one of its commercial channels, and move one of its 'educational' programs on to one of the City's PEG channels. Regal said the parties could 'paper over the deal' to make it look like there was no quid pro quo. Time Warner's response was that what the City was proposing was unacceptable and illegal. Time Warner's counsel, Alan Arffa, began reading provisions of the Cable Act that prohibited the City from dictating the programming that a cable operator should carry. Sinel interrupted him. 'You don't have to lecture us on the First Amendment and the law, we know what the law says. The mayor's office is fully aware of the risks involved here. We're willing to take those risks. The question is, is Time Warner willing to take those risks?'

The risk, as Judge Dennis Cote would point out a month later, was that the City's proposal might break the Cable Act. The meeting ended quickly, neither side conceding. That night Murdoch hosted a launch party for Fox News in a marquee outside the News Corp offices on 48th Street that drew an A-list of luminaries including Walter Cronkite, Connie Chung, Barbara Walters, Oscar de la Renta, Governor George Pataki and Senator Al D'Amato. In front of the glittering crowd Giuliani and Pataki officially welcomed Murdoch and Ailes and their new cable operation, which the mayor said was of 'incalculable value to the people of the city'. (Next morning both Pataki and D'Amato would call Levin to complain about Time Warner's decision to exclude Fox News.) Arthur Siskind made a beeline for Dennis Vacco, the state attorney general, as Murdoch escorted Fran Reiter though the crowd.

Earlier that evening, Parsons had called Reiter to say that while he believed the City's actions on behalf of Fox were inappropriate, he hoped Time Warner could avoid a head-on collision with the City. Reiter said the meeting had been 'very unpleasant and unnecessary', because she recognised Time Warner's right not to carry Fox News. However, she pushed for Levin to call Murdoch and arrange a meeting. She said she was going to write a letter the next day with a new suggestion, under which the City would seek a waiver from Time Warner to run Fox News directly on one of the City's PEG channels. Parsons said any negotiations would have to wait until after the Time Warner/TBS merger was finalised nine days later, on 10 October. Reiter replied that Fox News planned to raise the issue at the public hearing that was to be held the following Monday into whether the City would reaffirm the cable franchise after the merger. She said that 'that would be a problem for Time Warner'. In addition, the cable franchises were up for their regular renewal in 1998 and Time Warner 'would not want the Fox News Channel to cloud the renewal decision'.

The pressure on Time Warner was unrelenting, a continuing effort 'by fair means or foul', Judge Denise Cote later found, to force Time Warner to carry Fox News. The strategy, it would later be claimed in court, was 'to beat Time Warner over the head to force Time Warner to carry Fox News and to retaliate for refusing to do so . . . and to keep beating Time Warner until Time Warner carried Fox News.'

On Wednesday Reiter sent Time Warner the letter she had promised. On Thursday Giuliani called a conference with Reiter and the City's lawyers at Gracie Mansion to review the position. When news of the latest exchange leaked to the press, an angry Gerry Levin ordered his lawyers to send back a terse rejection of Reiter's latest proposal. It was probably on that day, Judge Cote later found, that a decision was made 'at the deputy mayor level or higher' that, as Siskind had urged, the City would not re-endorse the Time Warner cable franchise after the merger with Turner Broadcasting unless Time Warner put Fox News on the system.

That night Sinel phoned Time Warner's outside counsel Alan Arffa and warned that the City might raise antitrust objections to the Time Warner merger. The next day the City wrote again to Parsons urging him to reconsider its position, on the grounds of Time Warner's 'good corporate citizenship'.

At 6 a.m. on Monday 7 October, Fox News went to air with 18 million subscribers, thanks to a string of hastily-cobbled-together distribution agreements with smaller cable companies. That morning, in rowdy scenes, Fox News lawyers launched a broadside at Time Warner at the public hearing over the cable franchise. Two days later the mayor put any decision on the franchise on ice, leaving Time Warner out in the cold. On Tuesday 8 October, the first subpoenas hit Time Warner. The Attorney General Dennis Vacco's office announced an antitrust investigation into Time Warner's cable programming decisions. The same day Fox News sued Time Warner, Turner Broadcasting and Ted Turner to stop the merger. The suit was 'utter foolishness', a Time Warner spokesman said. Ted Turner called the suit 'a frivolous piece of junk.'

City Hall and Time Warner were now so close to all-out war there seemed no way to pull back. On Wednesday 9 October Time Warner received another letter from the City, this one saying that even if Time Warner refused its consent, it planned to run Fox News and the Bloomberg business news channel on its PEG channels anyway. Including Bloomberg in the scheme was to demonstrate that the City was not merely favouring Fox News. On Wednesday 10 October the Time Warner merger was finally consummated. At 10.48 p.m. that evening, the City began transmitting Bloomberg on one of its PEG channels. It planned to begin running Fox News the next day. But an hour later, just before midnight, an attorney dropped Time Warner's lawsuit against the City through the mail slot of the federal court in Foley Square.

The dispute was about 'very fundamental issues regarding freedom of the press and the rights of the people,' Richard Parsons said. 'The City has basically gone into the news business.'

The next morning Judge Cote granted Time Warner a temporary injunction blocking the city from running Fox News or Bloomberg. She ordered both sides to return to court two weeks later. In her subsequent judgment on 6 November she found that there was 'compelling evidence' that the City had abused its power, and had acted to coerce and to punish Time Warner over its refusal to carry Fox News. 'The City's purpose in acting to compel Time Warner to give it one of its commercial stations was to reward a friend and to further a particular viewpoint,' she said.

Fox News 'is not persuasive it its claim that its dealings with the City do not constitute corruption,' Judge Jack Weinstein found on 10 April 1997 in the Fox case against Time Warner.

New York was left to wonder at the events that had left its mayor, Rudy Giuliani, the former mob-busting US attorney, fighting Rupert Murdoch's battle for him with the biggest media group in the world. Why had he got so involved? There was a further irony that much of the script here seemed to have been written by Arthur Siskind, a man who in the mid-1980s had been under scrutiny by Giuliani's office as US Attorney for New York, in the Wedtech scandal.

'I don't think there was ever any serious consideration given to bringing charges against myself or against Squadron Ellenoff,' Siskind said in November 1996. 'I spoke to Giuliani at a lunch today and we had a little laugh that anybody could be bringing up that old matter.' He was similarly dismissive of any suggestion that Giuliani had favoured News Corp in the latest tussle: 'Nobody buys Rudy Giuliani.'

On Friday 18 October, Ted Turner gave a colourful deposition to the City's lawyers, in which he again described Murdoch as Hitler. The legal battle would grind on, but this bout had reached the end game. Other parts of the News Corp empire required attention. On Tuesday 15 October Murdoch was in Australia for the News Corp annual meeting, where in the course of an upbeat profit forecast for the group he mentioned that News Corp was a couple of weeks away from floating off part of its Israeli technology and encryption arm. This breezy bit of news generally went down well with the financial press. In fact, the announcement turned out to be a really, really bad idea. It woke a nightmare from News Corp's past called Michael Clinger.

CHAPTER NINE

WIRED

London, 31 March 1995

By the mid-1990s, one of the critical side-effects of the Information Revolution was that the business of keeping secrets – running a commercial encryption system – was now worth a lot of money. News Datacom and its related company, News Digital Systems, were valued at close to $1 billion. News Datacom had become Murdoch's technological edge in the twenty-first century, developing the technology – the set-top boxes – to decode his television signals, and the encryption systems to control the next generation of digital broadcasting. It was the key to everything Murdoch was planning. With luck, it could lock Murdoch into the new digital environment, and lock his rivals out. To safeguard that future, in 1995 Murdoch launched an extraordinary international manhunt.

The great pursuit began as the result of a meeting in a room at the Four Seasons Hotel in London. Peter Stehrenberger, the secretary of News International, and Greg Clark, the president of Murdoch's high-tech arm, News Technology Group, had shown up for an appointment that even at the time must have seemed peculiar. They were meeting an Israeli lawyer called Abraham Nantel, who had written to Stehrenberger to request the meeting. He wanted to talk about some shady dealings involving News Datacom. Nantel acted for an Israeli inventor called Ben Zion Kornizky. Nantel stressed that the decision to approach News Corporation was his suggestion, not his client's. Nantel, it seemed, had flown from Tel Aviv to London to see Stehrenberger and Clark off his own bat. Having come that far, he had decided that he couldn't make it a bit further to the News

International offices at Wapping. Even at this stage, the affair seems to have been governed by an obsession with secrecy.

The meeting at the Four Seasons on 31 March 1995 lasted an hour and a quarter, during which Nantel said his client, Kornizky, had been 'entrapped' in a business relationship with a ghost from News Corporation's past called Michael Clinger, who had taken control of a start-up company that was developing one of Kornizky's inventions. Kornizky was distressed and wanted revenge – which seemed pretty much the reaction of almost anyone who had ever done business with Clinger.

Peter Stehrenberger was aware of some of Clinger's wretched history, but believed that after the buyout in 1992 Clinger had had no further connection with News Datacom. Nantel told Stehrenberger and Clark that this wasn't true. Through a series of dummy companies in the Channel Islands and other tax havens, Clinger still controlled the assembly of every smart card that News Datacom produced. He was able to do this because, before News Datacom could program its smart cards for pay-television operators like BSkyB, it paid an outside firm to physically put the smart cards together. News Corp had never realised that Phoenix Micro Inc, the Jersey company which did this work, was controlled by Clinger, who took 60 per cent of the profits. News Datacom had tried for years to find another supplier, without success. According to Nantel, Clinger had boasted that, with the help of Israeli accomplices still working for News Datacom, he was inflating the price that News Datacom was paying for the assembled smart cards. In addition, his accomplices were able to ensure no one passed the testing needed to qualify as an alternative source of supply of smart cards for News Datacom. When one London-based executive with the News Datacom group seemed to be trying a little too hard to find another supplier, Clinger was able to engineer his replacement. The payoff from all this was that, with News Datacom expanding its range of customers beyond BSkyB in Britain, to DirecTV in the United States, and other pay-television operators around the world, Clinger could virtually name his own price for supplying the cards. It was a classic scam.

The only evidence that Nantel offered for these claims was stories that Kornizky had heard, and conversations he had had with Clinger. The case was circumstantial. However, alarm bells were ringing for Peter Stehrenberger and Clark. Greg Clark wrote in his notes on the meeting, 'Peter is aware that Gus Fischer recently had a meeting with Leo Krieger (a former News Datacom accountant) where Leo offered information useful to News and damaging to Clinger.' The problem was that Gus Fischer, News Corp's former chief operating officer, was no longer on the team. He had resigned two weeks earlier, part of the management exodus that claimed all the News International executive directors except Stehrenberger in an 18-month period. Details of Fischer's meeting with Krieger would emerge three years later when a trainee with one of the legal firms acting for News Corp pressed the wrong button on a fax machine.

Leo Krieger had been Michael Clinger's business partner and closest friend until the two had had a spectacular falling out over Clinger's wife, Niva Von Wiesl. Clinger had walked out on Von Wiesl when she was pregnant with their third child, and had moved in with a new girlfriend, Daphna Koszniak. Subsequently, Krieger developed a relationship with Von Wiesl. This enraged Clinger, who began harassing the couple. Clinger fought out a bitter divorce with his wife, and married Koszniak. But he continued the harassment of Krieger and his ex-wife. Krieger responded by blowing the whistle on his former partner. He met with Fischer, and told him that Clinger was stealing News Datacom blind, and for $1 million in cash he was prepared to supply tapes of bugged telephone conversations to prove it.

Fischer's sudden exit from News put Krieger's claims on hold. It was the Nantel meeting several weeks later that stirred Stehrenberger and Arthur Siskind into action. They renewed contact with Krieger, where their first move was to beat his price for information down. After a little haggling they agreed to pay him $312,500 for his help in the investigation, plus a success fee based on a share of any funds retrieved. An affidavit by Siskind underlined the fevered emotions running underneath the case. Siskind told the High Court that part of the reason that News was paying Krieger was 'to enable him to take steps to protect himself and Mr Clinger's former wife, which protection Mr Krieger believes to be necessary as a result of his co-operation with (News)'.

Despite the arrangement with Krieger, Siskind's main hope of proving Clinger's fraudulent behaviour was through Argen Limited, the private investigators he had hired to investigate the claims against Clinger. In three decades Argen had carved out a reputation as one of Britain's largest and most discreet private investigation firms, operating in five countries. Financial investigations at Argen were the province of Jonathon Edwards, who had a background as a lawyer, accountant and merchant banker.

Argen Limited found Michael Clinger's tracks led deep into the tax haven archipelago. They tracked money flows through the Netherland Antilles, the British Virgin Islands, the Channel Islands, Bermuda, Liberia and Panama. They obtained confidential bank documents, bank transfer details, telephone records and restricted court documents, to build up a remarkably detailed picture of where Michael Clinger went, whom he met, and what he said. 'We know everything about him,' Siskind boasted in 1997. News were able to find out about the details of Clinger's marriage settlement locked in an Israeli court safe, and even the $250,000 Swiss glass staircase he had installed in his $1.5 million home in Jerusalem.

In February 1996, News Datacom and News International sued Clinger in the High Court in London for £19 million in damages from fraudulent profits. News claimed that Clinger had overcharged News Datacom at least £1 apiece on more than 19 million assembled smart cards. By 1997, Siskind would be counting the cost of the international manhunt, even though the investigation gave widespread support to Krieger's conspiracy allegations. Legal costs in the eventual trial were estimated at £2 million by a News lawyer. But the real cost of the inquiry was the light that it shone on the secret side of the News empire. For a brief time it put the News archipelago into the spotlight.

'There is a message to be sent here,' Siskind said when queried about the extent of the News investigation. 'Despite the economics of the return, we feel very strongly about people who seek to defraud the company . . . We will not allow ourselves to be extorted by anybody.'

By late 1996, journalists were expressing concern about how News had acquired its information on Clinger. Siskind, who oversaw the investigation, had developed a prickly relationship with media covering the case, in particular *Financial Times* journalist William Lewis in London. Clay Harris, the head of the *Financial Times* investigations unit, described exchanges between Lewis and Siskind as low-level hazing, with Siskind indicating a surprising knowledge of Lewis' personal circumstances – for example referring in conversations with Lewis to his recent marriage, his wife's name, and her place of business. When questioned in November 1996 about how he had learned details of the personal life of a journalist, Siskind and News lawyer Eugenie Gavenchak said that any personal information about Lewis and his family came purely from News Corporation's surveillance of Clinger. 'We have not engaged in any illegal act . . . Our instructions (to our agents) are not to engage in any illegal acts,' Siskind said.

The emotional temperature in the case ran high. In a separate action Bruce Hundertmark had sued Clinger in Israel. He said he was entitled to half of the £5 million Clinger had received from the News Datacom buyout in 1992. A lawyer involved in the case had attempted to commit suicide. Hundertmark was anxious about his personal safety. In late 1995, he had been attacked by two men with knives outside a hotel in Djakarta.

Several months later someone had caused $A180,000 of damage to his house in Australia. There was nothing to suggest either incident was related to the case, but they had unsettled him.

The case took a curious twist. In mid-1995, Clinger developed an acute case of moral sensibility around the time that the Israeli Tax Authority began examining his personal tax returns for previous years. Clinger was suspected of having under-reported his income. The upshot from the conversations which followed was that Clinger, who had already heard whispers of the News investigations, offered to share with the tax man how it was that News Datacom paid so little tax. The News Datacom companies in 1992 had been reorganised as offshore companies which paid for research to be conducted in Israel on a cost-plus basis. Any profits which accrued would be offshore, beyond the reach of the Israeli tax authority. Siskind described this as standard practice for research companies in Israel, including Intel.

On 10 September 1995, Clinger signed an agreement to assist the Israeli Tax Authority in a secret investigation of News Datacom. Tax officers and police staged a series of dawn raids on Krieger's home in Jerusalem, as part of twin investigations into where the telephone tapes that Krieger had offered to News Corp had come from, and into Clinger's allegations that Krieger had evaded personal income tax. In June 1996, Clinger's lawyers disclosed the existence of the agreement in the High Court in London. At the time Arthur Siskind said he had asked the Israelis on several occasions whether they were investigating News Datacom, and was assured they were not. The next thing that happened was that, after a 12-month investigation, the Israeli Tax Authority raided the News Datacom offices.

The immediate trigger was Rupert Murdoch's revelation on 15 October 1996 that he was about to float off News Datacom. The new corporate structure would insulate News Datacom's taxable income in a British holding company while realising more than half a billion dollars of untaxed capital gains. The news galvanised *Mas Hachnasa*, the Israeli tax office. By the evening of Thursday, 17 October, the Israeli chief of intelligence, Daniel Vash, had signed a warrant to search the News Datacom offices and to hold seven News Corp executives, including Rupert Murdoch, for questioning, on suspicion of tax evasion. The warrant was stamped by the President of the Law Court in Jerusalem. The Tax Commissioner, Doron Levy, sat on the warrant through Friday as political arguments raged over whether the warrants should be executed. The green light was given by Friday evening, and tax officers were briefed for a mass raid on the News offices early Sunday morning, immediately after the Israeli Sabbath.

The Israelis know how to mount a raid. Early on Sunday morning, 20

October, they sealed off the block around the News Datacom office building at Har Hotzvim on the outskirts of Jerusalem. At a time when most taxpayers in the western world were still tucked in bed in the sure knowledge that the wheels of the tax man may grind exceeding small but they don't grind on the weekend, 75 Israeli tax inspectors thundered through the News Datacom office in Jerusalem. In simultaneous raids they also hit the News Datacom warehouse in Tel Aviv, the offices of three sets of News Datacom lawyers, and the News Datacom accountants.

It was one of the most widely publicised tax raids in history. Radio, television and print journalists were on hand to record all that happened in loving detail. Newspapers around the world ran pictures of tax officers carrying boxes of documents out of the News building at Har Hotzvim, on the edge of Jerusalem, with claims that News Datacom had not reported $150 million of earnings. The story was helped by the fact that, ever since the mid-1980s, News Corporation accountants, by a number of shrewd but legal financial moves, had made sure that News never paid more than about 10 cents on the dollar in corporate income tax. The accountants had saved News $1 billion in tax payments. Then there was the search warrant itself. Rupert Murdoch's name was on the Israeli document, which meant that he could be held and questioned, but by the time the story was picked up in Britain, the search warrant had somehow (incorrectly) become an *arrest* warrant for the media baron.

Arthur Siskind was called in the early hours of Sunday morning in New York, and Rupert Murdoch in the early afternoon in Sydney, with the news that Israeli tax officers were carting financial records off in trucks. News Corporation executives were furious. 'Mr Clinger has the tiger by the tail,' Siskind said grittily. News denied all claims, protesting loudly that this was a set-up, a piece of mischievous harassment orchestrated by a 'former News Datacom executive' who was already on the run from US authorities. Back in 1992 News Corp might have appeared blasé about Clinger's fugitive status. Now News Corp's view was much clearer: Clinger needed to be behind bars.

Eventually the frenzied media coverage subsided. No further public statements were made. Several weeks later the Israeli tax officers, wading through the mountain of material taken from News Datacom, made a discovery which while very interesting had nothing to do with tax. It would take some weeks more before the Israeli bureaucracy decided what to do with the discovery.

London, 2 February 1997

By February 1997, Audley Sheppard had been a London partner at Clifford Chance, one of the largest law firms in the world, for two years. At 36 years old he was a solidly built, reassuring figure for clients, with a faint New Zealand accent that he had retained through a decade living in Britain. His problem was that, a year into this most bitter of court cases, he still didn't know how much he trusted his client. Trust is not an essential ingredient in the lawyer-client relationship. It becomes an issue only when the lawyer has to go out on a limb for the person he is representing . . . which in Audley Sheppard's case was Michael Clinger.

In taking on the Clinger case, Sheppard had found himself in a surreal landscape. The court filings on Clinger's case in the British High Court read more like something out of a *film noir*, at every turn becoming more and more bizarre as they documented a surreal investigation by News Corporation lawyers and private investigators that took them through the tax havens of the world and into the shadowy corners of the global media group itself. Preliminary hearings at London's Old Bailey had raised claims and counterclaims of death threats, violence and intimidation, suicide attempts, blackmail and doctored evidence. The depth of bad feeling on each side of the case was like nothing Sheppard had ever seen – and the hearing date was still a year away. It wasn't going to get any better. Sheppard had just discovered that someone was tapping his phone. The question on Sunday 2 February 1997 was what should he do with this information.

Ever since God created trial lawyers (a date which most Hebrew scholars site in the Genesis account somewhere between the bits about lords of the earth and every crawling thing), the British justice system has wrestled with the seminal problem of what to do on Sundays. From ten-thirty on Monday mornings, British courts dispense justice without fear or favour, with a dignity and ritual in keeping with their 800-year history. They do this right up until Friday afternoon. If the God-fearing architects who designed the system centuries ago had a fault, it is that they took the commandment to rest on the seventh day a trifle broadly. From four-thirty on Fridays to ten-thirty Monday morning, the British court system goes into recess. During this time it is difficult to do anything more than secure bail on a drunk and disorderly charge. Officially at least, Britain's judges and their associates, the court system's Recorders, its magistrates and administrative staff, its Queen's Counsels, its junior barristers and solicitors, are at rest. And, as Isaac Newton long ago observed, objects at rest like to remain at rest.

Nevertheless, if the case is urgent enough and the lawyer is resolute enough, British justice provides a way to obtain an emergency court order. It means approaching the duty judge rostered for that weekend. There are two rules for young lawyers approaching the High Court duty judge. The first is – don't try it. The second is – if you do, your reasons need to be compelling and dire. On Sunday 2 February 1997, the duty judge for the Chancery Division of the High Court was Justice Evans-Lombe. From the moment on Sunday morning when Evans-Lombe picked up the phone at his home at Marlingford Hall in Norwich and heard the reference to Rupert Murdoch, he knew Audley Sheppard had put him in the hot seat. Sheppard told Evans-Lombe that it looked like someone at News Datacom had been running a major bugging and surveillance operation.

Sheppard asked Evans-Lombe for an immediate order restraining News Corporation and its lawyers from destroying or disposing of any tape recordings, transcripts or other records of telephone conversations between Mr Clinger and his lawyers. Sheppard faxed Evans-Lombe a series of affidavits sworn by Clinger and his Jerusalem lawyer, Michael Kirsch. (Kirsch for most of the previous ten years had been the District Attorney of Jerusalem.) According to the affidavits, Clinger had been called to the offices of Israel's National Serious Crime Unit on 12 January 1997. There he had been shown a series of tapes that he was told had been seized by the Israeli tax inspectors when they raided the News Datacom offices three months before. They had been found in the office of News Datacom's managing director, former IBM vice-president Abe Peled, in his office safe.

The tapes found in Peled's office contained recordings of an extensive series of bugged telephone conversations between Clinger and his lawyers, and appeared to be the product of a major illegal telephone-tapping operation. Clinger had apparently listened to recordings of 15 telephone conversations involving himself on a tape marked 23A. Five of these conversations, which had taken place around late September 1996, were with his lawyers at Clifford Chance. Others involved Clinger and his American attorneys. Kirsch later heard the same tapes and verified a rough transcript Clinger had made of his taped conversations. The Jerusalem District Attorney confirmed to Sheppard in London that Sheppard's voice was on tapes found in the News Datacom office.

It wasn't just Clinger and his lawyers whose conversations had been recorded. Other tapes, it would emerge, included conversations between Israeli tax officers talking about their News Corporation investigation, and telephone calls from Israeli journalists. Within days, the Israeli media would report police raids on several private-investigation firms employed by News

Corporation including an outfit called Shaffron, run by Reuven Hazak, the former deputy head of Israel's security agency, Shin Bet. Under questioning later by the National Serious Crime Unit, both Abe Peled and Hazak would deny knowledge of any tapes. Charges relating to earlier wiretapping were later laid against Clinger's former friend, Leo Krieger.

Clinger's lawyers were undecided about what to do with this information when they received it in mid-January 1997. However, on Thursday, 30 January, Clinger had been called back to the offices of the National Serious Crime Unit. While there he said he was shown a fax apparently addressed to a News Corp executive and an adviser, also found in Peled's office in the tax raid. The fax contained a transcript of one of Clinger's conversations with Sheppard.

Clinger's evidence of the fax lifted the matter into a different league. It wasn't the job of the High Court to look at bugging allegations in overseas countries. But a breach of legal privilege – the confidentiality of private communications between Clinger and his British lawyers – was a different matter. Initially it appeared that unnamed private agents employed by News Corporation might have gone beyond their brief. But copies of transcripts in the hands of senior News lawyers and executives indicated something more than a rogue operation out of control. It suggested an organised strategy. If true, it raised the possibility that information that had been illegally obtained by its agents had reached senior levels at News. Was there a risk that this was part of a pattern of illegal activity coordinated at the highest levels of News Corporation?

The bugging allegations were dynamite. But were they true? All hell would break loose when the court papers were served on News Corporation and Allen & Overy the next day. In angry court scenes the News lawyers would argue flatly that the tapes did not exist; and that if they did, then Clinger was the wiretapper. Peled, and those allegedly named on Clinger's fax all signed affidavits denying any knowledge of the tapes. In response to a query, Arthur Siskind's assistant, Eugenie Gavenchak responded:

> If any tape recordings of any conversations do exist, it is clear to us that Mr Clinger was responsible for making them. If any tapes were indeed found within our company's offices, they were planted there. Mr Clinger has failed to produce any evidence of this purported fax, other than his own word, the trustworthiness of which needs no comment.

Justice Evans-Lombe was troubled by the scope of the allegations on that Sunday. Would senior lawyers really be a party to actions of this sort? It seemed improbable. As a witness, Clinger had little claim to credibility. In relation to other testimony the regular case judge, Justice Lindsay, would later describe Clinger as a skilled liar. But the existence and illegal content of the tapes – found in the chief executive's office in a company whose business is all about secrecy and tight security – had been attested to by Sheppard in London, by the current Jerusalem District Attorney, and by Clinger's Israeli lawyer, Michael Kirsch, the former Jerusalem District Attorney. What was unsupported was Clinger's claim about seeing the fax, which connected the tapes to the News lawyers. Unless he could produce the fax, this claim would be discounted. At the same time, News Corporation had its own questions to answer. Clinger was a fraud and a charlatan, but what did that say about News Corporation, his former employer, or the way it dealt with its business opponents? From 1990 to the end of 1991, Clinger had run an important arm of News Corp's business, representing News before regulators and senior government officials around the world, *while he was on the run*. Knowingly or not, News Corp employed a fugitive.

The role of weekend duty judge does not extend to making final judgments. Evans-Lombe signed the interim orders Sheppard sought, passing on the job of sorting through the allegations to Justice Lindsay, the judge presiding over the case.

CHAPTER TEN

THE POKER PLAYER

New York/Denver, 2–24 February 1997

For a crisis junkie like Rupert Murdoch, there is something inspiring about New York, which evokes some of his most brilliant pieces of damage control – intuitive counterpunches that sometimes provide him with a solution before he's even aware he has a problem. In New York, Murdoch can be anything and anyone that he wants to be. And on Sunday, 2 February 1997, Rupert Murdoch was a Jewish-American hero.

In the previous days, as Audley Sheppard was planning the application he would make to Justice Evans-Lombe in London, Murdoch had been the guest of honour of the King David Society, the big-money patrons group for the United Jewish Appeal. Murdoch had been presented with two scrolls of Jewish scripture in recognition of his recent philanthropic efforts. These must have been substantial, as the basic requirement for the lowliest society member is a $25,000 minimum contribution to the United Jewish Appeal each year. The night was just the beginning of honours for Murdoch the philanthropist. The big news of the evening was that in three months' time, the United Jewish Appeal would name Murdoch Humanitarian of the Year. The presentation on 29 May would consist of a gala dinner at the Waldorf-Astoria, where he would again be guest of honour, a night of tributes that would climax in a personal eulogy from Israeli Prime Minister, Benjamin Netanyahu. The honour was a tribute not just to the lobbying efforts of Murdoch's New York lawyer, Howard Squadron, a former United Jewish Appeal president, and News senior vice president Eric Breindel (a leading figure in the United Jewish Appeal's Entertainment and Music Industries division), after News Corporation's

Jerusalem tax débâcle the previous October; but also to his own genuine admiration for the Israeli spirit and an untiring campaign by Murdoch since the 1970s to draw close to the Jewish community.

Murdoch himself attributed the bestowing of honours to outrage in the Jewish community over his brawl with Ted Turner in October 1996 over Fox News, when Turner compared Murdoch to Hitler. He told William Shawcross in 1999: 'They were so outraged that they gave me a great dinner, with Henry Kissinger making me Humanitarian of the Year, purely to stick their finger in Ted Turner's eye.' What would have been almost as satisfying was that Sumner Redstone, the crusty head of Viacom, who four months before had been planning to sue Murdoch in one of the minor turf wars that the media business throws up, would be United Jewish Appeal chairman for the occasion. The invitations to Murdoch's big night would be sent out under Redstone's name.

Murdoch would not learn of Clinger's allegations, or the interim orders by Justice Evans-Lombe in London, until Monday 3 February, when Sheppard served the papers on the News Corp lawyers. However, it is unlikely that Murdoch would have spent a great deal of Sunday thinking about his Israeli problems if he had known. Armed with the United Jewish Appeal honour and the personal involvement of the Israeli Prime Minister, Murdoch had the perfect counter to anything that Michael Clinger could throw at him in Israel.

The problem that Clinger posed was closer to home, in the greater drama that was gripping Murdoch and his media empire in the US. For no matter how great a media organisation's reach or power, no matter how many countries or deals in which it is involved, it remains intensely vulnerable in one area: public confidence. This is not merely a matter of maintaining the confidence of its bankers – though even here News was struggling. It is also a question of probity. Broadcasting licences around the world are granted on the basis that regulatory authorities believe a media group is fit and proper to be entrusted with such a licence. It is a position of public trust. Any accusation that it is involved in illegal activities such as Michael Clinger had just alleged in the High Court in London, even if it is baseless, poses a threat to the group's future.

For Murdoch on that first weekend in February, Israel and the United Jewish Appeal and everything else on the empire's agenda was just a sideshow. Because Murdoch was at that moment involved in the ultimate high-altitude property deal. And the issue which had his complete attention was the problem of how to pay for it. Rupert Murdoch had 22 days to find $4 billion. Whatever else he did, by 24 February he needed to have the money or else have a great story about how he was going to get the money.

Back in the 1970s, the pioneers of cable television were stringing wire along telephone poles, in hock to their ears to connect up another street, another suburb, another town. Even as the cable networks inched slowly outward, another breed of entrepreneur was looking at the sky and dreaming bigger dreams. A cable company could provide subscription television for a town, for a region, for a state. But if you put a satellite up in the sky, you could broadcast to all of America. As a dream, it was all the more appealing because it was hopelessly impractical. The two movements – the cable pioneers and the satellite dreamers – produced two minor but significant waves of migration west.

In 1972 an executive at General Instrument Corporation, John Malone, packed up his family and moved from Connecticut to Denver to head up a struggling cable outfit called Tele-Communications Inc for a cable entrepreneur called Bob Magness. Denver was a natural draw for cable operators because the mountainous terrain on the east of the Rockies made television reception difficult. Tele-Communications Inc had such chronic debt problems that for years Magness and Malone made sure their offices always had a back door, to evade overzealous creditors.

By 1990 John Malone and Tele-Communications Inc decided what went into the television sets of one in four US cable households and more than half of Britain's cable households – and what didn't. Malone's power didn't just rest upon his personal wealth and Tele-Communications Inc's global reach. In three decades he had shown a remarkable ability to make the strategic play, to out-think his rivals, to be always one step ahead of the main game. He was the guy with his feet on the ground, the big man with the crooked grin who always looked like he was on the verge of doing something downright tricky. Malone's unfailing acumen was one of the certainties of life.

If Rupert Murdoch has ever had a friend in the business world, it is John Malone. The two men would like each other if only they could afford to. Their relationship is based as much on deep distrust as it is on mutual respect. The pair are similar in many ways. Both are risk-takers, pioneers, over-achievers. Both have worked up a worldwide media empire out of a minor provincial operation.

Malone, like Murdoch, knows the disappointments in store for anyone who bets their future too heavily on technology. It was Malone in 1992 who promised 500 channels to his cable subscribers. Five years later 500 channels seemed as far away as ever. Malone's hardware supplier General Instruments and its subsidiary Jerrard Electronics were struggling with huge technical hurdles to produce a set-top box for the new digital universe.

In 1980 another executive packed up his possessions and headed west. A colourful, knockabout character with an intermittent Tennessee drawl, Charles W. Ergen was once thrown off the Las Vegas Strip for card counting. He cultivated the down-home image, a colleague once saying of him 'I don't think I've ever seen Charlie with a suit and tie. He wears sweaters and button-down collar shirts and Nikes. That's Charlie.' Stories about Ergen centre on his skills at blackjack and poker rather than his Ivy League education or his work in Dallas as a financial analyst for snack-food group Frito-Lay, Inc.

The story goes that at some time during a poker game in 1980, Ergen formed the resolve to follow a long-held dream about getting into satellites. It had had its roots (or so he would later tell the story) on the night of 4 October 1957, when as a four-year-old he stood beside his father near their home in Oak Ridge, Tennessee, and watched the world's first satellite, *Sputnik 1*, streak across the sky, orbiting the earth every 96 minutes.

In 1980 he and his wife and business partner, Cantey, packed up, and together with another poker buddy, James DeFranco, headed west to sell satellite dishes. Ergen was 27. The three partners had $50,000. They went to Denver and opened a shop because they figured, like the cable guys before them, that the mountainous terrain east of the Rockies made television reception difficult. In addition, cable would only service larger communities.

To pick up broadcasts from the low-power satellites in operation in 1980 you needed a satellite dish that cost $30,000 and was ten feet across, turning your roofline into what looked like a deep-space research project. The effect was even more compelling of you lived in an apartment. 'We honestly believed people would line up to buy them,' Ergen said. Nobody did. Undeterred, Ergen and DeFranco packed a satellite dish on a trailer and headed for Aspen. No one was buying in Aspen either, but two people stopped them on the way to order a dish. Ergen and DeFranco were down to their last $5,000 and were delivering one of the only two satellite dishes they had when disaster struck. 'A gust of wind came along and flipped the dish over,' Ergen said later. 'It was destroyed.' It was only the successful sale of the last remaining dish that kept the business solvent.

As satellite dishes came down in price and size, Ergen turned to making them himself. By the late 1980s, he had a $200 million international business and had made and sold almost a third of the million satellite dishes in the United States. Originally Ergen's company was called Ecosphere, but he changed it to Echostar Communications.

In 1983 Ergen heard about a new sort of high-power satellite broadcasting called Ku-band, which could be picked up with a satellite dish only fifteen to eighteen inches across. Ergen believed Direct Broadcast Satellite (DBS), as the new system was called, would be a huge money machine. He began acquiring DBS transponder frequencies – even as John Malone was jeering that DBS stood for Don't Be Stupid.

'In Monopoly, the player who usually wins is the person who buys the most deeds,' Ergen said. 'We have more spectrum than any other DBS provider.'

In 1992 Ergen began ordering satellites.

High-power Ku-band satellites pump out so much power that to prevent interference with each other, international convention requires that they be kept at least nine degrees of longitude apart. At ground level in the United States this is about 350 miles. In space it works out to a minimum of 2,000 miles of separation. What this means is that there are a limited number of satellite slots that can cover all of the continental United States – known as CONUS slots. Too far east or west, and the curvature of the Earth blocks off part of the country from the line of sight that the satellite needs for its broadcasts. This is important, because if you spend half a billion dollars putting up satellites, it is a bit dismaying to find that half your audience can't see you. If you want a chance at getting your money back on the investment, you need to reach as many people as you can. After parcelling out the various orbital slots and frequencies with Canada and Mexico in the 1980s, the high-power Ku-band slots above the United States reduced to just three.

If you take a map of the United States and draw a line from 100 miles east of Phoenix, Arizona, running north to the eastern edge of Yellowstone National Park, and on into Canada, passing east of Medicine Hat, you will have a rough marker for the line that geographers calls 110 degrees west longitude. For the most part it is rugged country, marked with tight elevation contour lines that mapmakers use to denote extremely mountainous terrain. There are a lot of cable customers on 110WL. Besides 110WL the Ku-band slots were 101WL (350 miles to the east), and 119WL (350 miles to the west). Each slot carries the right to broadcast over 32 transponder frequencies. So there are 96 frequencies in total. If you want to run a big US satellite television operation, these are the slots you have to have.

The thing about geostationary real estate is that it obeys the rules of property investment everywhere. It begins and ends with position. You pay for the view, and you pay to make sure your view can't be spoiled by developers (or in this case by a high-power satellite parked next door drowning out your signal). And you still know that, at the end of the day, the government can make or break your fortune with a re-zoning or licensing decision. This was the sad lament of Daniel H. Garner.

Garner was an Arkansas entrepreneur who picked up the rights to the prime 110WL satellite slot for nothing in the 1980s. In 1994 he was all set to make a killing by selling the licence to John Malone, who was in a partnership of other cable operators with a satellite service called Primestar. However, on 28 April 1995, before the deal was consummated, the Federal Communication Commission took Garner's satellite licence back because he hadn't done anything with it. The announcement went largely unnoticed: media interest at the time was focused on the Federal Communication Commission inquiry into foreign ownership of Murdoch's Fox network, which was due to report within days.

The loss of Garner's satellite licence was a major problem for John Malone and Primestar. Malone had already ordered two satellites for the 110WL slot, which he had graciously allowed his partners to pay for. Now he had two satellites worth half a billion dollars and nowhere to put them. Resting between engagements, as they say in the entertainment business.

It was a bit more than bad luck. MCI, the long-distance telephone group, had lobbied the Federal Communication Commission heavily to revoke Garner's licence. On 10 May 1995, twelve days after the Federal Communication Commission moved on Garner, MCI chief executive Bert Roberts announced a $2 billion strategic partnership with Rupert Murdoch. On 4 May the Federal Communication Commission had found Murdoch's Fox television group was in breach of the foreign ownership restrictions, but granted Fox a waiver to these. The news of Murdoch's MCI alliance produced stunned silence at a cable convention in Dallas that day. John Malone would not speak with reporters, instead pulling into a tight huddle with his executives in the middle of the room. When he emerged Malone looked visibly shaken. 'I'm not worried about Bert Roberts, but Rupert scares the hell out of me,' Malone said. 'He's my partner, incidentally.'

The cable operators suspected that Murdoch had been calling the shots in MCI's strike against Garner. Remarkably, at the very time when Murdoch's whole future in America was under threat from the Federal Communication Commission's inquiry into the foreign ownership of Fox, he had stage-managed a stunning counter-strike against the cable industry.

In late 1995 the Federal Communication Commission solved the problem of what to do with Garner's satellite licence by announcing that it would auction off 28 of the 32 transponder frequencies at 110WL. The new licence carried the right to hang a string of high-power satellites in geostationary orbit 22,300 miles above the line on the map that is 110WL. With digital technology, each transponder could broadcast eight to ten channels of crystal-clear television to a pizza-sized satellite dish on top of any home in America. Whoever ended up with the 110WL slot could launch a Direct Broadcast Satellite television service with 280 channels.

So the fate of this key piece of America's media future was decided in the drab Federal Communication Commission auction offices on Massachusetts Avenue in Washington on a cold day in January 1996. The two major bidders were John Malone who through his Tele-Communications Inc Technology Ventures was bidding on behalf of Primestar; and Murdoch. The actual bidder would be MCI, but in the News/MCI relationship, MCI was just the money. Charlie Ergen was also a bidder. Ergen had picked up a lot of spectrum over the years, including FCC licences for 21 of the 32 frequencies at 119WL, and one frequency at 110WL. In December 1995 he had put all his hopes on a Lockheed Martin satellite loaded on top of a Chinese Long March 2E rocket – the launch vehicle with the best track record for exploding and killing ground crew. 'I was pretty confident but still counting the fingers and toes and breathing a sigh of relief when it went off,' he said.

Ergen was set to launch Echostar's Dish Network with the new satellite on 3 March, five weeks after the auction. He came to Washington with Echostar director Jim DeFranco, his old poker-game buddy. Ergen and DeFranco had no backers and not much money, two outsiders who had made it to the big table. 'Both of us felt we'd been training our whole lives to be in a big poker game with people like Rupert Murdoch and John Malone,' Ergen said later.

MCI lodged its opening bid of $125 million at 9.36 a.m. on Thursday, 24 January. Eleven minutes later, TCI topped it with a bid of $201 million. The bidding continued through the morning, a silent affair with bidding teams in separate rooms, lodging bids electronically or using waivers to sit out a half-hour round. Just after lunch TCI made its last bid, at $297.7 million. By 3 p.m. TCI had run out of waivers and was officially out of the auction. 'We weren't going to bid just anything,' said TCI senior vice president David Beddow. MCI had the bid at $332 million. Now there was just Echostar still bidding.

Charlie Ergen was a stayer. Throughout the day he had kept coming back with aggressive calls. At 3.48 p.m. MCI went for the big hit. It lifted the bidding more than $100 million to $450 million. It looked like a killer bid. Ergen exercised a waiver and made no counter-offer in the next round. Such a sum seemed way beyond his financial reach, and the auction looked like it was all over. It was 4.30 p.m. Mercifully, proceedings were adjourned until the next day. Ergen and DeFranco had a night to stew over their next move before they were expected to throw in the towel.

At 9.02 the next morning, Ergen came back at MCI with a higher bid. And he kept on bidding. For the executives in the MCI bidding room looking at their electronic screens, working the cell phones for instructions from Bert Roberts and Rupert Murdoch, the auction had become a nightmare. MCI and News desperately wanted to get into the US satellite business. But just how high would the two crazy men in the other bidding room go? Who was really behind them? Or were they just bluffing? '[Ergen] is a smart guy. If he's bidding this high, he has someone else's money behind him. Echostar just doesn't have the resources,' DBS consultant Michael Alpert had said the previous night, before the bidding had reached stratospheric levels.

Was Ergen bluffing? In some ways, this question is a little like asking a poker player who has just stared down his opponent what his cards were. Ergen himself denies any suggestion of bluffing. He said later that he had always intended to bid up to $650 million, but no further. He didn't have someone behind him, but he figured that he had nothing to lose. If he won the auction, unlike his opponents he had a satellite ready to launch straight into the slot – though it is hard to see how Echostar could have paid for the licence and not gone broke. If Ergen lost, he would still cost his opposition a bucketload of money. 'DeFranco and I, from playing poker, had learned the discipline of not being emotional about what your cards are,' he said.

It was only when MCI took its bid to $682.5 million just after 11 a.m. that Ergen folded. He had lost the fight. But he had forced MCI and Murdoch to pay an astonishing price for the licence.

After lunch, Ergen and MCI resumed hostilities over another, less desirable slot, at 148WL. In another day and a half of torrid bidding, MCI forced Ergen from his opening bid of $101,888 all the way up to $52.3 million before MCI folded. Ergen wasn't worried. His stock price jumped 27 per cent – unlike MCI stock, which slumped. MCI's winning bid was all the more remarkable, because News Corp and MCI would be starting so far behind their competitors. DirecTV, a subsidiary of General Motors, had launched the first DBS service in March 1994, and already had 1.8 million subscribers. Four other DBS services had followed DirecTV – US

Satellite Broadcasting, Primestar (which upgraded its existing analogue system to digital), Echostar's DISH network, and Alphastar.

'There is no business model that anyone has seen to spend that much money with three years getting to market and still make a profit,' Bob Schermar, publisher of *Satellite Business News*, said on the Thursday night, when MCI's bid was just $450 million. One of the only people who liked the deal was Charlie Ergen. 'The price MCI paid was a bargain, it's a very valuable spectrum,' he said.

In starting a new DBS operation to be called AskyB, MCI and News Corp would be taking on well entrenched rivals who had picked up their own FCC licences for next to nothing. It would be two years and another $600 million before MCI and News could get satellites into orbit and begin their new DBS service, up to four years behind their competitors. MCI had paid a deposit on the licence price immediately after the auction.

On 6 December 1996, after being held up by various appeals, the Federal Communication Commission announced that the 110WL licence was ready to grant. This meant that MCI now had a week to pay up the balance. So it was particularly unfortunate that in November Roberts had announced that MCI was pulling out of the partnership and was no longer prepared to provide the $4 billion funding that Murdoch needed.

In hindsight, the breakdown of the relationship between Bert Roberts and Rupert Murdoch looks like pure carelessness. The Federal Communication Commission auction débâcle had planted the seeds of disenchantment for Roberts, but it was a series of highhanded moves by Murdoch that had finally soured the alliance.

MCI's withdrawal announcement knocked the News Corp share price, and the stock continued sliding. The mood among investors was that if God had wanted people to go into space, he would have given them more money. They were worried that ASkyB would become a financial black hole. Its satellites wouldn't be in operation until 1998 and it was unclear how Murdoch was going to pay for it all. Murdoch was already involved in satellite start-ups in Japan, Mexico and Argentina, and his Star TV satellite operation in Hong Kong was still losing steadily. He had spent $500 million launching his Fox News cable channel in October. Now there was the ASkyB problem. Financially Murdoch was more exposed than he had been since his debt crisis six years before. It wasn't life-threatening yet, but negative sentiment for a stock can grown quickly.

It wasn't just investors who were concerned. Credit agencies were worried as well. The Federal Communication Commission formally granted the 110WL licence on 20 December 1996. Three days later,

Standard & Poor's announced that it was putting News Corp on negative credit watch. If News Corp lost its BBB credit rating, News debt and stock would no longer be investment grade, they would be junk bonds. News Corp carried $9 billion of investment-grade debt. Keeping that investment status was a condition of the loans and losing it would actually put much of the debt into default. It was the nightmare scenario: Murdoch could be facing an instant debt crisis.

Mere mortals and minor media executives flinch at prospects like this. But Murdoch knew all about debt crises. He had been down this road before. So he knew what the solution was. He needed to call a meeting. Two days before the Federal Communication Commission announcement on 6 December that the 110WL licence was ready to grant, 300 fund managers, media analysts and bankers around the world had begun receiving invitations to a special investment conference. Murdoch would host the conference on a sound stage at the Twentieth Century Fox studios in Los Angeles on 24 February 1997. More than twenty News Corp executives would brief analysts and bankers on all aspects of the company and its many ventures, and in particular explain the group's US satellite strategy. If analysts would only be patient, all would be revealed. News had never before done anything so elaborate. The major effect of announcing the conference was that it bought Murdoch some time. It meant that he had three months to come up with another deep pocket to pay for ASkyB.

Murdoch tried his darnedest to do just that. He approached his satellite rivals, he talked with the telephone companies, he explored an Initial Public Offering to float 30 per cent of ASkyB to the American public. Nothing worked. '[Murdoch] extracts so much blood that it's going to be very difficult for anybody to cut a deal with him that makes any sense,' one telephone company executive complained.

No one was buying. In the US winter of 1996–97, the entire entertainment industry was toast. In the middle of the biggest share boom in history, Wall Street was sick of the entertainment industry's high promises, huge debt levels, and low profits. The growth rate of people subscribing to DBS services was falling, and the cable industry was in retreat. John Malone had frozen TCI's rollout of fibre-optic cable. 'Our big capital spending days as a cable company are over,' Malone told a Bear, Stearns conference in October, before cutting 2,500 jobs at TCI. Time Warner chairman Gerry Levin had announced that Time Inc would sell off parts of its cable network because of cable's high capital demands. Time Warner's long-term debt already stood at $17.5 billion. Across the country, after three turbulent years, media mergers were off the agenda. 'The fever has broken,' one investment banker said.

By 2 February 1997, Murdoch had just 22 days to sort out his satellite problems before he fronted with analysts on 24 February. If he didn't have a credible strategy for ASkyB by then, the exodus by investors from his stock would be a stampede and he would have to write off many of his current ambitious plans. But Murdoch had one last card to play. There was one person in the industry who needed money even more than Murdoch did: his old nemesis, Charlie Ergen, whose Dish network was now the third largest DBS operator. Ergen's money problems were growing bigger and bigger with each passing day. Murdoch might finally be able to cut a deal with him. Murdoch's own financial worries were all about confidence. If Murdoch could unveil an alliance with Charlie Ergen, he wouldn't have any more money, but he would have a great story to sell to the analysts.

The timing was tight. So from the moment that Audley Sheppard's High Court injunction landed on Murdoch's London lawyers on Monday, 3 February, Murdoch knew he had only days to kick this messy Israeli wire-tapping affair out of existence. The scale of what he was about to attempt was too great, the negotiations he would be undertaking too sensitive, to be distracted by ugly unproven court allegations that News had been bugging business opponents and foreign governments.

Murdoch already had a containment strategy working in Israel. In mid-January, Israeli police had requested an interview with Abe Peled, the head of News Datacom, in whose office the tapes had been found. News Datacom told the Israeli Serious Crime Squad that Peled's duties abroad would keep him from returning to Israel until March. The unavailability of the chief witness would put the Israeli police investigation on hold through February.

Meanwhile in London, Murdoch's lawyers launched a ferocious attack on Michael Clinger before Justice Lindsay, the regular High Court judge assigned to the case. They challenged Clinger to produce details to support his phone-tapping allegations, including the damning fax he claimed to have seen in the National Serious Crime Unit office. Clinger was not able to do so. He said it was in police hands. On 10 February, the High Court suspended any further hearings on the matter until the trial, accepting the News lawyers' assurances that they knew nothing of any bugging.

'It seems to me that the proper approach is to treat the plaintiffs' answer on affidavit that there is no privileged information that has come to or is in their hands as conclusive,' Justice Lindsay found. He did extend the injunction on the News Corporation companies, but reduced this to an undertaking in the case of the News lawyers that any such material, if located, would be presented to the court. The judgment was never reported in Britain. In London, bugging was a dead letter.

Within hours of Justice Lindsay's judgment on 10 February, Murdoch had telephoned Charlie Ergen at Echostar's headquarters in Denver, to arrange a crash meeting. Three days later, on Thursday, 13 February, Murdoch flew into Denver with a team of News executives to meet Ergen. Murdoch's great American gamble had begun. Murdoch was days away from the worst – and the best – business decision of his life.

It was an interesting pairing in the Echostar offices. On one side of the table was Charlie Ergen, 44 years old, determinedly casual. Opposite him was Rupert Murdoch, the man never seen in public without a white shirt and tie. For all of his career, Charlie Ergen had done things his way. Like Murdoch he was a gambler, he challenged conventional wisdom, he had regularly put the future of his company on the line, he ran his company like a personal fief. He ran to win. In another lifetime Ergen and Murdoch could even have been friends. But in decades of wheeling and dealing, Rupert Murdoch had never been known to forget a wrong. He took losing money very, very personally. The thing which would always niggle below the surface of any relationship between the pair was that at the auction for 110WL spectrum twelve months before, Ergen's poker skills had cost Murdoch $350 million – the difference between TCI's last bid and what Ergen had pushed MCI up to. Ergen's bidding had crippled the MCI/News partnership. Murdoch would remember that for a long time.

So it was a measure of Rupert Murdoch's situation, and his supreme ability to do whatever he needed to do to survive, that this meeting in Denver a year later was even taking place, that he was sitting down with this man who had been the cause of so many of his problems. With him were Chase Carey, who had recently been named co-chief operating officer of News Corporation, who still ran the Fox television network; Preston Padden, a former Washington lobbyist who was head of ASkyB, whose work corralling the Fox television affiliates had won him a tough reputation; and News Corp counsel Arthur Siskind.

On the other side of the table were Ergen, Echostar's legal counsel David Moskowitz, and Echostar executive vice-president Carl Vogel. Vogel was given much of the credit by analysts for turning Echostar into a bankable proposition. Vogel had taken a big risk three years before to leave his position as president of programming at Jones Intercable in Denver to join a shaky satellite start-up. 'Some people thought I had taken leave of my senses,' Vogel said later.

Each side needed to calculate how desperate the people on the other side of the room were. The Echostar team knew Murdoch had a problem with ASkyB, but didn't realise how poisonous the relationship between Murdoch and his partner, MCI, had become. On the financial side, News Corporation's accounting disguised the size of Murdoch's gambles. A week before News Corp had reported a $350 million net profit for the last six months, under Australian accounting, on the way to a healthy 1997 profit. Under US accounting, however, the return for the full year was three quarters of a billion dollars less than Murdoch had reported, and News was losing money.

Echostar's situation was even more precarious. The Dish network had 430,000 subscribers, but it was burning up $5 million a week. Its liabilities were already $70 million more than its assets, and Ergen needed to find another $200 million quickly to pay for his next two satellites. If Ergen didn't find more money by June, Echostar would hit the wall.

Echostar needed Murdoch. But corporate deal-making is never just about deals. Something much more personal was at stake here. For Murdoch, winning Echostar was about winning over Charlie Ergen. Murdoch told Ergen that he shared his vision, and wanted to join him. Previously talks between Ergen and Murdoch had been about buying Ergen out. Now Murdoch was talking partnership, a meeting of equals, and bringing his legendary powers of persuasion to bear.

'Charlie, you remind me of myself when I was younger,' Murdoch told Ergen over dinner.

'The personal chemistry with Rupert is very positive,' Ergen would say days later. 'We've known each other for quite a while now, and I have followed Sky's progress in Britain very closely . . . We matched up personally, we are both individuals who have attacked monopolies and oligopolies.'

In formal meetings, over the telephone, and at Ergen's home, the two principals talked about their shared frustrations with the cable industry, their career experiences, Ergen's precarious early days and Murdoch's own close encounters with penury, including his debt crisis at the end of 1990. Like everyone else in the world, Ergen had heard the story about how a bank in Pittsburgh had almost sent Murdoch to the wall over a $10 million loan.

'[He was] one little bank away, and we watched it all, and one of the conversations that Rupert and I had was that it makes more sense to do something today when we are both financially sound than when we are laying on the ground bleeding,' Ergen said.

Beyond the pleasantries there was the sales pitch. This meeting was about a merger. Preston Padden had a little survey of 1,200 cable customers that he would present 11 days later at the News Corp's analysts' conference. The survey showed that 52 per cent of cable customers, offered the service which Echostar and ASkyB together would be able to provide, said they would immediately cancel cable and switch to Sky, as the new service would be called. Sky would own seven satellites and 49 of the 96 CONUS transponder frequencies. Echostar already offered its customers 120 channels. Sky would offer America 500 DBS television channels of crystal clarity, including for the first time local channels and video on demand.

Ergen would say later:

Our competition isn't so much the other guys in this industry – it's the cable guys who have 65 million people paying for TV today with old analog cable, monopolistic, high-priced, archaic systems.

It costs me $5 per person to send signals to everyone in the whole United States. The cost for cable companies to rewire digitally is $600 per home, and they must pass every house in a neighbourhood even if the residents aren't customers.

Sky's edge was that, with so many satellites and television channels, Sky could give customers most of their local free-to-air television stations in the same package. DBS customers would not have to have one system for satellite and another antenna linked up for local stations. At long last, like cable, DBS would be able to offer it all in one system.

Before Sky could do this, however, the US Congress would need to change the law to enable satellites to retransmit local broadcasts – and this would be the tricky part. But Murdoch and Ergen both believed that Congress could be persuaded. The market penetration would be huge. Under the News business plan, Sky would lose $500 million in its first year, but would break even in 1999 with three million subscribers. By 2002 Sky would be generating $1.2 billion in operating profits. By 2005, subscriber numbers were expected to pass 15 million.

At some point during the series of talks he had with Murdoch Charlie Ergen became a true believer. He said later:

News Corp made sense as a strategic partner because they brought things other people couldn't – satellite capacity, programming content, worldwide expertise. They know more about DBS than anybody, and they brought capital. We made sense because we got them in the marketplace today, as opposed to a year from now. It's certainly an equal partnership, and it's certainly complementary.

There was a little friction on technology. Murdoch wanted the merged venture to use the smart card encryption developed by News Datacom and News Digital Systems (which had been renamed NDS after the unpleasant publicity of the Israeli tax raid in October). Ergen had made his fortune making satellite equipment and had his own Swiss encryption technology, which he believed was better and which he wanted to keep. No mention was made of the bugging allegations in the British High Court, or the investigation by the Israeli Serious Crime Unit.

There are usually two danger points in any merger negotiations: the first is agreeing on the money. With Sky the money was fixed up. Echostar stock was at $15, and News and MCI would buy half the company for $1.2 billion at $25 and pump in $200 million cash by May. But a real deal-breaker can also be the floor plan. No matter how exciting the concept, or how appealing the deal is, there comes a moment when each member of any negotiating team sits back and begins to wonder what their role will be in the bigger, better enterprise. After the merger happens, where are they going to *sit*? In the new head office, who is going to end up without a chair?

Ergen insisted that he retain control of the new entity. He wanted to run Sky and to retain Echostar management, or the deal was off. Murdoch didn't like it, and said he would think about it. He flew back to Los Angeles, but called Ergen back a couple of days later. They agreed that Murdoch would be chairman of Sky, Ergen would be president and Chief Executive Officer. News Corp would appoint Sky's Chief Financial Officer.

Murdoch then added a condition of his own. This thing had to be a done deal by Monday 24 February, in time to present it to the analysts and fund managers at the News Corp conference at Twentieth Century Fox. Ergen's merchant bankers told him this was madness – there was no time for a full-scale contract, and announcing a deal with News would cut off any other possible funding lifeline for Echostar. Committing to Sky without a full contract would leave Ergen out of money and completely in Murdoch's power if Ergen's fellow visionary decided to renegotiate the deal. Ergen overruled his advisers and put all of his chips on Murdoch.

A binding letter agreement was drawn up and signed on Thursday, 20 February. Ergen agreed to use the NDS encryption technology under strict conditions. Under the letter agreement, News and Echostar executives were to complete their due diligence checks on each other by 7 March. Despite the critical importance that News attached to the News Datacom technology in this deal, Echostar and its due-diligence committee were not told of the Israeli inquiry into News Datacom, nor of the police interest in its chief executive. During the due diligence period, News Datacom chief Abe Peled would be interviewed by Israeli police on 2 March after a formal caution that he was suspected of wiretapping, but Echostar was not informed.

Show Time, 24 February 1997

Late in the afternoon of Monday, 24 February, four days after the letter agreement between Fox and Echostar had been signed, analysts in the final session of the News conference in Los Angeles were probably thinking about catching return flights. It was then that Murdoch and Ergen stood up and shocked their audience of 300 with news of their Sky deal.

'Our goal is not to be complementary to cable,' said Charlie Ergen at the press conference afterwards, 'We want to *eliminate* cable.'

'Four years ago the cable industry promised 500 channels, and it's Sky that will deliver on the promise,' Echostar's Carl Vogel said as he stood beside Ergen.

'At that point, the cable guys will be calling for Dr Kevorkian,' said Preston Padden, renamed head of global satellite operations for News.

The cable operators immediately rechristened the Sky venture 'Deathstar' but would not share Padden's enthusiasm for euthanasia.

Murdoch raised a laugh with a not very cryptic reference to his flight with Ted Turner to get Time Warner to carry Fox News in New York. Sky was all about 'access to, not control of, distribution outlets – we never want to be beholden to greedy gatekeepers,' he said.

Ergen fended off questions about how the deal was put together. 'Rupert may have known about the deal two weeks ago, but I only found out about it a day or so ago,' he told News Corp journalists, a little disingenuously.

The most aggressive comments came from Preston Padden, the head of satellite operations at News Corp. In the past, critics who disliked his abrasive style had described him as Rupert Murdoch's attack dog. 'Our goal is to come to market with a television product so superior, and a consumer proposition so compelling, that a substantial number of 70 million households stop writing their cheques to their current service – usually cable – and start writing them to Sky,' Padden told the audience. Afterwards, it was Padden's speech that those in the audience remembered best, and the cable industry hated most.

'The presentation of the deal (by Padden) was the most egregiously stupid presentation by a corporate executive that I've ever seen,' said Gordon Crawford, senior vice president of Capital Research and Management Co. 'I went up to Rupert afterward and told him that talk was going to cost him a lot. I don't think he realised that the cable industry is this small club of individuals whose net worth is tied up in their companies, and how pissed they would be.'

Murdoch laughed and conceded Padden had gone too far, though he himself had been beating the same drum. 'We're aiming for the big cable market, 65 million homes,' Murdoch told journalists. 'We expect to have a good 50 per cent of all new satellite customers from here on.'

Once again the cable industry was stunned. Within hours they had nicknamed the Sky merger 'Deathstar'. The prices of cables stocks dived. An industry trade weekly, *Multichannel News*, ran a cartoon of a small cable operator considering two options on a blackboard: 'Plan A: Hope Murdoch's plans to air local broadcast signals on Sky aren't realised. Plan B: Build altar; say prayers.' Here was the man who had miraculously smuggled Dan Garner's satellite slot away from the cable operators, who had gouged them on fees to run his f/X channel, who had started a fourth television network from scratch when no one had believed it was possible, who had built the biggest satellite operation in the world, now openly promising to drive them out of business.

John Malone was one of the first to tell Murdoch just how foolish he had been. Malone had known about the Sky merger before it was made because he and Murdoch had held another of their regular mini-summits in mid-February. As always, their discussions had covered the world. They'd talked about Fox News, Murdoch's interest in buying Pat Robertson's Family Channel, and their satellite joint ventures in Latin America. In particular, they talked about Murdoch buying Malone out of the Fox Sports joint venture. It was a deal that would put a billion dollars into Liberty Media, and get Malone out of a hole. With that money he could buy out the controlling bloc of Tele-Communications Inc stock held by the Magness estate – which otherwise would be sold on the market to pay inheritance taxes. Murdoch would have been aware of the huge favour he was doing Malone with the Fox Sports deal. It was during these talks that Murdoch broke the bad news that went with it. He casually told Malone that he was about to announce a satellite partnership with Charlie Ergen.

Malone's lieutenant Peter Barton told *Denver Post* journalist Stephen Keating, 'Rupert told us he was doing the deal with Charlie. I remember looking at him and telling him he was nuts. John said, 'Let's move on.' But John was quite pissed about this. It coloured the meeting.'

Malone was less stoic after the theatrical announcement of the merger on 24 February. He swore at Murdoch in a meeting several days later. 'Rupert,' Malone said, 'we're trying to sell affiliation on f/X and Fox News and Fox Sports and having you as a partner under these conditions is not an asset.'

The question was, did Murdoch and his executives really believe the claims that they were making? 'Rupert Murdoch is an old friend,' said TCI's new president, Leo Hindery. 'I applaud his strategic initiative. I am more than a little annoyed by the anti-cable rhetoric.' Hindery went to the post-announcement meeting with Malone determined to clarify if News Corp's 'public rhetoric' was the same as its 'internal rhetoric'. That is, did they mean what they were saying? Hindery said he went away relieved that they didn't.

Behind all the drama on the Fox sound stage that day, the new partners' real views of the future were more modest than they were letting on. In a year, Echostar had clawed its way to a subscriber base of 400,000. This was still way behind its major competitor, Hughes Corporation's DirecTV, which had 3 million subscribers. No matter what Sky did with new technology, local programming and 500 channels, its internal forecasts suggested DirecTV would stay ahead of them. The Sky business plan that Murdoch and Ergen announced with such gusto to the world on 24 February was for Sky to have 8 million customers within five years. But this represented only 38 per cent of the market. Its DBS rivals – chiefly DirecTV – would have 13 million subscribers. This would be devastating for cable operators, who faced losing a third of their customers. But they would not be losing most of them to Sky. When Murdoch said, 'We expect to have a good 50 per cent of all new satellite customers from here on,' he meant that the aim was merely to try and keep up with DirecTV. The big threat to cable would come not from Murdoch, but from General Motors, DirecTV's ultimate parent. But on 24 February Murdoch convinced the world exactly the reverse.

A headline in an industry magazine, *Cablevision*, summarised the rising tide of indignation and outrage among cable operators: 'Cable to Murdoch: Drop Dead.' For the moment, the threat of Murdoch had put cable operators on the defensive. But it was only a question of time before they rallied, the wagons came out of the circle, and the irate cable operators mounted a counter-attack. In the narrow window of opportunity that this gave him, Murdoch had to find some powerful allies. He needed a political fix; and no matter how daunting the task, he needed it quickly. Success or failure in the battle to make the Sky merger work lay in how Murdoch fared in Washington.

CHAPTER ELEVEN

DIVIDED ROYALTIES

Rupert Murdoch at his best is probably when he is cornered or when he does have great adversity going against him. And maybe it's his moment of greatest pleasure.

Barry Diller

Washington, March–April 1997

When Rupert Murdoch went to Washington in March 1997, he faced one of the most delicate tasks in modern politics. He needed a change to the copyright laws that would allow his Sky satellite operation to beam local television programming down to its customers across America – and he needed it in a hurry. He hoped to have the new laws in place by April, tacked on to the end of a $4 billion appropriations bill to fund US troops in Bosnia and disaster relief in the American Midwest.

As one lobbyist put it at the time, 'Historically, copyright legislation is the most difficult legislation to get through Congress . . . it will take some pretty creative strategising for them to get their proposal through.' The difficulty is that copyright holders range from local television stations to networks to movie producers to sports leagues. The information economy is based first of all upon an economy of information . . . of regulating the commercial returns from media. The entertainment industry is based upon tightly defined market territories. If the boundaries are rewritten – and with satellite television boundaries may cease to exist – the immediate questions are: Who pays the royalties, who gets paid and how much do they get paid? Rewriting the copyright laws is like rearranging the deck chairs for everyone in the entertainment industry. Nobody wants to move.

And it was a bad time for Murdoch to be asking for political favours. In the early months of 1997 a sea change was buffeting conservative politics. The current malaise could be seen most clearly in the woes that had overtaken Speaker Newt Gingrich. Back when the Republicans had swept to power in September 1994 to win both Houses of Congress, Gingrich had been the man of the hour, the architect of a historic victory. His 'Contract with America' manifesto had been the platform for the Republican revolution and Gingrich had seemed an unstoppable colossus, a man tipped to succeed Bill Clinton as President.

That was 1994. When Murdoch came to Washington in 1997, the picture was not so happy. King Newt was being blamed for a string of Republican disasters. There had been the failed stand-off with Clinton that Gingrich masterminded in late 1995, when Congress refused to pass the Federal Budget until Clinton cut spending. And hold-ups with Republican legislation; filibustering in the Senate; party losses in the 1996 elections and Clinton's landslide victory to win a second term: all had stirred discontent with the Speaker's leadership. In January 1997, the House ethics committee fined Gingrich $300,000 for misleading information he supplied during an investigation of his finances. Some Republican kingmakers had even begun an internal debate about the virtues of regicide.

One of Gingrich's most vehement critics was William Kristol, a leading light among the new conservatives, the so-called neo-cons. By March 1997, Kristol was calling openly for Gingrich to resign in the right-wing magazine written for Washington insiders called the *Weekly Standard*. The cover line on the 20 March issue of the *Weekly Standard* was 'Newt Melts', and featured an opinion piece by New York Republican Peter King, who described Gingrich as 'roadkill on the highway of American politics'. Gingrich was on a trip to China at the time, but he was so incensed at the King article that at Elmendorf air force base on his way home he called Rush Limbaugh's radio program to attack Kristol. 'I don't know of any conservative person who is a serious person who isn't, frankly, worried about what's happening at the *Weekly Standard*, and Kristol's passion for destroying Republicans,' Gingrich thundered.

The spat degenerated. Gingrich went on to defend his record and show that he had regained his old fire and reforming zeal at a Washington dinner for his political action committee, GOPAC, at the Ritz Carlton Hotel on 3 April. In passing, Gingrich cited the high sales in Mongolia of the book *Contract with America*, which he said had even been distributed by camels and horses. 'Isn't it exciting to know that not only in America but in Mongolia, ideas are working,' Gingrich said. It was perhaps a mistake that Gingrich brought along a ceremonial Mongolian hat to the conference, a triumph of burgundy velvet and gold shaped like a crown, as the press gleefully reported.

'In two years we've come from Contract with America to Contract with Mongolia,' Kristol sniffed disdainfully.

The difficulty for Rupert Murdoch in this little spat was that he had a reputation as one of the most interventionist newspaper proprietors in the world. And Bill Kristol worked for him. Murdoch had given Kristol a budget of $3 million to launch the *Weekly Standard* 18 months before, to give Murdoch an authoritative voice in Washington among the neo-cons. Murdoch said at the time he didn't expect to make money from the *Standard*, it was 'a bit of a hobby'. He said he thought it would be fun. There was no indication that Murdoch was telling Kristol what to write, but given News Corp's track record, one could never be sure. At the very least, the question for Gingrich would be why Murdoch didn't rein Kristol in, once the attacks on him started.

Gingrich's position *vis a vis* Rupert Murdoch had become very peculiar, and went to the heart of the pressures gripping Republican politicians in Washington. And if there was anyone in America that Gingrich could blame for starting him on the slippery slope that led to his predicament, other than himself, it was arguably his erstwhile admirer and new friend, Rupert Murdoch. The key to understanding Murdoch's political problems in March 1997 lies in the history of America's conservative politics.

Murdoch has always had a remarkable effect on politicians. Unlike many chief executives, Murdoch has made a habit of descending regularly upon Washington to argue his concern of the moment in person. In some conservative circles, Murdoch has superstar status. One lobbyist told of a legislator who virtually went into shock after running into Murdoch walking through Congress one day. 'It was like he'd seen the Second Coming,' the lobbyist told reporters. There was a flip side to Murdoch's notoriety. Over the years he had made so many cosy deals with political leaders of all ideological persuasion, and his reputation had so far preceded him, that for his Democrat critics, merely seeing him speak with a politician could raise grave suspicions. Somehow, Murdoch must be pulling another fast one.

The American swing to the right in November 1994 was not simply a matter of choosing different politicians. It was a quest for new ideas. Newt Gingrich came to office on a wave of public hostility to self-serving incumbents and party machines. Main Street America wanted to see power taken away from the traditional power-brokers, including lobbyists, committee chairmen and committee staff. A major part of the power taken from House and Senate committees was subsumed by Newt Gingrich himself.

The Republican victory in 1994 came at a critical time. A new crop of legislators faced the task of coming to terms with the broader issues facing American society and its economy. Their lofty concern was shaping (or reshaping) America's future. A major part of that future would be determined by the technologies emerging out of Silicon Valley and communications labs around the country. What was the role of government in the uncharted new world that information technology promised? Did Congress know any more about where technology was going than the media industry leaders who met at Herb Allen's conference at Sun Valley each July? How did one make sense of the changes that technology was bringing to society? Where did the future lie? These were questions of some immediacy, because Congress was about to embark on the first major overhaul in decades of the Telecommunications Act. Matters of ideology here would translate into market movements worth billions of dollars. The Republican view of technology would be shaped by the conservative policy institutes.

At the end of the twentieth century, most visions of the future lay somewhere between two extremes. On the one hand was the dark, European pessimism formulated by writers like George Orwell, whose book *Nineteen Eighty-Four* painted a future where technology is used to control the populace, and Britain is reduced to an outpost named Runway One. The book deals with the nature of power and the way it has come to pervade our intimate spaces; but it is the vision of Big Brother as the hand behind technology, using telescreens in each home to spy upon and brainwash the population, that has become the book's most memorable image. Opposed to that view, at the other end of the soothsaying spectrum, was the long tradition of American optimism, which suggested that with technology, the only thing that Americans had to fear was fear itself. It was this latter view that was propagated by the right-wing think-tanks and policy institutes that had driven the Gingrich revolution. Their initial goal was to discredit the pervasive scepticism about technology as Big Brother that Orwell's work had produced.

It was a battle of ideas and world views where no quarter would be offered, and there were no non-combatants. When Charles William Maynes retired in 1997 after 17 years as editor of *Foreign Policy*, he complained that the 'non-partisan specialists' that had traditionally advised policymakers in all camps had been replaced by a new breed of 'combat intellectuals'. 'In today's Washington, ideas are no longer tools made available to everybody. Rather, they are weapons crafted for one's political allies.'

The conservative policy institutes' views on technology and their pervasive influence, which tended to correspond happily with the views of the technology companies that supported them so generously, can be best appreciated through the words of their most high-profile advocate.

Rupert Murdoch made the best known political speech of his life in London's Banqueting Hall on 2 September 1993. Ostensibly he was there to unveil a new package of pay-television channels for BSkyB. His address, which would set out his vision for the future of world media, was being broadcast by satellite to little groups of investors and media analysts at sites around the world.

Murdoch told his worldwide audience:

> We are on the edge of a new technological revolution . . . For years man has been both beguiled and frightened by new technologies, and with reason . . . Television created both a new means of entertaining and informing huge numbers of people, and the possibilities of totalitarian control by Big Brother laid out by George Orwell in his frightening *Nineteen Eighty-Four*. We are almost a decade beyond Orwell's famous date and he has been proved wrong. Advances in the technology of telecommunications have proved an unambiguous threat to totalitarian regimes everywhere.

There was much more. Telecommunications technology had been critical to the enormous spread of political freedom in recent years:

> I must add (with maybe a tiny touch of regret) that this technology has also liberated people from the once-powerful media barons . . . The media mogul has been replaced by a bevy of harassed and sometimes confused media executives, trying to guess what the public wants.

Consumers were in control, Murdoch said, technology was 'galloping over the old regulatory machinery, in many countries rendering it almost obsolete'.

At least, that is the way the speech appeared in the next day's edition of *The Times*. Because it was Rupert Murdoch, he didn't quite say it like that. Before launching into the speech Murdoch paused to look around at the Rubens paintings that decorate the Banqueting Hall, savouring the moment. 'I am particularly fond of 'Hercules Crushing Envy', from which we have suffered much,' he began reflectively. 'And 'Minerva Crushing

Ignorance', from which we have suffered even more.' The speech went down well with the satellite audience, particularly the cut-away shots of BSkyB chief Sam Chisholm looking most unamused when Murdoch referred to 'harrassed and sometimes confused media executives'.

The speech was a disaster for Murdoch. A month later the Chinese government, alerted by Murdoch's widely reported comments, dealt with the unambiguous threat to totalitarian regimes everywhere by banning all satellite dishes in China. Murdoch had paid $825 million to buy Star TV in Hong Kong, principally so that he could broadcast to the mainland. The Chinese ban threatened to turn this whole investment into a complete loss. In what appeared to be a bid to assuage Chinese concerns, Murdoch dropped the highly critical BBC World Service from the Star platform, but Beijing was unmoved. He spent the rest of the decade attempting to re-establish links with Chinese leaders, as Star continued to notch up $100 million in operating losses year after year. And Murdoch stopped mixing business with foreign politics. Advocating political change through technology was just too volatile a subject to bring up. When it came to learning painful lessons, Rupert Murdoch never needed to be told twice. The puzzle then was why, a year after the Banqueting Hall fiasco, Murdoch returned to the same dangerous ideological ground.

Murdoch was in Melbourne on 20 October 1994 to give the John Bonython lecture at the Centre for Independent Studies, a policy institute modelled on the Institute for Economic Affairs in London. His theme was the arrival of the 'Century of Networking'. 'Those of us who make our living by putting news and ideas and their audiences together face changes, triggered by science, that are no longer differences in degree: they amount to differences in kind,' he said. George Orwell misunderstood the future, Murdoch argued, because he got it all wrong about technology. Ignorance was not strength, as Orwell asserted; freedom was not slavery. Rather than becoming Big Brother, technology was liberating people, producing an anarchistic media environment with no barriers to entry.

This was an area with red flags all over it for Murdoch. Essentially it was the same argument he had put the year before at the Banqueting Hall. And while he was being careful to avoid politics, if you gave the underlying theme the smallest nudge you would be back with technology as the great threat to totalitarian regimes. Asian governments could read the subtext of a speech. Murdoch's actions over Star TV and the BBC had shown he was too pragmatic to walk into danger needlessly, and this was clearly dangerous. Why then was he playing with fire like this, two weeks before the US Congressional elections?

Murdoch drew his argument from the early galley proofs of a book published that month by Peter Huber, a lawyer with a US think-tank, the Manhattan Institute for Policy Research (Huber's thesis had been kicking around in various forums for more than a year, and also appears to have been the major source for Murdoch's 1993 London speech). Huber had written his book, *Orwell's Revenge: The Nineteen Eighty-Four Palimpsest*, by using a computer to recombine a wide range of Orwell's works to produce a happier version of *Nineteen Eighty-Four*, interspersed with chapters of his own analysis of where the technological revolution was going. In fact Huber had drawn so heavily from Orwell that he ended up paying a quarter of his royalties on the book to Orwell's estate.

Huber wrote:

Nineteen Eighty-Four is still the most important book published since [World War II]. Orwell's technotic vision still casts a dark shadow over every advance in telegraphy, telemetry, telephony, and television – which is to say, every facet of teletechnology, every yard of the information superhighway, that is transforming our lives today.

One of the themes in *Nineteen Eighty-Four* is the way that those in power in a society can rewrite history to suit their own ends. Winston Smith, the book's hero, spends his days at the office rewriting old newspaper clips. That way every Party prophecy is always vindicated: 'Who controls the past controls the future; who controls the present controls the past.' Huber's novel approach was to rewrite the history of *Nineteen Eighty-Four* itself, to give the book a feel-good Hollywood ending. Huber's argument was that technology is essentially anarchistic – and that proves to be society's salvation. Orwell's unhappy citizens discover that the telescreens that Big Brother uses to control them are actually interactive. They use them to communicate with each other. The network becomes in effect the World Wide Web. They develop street markets, entrepreneurial spirit and free enterprise become rampant, and authoritarianism curls up its toes and calls it a day.

Huber's focus was on the way technology empowers private citizens. 'We are all becoming broadcasters in our own rights, with our PCs and broadband connections between them,' Huber said in an interview in early 1995 on *The Progress Report with Newt Gingrich*, a US cable television show sponsored by Gingrich's Progress and Freedom Foundation. 'We are all gaining inch by inch the power of a Dan Rather or a Peter Jennings.'

Huber was less clear about the position of chief programmer in this brave new network. Michael Vlahos, the show's host, asked him:

It seems as though there is an opportunity for a kind of re-creation of the kind of gatekeeper system, for example, that you have in Hollywood, where in order to be an actor you have to go through certain agents or through certain casting people . . . a whole system that kind of gets you to where you can begin to have a chance to make it.

This was a gift to Huber, ready for him to pat away with a stock answer. Instead Huber fudged. The question was about access to networks, and he ended up talking about good and evil:

The power to project yourself at a distance . . . amplifies both the power to do it well and honestly and the power to do it badly . . . The technology always amplifies both. But there – what it does seem clear to me is that it amplifies the good overall. The good and the honest and the productive people get more out of it than the cheaters and the malefactors because – I mean, that's just the way.

Huber's description of the moral dimensions of the Information Revolution must have seemed awkward even at the time. Today it sounds uncomfortably like a religious position, a statement of faith. One of the pillars of America's freedom of speech laws is the belief by US courts that good ideas push out bad ideas. It is a given. This belief is what makes freedom of speech possible, and it is why censorship is unnecessary. The paradigm has proved a little less robust when libertarians go on to apply the same concept to commerce, and argue that good business practices drive out bad business practices – and therefore there is no need for government to regulate business in any way. This is not a given. So is the new media a form of expression, or a business enterprise? For Huber, the Information Revolution was all about communication – so governments should stay out of it. Wall Street, on the other hand, was about to discover that the revolution was really all about business. Technology was the road to El Dorado.

Huber was speaking on the brink of the greatest wealth transfer in human history, the Net stock bubble that would trigger the most giddy pursuit of money seen in modern times. Probably 1995 was the latest that anyone could still describe the Internet in the disinterested, altruistic terms of its government and academic origins. Indeed, in September 1995 Huber was described as lamenting at a Progress and Freedom Foundation conference in Aspen that 'the current view of the World Wide Web as a marketplace was that it was full of deceit: a global bazaar full of mistrust.' It would not be long, however, he assured his audience, before the transparent nature of the Web transformed into a place for 'higher levels of integrity and loyalty'.

Rupert Murdoch has been accused of many things in his life, but never of being a wild-eyed optimist. His life story has been a struggle against being locked out by media gatekeepers. 'I have fought against them all my life,' he said of his first monolithic business rivals in Australia in the 1970s. He has described his life as a series of interlocking wars; he likes to describe his use of sport as a 'battering ram' to break into markets. In the mid-1990s he and his rivals were in the process of spending billions of dollars to ensure that whatever twist or turn that the Information Revolution took going into the next century, they would hold the keys of the kingdom. It was the reverse of what Peter Huber was arguing. Why then was Murdoch going out of his way in October 1994, at some risk to himself, to publicise and endorse a libertarian philosophy to which in practice he was so fundamentally opposed?

Besides his policy work, Huber was a partner at Washington law firm Kellogg, Huber, Hansen & Evans, which represented the regional Baby Bell telephone companies in their efforts to roll back some of the restrictions of the consent decrees that broke up AT&T. Huber's high media profile underlined how influential he had become in Gingrich's circle of advisers, and as one of the architects of Republican strategy on telecommunications reform. The real attraction of Huber's thesis was the political agenda it carried. If technology is anarchistic, then any attempt at government regulation is at best futile. At worst it might be detrimental for society as a whole. Huber co-authored an influential study for the Progress and Freedom Foundation released in February 1995 which argued that Congress should allow the Baby Bells to enter the lucrative long-distance market, and also to compete with cable companies. 'We should do everything possible to unleash cable companies to attack phone companies and unleash phone companies to attack cable companies,' Huber said. Most important of all, Congress should abolish the Federal Communication Commission (FCC) entirely, a cause which Huber championed at every opportunity and eventually turned into a 1997 book. So in terms of Realpolitik, Huber's attack on Orwell was really an assault on the FCC.

Rupert Murdoch had never been on the best of terms with the FCC. Each year since 1986, the FCC would later conclude, his media empire had misreported to the FCC the level of foreign ownership and control of the Fox television stations. In 1993 when he spoke at the Banqueting Hall, Murdoch was opposed to the FCC in principle. But Huber's anti-Orwell rhetoric applied nicely to any government involvement in the media. And while Murdoch might be only opposed to the FCC in principle, he had far stronger feelings about the government-owned BBC. His newspapers had run virulent anti-BBC editorials for a quarter of a century.

Thirteen months later, when Murdoch spoke in Melbourne in October 1994, the FCC problem had grown far more specific. After prodding by the National Association for the Advancement of Colored Peoples (NAACP), the FCC had forced News Corp to disclose for the first time the foreign ownership of the Fox stations. The FCC was mulling over whether to launch an inquiry. For Murdoch, taking up Huber's thesis about technology not only brought him into the policy network around Newt Gingrich; it also provided an oblique way to undermine the federal agency that was investigating him. For libertarians like Huber, it was a natural consequence: if George Orwell was wrong about technology, then a government regulator like the FCC was unnecessary and should be killed off immediately. In Murdoch's view that could not be soon enough. Murdoch pressed the attack on Orwell perhaps out of conviction; certainly out of self-interest.

In mid-November 1994 the FCC problem grew even more threatening for Murdoch, after NBC launched a strident complaint against the Fox stations. Relations between NBC and Fox executives had become poisonous, with reports of heated telephone calls, and an alleged confrontation (later denied) where NBC president Robert C. Wright 'jabbed his finger at Mr Murdoch's chest,' complaining that he had been forced to spend hundreds of millions of dollars to keep NBC's affiliates from defecting to Fox. NBC was pressing the FCC to open a full inquiry into Fox's foreign ownership.

Murdoch was already heading for Washington. Preston Padden had scheduled a whistlestop tour of the Capitol for late November 1994, three weeks after the Republican landslide win. Padden set up eighteen meetings over three days for Murdoch with Republican and Democrat leaders. While these were purely courtesy calls, it was only natural that the conversations would turn to the FCC inquiry, at least in passing. The key players to see would be Bob Dole, the Republican Senate Leader; Jack Fields, the chairman of the House Telecommunications Subcommittee; Thomas Bliley, a Republican from Virginia picked by Gingrich to chair the House Commerce Committee; Senator Larry Pressler, the amiable chairman of the Senate Commerce Committee; and the face of resurgent Republicanism himself, Newt Gingrich.

On the hectic Monday afternoon of 28 November 1994, Speaker-elect Gingrich was still operating out of his cramped Capitol office. His new staff would have no offices until he was formally elected Speaker two months later. In the meantime Gingrich's one-room office was awash with papers. New telephone lines were being installed, and some of Gingrich's aides were operating without desks, off the floor. Gingrich arrived late. He took a look at the wild scene in his office, and waved his next appointment, down the hall to a reception room, which was being set up for a Democrat dinner function. As he walked down the corridor with Rupert Murdoch, Gingrich had no idea how much this new relationship was going to cost him.

In November 1994, the goal for which Gingrich had been striving for two decades was finally within his reach. Ever since the former Georgia college professor had won a seat in Congress in 1978 he had worked tirelessly to discredit the ruling Democrats, attacking their ethics and values. The highpoint was in 1988, when he had filed a complaint against Speaker Jim Wright. Wright later resigned over a string of ethics charges, including improper benefits from book royalties. Through the 1990s, Gingrich's political action committee, GOPAC had sent monthly audio tapes on tactics and vision to 28,000 supporters. Gingrich's recurring theme was the corruption of the incumbent Democrats and the welfare state. He advised aspiring Republican candidates to use words such as 'bizarre', 'sick', 'self-serving' and 'cheat' to describe liberals and Democrats.

Gingrich was a man of immense energy. In 1994 besides leading his Party as minority whip, teaching a college course and mixing regular television appearances with political speeches and masterminding a sweeping political change through America, Gingrich had not neglected his hobbies. He liked to write books. His publisher, Jim Baen of Baen Publications, was finalising his latest effort, a steamy historical novel called 1945. Early reports described the book as a bodice ripper, and Gingrich and Baen were toning down some of the bedroom scenes. The book would earn Gingrich a princely $8,000 in royalties the following year. But back in June 1994, one of Gingrich's aides, Jeff Eisenach (who had founded the Progress and Freedom Foundation the year before), had set up a meeting between Gingrich and a New York literary agent, Lynn Chu, to discuss a more lucrative writing opportunity. Chu and her husband Glen Hartley represented a high-profile stable of writers including literary critic Harold Bloom and conservatives David Brocks, Thomas Sowell and Irving Kristol. In June 1994, Chu told Gingrich that he could expect to earn up to $2 million from a book that, as he later put it, 'described what we need to do to renew American civilization'. Gingrich said, in effect, 'Get serious.'

The book floated around as an idea until August when Chu had lunch with Adrian Zackheim, executive editor at HarperCollins US, who expressed interest. HarperCollins had a fascination with books by powerful politicians. Previously it had published memoirs by British Prime Minister Margaret Thatcher, Soviet President Mikhail Gorbachev, and a biography of Chinese leader Deng Xiaoping written by his daughter. 'They were very excited, and we were happy to pursue it with them,' Chu said later. 'We knew they were a good house, they responded to the numbers we were pitching out . . . Sometimes it all happens one-on-one like that.'

By late November, Chu and Eisenach had turned the idea into a seventeen-page proposal, *To Renew America*, for Zackheim. The situation was not yet resolved, but Gingrich was facing the pleasant prospect that HarperCollins was about to make him richer than he had ever been. As both sides tell it, the meeting that followed between Gingrich and Murdoch was one of the most confused exchanges in modern politics. It was a seven-figure misunderstanding. Gingrich did not know that Murdoch owned HarperCollins, so he could not know that the man he accompanied down the corridor was about to pay him $2 million; and Murdoch for his part didn't know that HarperCollins was talking to Chu, so he could hardly be asking for any special political favours.

It was, as Padden described it later, 'the most insignificant meeting in the history of the world'. Murdoch and Gingrich spoke for about a quarter of an hour. Padden and Binzell were also present, as was Gingrich's aide Greg Wright. 'It was a ten minute meeting – maximum,' Murdoch told Ken Auletta at the *New Yorker*. 'We met in the hall, because there were too many people in his office. It was just chitchat. We talked about the chances of his getting his Contract with America passed.'

Initially, spokesman for both men denied that Fox's FCC problems were raised at the meeting. However, six weeks later Preston conceded, 'Right at the end I interjected that NBC was trashing us all over Capitol Hill, and it was just sour grapes because we were hurting them in the marketplace.'

Gingrich said, 'They said something about, 'We're in this big fight with NBC,' and I said, 'Fine, I don't care.' I never got involved in individual cases like that . . . The truth is, I don't remember anything about his problems with the FCC.'

Chu told the *New York Times* that she was not formally appointed Gingrich's agent until three days later on Thursday 1 December, 'and that's when I immediately began talking money.' On 9 December, HarperCollins' senior vice president Jack McKeown told dozens of the company's employees at their winter sales conference that HarperCollins had won the Gingrich book with a $2 million advance.

On 7 December the FCC announced it was holding a formal inquiry into Fox, and Republicans began coming out in support of Murdoch. The next day Mike Riley, a Republican Congressman from Texas and a senior member of the House Telecommunications subcommittee, announced he would be introducing legislation to overturn the foreign ownership laws on television stations. *Daily Variety* reported that Republicans were prepared to rally around the Fox cause, and in the weeks that followed, Larry Pressler, Thomas Bliley and Jack Fields all came out in support of Fox.

Gingrich meanwhile had had second thoughts about the $2 million advance. He had spoken to his friends Alvin and Heidi Toffler, and to former secretary of education Bill Bennett, who told him there was more money out there. Only Gingrich's fiction publisher, Jim Baen, told him to take the money and run. On the afternoon of 20 December, Chu held a telephone auction with publishing houses including Doubleday, Simon & Schuster, Putnam and Little, Brown. Such was HarperCollins' enthusiasm for the book that the bid price escalated sharply – so sharply that only one other publisher, Penguin USA chief Peter Mayer, managed to lodge a bid, believed to about $4 million for two books. HarperCollins won with a bid for $4.5 million two-book deal, including a Gingrich reader. Again, Murdoch said he knew nothing about the negotiations. 'I was telephoned in Beijing on Christmas Eve and told that it had happened,' Murdoch told Ken Auletta in mid-1995. 'Howard Rubenstein called me. I went crazy. I knew critics would explode.'

This is a curious account. The call on 24 December by Rubenstein, New York's master spin doctor, would not have been to tell Murdoch that HarperCollins had made a rather large publication advance. The call can only have been about damage control, because in the intervening four days the critics had already exploded. On 22 December, Democrat Minority Whip David Bonior had launched a devastating attack on Gingrich with a press conference script that read straight out of pantomime. He began:

> I'm so sorry that I'm late. I know I've kept you waiting, but I just received this gift from Santa before we went away for the Christmas holidays, and I'd like to open it up and share it with you. Oops, it's for the other minority whip, Mr Gingrich, who will be the next Speaker. It's a cheque for $4 million from Rupert Murdoch. Would you like to see it?

Bonior suggested a link between the book contract and Republican support for Murdoch and Fox. But was this really the sort of improper payment or bribe that Bonior was suggesting? Gingrich gave every impression that he believed that $4.5 million was the fair market price for his writing, and thus Murdoch was entitled to no special favours. Murdoch says he knew nothing about the deal. Having said that, Gingrich had a history of difficulty in distinguishing between his personal ambitions and his public duties – particularly in using tax-free donations to fund political activities. He had also been criticised for the favourable mentions he regularly gave in his college course to companies that sponsored him. Murdoch, for his part, had a history of publishing books by political leaders while they were still in power. In February 1995, Murdoch would host a New York launch for a book by Deng Xiaping's daughter, as well as a 30-member Chinese delegation to Sydney. An improper payment exists in the eye of the beholder. It is a state of mind. It only takes one person in such a deal to feel that is an improper transaction for it to be an improper transaction for both parties. There is no evidence here that either Murdoch or HarperCollins executives or Gingrich viewed this as being in any way improper. What can be said is that committing to a book deal of this magnitude was most unwise.

In the furore that followed, Gingrich found himself under fire even from Republican ranks for the sheer size of the advance. Eight days later he announced that he would forgo the $4.5 million. Instead he would settle for $1 up front, with royalties based on book sales. That was not enough to stop a House ethics committee investigation into the original book deal. *To Renew America* went on sale the following August, just as Gingrich was testifying about the deal before the ethics inquiry. The book proved to be a bestseller, but it wasn't enough of a bestseller to recoup what Gingrich had given up. Gingrich grossed $1.47 million in royalties for *To Renew America*, and another $163,500 on the second book, *Lessons Learned the Hard Way*, a total of $1.64 million.

Gingrich had always been strapped for money. Now the Murdoch factor had cost him a fortune. If Gingrich had accepted the Penguin bid for $4 million, the deal would not have been such a *cause célèbre* and may well have survived. But the advance wasn't the only loss. Gingrich's agent Lynn Chu operated on a 15 per cent commission. On the royalties Gingrich actually received that would have come to $245,000. The difficulty here was that Chu had acted in good faith and produced a $4.5 million advance that Gingrich then declined. She was still entitled to her 15 per cent fee of the original deal. That came to $675,000. Gingrich had to pay Chu an extra $430,000.

The repercussions continued. Gingrich was cleared by the ethics committee over the book deal, but ethics inquiries are hard things to stop.

The sheer momentum that the Murdoch controversy had produced meant that the committee kept looking at other complaints that the Democrats had tacked on to the investigation. Without the Murdoch book deal, it is doubtful there would have been the will to launch an inquiry into the secondary complaints. These related to Gingrich's fund-raising practices. It was this long-simmering inquiry that finally resulted in the £300,000 fine imposed on Gingrich in January 1997. At this point, after paying Chu and his co-writer, Newt had netted $656,000 from *To Renew America*, a long way short of his original fond hopes in 1994. And in early 1997, as Gingrich explored avenues to raise the $300,000 he needed to pay his ethics committee fine, he realised that his only major prospect for producing big money was from more book royalties. He needed to write the second book for HarperCollins to pay his ethics fine. (*Lessons Learned the Hard Way* was published in 1998, and earned $163,500 in royalties. Gingrich's career prospects were not helped by his decision to dedicate the book in loving terms to his wife Marianne, when he had been having an affair with an Agriculture Committee clerk and former intern, Callista Bisek, since 1993.) Thus in 1997 Gingrich's financial future once again lay with Rupert Murdoch, the man whose manoeuvrings had brought Gingrich to this pass in the first place. And now Murdoch's editor was making fun of his Mongolian hat.

Gingrich was hardly in a position to criticise Murdoch, whom he had hit six months before for a $1 million donation to the Republican Party in California. Instead, Gingrich raged against Kristol and his 'ABC bosses', a reference to Kristol's regular television spot. So if Murdoch was looking for a political miracle in 1997 to save his satellite hopes, it would not be coming from Gingrich. It was not just a matter of whether he would be inclined to give Murdoch a miracle. The question was whether Gingrich still had the power to pull one off. It wasn't the only setback.

Besides his small team of in-house lobbyists, Murdoch's biggest ally in Washington was the tobacco industry. Murdoch had been on the board of Philip Morris Tobacco Co since 1989. Philip Morris chairman H.W.H. Maxwell had sat on the News Corp board since 1992. The relationship was more than just the natural attraction between a media group and a major advertiser with an image problem. The tobacco industry hired the best lobbyists and spin doctors in Washington, and they had close links with Southern politicians. Murdoch's pro-tobacco stance made him a natural fit for the Cato Institute, a high-profile conservative think-tank whose major contributors included R.J. Reynolds and Philip Morris. Murdoch joined John Malone on the Cato board in September 1997.

Unfortunately for Murdoch, Larry Pressler, chairman of the Senate Commerce Committee, lost his seat in the November 1996 elections. The new head of the Commerce Committee was John McCain. While Thomas Bliley, the head of the House Commerce Committee, liked to describe himself as 'one of the tobacco industry's best friends', McCain would show himself to be one of the tobacco lobby's worst nightmares with a 1998 bill that if passed would have cost tobacco companies $518 billion. So Murdoch's tobacco lobbyists were not the ideal advocates for Murdoch's present dilemma.

Murdoch had bolstered his lobbying arm by engaging Perry & Romani Associates. Its star recruit was Dennis DeConcini, former Democrat chairman of the Senate Copyright Committee. DeConcini, like John McCain, was one of the Keating Five, politicians who received donations from Charles H. Keating, later convicted of fraud after his Lincoln Savings & Loan lost $2.5 billion. While DeConcini resigned after he was criticised by the ethics committee, McCain emerged largely unscathed. However, it was still a sensitive subject for McCain. It made DeConcini as awkward an advocate as Murdoch's tobacco lobbyists.

The biggest thing that Murdoch had going for him was the way Congress hated cable companies. After all the deliberations that went in the 1996 Telecommunications Act, the bill had turned out to be a damp squib. The Progress and Freedom Foundation and the various right-wing think-tanks had assured Republicans that lifting price restrictions would trigger cutthroat competition between cable guys and telephone companies, and see telephone and cable prices slashed. Nothing like that had happened. No credible rival to cable had emerged, and cable operators had celebrated by raising cable fees by an average of 10 per cent that year. Many Republicans felt like they had been sold a pup. 'If anyone ever says they really believed real (telco) competition was going to come from cable, they are either stupid or disingenuous,' said one government insider. One of those most upset was John McCain. Murdoch went to Washington on 6 March to brief him on the Sky merger and the competition this would pose to cable operators. The telcos had done nothing more than make promises about providing competition. Murdoch was about to really do it. McCain was sympathetic but non-committal.

Murdoch had decided on a crash-through strategy. A conventional change to the copyright law could be bounced around committees for years. Rather than have the issue bogged down in Orrin Hatch's Senate Copyright Committee, Murdoch would use his friends in Congress to press the measure as a matter of urgency, tacking it on to an appropriations bill.

The downside was that if this strategy failed, the issue would end up back with the disgruntled committee chairman whose power he had tried to subvert.

At McCain's invitation, Murdoch returned to Washington on 10 April to appear before a Commerce Committee hearing into the rise in cable rates. 'Congress must clarify that satellite competitors like Sky are legally entitled to carry local broadcast stations the same way that cable and wireless cable systems can do today,' he said. Murdoch went on to portray himself as the persistent underdog. When Fox TV was launched, he said, 'The critics laughed so loudly I still have a slight ringing in my ear.' He had launched Fox News six months before 'despite a firmly entrenched competitor in CNN and in another younger but widely hyped competitor, MSNBC.' Even if it succeeded, he said, Sky would

hardly put cable out of business. But eight million customers can provide a profitable business for us, a choice for customers and an improved cable product for those who might be unwise enough to reject the Sky service and stick with cable . . . Sky is willing to risk a $3 billion capital investment to bring consumers a better choice now. If you give us the legal authority, the rest is up to us.

Murdoch is a persuasive advocate. 'There is this premise that Rupert Murdoch is the White Knight, and that he's the only one who knows how to provide competition,' complained Stephen Effros, president of the Cable Telecommunications Association. 'It's a silly premise.' Meanwhile National Cable Television Association president Decker Anstrom was insisting Sky had to provide 'more specific information about its business plan, about its technology and about the specific legislation it's looking for. Otherwise (Murdoch is) making nothing more than some vague assurances.'

Yet while Murdoch was touching a chord, it had become clear by 10 April that he was unlikely to win the fast-track legislation he was seeking. 'It's too much, too soon for one person to pull off, even for Murdoch,' Lehman Brothers analyst Kim Wallace told reporters. 'He'll have to kiss the rings of twenty or thirty people but he will prevail (by the end of the year).'

That same day, Orrin Hatch wrote to Senate Appropriations Committee chairman Ted Stevens objecting to tacking copyright amendments to an appropriations bill, as 'copyright issues are complex and deserve a full airing.' Murdoch said he welcomed 'all the hearings in the world,' although 'what a delay does is let our competitors catch up with us.'

In reality the game was already over. The window of opportunity that Murdoch had been chasing was closed. Typically, the first person to realise this was Murdoch himself. Within a day of his appearance before McCain's committee on 10 April, reports circulated that Murdoch had begun talking to his cable rivals about cutting a new satellite deal, even before he went to Washington. Murdoch had already conceded he was facing a humiliating defeat.

For a minor media mogul, this might have been a debilitating setback. But one thing that running a worldwide empire like News Corp had shown Murdoch is that the game always goes on, somewhere else in the world. At the same time that he was wooing Republicans, Murdoch was helping to engineer a different political revolution in Britain. In London on Monday 17 March, the British Prime Minister John Major called a general election for 1 May. Murdoch's *Sun* newspaper had supported the Conservative Party since the 1970s. On the British election day in 1992, the *Sun* had run a page-one picture of Labour leader Neil Kinnock's head squeezed into a light bulb. The headline read: 'If Kinnock wins today, will the last person to leave Britain please turn out the lights.' When Major won a surprise victory for the Conservative Party that year, the *Sun* crowed, 'It was the *Sun* wot won it.' On 18 March 1997, six days before the *Weekly Standard* in Washington ran the 'Newt Melts' cover accusing Gingrich of not being right-wing enough, the *Sun* began day one of the British general election between Major and Labour's Tony Blair by dumping the Conservatives: 'The Sun Backs Blair.' Days later in Sydney, News Corporation attacked another conservative government, with muted criticism of Australian Prime Minister John Howard. In the courtly conversational style of local News chief Ken Cowley, it hardly ranked as a threat: more a promise to be brutal with a fluffy pillow.

By the middle of March, the dismayed cable industry had regrouped. On 17 March it roared into New Orleans, twenty thousand strong, for the three-day annual conference of the National Cable Television Association (NCTA). Ted Turner took the stage on the final day for an interview with Larry King, under stern riding orders from NCTA chief Decker Anstrom not to trash Murdoch. Nevertheless Turner could not resist a jibe, saying:

> Nothing that (Murdoch) does particularly surprises me because he just turned 66 and he's running out of time. He's got to do it quickly before he passes on. As hard as he works, you know, he could have a

stroke or a heart attack at any time. That's okay, isn't it, Decker? This nice man could trip and fall . . . a hundred stories.

Ted Turner should have quit while he was ahead. He went on to defend Time Warner's broken promise to run Fox News on its New York cable net: '. . . You don't have a deal in this country until you have a signed contract. A promise doesn't mean diddly poo. I never sued anybody over a promise. I promised to be faithful to my *wife*.'

A little pause followed, as the penny dropped for Turner that Jane Fonda was in the audience. '. . . Uh, not this wife. But everybody makes promises they haven't kept.'

Turner resolved the minor hiatus that his gaffe produced by returning to his favourite theme. 'We're going to make it as tough as we possibly can (for Murdoch), kind of like the Russian army did to the German army . . . Either he's going to go hungry or we are. He's the one that cast down the gauntlet.'

Gerry Levin was more prosaic about Sky: 'It's never going to get off the ground. It's over-hyped. They have too many problems to overcome.' But behind the bravado, the industry was in deep turmoil. 'Every meeting we've had, Murdoch is the topic of discussion,' one industry official said.

What would trigger a rebound in cable stocks? 'If Rupert Murdoch gets malaria,' said cable industry guru Paul Kagan.

John Malone's warning about the threat to Murdoch's cable programming had been realised. A week after the announcement of the Echostar merger, Jeff Marcus, the head of the country's ninth largest cable group, Marcus Cable, cancelled appointments with News Corp executives to carry f/X on more of his systems. Marcus flatly refused to see Murdoch's people.

News Corp had $2.5 billion tied up in Fox News, Fox Sports and f/X in partnership with Malone. Malone later testified, 'Most of the large cable operators were giving (Murdoch) a slow no on carrying his channels.' Like Marcus, they would not even discuss carrying Murdoch's programming.

'I don't think, generally, people want to buy bullets for the gun that's going to shoot them,' said Glenn Jones, head of Jones Intercable, when asked about carrying Fox News for his 1.5 million subscribers.

The five cable partners in Primestar had met before Turner's speech on 19 March. 'Time to market is critical to gain market share, blunt ASkyB entry,' Malone noted tersely in a memo the next day. Malone's memo suggests that the cable operators would try to minimise ASkyB's impact by delaying the launch as long as possible.

Dan O'Brien, the Time Warner representative on the Primestar committee, noted at a partners' meeting a week later: '(ASkyB) will be a formidable competitor.' He expected News Corp to have prices lower than everyone else's.

Murdoch was beginning to realise the full cost of what he was doing. The bottom line was that a $2.5 billion stake in cable channel programming was being threatened by his $1 billion investment in satellite television. The programming problems had grown so serious that in late March he went to Malone for advice. Leo Hindery, TCI's determinedly amiable president, described the outcome of the meeting as 'both organisations saying, 'Let's talk. Let's not whale on each other.' ' Malone was actually a little more blunt than this. He told Murdoch flatly that the whole Echostar merger proposal was 'lunacy'.

Murdoch's response, even in the deadening tones of a Justice Department legal document filed 14 months later, still carries the desperate flavour of that moment. 'Well then, help me get out of it; help me find something else to do,' Murdoch told Malone. 'What is Plan B?'

Malone has never said quite what Plan B was. But on 26 March he discussed the Murdoch's options with Bob Scherman's Washington trade publication, *Satellite Business News*. 'Rupert is so aggressive that he doesn't really make a good partner,' said Malone. He thought the ASkyB strategy would probably work for some markets, saying: 'I wouldn't be surprised to see them target a few markets, really drive hard in those markets, and Rupert try to make a deal for distribution.' Malone apparently saw Murdoch's strategy as a squeeze play, where the quid pro quo Murdoch was offering was to go easy on pushing his satellite service. 'There's some kind of peace in which Rupert gets what he wants, which is broader distribution of his programming networks in exchange for which he's not quite as aggressive (in DBS).'

Malone had outlined the basic ingredients for an armed truce. Murdoch would ease up on the cable industry, and in return the cable guys would run his channels. But a player as sophisticated as Malone could extract more out of this than just the pleasure of seeing his friend Rupert made to eat a little humble pie. Malone could also use the situation to change the balance of power in Primestar, where TCI and Time Warner each held a 21 per cent stake. It was a lever to make Gerry Levin at Time Warner more amenable.

Malone continued:

You don't take Rupert lightly. It may actually be the kind of rallying cry Primestar and the cable operators need in order to really see the threat that is there. So Rupert may be doing us a huge favour by pointing out to us our vulnerabilities and rallying us . . . I suspect that the external threat of Rupert Murdoch to CNN may be about to cause them [Time Warner] to be a little more willing to reach the combinations with TCI and the rest of the industry and maybe have a united front in Primestar.

For whatever reason, a week and a half later, Murdoch appears to have concluded that the conflict required a more drastic resolution. It is hard not to feel some sympathy for Charlie Ergen, Murdoch's erstwhile partner at Echostar, as events unfolded in April. Murdoch's presentation to the Commerce Committee on 10 April was supposed to be the lynchpin of the campaign to win Capitol Hill over to the anti-cable cause. But the following day, David Lieberman in *USA Today* reported that Murdoch had had another meeting earlier that week with Malone, when Murdoch had been proposing quite a different agenda. He had discussed dumping Echostar and instead folding ASkyB into Primestar with the cable operators. Bob Scherman at *Satellite Business News* ran the same story. He said Murdoch met with Malone and Hindery in New York on Tuesday 8 April.

What was Charlie Ergen to think? When Murdoch read the *USA Today* story he left a message on Ergen's answering machine saying that he had not had discussions with the Primestar partners in more than a year. Preston Padden also denied any meeting: 'This is someone's fantasy.' Then Ted Turner called Ergen to tell him that News Corp officials had approached Time Warner. 'He called to say that News Corp was throwing us over- board and that they were meeting with Levin to talk about a Primestar/ News Corp deal,' Ergen later told *Denver Post* journalist Stephen Keating. Clearly Turner wanted to scupper any Primestar deal.

In Washington, Murdoch's lobbying campaign was dead in the water. The stories that the cable companies had circulated about Murdoch's secret New York meeting with them, whether true or not, had killed any hope of a quick political fix using a clause tracked on to the appropriations bills. The stories kept coming. *Multichannel News* also reported Murdoch's offer to fold ASkyB into Primestar. 'Rupert's desperate,' a senior cable executive said. Primestar chairman, Jim Gray, a former Time Warner executive, was dismissive. He said he wasn't in the room when the Murdoch pitch was made. 'I haven't heard anything serious like that coming from the partners, and my own view is that there's a low probability that anything will happen in that area,' he said.

The question was, if the cable operators had stalled Murdoch in Washington, did they still need to negotiate with him? The cable guys had beaten Murdoch. Now they wanted to roast him, to leave him swinging with a satellite licence and satellites that he couldn't afford and no one wanted. Discussions between News Corp and Primestar that spring were handled mainly by Leo Hindery and Chase Carey. Hindery was 'a peacemaker . . . He kept trying to convince everybody that there was more profit in peace than war,' Malone said later. Malone was hauled out for the heavy meetings with Time Warner and several other Primestar partners where he was 'a proponent of, at least, exploring whether or not we could make peace (with Murdoch).'

For Charlie Ergen, with April came the slow and bitter realisation that his satellite dream team was not going to reach orbit. Murdoch would cast him adrift, in desperate financial straits, and the only thing that Ergen had going for him was his sheer cussedness and ornery determination. Back on 7 March, Echostar and News, after taking advice from tax lawyers and the FCC, had agreed to restructure the deal and draw up a new terms sheet. But lawyers on the two sides could not agree, and draft versions kept bouncing back and forth between the two sides. The worrying thing was that if News Corp took the view that the original letter agreement had been abandoned – as it would – and no subsequent agreement had been finalised, where would that leave Charlie Ergen? What would stop Murdoch walking away from the table?

Ergen and Padden, who headed News Corp's satellite operations, fought over everything, including whether to lay linoleum or carpet in the Phoenix uplink centre. From 7 April, the day before Murdoch's reported meeting with Malone in New York, News Corp had been insisting that the new Sky operation use News Datacom's encryption and conditional access system. Ergen wanted to continue with the Swiss Nagra SA system that Echostar used. He argued that hackers had broken the News Datacom encryption. Padden responded that Echostar was Nagra's only customer, with only 400,000 subscribers. On 17 April, in a torrid meeting at Echostar's headquarters between Ergen and Murdoch and their executives, Padden stormed out. He didn't return.

On 25 April, Murdoch wrote to Ergen highlighting the News Datacom issue among a range of issues needed to be resolved: '(News Corporation) cannot agree to making a vast investment in Echostar on the basis of (the Nagra) technology . . . We cannot go forward in our partnership using this technology.'

Meanwhile, Echostar stock had dropped from $27 to $14. The critical date would be 1 May, when News Corp was due under the original letter agreement to make a $200 million loan to Echostar to keep it going, and file for federal approval for the deal. Thursday 1 May was the event horizon, the point of no return for the entire deal. Once Murdoch had put down some hard money, he would be committed. As it turned out, no money was forthcoming for Ergen that day. The rumour mill ratcheted up a cog.

On the evening of 1 May, when asked about the Sky deal, Malone responded: 'It's dead.' Preston Padden appears to have come to the same conclusion. He resigned from News Corp, telling reporters, 'The reality that I did not have a job was apparent nearly to everybody else in the world before I figured it out.' It was not an easy parting for the man who a year before had said he was with News Corp 'for life', who had regularly had his boss as a house guest when Murdoch went to Washington.

'From what I understand, Murdoch placed a call to Ted Turner on Tuesday of this week (29 April) suggesting that they make peace,' UBS Securities analyst Rick Westerman told CNN. 'I understand that Murdoch met with Gerry Levin, the CEO of Time Warner, on Wednesday and there were discussions with respect to the potential satellite relationship going forward.'

Ergen was still alive and kicking, trying to revive the deal. The following Monday, 5 May, Echostar demanded that News Corp make good on its commitment to loan the $200 million, to stop Echostar going broke. Though Ergen didn't know it, on Tuesday News Corp sealed a deal with MCI for News Corp to take 90 per cent of ASkyB. On Tuesday afternoon, after further exchanges, Chase Carey flew in to Denver International Airport, where he met Ergen and told him bluntly that if he wanted the merger to go ahead, he would have to resign. The new venture had to be headed by a News Corp executive, or News would go its own way. Ergen said he still wanted to go ahead, but wanted time to consider. Carey said he would call him the next day. But he never made the call. The momentum towards the courtroom had become unstoppable.

By Wednesday 7 May, the first legal skirmishes had begun. On Friday morning News Corp finally signalled that the alliance was over when six News Corp employees left the Echostar offices. That night Echostar staff drove to the home of the chief deputy clerk for the US District of Denver and filed paperwork for a writ at his kitchen table. Charlie Ergen was suing News Corp and Rupert Murdoch for $5 billion. The question was whether Echostar would stay solvent long enough to get the case to court.

News and Echostar lawyers would spend much of the next eighteen months deposing each other and everyone else connected with the deal. The onerous terms exacted by Ergen when the suit was settled in late 1998 would cost News Corporation and MCI $3.5 billion.

And Charlie Ergen? He thought he knew Rupert Murdoch. For months after the deal came apart, as Echostar struggled for survival, Ergen would keep that signed agreement with Murdoch on his desk. He would look at it every day and wonder: What could have been? Where did it go wrong? In his darker moments he would wonder whether Murdoch had ever intended to go through with Sky, whether he had been used as a pawn in a wider game. Even whether it was all some sort of hideous revenge for the 110WL auction.

CHAPTER TWELVE

THE TESTING OF PAT

Virginia Beach, Virginia Feb–June 1997

Some telephone calls should never be answered. One day in the depths of the North American winter of 1997 Rupert Murdoch picked up the telephone and said, 'Hello, Pat,' though he should have known better.

America's most influential religious figure was on the other end of the line. Murdoch had never made a secret of his admiration for Pat Robertson, the one-time Baptist minister who became a television evangelist, then a politician, remaining always a businessman. Murdoch had known Robertson since 1986, when Robertson sold his Boston television station, Channel 25, to Fox. 'You can say what you like, he's right on all the issues,' Murdoch said of Robertson during Robertson's unsuccessful presidential campaign in 1988. Now Robertson was calling Murdoch again about another business opportunity.

What was Rupert Murdoch doing? His family background should have warned him of the danger he was facing. Murdoch had enough low church men among his ancestors to know the folly of the course before him. His roots would have told him that it is a basic premise of Protestant free enterprise that you never, ever do business with the preacher. Because when you do, and the preacher gets a fatal attack of scruples, you know it will cost you a lot of money. In the next four months, Pat Robertson's inner struggle to do the right thing would cost Rupert Murdoch $1 billion. It would also play a critical role in resolving the battle for cable networks, the future of satellite television, and the economics of sport. The outcome would be determined by a bizarre string of events that reached as far as a hotel room in Zaire. Even in the topsy turvy worlds of the Murdoch empire, this would be a remarkable outcome. The conflict was a subtle one, which needs to be examined one strand at a time. It begins with the peculiar character of Marion Gordon Robertson, the tall silver-haired figure who has always been known as Pat.

Pat Robertson in his own way is as much a pioneer of the cable industry as Ted Turner or Gerry Levin or John Malone. Robertson was fresh out of seminary in 1959 when he came to believe that God was telling him to buy a defunct UHF television station in Plymouth, Virginia, for $37,000. Soon after the station went to air in 1961, Robertson hired Jim and Tammy Bakker, a husband and wife team on the revival preaching circuit, to do a puppet show. With the station's finances in disrepair, Jimmy Bakker launched a tearful appeal that drew in a surge of donations. Subsequently Bakker and Robertson launched a show called the *700 Club*, which aimed at raising 700 supporters willing to pledge $10 a month. Robertson never looked back. In 1977 he launched America's first general entertainment cable channel with a risible 16,000 subscribers. Five years later his audience had grown to 15 million, and no one was laughing.

Robertson was part of a wave of televangelists who took America's airwaves by storm in the 1970s and early 1980s. Jimmy Swaggart, Robert Schuller, Jim Bakker, Oral Roberts and Jerry Falwell became household names. By the mid-1980s, Christian preachers had 62 national syndicated shows. The virtual realities of modern media held no fears for the televangelists, as they contemplated the television programs forged by faith, the cable networks not made with hands. In 1985 a Nielsen survey of the top ten religious shows reported that 21 per cent of America's television households were tuning in to Christian TV for at least six minutes a week, and 40 per cent of households watched at least six minutes a month. These huge numbers marked a major social phenomenon. The televangelists 'have greater unrestricted access to media than any other interest group in America,' sociologist Jeffrey Hadden of the University of Virginia told *Time*. The head of National Religious Broadcasters, Reverend Ben Armstrong, claimed the televangelists had 'done what Ted Turner tried to do and Rupert Murdoch wants to do – create an alternative fourth network.'

Armstrong's claim was not without substance. Whether you loved or hated television preachers (and most people settled for one or the other), they had become arguably the only non-commercial group to make serious inroads into the American television industry. But already by the mid-1980s, waves of change were beginning to buffet them as the information revolution gathered speed. How the virtual cathedral weathered this sea change would say much for the future of independent voices in traditional media. And how the televangelists survived would turn largely on the flamboyant, passionate figure who towered above them all, Pat Robertson, whose audience was almost double that of his closest rival.

The most distinctive feature of Pat Robertson has always been his mouth. When the Bank of Scotland pulled out of an online banking alliance with him in June 1999 over his outspoken comments, Robertson said 'you can't believe how strong the homosexuals are' in 'that dark land' of Scotland. His 1991 book, *New World Order*, described world finances as being controlled by a Jewish-led conspiracy. He advocates using political assassination against foreign heads of state. He sees feminism as a 'socialist anti-family political movement that encourages women to leave their husbands, kill their children, practise witchcraft, destroy capitalism and become lesbians.' It isn't just gays, feminists, child molesters and Democrats who arouse his ire (not necessarily in that order). 'You're supposed to be nice to Episcopalians, Presbyterians and Methodists,' he told the *Observer*. 'Nonsense. I don't have to be nice to the spirit of the Antichrist.' That was around the time he was quietly shuffled off the Laura Ashley board.

Not that Robertson always means quite what he says. 'I have been on TV now for almost 40 years, I do a one-hour show every day and it is easy to make what I believe are malapropisms,' he said in 1999, by way of explanation. 'I speak from the heart often, and many times these statements need clarification and if brought out of context can easily be misunderstood.'

Robertson's point about context is significant, because if there is one person whose rambling, stream-of-consciousness diatribes bear comparison with Robertson's, it is that other fine Southern gentleman, Ted Turner. The similarities between the two men go deeper than sharing a flair for over-dramatic language and the outrageous phrase. Each used public appeals for money to keep their first television stations afloat, and each went on to found a cable network. Both men are plugged into a tradition of Southern rhetoric that is easy for outsiders to dismiss and underestimate.

Robertson was on the brink of launching into politics when Murdoch bought his Boston television station in 1986. The 1988 bid for the Republican presidential nomination proved one of the pivotal experiences of Robertson's career. In nine of the first ten primaries in the south, Robertson beat frontrunner George Bush, before Super Tuesday blew away his hopes. Robertson was in Washington for the Bush inauguration in January 1989. He was mulling over his political prospects and his mailing list of three million conservative Christian voters when a young conservative activist, Ralph E. Reed Junior, convinced him to found a new religious political group, the Christian Coalition. It would go on to become one of the most powerful supporters for America's move to the right in the 1990s.

Of more immediate importance were the problems at the Christian Broadcasting Network. In 1988, with Robertson away campaigning, donations raised by the *700 Club* dropped 36 per cent. Who was responsible? The revivalist tradition from which Robertson springs has always struggled with the tension between the natural and the supernatural, between belief in God's power and personal agency. A popular expression in fundamentalist circles summed up this tension: 'You must pray as it all depends upon God. Then you must go out and work as if it all depends upon you.' The big drop in donations to the *700 Club* made it appear that, at the Christian Broadcasting Network (CBN) at least, it all depended upon Pat.

'What are we going to do when Pat Robertson is gone?' CBN's chief financial officer, Robert M Prigmore, said in 1994, 'Pat's not going to live forever.'

'It was an eye-opener of how dependent we are on Pat and the money he raises for the ongoing ministry,' CBN director Harold Bredesen said in 1994. 'We realised our need for alternate funding.'

CBN needed to become more commercial. At the same time, the profits that the Family Channel were notching up were beginning to threaten CBN's tax-free status as a charity. The solution to all this was for CBN to sell the Family Channel; and the most suitable buyer would be itself. In early 1990, CBN sold the Family Channel into a new company called International Family Entertainment (IFE) in return for $250 million of convertible debt. All of the initial stock in IFE was held by Pat Robertson, who invested $100,000, and his son Tim, who kicked in $50,000. Robertson senior's stock was held by a trust he controlled that would revert to CBN when Robertson turned 80, 20 years later. One aspect of this arrangement was that, while Robertson would have complete control of the investments held by the trust, he could always say that no matter what he did privately, the money would always end up with CBN.

Two years later when IFE and CBN raised $187.5 million in an Initial Public Offering, Pat and Tim Robertson ended up with super-voting stock in IFE worth $62.5 million.

Tim Robertson continued to craft the Family Channel into a general entertainment network that ran old family fare like *Bonanza*, *The Waltons*, *The Three Stooges*, and the *Mary Tyler Moore Show*. 'I make no bones about it, I am a person of faith, and I have very deeply held-religious beliefs, but I don't use the channel as my pulpit,' Tim Robertson told the *Boston Herald*. Robertson described his ideal viewer as a mother, aged between 25 and 54, who was seeking entertainment suitable for young children but was leery of the content of most TV shows.

The Family Channel went on to cable in Britain in 1993, and to satellite in Latin America in 1995. By then, the Robertsons had made the Family Channel one of the top ten television brands in the world, a fact which advertisers conceded sometimes with gritted teeth.

'We buy it [the Family Channel],' Grey Advertising senior vice president Jon Mandel told *Multichannel News*. 'Even though the worst piece of garbage ever run on TV is the *700 Club*, it doesn't carry commercials, anyway.'

By 1996, Pat Robertson had become a man of many parts. From his base in Virginia Beach, besides IFE he also presided over Christian Broadcasting Network, which produced the *700 Club* show and also owned a string of commercial ventures that included a hotel, a theme park, an unsuccessful vitamin and cosmetics business and a retirement village. Nearby was Regent University, the college Robertson had founded. And just along the road was the headquarters of Robertson's relief agency, Operation Blessing International. But by late 1996, press attention was focusing on Pat Robertson's private business interest – in particular his diamond mining operation in Zaire.

'I personally funded huge shipments of medical supplies to the refugees from Rwanda as well as the victims of the Ebola outbreak in Kikwit,' Robertson said later. 'It was obvious that private charity could not sustain the enormous need that existed in the country, and I was attempting to make investments in timber, mining and agriculture which would be self-sustaining. Regrettably, the chaotic political situation in that nation made such ventures impossible.'

In the early 1990s, Robertson had established a cordial relationship with the brutal dictator of Zaire, President Mobutu Sese Seko, who granted a diamond mining concession on a river in the south-east of Zaire to a corporation that Robertson owned called African Development Company. The concession turned out to be something of a dud. Robertson flew in dredges that didn't work, diamond grades were poor, and eventually he pulled out after writing off losses that some estimates put as high as $7 million. But the link raised questions about what Robertson was doing in business deals with Mobutu. There had been some curious incidents.

Kinshasa, Zaire, 23 March 1993

The door on Leslie Naghiu's hotel room was unlocked, but this didn't trouble him. Even the most dependable of hotel maids can forget to lock a room after they come in to turn down the sheets, and he was glad to be back in familiar surroundings. He had just completed a trip to the back blocks outside of Kinshasa, through military checkpoints where soldiers had been known to beat up and rob foreigners. That was why he had left his attaché case behind in his room on the nineteenth floor.

Naghiu shuffled in to the dark room and felt for the light switch. It wasn't working. Naghiu fumbled around and finally located a floor lamp. It was then that he saw the clothing strewn about the room, his large suitcase open, and a man crouched beside it . . . a man who, even as Naghiu saw him, rose and lunged at him with a knife. In the fierce struggle that followed, the knife caught Naghiu above the ear on the left side of his head, and then again on the right forearm. And then Naghiu realised that a second man was coming towards him out of the bathroom. Amid a flurry of blows a wider darkness engulfed him, and Naghiu slumped to the floor unconscious, where his companions later found him.

The incident was revisited in the Delaware District Court in February 1996 when Naghiu, who worked for the Christian Broadcasting Network as 'director of executive protection' for Pat Robertson, sued the Intercontinental Hotels Group for personal injuries and the loss of $146,000. The money had been in the briefcase stolen from him during the attack in his hotel room in March 1993. According to Judge Murray M. Schwartz, who described the events in the case as 'rich with intrigue,' Naghiu had flown to Zaire with other CBN staff that month 'to purchase diamonds and render humanitarian aid'.

As one does. Naghiu carried $100,000 in an attaché case. While in Zaire he had received another $46,000 'as proceeds of a diamond transaction', Judge Schwartz found.

Pat Robertson said later:

To the best of my knowledge, (Mr Naghiu's) medical expenses were paid by insurance which we had provided for him, and he was given a retirement settlement from our organisation to compensate for his severe injury in excess of $500,000. Today I am still at a loss to understand why he did not prevail in the case against the Intercontinental Hotel Company, which, in my opinion, was clearly negligent in permitting one of its guests to be attacked, brutally beaten, and robbed in his room in their hotel.

Judge Schwartz dismissed Naghiu's claim for compensation against the hotel on the grounds that he did not own the money that was stolen. He also found it 'noteworthy' that the hotel group had twice requested, without success, for paper records to show where the money came from, who owned it, or to prove if it even existed. Further, despite repeated requests, Naghiu had not been able to produce evidence that he or CBN had declared the money when he left the US, as required by US law and the Customs Service.

It really was most peculiar. Did the money in the suitcase belong to Pat Robertson's private companies, or to the tax-exempt CBN organisation, or to Operation Blessing, CBN's relief agency? Why didn't the real owner of the money bring the lawsuit? If it was money connected with Robertson's private businesses, as seemed likely, what were CBN staff or relief workers doing handling it – and being knocked unconscious for it?

What significance did all this have? In 1996, the answer was, not very much. There was nothing illegal or improper about being robbed in a hotel room. But the virtual cathedral of the televangelists ran on appearances – or at least its leaders seemed to believe it did. When asked about his mining interests in 1999, Robertson explained:

> You can look at it one way and say this is a wonderful thing you're doing, taking your money to try and make some profit in order to help people who are desperately poor. The other side is that it is not right. But if I please the Lord and I do what he says then he will take care of me.

The sort of questions that were being raised about Robertson's diamond operations had the potential to damage the relationship of trust that Robertson, the *700 Club*, CBN and Operation Blessing had with their donors. And donations were the lifeblood of the Robertson group. Robertson was already struggling with bad press because of an ongoing tax audit by the Internal Revenue Service over several million dollars of CBN funds that had been channelled into his presidential campaign in 1988, and the Christian Coalition's ties with the Republican Party. Then there was the messy lawsuit lodged by three members of the Regent University law school, after Robertson wrote an open letter that suggested they were the worst law professors in the history of Western jurisprudence. There had been a messy scene in a Virginia courtroom when a process server had tried to serve a court order at Robertson, chasing Robertson around a table in a conference room, papers and coffee cups spilling over, some spirited pushing and shoving, while Robertson's bodyguard threatened to beat the process server up. All in all, by early 1997 a little more bad press was the last thing that Pat Robertson needed. This provides one possible explanation for the remarkable turn that events would later take. In the meantime, Pat Robertson had had a close encounter of an entirely different kind. In early January 1996, Rupert Murdoch had telephoned Robertson. His old friend had an idea for him. It was a world away from the comfortable values of the Family Channel.

If anyone knew the frustrations of seeking media access in the 1990s, it was Murdoch. He had had to scrap and scrape to win affiliates for the Fox network. He had just committed to launch Fox News, an outlay that would grow to more than $500 million. And at the same time he had decided to launch a cable channel with children's programming called Fox Kids. It was the brainchild of an aggressive Egyptian-born Israeli American called Haim Saban.

Saban, like Robertson, had carved a business empire out of a niche in the media industry, but he had taken a very different route. The international growth of the US entertainment industry has produced opportunities for entrepreneurs at every frontier. The dubbing down of America is very big business. Every time a book or film or television program or song crosses national and language frontiers, there is work for a little community of specialists who can translate or dub the work, to make it acceptable and sellable in another culture. Saban was a linguistic arbitrageur. Born in Alexandria in 1944, his family moved to Israel in the 1950s, where he grew up in modest circumstances. Like many people from Alexandria he was a polyglot, able to switch at will between English, French, Hebrew, Arabic, Spanish and Italian.

In 1980, having spent many years building one of the largest music businesses in France, Saban moved to Los Angeles. He said later he had barely enough money to buy a hilltop house in Hollywood and a Rolls Royce. At least he had enough left to insist on personalised number plates: 1 RSK TKR. He scrounged and pushed his way into music work in Hollywood, then into producing a children's show for NBC called *Captain Kidd*. US domestic sales covered the $200,000 cost of producing each episode and gave Saban a $50,000 profit. It was the overseas sales, where he could earn another $70,000, that became the major profit driver of such productions. In 1986 he secured the rights to a Japanese children's action show called *Macron 1*, to be dubbed into English. It was on the same trip to Japan that Saban came across episodes of Japanese fantasy shows from the 1960s and 1970s, on which he quietly took an option for distribution rights outside Japan. They were pretty horrible really, at least to Western eyes. But they had some expensive special effects fight scenes between giant dinosaurs and huge robots intercut with human figures. The thought stayed with Saban that the figures had helmets on. Once you put a helmet on a figure, it could be anyone underneath.

For the next six years, he played around with the idea of producing a cheap-as-dirt children's program by shooting a few scenes of American teenagers changing into bright costumes, then inter-cutting the special effects shots from the old Japanese shows of the 1970s. He pitched the idea to a succession of network programmers over the years, all of whom found the idea too awful to contemplate, until in 1992 he found someone desperate to try something loopy and unusual in children's programming. Margaret Loesch, programmer for Fox Children, loved the idea. In 1985 when she was president of Marvel Comics' television production company, Leosch had actually spotted the same Japanese program – a year before Saban – and had paid $25,000 to have a pilot dubbed into English. US network executives hated it. 'One network executive asked, "How could you bring us this piece of garbage?" ' Loesch said later. So when Loesch signed up Saban to produce another US version of the same show, her colleagues, the staff and her boss thought she was out of her mind. 'They basically thought I had finally lost it,' she said. A week before it went to air in September 1993, the new head of Fox programming, Lucy Salhany, watched a video of the pilot and faxed Loesch to tell her to dump the show. 'Maybe I'm too old, but this will be a disaster,' Sahany wrote.

'You're right – you're too old,' Loesch faxed back. 'Kids will like it, and I've got a back-up if they don't. Please let me go ahead.'

Salhany relented.

Over the years Saban had worked through a series of names for the show. The original Japanese name, *Che Je Yu Rangers*, didn't really have the southern California feel he was looking for. *Galaxy Rangers* was an early attempt at the naming problem, but this was also discarded. To beef up the action sequences Saban had contracted to buy in footage from other Japanese programs including *Kaku Rangers*, *Dai Rangers*, *Spielvan* and *Metalder* or *Megaman*. Saban included a campy script to pull this hotch potch of material together, and for a name eventually settled on the *Mighty Morphin Power Rangers*. In September 1993, even as Fox worked on contingency plans for what to do when the show bombed, the Mighty Morphin Power Rangers took America by storm. They became the most popular children's programming in forty countries, on the way to pulling $5 billion in merchandising sales. Power Rangers became the most popular action figures of the decade, beating Batman, Star Wars and World Wrestling Federation figures out of the park. In 1995 alone, US merchandising sales topped $1 billion. World sales were probably double that. *Power Rangers* made Fox Children's Network the highest rating children's programming on broadcast television. Only Nickelodeon on cable had higher ratings for children aged two to eleven. The Rangers also made Haim Saban a major Hollywood player.

In 1992 Saban's company, Saban Entertainment, had been a solid little production house. It notched up $48 million in US and foreign sales that year from its stable of children's television programs ranging from Marvel Comics' *X Men*, *The Tick* ('a garden variety giant 400-pound crime fighter') to *Goosebumps*. The company's net profit was a modest $4 million. In a two-and-a-half year period ending in October 1995, Saban's operating profits totalled $224 million, driven by the $290 million that the company earned from the *Power Rangers*. It wasn't the television shows that made the money – it was the royalties from Bandai America, which made the Power Rangers action figures. In 1995 only a quarter of Saban Entertainment's sales came from television deals. Two thirds of the company's income – or $164 million – came from merchandising and licensing.

Haim Saban had developed a distribution system that could take programming unique to one country and extract profits from it in dozens of countries around the world. He had become an expert at 'freshening' old programs with new scripts, voices and music. He knew that all popular fads have a use-by date, even the Power Rangers, so his stated policy was to refresh the Power Ranger characters by 'changing their costumes and ethnicity'. Even so, by late 1995 the Ranger had peaked. That was when Saban put the squeeze on Rupert Murdoch.

It wasn't just Haim Saban that had been making money out of the Power Rangers. Fox Children's Network (FCN) had earned $85 million in the same two-and-a-half year period to October 1995 from them. Murdoch wanted to replicate the runaway ratings success of FCN on cable. At the same time that Murdoch was planning his Fox News cable channel in late 1995 and 1996, he had a covert operation going to set up a cable channel called Fox Kids. He believed Saban's involvement would be critical to the success of the venture. Saban was interested, but he wanted to be an equal partner. So in mid-1995, Saban and Murdoch agreed to merge Saban

Entertainment with Fox Children's Network. Saban and Fox would each hold just under 50 per cent of the new company, Fox Kids Worldwide. Murdoch's merchant bankers Allen & Co would hold the balance of the shares, which would keep the deal off the News Corp balance sheet. The deal valued Saban Entertainment at close to $1 billion.

The plan was to float Fox Kids worldwide within a year, which would give Saban the big cash payout he was looking for. In the meantime, Murdoch paid $80 million cash to Saban and the minority shareholders in Saban Entertainment. Stan Shuman at Allen & Co didn't just help to organise the deal. Wearing his other hat as a Democratic Party fundraiser, he helped Saban become one of President Clinton's major fundraisers in Hollywood, an outcome that must have been as gratifying to Shuman as it was annoying to Murdoch.

By the end of 1995, the Fox Kids deal had been hammered out. The only problem was how the new children's cable channel would be distributed. So in January 1996 Murdoch quietly called his old friend Pat Robertson to put an idea to him. Robertson's company, IFE, needed cash to upgrade its programming. Regent College and Christian Broadcasting Network were also strapped for cash. Murdoch was prepared to pay cable operations to carry Fox News. In a variation on the same theme, Murdoch suggested to Robertson that he would pay IFE to run Fox Kids on the Family Channel through the day up to 6 p.m. Overnight Fox Kids would have 59 million subscribers, putting it well ahead of the Disney Channel with 28 million subscribers, and in striking distance of Nickelodoen with 72 million subscribers.

Robertson liked the idea, but didn't commit himself. Instead, the IFE board appointed Goldman Sachs to find someone prepared to pump $350 million into the company. It was an almost impossible task, because on the one hand Robertson insisted that at the end of the day he had to retain control of the company. That way, he could ensure that the new management would not drop the *700 Club*. On the other hand, John Malone at TCI reminded IFE that he had pre-emptive rights over any stock to be sold. He would block any new investor holding a larger stake than TCI.

Whatever financial structure emerged, Pat Robertson and John Malone both had to be happy at the end of the day. The struggle to achieve this would throw off a bewildering series of failed deals – and drive off almost all of IFE's suitors. The key to following the saga that unfolded is seeing in each deal how much money ended up on Pat Robertson's side of the table – and how much it was going to cost Rupert Murdoch.

Goldman Sachs talked to NBC, to CBS and to Universal Studios, but in the end they all wanted to take control of IFE. Only Murdoch was prepared to leave Robertson in charge. Goldman Sachs proposed a $643 million takeover scheme. IFE stockholders would be offered between $20 and $21 a share. Regent College and CBN would walk away with $166 million between them. Pat and Tim Robertson would not receive any money. They would hold on to their super voting shares and 20 per cent of the company. The money to fund the takeover would come from bank borrowings, a $110 million cash contribution from TCI, and $350 million from the new investor, News Corp. By August 1996 Murdoch was chafing at the delays, and offered to sweeten the deal by pumping another $150 million of subordinated debt into IFE. This took the total cost to Murdoch of carrying Fox Kids to the Family Channel's 59 million subscribers to $500 million. This was still a much faster and more effective way of getting on to cable than the $10 a head inducement Murdoch was offering cable operators to run Fox News.

By 20 December 1996, all parties were ready to draw up a formal proposal. The final meeting was set down in Los Angeles for the week of 3 February 1997. But Pat Robertson got cold feet. Caught between two powerful figures like Murdoch and Malone, Robertson feared that he would lose control of the Family Channel, and if the *700 Club* survived at all it would end up rescheduled into the 2 a.m. slot. At the last minute Robertson refused to sign the papers and called off the deal.

Malone had had enough. He told Robertson he was prepared to step away from the deal if someone made him an offer. At this point the deal was dead. 'I think it's firmly on the rocks,' a source told the *Hollywood Reporter*. Over more than a year, Robertson had proved a demanding, frustrating negotiator. He had picked and fiddled with details of the deal, trying to lever out more money and greater control. He was just too much trouble. This was the point where Rupert Murdoch should have cut his losses and run. Instead, when Pat Robertson phoned Murdoch in mid-February to talk him into reviving the deal and buying out Malone, Regent College and CBN, Murdoch said he would see what he could do. As he discussed it with Malone, Murdoch decided he could break the deadlock by throwing some money into the pot for Pat Robertson himself. Mistakes like this are what come from answering telephones.

Rupert Murdoch maintains the frenetic sort of schedule that would put most people on Prozac. But Murdoch's manoeuvres in February 1997 were bewildering even by his standards. In Israel his group had been accused of bugging business opponents and government officials. In Denver, Charlie Ergen believed Murdoch was offering him the deal of his life with the Sky merger. Meanwhile Pat Robertson was on the phone demanding a new deal. So was Peter O'Malley, the owner of America's best-known baseball team, the Dodgers, which Murdoch had decided he wanted to buy. In the back of his mind was a coupon and inserts business called Heritage Media, that he would buy for $1.4 billion on 17 March. And then there was the little problem with John Malone.

Malone was angry. The Echostar merger announcement had come halfway through the convoluted negotiations over IFE and Fox Sports. In trumpeting the power of the new Sky alliance, Murdoch's executives had gone out of their way to describe how they were going to destroy the cable industry . . . and that would include the largest cable company, John Malone's TCI. The first consequence was that Murdoch could kiss goodbye to any plans he had for buying Pat Robertson's Family Channel.

'We were really neutral in it,' Malone said much later, of the IFE negotiations. 'The only thing we said is that while Rupert was working out his difference with the cable industry, on the satellite side, we wouldn't let any deal happen. Once the satellite deal got worked out, we simply took our foot off it and said, 'It's open to the highest bidder, but it's Pat call.'

This is the sort of magnanimous understatement that is only made in retrospect after a peace settlement. At the time, the emotional temperature was much higher, the antagonism much stronger. The bottom line was: nothing was going to happen with the Family Channel as long as cable operators like Malone were facing the Sky merger. Murdoch wasn't taking the pressure lying down. If the IFE deal was off, and cable operators were threatening not to run his programming, then Murdoch wasn't going to buy Liberty Media's half share in Fox Sports that Malone wanted to sell.

'We want to remain partners with them,' Murdoch told journalists rather archly. 'We don't want to lose their carriage.'

The script was playing out like one of the remakes of the Hollywood classic where two people who dislike each other are handcuffed together, forced to co-operate. No matter how irritated Murdoch and Malone were with each other, the reality was that they were irretrievably bound together. And both men were too smart not to realise this after the first annoyance had worn off. It was this wider confluence of interests that brought them together again in late March to say, as Leo Hindery later put it, 'Let's talk. Let's not whale on each other.'

It was at this meeting that Murdoch made his plaintive appeal to Malone over the Echostar deal, 'Well, then, help me get out of it; help me find something else to do. What is Plan B?'

By that stage, it was as important to John Malone as it was to Rupert

Murdoch to find a way out of the mess. The satellite and cable industries were looking down the barrel of a crippling price war that could have a devastating impact on the whole future of the communications revolution. More to the point, it would have a devastating impact on Murdoch's and Malone's businesses. So the two men kept talking.

And Murdoch kept talking to Pat Robertson. Under the new deal for IFE that Murdoch put to Robertson, Fox Kids would not be putting any more money on the table than last time. The difference was where the money would go. There would be no general takeover bid. Instead all the cash went to Pat Robertson and his assorted interests. No one else would get a red cent. The payout went like this: Fox Kids would buy CBN's stock at $26 a share and Regent College's stock at $24 a share. Malone's TCI would be paid out at $26 a share in convertible notes in Fox Kids. Then Pat and Tim Robertson would sell their super-voting stock for $70 a share. So Regent and CBN would end up with $203 million, and the Robertsons would end up with $350 million, paid out three years later. They would have certain governance rights over the Family Channel. And the *700 Club* would stay at 10 p.m. each night. For decades Murdoch had based his business strategy on the belief that every man or woman has a price. Rupert thought he had his friend Pat pegged. For $350 million, the least that Pat Robertson could do was to come quietly.

Murdoch joined Fox executives to make a presentation to the IFE board in New York on 8 April. As Malone would be taking convertible notes, Murdoch would only be paying out $550 million cash, which was little more than he had been planning to pay previously. The independent directors pointed out that most of the money now went to the Robertsons personally. The board didn't like it, but the deal was a private one between shareholders that didn't require board approval.

·Malone was also in New York for the IFE board meeting. That was how the two men came to have their famous 8 April encounter which proved so fatal to Murdoch's Washington campaign, where Murdoch offered to dump the Echostar merger and offer his ASkyB satellite slot to the cable operators' Primestar instead. Meanwhile, negotiations with Pat Robertson had turned a little sticky.

Through April, Robertson continued to bicker over the terms of the buyout that Murdoch was offering. Various combinations were floated for the Robertsons' $350 million payout. The Robertsons were conscious that this deal might not be looked upon quite so warmly by the rest of the IFE stockholders, who would receive nothing. In late April Pat Robertson levelled a new demand at Murdoch. Any deal would also have to have something in it for the rest of the stockholders. They would need to be offered at least $24 a share for their B class stock. This hadn't been part of Rupert Murdoch's plan. The whole idea of buying out the Robertsons was to avoid paying anything to anyone else and getting involved in a full-scale takeover bid. Extending a general offer like that would cost News Corp another $630 million. As the Robertsons also held a swag of B shares and options, it would also put another $60 million in their pockets. If IFE were in play, who knows what other bidders might emerge?

At the start of May, just as Murdoch was grappling with the implications of Pat Robertson's latest demand and killing off his alliance with Charlie Ergen, something remarkable happened. Murdoch and Haim Saban went to meet with Robertson and CBN management on 2 May to work out a final form for the deal, when Robertson made an extraordinary offer. Robertson said he believed it was important to be fair to all the IFE stockholders. That was why he was insisting that Fox Kids should make an offer for all the IFE stock. Even so, it just didn't seem right to Pat Robertson that he should receive $70 a share for his super-voting A stock, when all the B stockholders received only $24 for their B stock. In fact, it was forbidden by IFE's certificate of incorporation, which stated: 'In the event of a merger or consolidation (all classes of shareholders) shall be entitled to receive the same per share consideration.'

Any decent corporate lawyer could find a loophole to get around this restriction, but it was a matter of principle. Pat Robertson felt so strongly about the need to be fair to everybody that he was willing to accept less money for himself, so that Murdoch could offer more to the other shareholders. It would not cost Murdoch anything extra, it was merely a redistribution of the payout.

Robertson said later:

I was offered a substantial premium for the controlling shares of IFE that would have amounted to a huge windfall for my son and me. Instead of taking that personal financial windfall, it seemed only proper that all the shareholders should benefit from the sale on an equal basis with the controlling A shares, and that there would be no control premium offered.

This was a remarkable gesture. Robertson was offering to accept only $40 for his super-voting stock, which would cut his payout by $150 million. Sharing that extra cash between the other stockholders would lift the price they received to $28 a share. While this would increase the payout for

Regent College and CBN and the Robertsons' own B stock, Pat and Tim would still end up a long way out of pocket. As a piece of corporate philanthropy, giving away $150 million for the sake of a principle is hard to beat. It is the sort of thing that restores one's faith in televangelism and virtual charity.

But why had Pat Robertson done it? Robertson is a complicated character, whose history shows both shrewdness and sincerity. Which side was at work here? It would be a brave reader who tries to second guess Robertson's motives in doing anything. But in the critical days at the end of April when Robertson experienced his change of heart, the Zaire connection had raised its head again. On Sunday 27 April, Robertson's local paper, the *Virginian Pilot*, ran a major story about three Caribou aircraft that Robertson's Operation Blessing aid agency had bought in 1994 for $1 million. The Caribou were old Vietnam War era cargo planes to be used for relief work in Zaire. Robertson announced on the *700 Club* that Operation Blessing was 'bringing in a couple of short-range STOL (short take-off and landing) aircraft that can get directly into those camps.' He then asked viewers to call a number that appeared on the screen. On another program Robertson said: 'There's the medical strike force in Goma with those people and now we've got a little small plane. We're doing a shuttle down to Bakavu so that we can take doctors and medicine back and forth from Goma to Bukavu . . . So please go to your phones. You can participate in Operation Blessing.'

The 27 April story in the *Virginian Pilot* quoted two of the pilots of the three planes who remembered one or two humanitarian flights but said that otherwise the planes had been used exclusively to haul equipment for Pat Robertson's private diamond mining operation. One pilot's flight logs referred to Robertson himself flying on one of the planes where the log entry read: 'Prayed for diamonds.'

Chief pilot Robert Hinkle told Bill Sizemore at the *Virginian Pilot*:

> We got over there and we had Operation Blessing painted on the tails of the aeroplanes, but we were doing no humanitarian work at all. We were just supplying the miners and flying the dredges from Kinshasa out to Tshikapa . . . After three months I had the workers in the hangar take the Operation Blessing off our tails, because I was embarrassed . . .

A CBN spokesman said that the planes had proven to be unsuitable for relief work and that Robertson's mining company had reimbursed

Operation Blessing for their use. Sizemore's story sparked a two-year government inquiry into whether Robertson or CBN had raised donations under false pretences. The Virginian Attorney General's office eventually cleared Robertson, who it said did not know that the statements he had made on the *700 Club* were wrong. Robertson had paid $572,597 to Operation Blessing to reimburse it for the use of the planes. Some $400,000 of this amount was paid in August 1997, two months after the inquiry began.

'I've turned my other cheek so many times, my head is dizzy,' Robertson said in 1999 of the *Virginian Pilot*'s continued coverage of the affair. 'This is beyond the pale . . . they've tried to destroy a charity.'

No substantive adverse findings were ever made against Robertson, CBN or Operation Blessing. However, the Zaire story had wakened the old concerns about Robertson mixing his personal interests with those of his ministry. It suggested that Robertson had a knack for coming out ahead in any deal. The issue here was not whether using the planes to haul diamond dredges was really in any way improper. The virtual cathedral depended on public opinion. Perceptions were the issue here. And Pat Robertson was about to announce a deal where he and his son received $70 for each of their A class shares and walked away with $409 million in total, and everyone else was offered just $24 a share. The *Virginian Pilot* story touched off a storm of controversy about Robertson's business links. Six days later, Robertson met with Murdoch and made his remarkable offer to share $150 million of his payout with the other stockholders.

On one thing Robertson was perfectly clear, that his offer to Murdoch was not triggered by the adverse publicity, saying 'my relief efforts in Zaire had absolutely nothing to do with the IFE transaction. My motive in doing business in Zaire was to help people.'

Robertson like Murdoch is a complex character. Even if Robertson was influenced by the Zaire story, it still takes considerable character to walk away from such wealth.

'We gave up about $150 million in control premium, but after all, your reputation should be considered more important than money,' Robertson said.

A week later, Robertson changed his stance yet again.

Rupert Murdoch was in a difficult position. He was depending upon Pat Robertson to provide a home for his Fox Kids cable channel. He wasn't really happy about making a full-pitched bid for all IFE stock. It would cost a lot of money, and open up the door for other bidders to jump him. But faced with a preacher so obviously struggling to do the right thing by his stockholders, reducing his own payout to increase the price offered to everybody else, it was a little difficult to withdraw.

It got worse. By the week of 12 May, stories about the deal were in the press. On Wednesday 14 May, the *Wall Street Journal* reported a deal was imminent. No mention was made of the original $70 a share deal that Robertson had knocked back. The *Journal* only noted with some asperity that the Robertsons would receive $40 a share while all other stockholders would receive only $26 to $28 a share. This touched off a new storm of controversy. It wasn't just Robertson's preferential pricing that raised eyebrows. There was a more basic incongruity in this union between the violence underlying Fox Kids' *Power Rangers*, *X-Men* and *Goosebumps*, and the family values espoused in the *700 Club*, *Touched by an Angel* and reruns of the *Mary Tyler Moore Show*. It was a fairytale story line as old as the world: Heidi meets Godzilla, Beauty sells out to the Beast, King Kong runs away with Jessica Lange.

IFE's institutional shareholders were angry at the different prices. Mario Gabelli of Gabelli Funds waxed a little biblical himself. He would vote for the deal 'when hell freezes over,' he said. IFE's annual meeting was scheduled for the following Monday. On Friday 16 May, two days after the *Wall Street Journal* report, IFE announced that it was in talks with a potential bidder, but that any bid that eventuated would offer all stockholders the same price. Rather than $70 a share, Robertson would now receive only $28.50. The Robertsons would walk away with only $213 million, though the return for Regent College and CBN was up slightly, to $231 million.

For Murdoch, the downside to this new arrangement was that Pat Robertson now had a powerful incentive to extract the best possible price he could for IFE stock. Two weeks before, Robertson had quietly agreed to move the *700 Club* out of its spot in prime time at 10 p.m. each night, back to 11 p.m. This was the stumbling block that had driven off other suitors in the past. With that concession made, NBC, Sony, CBS and Universal Studios once again began circling IFE – and Fox Kids was now just one of the would-be bidders. But it was Michael Eisner at Disney that became the greatest threat to Fox.

The IFE board played hard ball. The Fox Kids bid stood at $28.50 a share. IFE told the suitors the company would open exclusive negotiations with the first bidder to offer $35 a share. The Fox Kids execs swallowed hard and said they would consider it. Murdoch had started this whole ball rolling with an offer to kick in $350 million to get Fox Kids programming on to cable. Even back in February, when the deal had looked like it was dead, Murdoch had only been contemplating paying out $500 million.

Now the total payout for IFE had risen to $1.7 billion. Counting in IFE's bank debt, the deal valued the company at an incredible $1.9 billion. Going back to do business with the preacher had cost Murdoch and Fox Kids $1.4 billion. Pat Robertson had suffered probably the most expensive attack of conscience in corporate history.

In the process, Pat Robertson had increased the payout for CBN and Regent University from $165 million back in February, to $284 million. Pat and Tim Robertson's payout for their A and B stock and options totalled $262 million. While Pat's stock was held by a trust that would go back to CBN in the year 2010, Tim Robertson would retain $113 million from his original $50,000 investment in IFE seven years before. For his stockholders, Robertson was a hero.

At the end of May, it looked like this fabulous bonanza would get even better. Michael Eisner flew secretly to meet Pat Robertson at Virginia Beach, where he offered to top Murdoch's price and bid $37 a share for IFE. It wasn't just that Eisner wanted a cable channel. By this time, frustrating Rupert Murdoch had become a passion with the head of Disney. The Eisner factor meant that the titanic struggles in early 1997 to determine the future of the world's media giants had become a whole new ball game.

CHAPTER THIRTEEN

MAN FOR ALL SEASONS

Los Angeles, January 1997

Even legends come to grief. On a wintry day in January 1997, Peter O'Malley announced he was calling it a day. He was selling the Dodgers at the end of the season. The baseball world went into shock. The Los Angeles Dodgers were the best known and best run baseball team in the world. They were the Manchester United of American sport. In the way that sporting teams can come to symbolise the aspirations and identity of their home town, the Dodgers were the face and pride of LA. And the O'Malleys had been an integral part of the Dodgers legend since Peter O'Malley's father Walter swung a deal with Los Angeles to move the Brooklyn Dodgers 3,000 miles away to the West Coast.

For days after Peter O'Malley's announcement on 7 January the press was filled with stories of unimaginable anguish. It was more than just sentiment over a lost ball park and ball team. The Dodgers had become a community undertaking. Sport is a passionate business. It shares some of the characteristics of religious wars in that it is essentially tribal in nature. No slight, no betrayal, no injustice is ever forgotten. And that is true when one is merely discussing sport in general. Baseball is a far more serious matter. It is the heart of the American sporting ethos. Oliver Wendell Holmes Junior, the Supreme Court Justice who reshaped the liberal tradition of law in American society, knew this. 'We are not mere grubbers in the muckheaps of the world,' he admonished his profession, with his eyes firmly set on an enlightened judiciary and the higher good of society. This clearly involved 'exhibitions of baseball', which he decreed at the turn of the century were 'purely state affairs', and as such were exempt from state and federal antitrust laws. One may conclude either that this was an inspired price of jurisprudence, or that Oliver Wendell Holmes was someone who really liked his baseball.

Baseball heroes like Babe Ruth or managers like the Dodgers' Tommy Lasorda had a quality of Everyman, transformed by a wonderful talent into towering figures. In the first half of the century the laws of symmetry required that to match the larger-than-life players, the owners of baseball teams must also be of corresponding size. Walter O'Malley was such a figure, with the charm and aggression of the black Irish. In 1958 O'Malley, who left Brooklyn because his plans for a new stadium were turned down, finagled his way into a land swap that left him with 300 acres of land set aside for cheap urban housing at Chavez Ravine. The Hispanic Americans still living on the land in a barrio called Palo Verde were duly evicted, and O'Malley proceeded to build a model baseball stadium without water fountains. It was an oversight over which he expressed surprise, but it meant thirsty fans could only buy Coca Cola or beer from his stalls. It was a manoeuvre known to movie-theatre managers as 'Coca Cola plumbing' and won him the nickname H2 O'Malley.

His son Peter was a different animal: unfailingly polite, reserved, precise, always formally dressed, with a manner kindly but patrician. Peter O'Malley grew up in baseball's First Family, and found it hard to emerge from the long shadow of his father. But he ran a good ball team. Dodger Stadium kept the price of its tickets low, it didn't festoon the ground with advertising or cannibalise the public stands to build lucrative corporate boxes. In many ways, though, by 1997 Peter O'Malley seemed to have lost his nerve.

'I think family ownership of sports today is probably a dying breed,' he said on 7 January as he announced his decision to sell. 'You need a broader base than an individual family to carry you through the storms. Groups or corporations are probably the way of the future.'

The furore over the sale subsided eventually. New York politicians talked about making a bid to win back their Dodgers, but they never did. Angelenos got used to the idea that a big corporation was probably going to end up with the ball team. The real consequences were much broader. What was less apparent at the time was that the geopolitics of sport in southern California – and in all of North America – had become dangerously unstable. The emerging alliances which sought to control the sports-entertainment-media business in America were on a collision course. They were one short step, one small space away from direct conflict. The significance of Peter O'Malley's announcement on

7 January was that his pending departure would force that final step on the road to war.

Rupert Murdoch was appropriately diffident about his interest in the Dodgers. At a panel discussion at the International Radio and Television Society in mid-January he downplayed any interest in bidding for the team, 'But I'm not saying that absolutely'. The first call to Peter O'Malley's office came some weeks later. Rupert Murdoch would like to have dinner with O'Malley. This was the logical way to start things, because the biggest hurdle facing anyone who wanted to buy the Dodgers was that first they had to sell themselves to Peter O'Malley. He was selling the family heirloom. This was not a conversation over a business lunch. A buyer would require exquisite negotiating skills, would have to use any prop or advantage that would give him the slightest edge. Murdoch's edge was 'the House'.

Barry Diller signed the papers to buy Jules Stein's mansion, Misty Mountain on Angelo Drive, for the Murdochs in September 1986. It is one of the great houses of Hollywood, filled with the requisite star-studded history. Celebrity architect Wallace Neff built it in 1926 for Fred Niblo, the director of silent films like *The Mask of Zorro* and *The Three Musketeers*. When Niblo fell on harder times with the rise of talkies in the 1930s, he rented the house out to Nelson Eddy and later to Katharine Hepburn. There, on the splendid lawn, Hepburn played croquet with Spencer Tracy. In 1940 Jules Stein, the founder of MCA Inc, now Paramount Studios, bought it and lived there until he died in 1980. His wife Doris died four years later, and the house went on the market. It stands on six acres on a hilltop off Benedict Canyon, overlooking Rudolph Valentino's house, Falcon's Lair. The house offers probably the best views in Los Angeles, with a panoramic sweep across the city and beyond to the Pacific Ocean. 'It was beautiful, you really had a sense of privacy, of being alone,' the Steins daughter, Jean, said of growing up there. Beyond the high walls, gates and security cameras a 600-foot driveway leads up to a two-storey Spanish-style mansion with a red roof and stone façade. The 14 rooms are based around a circular courtyard with a wishing well and Chinese elm at its centre. Murdoch paid $5.8 million for the house in 1986, and another $2 million for the antiques and art work that Jules Stein had collected for the house. 'My wife and I are extremely excited about it,' Murdoch said when he wrote to Neff's son about renovating the house after moving in. The house has four family bedrooms, three staff bedrooms, nine bathrooms, a pool, a screening room, two greenhouses and a formal English garden which Anna Murdoch managed.

It takes more than a bunch of bedrooms and a view to make an impression in Los Angeles. But even by Hollywood standards it was a magnificent setting. It served as a springboard for Anna's charity work that put her on hostesses' A List. It dazzled Murdoch's executives when they trooped to LA each year for the budget meetings. It was the perfect backdrop for relaxed business dinners where Rupert and Anna and their guests could stroll around the gardens past the Italian pines, or look out over the city from the terrace sipping Californian Chardonnay. It was a high, airy space where one could talk easily about the big picture. It was a place where a patrician like Peter O'Malley could feel at home around the smell of almost-old money.

Dodgers president Bob Graziano came with O'Malley for dinner at the Murdochs'. The entire evening was a triumph of composure for Murdoch. At the time he was deeply involved in the Sky merger deal with Charlie Ergen. He was still looking to stare down the cable operators who were after his hide, he was desperate to square off his exasperated partner John Malone, to win over Congress, and to tempt Pat Robinson. And he was doing his best to micro-manage the British general election. Somewhere along the line he found time to buy a coupon insert business called Heritage Media for $1.4 billion on 18 March. To have all this in the air, and to put it all aside for long enough to be the perfect host and tell Peter O'Malley exactly what he wanted to hear, required extraordinary self-control.

Peter Chernin was there that night, along with Murdoch's elder son Lachlan. At 25 years Lachlan was no stranger to the drama of haggling over sport. Two years earlier he had been part of the small News Corp team secretly signing up football players in hotel rooms across Australia, as News mounted a takeover bid on the country's major sporting code, rugby league. Tonight Murdoch Senior kept the conversation brisk with a string of questions.

'He wanted to know about my family and me and why I was selling the ball club,' O'Malley told the *Los Angeles Times* later. 'I told him I thought it was too high-risk a business for one family because there was no reason to believe player salaries would level off . . . I also told him about the tragic relation the owners have with the players. The lack of trust, and the animosity. I told him the truth.'

Though Murdoch had hated sport as a boy, as an adult he had quickly realised how sport stories sold newspapers. Reportedly he had never been to a game of baseball in his life. Yet on that night he spoke intelligently about the Dodgers' line-up – about Vin Scully, about catcher Mike Piazza whose contract was coming up for renegotiation, about the Japanese pitcher Hideo Nomo, and about the international prospects for baseball. 'I was astonished at his depth of knowledge – with all he's got going on – about the Dodgers,' O'Malley told Connie Bruck of the *New Yorker*.

In much the same way that he had with Charlie Ergen at Echostar, Murdoch managed to tap into O'Malley's dream for the future. O'Malley didn't want a personality to buy the Dodgers. He didn't want to sell the Dodgers as an adornment of the buyer's ego. 'He's not dancing on the roof of the dugout, or in the clubhouse filling out the line-up card,' he said of Murdoch. His host was able to share O'Malley's enthusiasm for promoting baseball internationally, because with his satellite and cable interests around the world Murdoch had a unique capacity to take the Dodgers around the world and back. Like many before him, he described his business relationship with Murdoch as a romance. 'The first time we met we had a common interest, a common focus,' O'Malley told Bruck. The night at Angelo Drive was a 'first date'.

For Rupert Murdoch, buying the Dodgers was not such a sentimental affair. It was merely an episode in his five-year odyssey to become the uncrowned sports czar of the world. Since 1992, Murdoch had spent $5 billion buying up sports programming rights. He had written off at least one fifth of this as losses even before the ink dried on some of the contracts. By 1997 his empire was paying more than $1 billion a year for sports rights, and Murdoch's appetite for sports programming was more voracious than it had ever been. To outsiders, the unfolding saga was a little like watching the luge at the Winter Olympics. The further down the track the competitor goes, the faster the sled moves, the tighter the turns seem, the more the risk of disaster grows. One mistake spells the difference between a medal-winning performance and ignominy. To use a less structured analogy, Murdoch had triggered an avalanche: the question was whether he could stay far enough ahead of it to avoid being buried.

It had begun at the Lancaster Hotel in London, just before noon on 18 May 1992. In a tense meeting, the chairmen of 21 first-division football clubs voted by the narrowest of margins to give Murdoch's BSkyB and the BBC exclusive broadcast rights for the new Premier League soccer competition. It was the climax of a furious months-long battle for the rights between Sam Chisholm at BSkyB and Independent Television (ITV). Two hours before the final vote Chisholm had telephoned Murdoch, waking him in the middle of the night in New York. Chisholm wanted to lift BSkyB's bid by £30 million to trump a revised offer that ITV had made an hour earlier. Murdoch gave a groggy approval. Chisholm's late counter bid won the day, so that BSkyB and the BBC won the Premier League broadcast rights for four seasons, for what then seemed the astronomical sum of £304 million.

Looking back, this seems to have been the sort of corporate masterstroke which is generally stumbled upon only by luck, and only by the very bold. Chisholm had been plagued by doubts about whether BSkyB could afford the Premier League rights. The bid would cost BSkyB £76 million a year, less the BBC's payment to run game highlights for its *Match of the Day* program. Chisholm's doubts were answered within weeks as BSkyB signed up one million subscribers ready to pay £5.99 a month for the sports channel. That came to almost £54 million a year of new income for BSkyB, almost overnight repaying most of the cost of winning the rights. Sport became a huge driver for BSkyB's subscriber numbers. As Murdoch said later, 'The Premier League was the really big move, it gave us a huge boost. That was a big deal, and it took off straight away.'

A year later, Murdoch turned his eyes towards America's National Football League (NFL). The Murdoch assault on sport – the transformation of the man who had always hated sport of any kind, into arguably the most influential person in sport in the world – came at an awkward time for the North American media industry. The big networks – NBC, ABC and CBS – were hurting from the inroads that cable television had been making on their audience for two decades. In the early 1990s the Big Three were winding back costs: cutting back on payments to their affiliates, and working to slow down the big growth in sports costs. While network executives were always 'slaveringly eager to . . . cut into each other's market share', as Murdoch put it, anyone could see the overall trend here. This was the sort of tacit consensus that game theory predicted, where it was in everyone's interest not to outbid each other. Everyone stood to lose from another cost blow out.

Murdoch recalled:

> The previous holders of the (NFL) rights were talking publicly about reducing prices. They were having public discussions about how to get the prices down, because they couldn't see what the NFL really meant to their networks. There were two companies that were for sale (CBS and NBC), and they were trying to increase their profits and their value to potential purchasers.

When Murdoch set out to win the free-to-air rights for the American Football Convention, one of the two divisions in the NFL, his first task was to convince Laurence Tisch at CBS, who had held these rights forever, not to bid against him. Tisch had to be convinced, according to George Vradenburg, a former CBS exec now at Fox, that 'Rupert was a crazy man'. In the previous term CBS had paid just over $1 billion for its four-year package of games, and had lost $150 million on the deal. That meant that for CBS, the rights had been worth only $850 million, or $212.5 million a season. Murdoch blew CBS away by bidding $395 million a season, for a total over four years of $1.58 billion. After that, CBS was never in the race. Once Murdoch had won, his first step was to write off $590 million as an upfront loss on the contract. This meant he was actually valuing it at less than the previous CBS deal (he later reduced the write-off to $350 million, under pressure from investors). But regardless of how he did the accounting, suddenly Rupert Murdoch was Mr Football.

The effect of the NFL contract in 1994 was as great for Fox as the Premier League had been for BSkyB. The ripples spread wider, because by making this outrageous deal work for him, Murdoch forced his rivals to follow him up the cost scale. He had changed the economics of sport. He had shown that the upfront losses in a rights deal weren't important. The critical thing was the ability to leverage off other gains from the rights – in this case, attracting new affiliates to Fox. By 1995 Murdoch had stepped up into a higher gear. In February he won a five-year deal for Fox with the National Hockey League for $155 million. In the three months following he committed more than $700 million to rugby league and rugby union. In November he bid $575 million to share Major League Baseball rights with CBS for five years. At the same time the regional sports nets that were about to become Fox Sports bid $129 million for cable rights to baseball. Murdoch immediately wrote off $80 million on the Fox Sports deal, and another $29 million on college football.

Then there were the deals that got away. In July 1995 the International Tennis Federation backed out of a plan to set up a new tour backed by Murdoch's money. In gold there was also a failed attempt backed by Greg Norman to finance a rival to the PGA tour. Then there were the Olympics. NBC paid $475 million for the broadcast rights for the 1996 Atlanta Olympics. In mid-1996 Murdoch bid $705 million for the 2000 Sydney Olympics, and NBC knew it had a fight on its hands. Eventually it won Sydney with a bid of $715 million. But in the process NBC had tied itself into a massive $3.57 billion deal to take broadcasting rights for five Summer and Winter Games from 2000 to 2008. Thwarted, Murdoch moved his sights across the Atlantic, where the European Broadcasting Union on behalf of state broadcasters throughout Europe including the BBC, had bid £961 million for a similar package to NBC's, running to 2008. Murdoch bid £1.3 billion for the package, but the anti-Murdoch factor defeated him. The International Olympic Committee stayed with the European Broadcasting Union. 'We sidestepped $400 million to have the assurances of maximum ratings,' said Jacques Rogge, head of the European National Olympic Committees. Even in defeat, however, Murdoch had forced the European Broadcasting Union to pay more than it ever had before for sports rights.

The sum effect of all this was that around the world, the price of programming rights for sports events was going through the roof. It was a redistribution of wealth from media groups to professional sports associations, clubs and sport stars. By the end of the decade, the flows of money that this process spun off to sporting groups were so great as to represent a form of social engineering. The catalyst for this had been the Murdoch effect – his demonstration that these rights were worth far more strategically than previously acknowledged. Whenever media groups bid against Murdoch, they were conscious that they were up against a rival who was prepared to offer what seemed crazy prices. The bidding strategy that this realisation produced for media groups in sports rights auctions around the world was simple and brutal: media groups would bid whatever it took to win the rights. If this proved beyond their reach, they would bid the cost of the rights up to ensure that the eventual winner was saddled with a crippling cost.

The difficulty in treating sport in this way is that it reduces any sporting code to a financial strategy. The world's love affair with sport, and the qualities that sporting contests can represent, are never quite that simple. Why does sport arouse such emotion? Four decades after the Dodgers moved to Los Angeles, why do Dodgers fans in Brooklyn still grieve the loss? Why do British soccer fans still feel so incensed about the 1998 battle to buy Manchester United? Murdoch's 1995 foray into Australian football would show the danger of forgetting that, at its best, sport is still a matter of the heart.

The pedant, the pariah and the polo player

Midway through 1995, Sydney legal circles were enjoying a delicious prospect. After three decades of armed truce, Rupert Murdoch and Kerry Packer were back at each other's throats. A lengthy court battle was shaping up between Australia's richest two sons before a deeply appreciative legal audience.

Kerry Packer is a very large man. He has never actually thrown anyone through the window, but former executives say that on occasion it has been a near thing. One failed business deal in 1988 reportedly ended in Packer wrestling with his former partner on the floor of his office in Sydney. Packer in a rage is a terrifying experience that leaves powerful executives white-faced and shaking.

He is not a man who believes in partial victories, or minor revenge. When he sued an Australian news program that accidentally slipped footage of Packer into a story about corporate crooks of the 1980s, he sued every person in the studio, from the executive producer down to the staff in the make-up room. In 1978, when the Australian Cricket Board refused to sell his Nine Network the broadcast rights that Packer wanted for cricket internationals (preferring that they remain with the government-owned ABC network with no commercial breaks), he revolutionised the sport by hiring most of the Australian team as well as the top cricketers around the world to set up his own competition, World Series Cricket. Two years later the cricket establishment caved in and Packer dictated terms for how the game would be run and televised.

Packer is entirely without pretension. He remarked after his near-fatal heart attack at a polo match in 1990, when his heart stopped for several minutes, 'I've been to the other side, and let me tell you son, there's fucking nothing there.' Since the late 1980s he has spent much of his time pursuing his passion for polo and gambling, a lifestyle that chews through more than $A100 million a year. He is alternately the saviour and the scourge of casinos around the world, where he has regularly won or lost $20 million in a night. Packer is not a gentle man. On one occasion in the high rollers room he turned on another gambler, who was making much of his own importance and his $100 million fortune. Clearly annoyed, Packer passed him a coin and growled, 'I'll toss you for it.'

Back in 1960, Rupert Murdoch's bouncers beat the stuffing out of Packer and his brother Clyde, after they and four other worthies had forcibly occupied a printing press owned by the Anglican Church, to stop Murdoch buying it. It was a confused, torrid affair with sins on both sides, that left the Packers limping off. By the 1970s, when Kerry had taken the helm of the Consolidated Press media group after his father's death, he and Rupert had concluded that media moguls didn't do stuff like that any more. Ever since, they had maintained a wary peace, meeting regularly to hatch elaborate schemes to take over Australia's media, most of which came to nothing. Murdoch was pre-eminent in print, with more than 70 per cent of Australian newspapers. Packer owned the country's leading television network, Channel Nine, which had been built up in the 1980s by Sam Chisholm, before he left to take over at BSkyB.

By 1994, powerful forces were testing this relationship. It came to a head over rugby league, one of the four codes of football played in Australia, and the major game in New South Wales and Queensland. While rugby union, the older game, was an amateur code associated in Australia with private schools, rugby league's heartland was the working-class suburbs of inner-city Sydney. In the 1980s and 1990s the game had emerged as a major business linked to clubs funded by slot gaming machines, though its critics claimed the Australian Rugby League was hidebound and Sydney-centric. The ARL's slick promotional campaigns featured Tina Turner singing 'Simply the Best' from the top of the Sydney Harbour Bridge, or held aloft in the arms of brawny footballers. For all that, it was still the people's game, and anyone who threatened it risked becoming a social pariah.

In 1995, Murdoch and Packer were locked in a ferocious battle over who would control the game. A case in the Federal Court would determine not merely who won the dispute, but the future of rugby league itself. And the thing that amused Sydney lawyers so mightily was that the case would be heard by Justice James Burchett. Those lawyers who liked to gossip gleefully reported that Justice Burchett had never dreamed of going to a football game in his life. He was bookish. A clever, conscientious judge, his critics said he had a reputation as a pedant, for being supercilious and even a trifle conceited.

The saga had begun on the night of Thursday 30 March 1995, when the players of the Sydney Bulldogs rugby league team finished a training session under lights at their Canterbury-Bankstown home ground. Their coach, Chris Anderson, told five of them he had something planned in the city for them after their showers, that there were some people he wanted them to meet. Late that night he took his leading players to a high-rise office in Sydney's central business district. One of the two men waiting for them in a conference room there was familiar to the players: John Ribot, the outspoken chief executive of the Brisbane club, who was the Australian Rugby League's chief critic. The man beside Ribot was less familiar: the 23-year-old figure of Lachlan Murdoch.

This move had been coming for more than a year. News Corporation had launched a cable television operation called Foxtel with the government-owned telephone giant Telstra. Foxtel badly needed a lever like football programming to boost subscriber numbers. Unfortunately, Kerry Packer had locked up all the television rights to the Australian Rugby League (ARL) until the year 2000. Packer has on-sold the pay-TV rights to

Telstra's cable competitor, Optus Vision, in which he had a 5 per cent stake. Ken Cowley, the managing director of News Limited (News Corp's Australian operating arm) had been leading a campaign to pressure the ARL to do a new deal with Foxtel.

This climaxed in a meeting with the ARL directors on 6 February 1995, when Cowley put a proposal to set up a new league with fewer teams, run in conjunction with News Limited. The alternative was for News to set up its own competition – in effect to apply the same tactic against the ARL and Packer that Packer himself had used in the 1970s against the Australian Cricket Board and the ABC. But this was an expensive last resort.

'I love the game, Ken,' Cowley had told the ARL chairman, Ken Arthurson, in November. 'I want you to know that I'd never do anything to harm it.'

At the February meeting, anxious to damp down any feeling of threat, Cowley told the ARL board, 'Whatever happens, there will never be a rebel league.'

Ken Arthurson, once a scrappy scrum half for South Sydney, spoke against the News Corp proposal for a smaller competition. After lunch it was Kerry Packer's turn to address the ARL directors. If Arthurson had played good cop, Packer played very very bad cop. He emphasised that his Channel Nine had contractual rights to broadcasting rugby league, and if the ARL didn't honour these rights he wouldn't just be suing the ARL and the clubs. He went around the table and told the directors, 'If anyone in this room thinks they don't have a contract with Channel Nine and tries to break it, I'll come after you personally.' At least this was the reported version of the threat. Packer has a gift for more colourful expression.

When Ken Arthurson phoned Cowley to inform him the ARL had rejected News' proposal, Cowley took his defeat gracefully. 'Ken, I'm disappointed in that,' he told Arthurson. While News would pursue the proposal, any further negotiation or approach 'would be made through the front door of the Australian Rugby League', Cowley promised Arthurson. He told News Corporation journalists that he loved the game of rugby league, and would not contemplate being a 'wrecker' of that game, by pursuing the concept of a rebel league. Although Packer had conceded that News was in a position to split the game, Cowley's 'refusal to damage the game came above (his) corporate ambition'.

'Accepting the honesty of Mr Cowley's statement at the time it was made, within a very short time it had been falsified,' Justice Burchett later found. News Limited's secret meetings with the clubs continued. Later, Arthurson testified that in mid-March Cowley repeated his promise to him not to make any further approaches to clubs. Rupert Murdoch made a more telling comment on 'Sixty Minutes' on Packer's Nine network on 19 March. When asked about a *Sydney Morning Herald* story headlined, 'Packer 1, Murdoch 0,' about the ARL's decision to reject the News plan, Murdoch responded that that was 'only the half-time score'.

In a meeting on 23 March, Cowley, Ribot and David Smith (the News executive heading the rugby league planning), presented a plan to Rupert Murdoch to commit $A60 million over four years to set up a rebel league competition. Cowley's promises would be disregarded. Smith's office was subsequently set up as a 'war room', lined with schedules of the plan to target the ARL's 'core playing strength'. Some 200 players would be offered two or three times their existing salaries to join the breakaway league. Travel documents were drawn up in false names for News executives involved in the swoop, in an operation that was characterised at every turn, Justice Burchett said, by 'secrecy, deceit and suddenness'. There was a certain indelicate timing in that this was taking place just as Federal Communication Commission staff were finalising their report in Washington on Murdoch's 1986 Metromedia deal, as to whether News Corporation's actions were characterised by a lack of candour. Meanwhile in London, Peter Stehrenberger was arranging his secret meeting with Abraham Nantel to talk about Michael Clinger.

On Tuesday 28 March, News signed up five of the ARL's top coaches on three-year contracts, including Chris Anderson at Canterbury-Bankstown. Two days later, Ribot and Lachlan Murdoch secretly flew to Sydney to target Anderson's team, the Bulldogs, who had won the ARL premiership the year before. Ribot met with Anderson at midday to discuss the plan to bring his players in late that night to sign them up for Super League, when Anderson himself would receive two cheques for $50,000 apiece.

That night in the Atanaskovic Hartnell offices, even as he offered the players more money than they had ever seen, Ribot would have been aware that he didn't have the players' full attention. One of them, Jerrard McCracken, known somewhat predictably as Crackers, had come in with another player, having left his Harley Davidson back at the football ground. Now, as Ribot ran sums of close to half a million dollars past him, Crackers was wondering if someone was going to pinch his bike. Another player wanted to call his wife to explain why he was late. Ribot didn't think this was a good idea. 'She'll be talking about it across the back fence,' he said. 'We don't want that.'

The details of that night are not entirely clear. Justice Burchett did not regard Ribot as a reliable witness. In the state Industrial Court, Justice Brian Hill said that parts of the evidence given by Ribot and the coach Chris Anderson were unconvincing. Lachlan Murdoch was never called to give his account. 'I had nothing to do with that,' Lachlan said in 1999, when asked a general question about his role in Super League.

What is generally agreed is that Ribot and Murdoch explained News Limited's plan to set up a new league, eventually called Super League, and asked each player individually to sign a playing contract. Players were offered salaries between $A150,000 and $A350,000, plus an immediate sign-on fee of between $A50,000 and $A100,000. 'This is Santa Claus in April,' Ribot repeatedly told the players. But it had to be signed that night, or they would 'miss the boat', he said. Signing was a formality, Ribot assured them, because their club could force them to play for Super League anyway, which was to be an elite competition – 'the best of the best'. Neither of these statements proved to be true, Justice Hill later found in the state Industrial Court.

The players had had no warning of what they were walking into. They were not able to make outside calls for legal or accounting advice when confronted late at night with complex legal documents, which their coach was urging them to sign. While Ribot later testified that he expressly offered any player who raised the matter the opportunity to have his manager present but the offer was declined, Justice Hill later found that these requests, 'were, in truth and substance, refused by Mr Ribot'.

There was not a lot of legal expertise in the room. By the time the players went home in the small hours of Friday morning, seven of them had signed up with Super League. The problem was, several of them had signed the wrong price of paper. Two of the players had signed the schedule to the contract but not the contract itself – one of them said later that the only documents he saw that night were a letter from News Limited dated the next day, and the contract schedule. At least four of the international players that signed had omitted to sign the Standard Terms page. The four subsequently had their contracts overturned by the state Industrial Court, which found that News had obtained their signatures by 'unconscionable dealing' and misrepresentations. 'None of (the four) read anything that night,' Justice Hill concluded.

The players went home with their sign-on cheques, but had to wait another three weeks to get a copy of the contract they had just supposedly signed. They were told to deny any connection with Super League, and were given a briefing pack that explained how to do this. If journalists asked them if they were in negotiations with News Limited, the suggested 'Player

Response to Media Questioning' was, 'There is no point in that, when I have a current contract which I am obliged to honour.'

That night was the beginning of a beautiful relationship between football players and the legal profession. In the next two years Sydney's senior silks and solicitors would get to know more about the personal idiosyncrasies and behaviour of the country's top football stars than they could ever have wished. The lawyers took some time to get used to living cheek by jowl, day after day, with large young men with a robust sense of humour, who would take to throwing around anything remotely ball-shaped during breaks in court proceedings. The ARL's lawyer, Mark O'Brien, said of the footballers he represented: 'Some of them can't even pack their bags without help.'

In the next 24 hours News signed up another 26 players in raids in Brisbane, Townsville and Perth for contracts as high as $A600,000 plus signing on fees of $A100,000 – huge sums in the previous rugby league economy. By that stage it had become clear that not all of Super League's new recruits were sticking to the suggested Player Response to Media Questioning. They had been blurting out details, and the story was splashed across the front pages of newspapers across the country.

It is difficult not to feel some sympathy for Geoff Cousins, the former advertising executive who started work for Foxtel's rival, Optus Vision, on 31 March. His first morning was a nightmare. He arrived at the office ready to take up a marvellous job as chief executive of a billion-dollar start-up for a new cable service, only to find that his rival, Foxtel, was in the process of pinching all his football programming. The job opportunity had become a billion-dollar crisis. Who was he going to call? Dumb question. The phone was already ringing. It was Kerry Packer on the line, and he was furious. It was worse when Packer arrived at Cousins' office in person. He was seven feet tall and he was waving a chequebook. It was a little time before it become apparent that it was Cousins' chequebook.

Cousins is a forceful character with a rasping voice who forged a highly successful career in advertising on a studied absence of personal charm. He approached media interviews like a marine charging up a hill. In an interview questioning his close links with Packer (he sat on the board of Packer's Consolidated Press Holdings group), his favourite gravelly responses were, 'Wrong', 'entirely wrong', 'absolutely incorrect', 'entirely the wrong construction', 'not right' and 'not relevant'. His best line was, 'Entirely wrong, fundamentally, basically wrong, improper, unethical and *illegal*.'

The News Limited operation depended upon a quick victory. The $60 million budget was not likely to go far if the ARL remained obdurate. What changed the picture was that by midday on 31 March, Cousins' first day on the job, Optus Vision and Packer's Nine Network had committed between $A10 million and $A13 million to support the ARL. Within days this grew to $A40 million. Most of that money would come not from Packer but from Cousins. Cousins had persuaded the Optus Vision shareholders, Cable & Wireless, Bell South and Continental Cablevision, that rugby league programming was more important for Optus Vision than it was for the Nine Network.

The next day ARL officials together with Packer's son James launched a counter-offensive, pressing large cash payments on football players who signed loyalty agreements to the ARL. The battle was joined in hotel rooms and clubhouses across the country. It split the league in two, both physically and emotionally.

'This battle split the entire country, fathers against sons, neighbours against neighbours, footballers against footballers,' said Arthurson. 'It ruined a lot of lives, mine included. And all because Rupert Murdoch wanted to control a sport that belonged to the people and was selfish enough to think he could own it for pay television.'

Eventually Super League and the ARL signed up 300 players apiece. In an effort to outflank the ARL, News Corporation had put rugby league associations around the world on its payroll, beginning with an £87 million deal for the English Rugby Football League to join a European Super League that transformed the code into a summer sport to coincide with the southern hemisphere winter.

The cost of the Super League exercise had soared past $A500 million, and the affair was headed for the Federal Court for resolution by Justice Burchett. Burchett may not have started off knowing much about football, but five months of hearings cured this. What became apparent when he handed down his judgment on 23 February 1996, was that he didn't like secret meetings, or News Limited's plan to take over the ARL by 'infiltration by the back door'. He did not accept the evidence given by several News Limited and Super League witnesses and he drew adverse inferences from the failure of Cowley and Smith to appear in the witness box. He gave the worst serving to Moore, the chief executive of Canterbury Bankstown, who was also an ARL director, over his efforts to recruit Chris Anderson for Super League:

Mr Moore had not less than an ordinary appreciation of right and wrong. He knew his duty. But, stripped of pretence in cross-examination, he was revealed as a man who had been overwhelmed by the magnitude of his temptation. He could not imagine the money being offered to his son-in-law, the Canterbury coach – not to himself – being refused. He was completely corrupted, and shut his eyes to his obligations to the club and to the (ARL). But those who suborned the coach, and at least indirectly Mr Moore, were acting with their eyes open. They knew they were asking officials of clubs to break their contracts . . . and their duty of fidelity. They were using the financial power of News Limited to corrupt targeted individuals.

Justice Burchett froze all further actions by the Super League companies that News Limited had set up until the year 2000, and left open a claim by the ARL for huge damages. It was a stunning win for the ARL. Arthur Siskind flew to Australia to supervise an appeal process to see what could be retrieved from the legal débâcle. News Limited was still in there punching, with talk of moves to circumvent Burchett's ruling with a new players' league.

The ARL's lawyer Mark O'Brien warned of dire consequences if Super League players even held a training session: 'The present directing minds of News Limited will be in contempt if this occurs. And that, of course, is Lachlan Murdoch, the man very much at the front of this fight, and Ken Cowley.'

When the case moved to the Appeals Court, exchanges were just as bitter, as the News Limited lawyers argued that Burchett had been swayed by the 'emotive' language used by the ARL's lead counsel, Bob Ellicott QC, which had appealed to the judge's heart rather than this head.

Ellicott, who was a former Federal Attorney General, argued that there was an 'ethical void' in News Corporation's corporate culture, together with a belief in 'the divine right of supernationals'. News seemed to believe 'that Rupert can do no wrong, Ken (Cowley) can do no wrong, and Lachlan can do no wrong'.

The issue at the heart of the Super League dispute was something that was causing heartache all over the world. What Burchett had to resolve was the complex question of who owns a sport – is it a commercial venture or a community enterprise, is it an undertaking based on mutual trust and confidence, or does the competitive arena extend to the way a sport is organised and run? At a more esoteric level, is it important for a sportsman to be honourable? Ultimately, Burchett's judgment seemed to hark back to Oliver Wendell Holmes' turn-of-the-century judgment that described baseball as an 'affair of state'. It was something beyond the common run of human experience, it was an exalted endeavour to which different rules must be applied. Burchett's findings ran into problems on appeal in part because of the way he defined the size of a market in applying trade-practice laws. But the heart of his judgment was that the way that rugby league was played in Australia by clubs together with the ARL was characterised by 'mutual trust that each is pursuing a common purpose'. One could call it the love of the sport. It made the ARL the basis of a joint venture, which placed fiduciary obligations upon ARL and club executives and employees. The secret meetings and plotting and late-night signings by coaches, players and club officials breached that fiduciary duty. In hindsight one might consider that Burchett had constructed an elaborate legal edifice which allowed him to protect an Australian social institution.

Perhaps it is significant that this lofty view was taken by a judge who himself had limited contact with the modern sporting world. On 4 October 1996 the Court of Appeal transformed the ARL's victory into a crushing defeat. Notwithstanding Ellicott's indignant arguments, the Court upheld News Limited on 60 out of 61 points of appeal against Justice Burchett's ruling. One of the critical findings was that the contractual uncertainty and internal squabbling of the ARL before the appearance of Super League did not constitute a joint venture based on mutual trust and confidence. Consequently there were no fiduciary duties of the sort described by Burchett. It followed that the directors of rebel clubs were not necessarily in breach of their duty to the ARL, and actions of the Super League coaches whom Burchett had criticised so sharply could be seen in a more acceptable light of looking after the interests of their players. 'Perhaps the criticism was too harsh,' the Appeal judges concluded.

In another of life's little ironies, the appeal judgment was released four days before Fox News sued Time Warner over Gerry Levin's broken promise to run Murdoch's news channel in New York. One may sneer that these are virtual ethics, to defend a broken promise in one country, and to claim damages from another broken promise in another country. But there was nothing unusual in either action. For better or worse, Murdoch was merely following best commercial practice. The Appeal Court decision in Sydney was based on the solid premise that at the end of the twentieth century, sports clubs were a business. Broken promises were regrettable, but not illegal. Once could as well quote Judge Jack Weinstein's District Court judgment in the Fox News case: 'They were hard-bitten executives steeled in such hagglings . . . The cajolery, as well as the blandishments, honeyed phrases and assurances that are to be expected in major negotiations of this sort in the media-entertainment field did not constitute fraud.'

Even allowing for different legal traditions, this was a judgment with resonance around the world. The commercialisation of the sporting ethos was not a matter to be obstructed by common law. Any such battles in future would be determined in the political arena, rather than the courtroom. This would take on great significance in 1998 in Britain, when Murdoch turned his eyes to Manchester United.

The turf war between Packer and Murdoch smouldered for two years. Various peace agreements were brokered during this time with the help of the two heirs apparent, Lachlan Murdoch and James Packer. These agreements foundered amid accusations on both sides of bad faith and broken promises, but there was too much at stake for the conflict to go on indefinitely. The two billionaires had had a marriage of convenience that lasted for three decades. Now both of them were facing difficult succession issues. Their sons' futures could be threatened by a long bruising war. Like two old sweethearts, Murdoch and Packer decided to patch things up, to stay together for the sake of the kids. On 16 January 1997 Murdoch and Packer signed an agreement which gave the Nine Network the free-to-air broadcast rights to Super League, and the right to buy half of the News stake in Foxtel at cost price.

'I would be telling a lie if I said I didn't feel deeply wounded and bitterly disappointed,' said Arthurson, who retired two months later. 'It's not really a great way to start the year, is it? Sometimes you really wonder what it's all about.'

News had lost an estimated $A500 million on Super League. Packer, by contrast, had lost very little, because it was Optus Vision, not Packer, who had been largely bankrolling the ARL. In fact, by buying the Foxtel stake at cost price Packer probably gained as much as Murdoch lost.

'It's a pity they couldn't have made the bloody deal in the first place,' Arthurson said. 'Then none of this would have happened.'

The ARL soldiered on for another season, as game attendance figures plummeted, before bowing to the inevitable and merging with Super League in 1998.

The downside to spending $5 billion on sporting rights around the world is that broadcasting contracts expire. The BSkyB contract had given the British football clubs more money than they had ever seen. But by the time the rights came up for re-negotiation in June 1996, the clubs were convinced that they had sold themselves short in 1992 – and BSkyB's rivals believed the same thing. They were prepared to offer enormous prices to oust BSkyB. To retain the rights, BSkyB had to pay more than double the previous price, for a total £674 million. And this was nothing to the huge bunfight looming when the National Football League rights came up for re-negotiation.

In the last half of 1997, a strange corporate madness seized the American broadcast industry. Speculation about the next round of National Football League contracts had been bubbling ever since Murdoch stole the broadcast rights to one of the two NFL divisions, the American Football Convention, from CBS in 1993. By 1997 the NFL contract negotiations – the broadcast rights for cable, for television networks on Sunday and Monday nights, and for the different NFL conventions – had become a blood sport. Michael Eisner at Disney and Rupert Murdoch had been meeting with NFL officials since March. Murdoch's success with Fox had convinced the NFL, like the Premier League in Britain, that it had undersold itself in its 1993 contract, which had raised a total $4.4 billion for the four seasons. This time the NFL was looking for real money.

'Out of the last negotiations three years ago, there was a feeling in the NFL front office that they undervalued the AFC rights in selling out to NBC (for an estimated $217 million per season),' an advertising executive told *Media Week*.

The existing four-year contract – thanks to the huge price rise that Murdoch had offered for Fox's share of NFL games – had paid $1.1 billion a season for football. The 1997 negotiations doubled that payment to $2.2 billion each season over eight years. Total payments came to $17.6 billion. The rights themselves hadn't changed. It was just that now the broadcasters would pay a staggering $8 billion more for them. It was straight wealth transfer, from the broadcasters to professional football players, who picked up 62 per cent of the NFL's gross revenues. The Murdoch effect – the compulsion for media moguls to keep up with Rupert, or merely the realisation that Murdoch had changed the economics of sport – had transferred $8 billion out of the media industry. The stock market values companies as a multiple of what they earn each year. Thus the full effect of the 1997 NFL renegotiation was to reduce the market value of the NFL broadcasters by up to $30 billion. The only people not complaining were the players, who would pocket an extra $5 billion.

The biggest loser was Michael Eisner at Disney. In 1993, ABC's *Monday Night Football* and the cable rights shared between ESPN and Ted Turner's TNT cost a total $1.97 billion, or $492 million a season. In January 1998, Eisner's ABC and ESPN retained the Monday football and pushed out TNT to take all of the cable rights for eight years for $9.2 billion. It came to $1.15 billion a year. The increase in the price of the rights over what

ABC, ESPN and TNT had paid previously came to an extra $658 million a season. That is, each year for the next eight years an extra $658 million would be taken out of Disney's cash flow. For that extra payout, Disney merely held on to its former position and gained half a season of cable rights. Eisner committed to this monster payment looking over his shoulder, feeling the breath of his rivals hot on his heels. Disney stock topped in May 1998. While other media stocks continued to soar, Disney dropped 40 per cent in the next year. There was plenty of bad news elsewhere at Disney to explain it, but the NFL rights were a quiet body blow from which Eisner would not recover.

CHAPTER FOURTEEN

THE MOUSE WARS

Los Angeles, January–June 1997

By January 1997, Michael Eisner was feeling the first twinges of concern that all was not well within the Magical Kingdom. The warning signs were faint. Earnings at the Walt Disney Company were still chugging along; the stock price would not peak for another year. There had been some little irritation over the departure of Eisner's second-in-command, Mike Ovitz. Eisner had hired Ovitz, his long-time friend, the head of Creative Artists Agency and the super-agent known as the king of Hollywood, in September 1995. Unfortunately for Eisner, Ovitz's employment contract had an extraordinarily generous payout clause.

In December 1995 Ovitz was fired. Two days after Christmas 1996, Disney lawyers wrote to Ovitz to confirm a payout of cash and Disney stock options valued at $140 million. It worked out at a little under $10 million a month for Ovitz's fourteen-and-a-half month tenure at Disney. The termination payment was 'larger than even the expert hired by the Disney Board to explain the contract imagined it to be, larger than almost anyone anywhere will receive in the lifetime of any of the parties, and perhaps larger than any ever paid,' Delaware Chancery Judge William B. Chandler III later concluded. For a group that minds its pennies the way Disney does it was very disconcerting. It was, as Eisner freely admitted to shareholders at the Disney annual meeting in February, 'Not good. A mistake. Won't happen again . . . Be angry. Be annoyed. God knows I am.'

Peter O'Malley's announcement on 7 January that he intended selling the Dodgers was the next bit of bad news for Eisner. Only months before, Disney had taken a controlling stake in the Anaheim Angels baseball team, unaware that a much more attractive prize would soon be coming on to the market. Now Eisner realised he had bought the wrong ball team.

Eisner's only consolation was to finalise a new stock option scheme for himself on 11 January, two weeks after Ovitz's payout, worth $198 million. Not that anyone grudged it to him. In twelve years Eisner had come to personify the transformation of Disney into one of the largest and most profitable media companies in the world. Eisner had started out in the 1960s as a television executive at the ABC network. He had gone on to be Barry Diller's second-in-command at Paramount Studios in the early 1980s, until both men had jumped ship – Diller to Twentieth Century Fox, and Eisner to head the demoralised Disney studios. Eisner made the better landing.

At the time of Eisner's arrival, the glory days of Disney's early years were long over. The company was even considering closing down its animation studio. Instead Eisner and the diminutive Jeff Katzenberg, whom Eisner had brought with him from Paramount, went back to Disney's core business. Eisner and Katzenberg – a serious figure in black-framed glasses and suits beside the elaborately casual figure of Eisner, who touched six foot three and on occasion wore socks that were too short – succeeded in turning Disney's animation business once again into the cornerstone of the entire group, a triumphant Mouse to Mouse resuscitation. Besides producing a string of animation hits including *The Lion King*, *Pocahontas* and *The Hunchback of Notre Dame*, Katzenberg re-released a series of Disney animated classics. Eisner extended that increased revenue into overseas distribution and into video sales. This in turn drew people to Disney's new theme parks. Then there were the Disney cruise ships. And the Mouse shops. By 1996 Eisner had opened 636 Disney stores around the world to sell the Disney merchandise that spun off the Disney films and programming. The group functioned as an integrated whole that had made Disney one of the best-known brand names in the world, and incidentally spun off enormous amounts of money.

Disney's corporate structure worked like a vine or climbing plant. Eisner kept finding new ways to leverage off the brand name, which was based upon the company's library of animated films. The heart of the Disney empire was 35 animated feature films made at enormous expense over six decades, which could be recycled for ever for each new generation of children between the age of two and eleven. The enormous power that this library gave Disney also made the company extremely vulnerable. Any threat to Disney's animated film business hit at the ground-root of the entire enterprise. If anything supplanted Disney films, the many branches of the empire could wither. The Mouse would fight ferociously to defend its franchise.

The strategy was so stunningly successful that by the mid-1990s the question for Michael Eisner was, what next? As he opined in his 1998 memoir *Work in Progress*, written with Tony Schwartz, 'Success invariably prompts restlessness. Absolute success often corrupts absolutely.' Eisner's emergency heart surgery in July 1994 had contributed to the unease. After experiencing chest pain on 15 July at Herb Allen's annual media conference, Eisner had been flown home for a quadruple coronary bypass. He wrote to the author Larry McMurtry: 'Something has happened to me that is a big deal. My life has a finite sense to it, and there is certainly a hollowness that comes with such realisations. I try not to think about it, but I think about it all the time.'

Eisner was still recuperating in early August when a simmering row came to a head over Katzenberg's determination to succeed Disney's president and chief operating officer, Frank Wells, who had died in a helicopter skiing accident in April. Perhaps the last straw for Katzenberg had been a *Newsweek* article on 1 August based on an interview Eisner had given a month before. Eisner had suggested to *Newsweek* that Disney should be modelled more along the lines of Rupert Murdoch's News Corporation, controlled by a strong leader without a second in command. Katzenberg's subsequent departure, which ended Hollywood's most successful working relationship, turned extraordinarily bitter. It would consume both men for years. In notes Schwartz made for Eisner's memoir, Eisner returned again and again to muse over the Katzenberg problem, as it had become. Besides his comment about 'the little midget', Eisner went on to claim, 'Jeffrey was my retriever.' And again, 'He was my pompom – I'm the cheerleader.'

In the giddy kaleidoscope of deal-making and breaking, alliance and mésalliance that the media industry had become, Eisner stood out as an old fashioned kind of guy. He was a good hater. Katzenberg had gone on to join David Geffen and Steven Spielberg in launching Dreamworks SKG. The new film studio became the epicentre of the anti-Eisner faction in Hollywood. 'He hates us and we hate him,' Spielberg was reported as saying. 'But he's a businessman. He'll buy our shows.'

'The more we go it alone, the better I feel,' Eisner told *Fortune* in 1998. 'Fighting and suing each other and making love – to me that's too schizophrenic. Either you love somebody or you hate somebody. I can't quite deal with this idea that you love them on Monday and hate them on Tuesday. But that is the business.'

The legal battles with Katzenberg over his termination payout would run through to August 1997, when Disney settled with an estimated payout of $100 million. Further disagreements over the share of profits to which Katzenberg was entitled from films such as *The Lion King* saw him back in court against Disney. Eisner finally settled in July 1999, paying Katzenberg a further $200 million. Team Disney had spent too much executive time on a fruitless quarrel. But in 1997, Eisner had bigger problems looming.

By the mid-1990s, Eisner had pushed the Disney brand about as far as it could go. There was a finite number of Disney stores and Disney theme parks and Disney cruise ships that the world could handle. The question was, where did he go from here? Eisner's view, as he put it to stockholders in the company's annual report in late 1996, was that Disney's history could be divided into three phases. There was the period Before Michael Eisner, which was the dismal history of Disney as a stagnant backwater up until 1983; there was the Early Michael Eisner, which was the spectacular turnaround of the next 12 years; then there was the Resurgent Michael Eisner. That was the new era he had ushered in with his deal with Warren Buffet at Sun Valley in 1995, for Disney to buy Capital Cities/ABC. The deal, which was finalised in early 1996, allied Hollywood's top studio with America's top network. Eisner had done it, he said, 'to protect the Mouse', to ensure Disney television programming could be distributed over the ABC network. But the real attraction of the deal, he always emphasised, was in acquiring ESPN, the world's premier cable sports network. ESPN already earned $600 million a year in cash flow. Eisner believed that figure could grow, that the future for Disney lay largely with the opportunities to expand ESPN, to launch ESPN Zone stores and spin off new cable channels like ESPN 2 and ESPN News. So for Eisner, sports programming was critical.

By the start of 1997, however, Eisner was beginning to realise the real cost of his executive squabbles. Disney's management instability in the mid-1990s had made Eisner take his eye off the ball. Disney was still churning out strong earnings, but in business after business, the growth areas were already staked out. In his own way, Eisner was facing a crisis of confidence, a test of nerve every bit as threatening as Peter O'Malley's at the Dodgers. Almost everywhere that Eisner looked for new opportunities in 1997, someone else had got there first. What was frustrating was that it was always the same someone. The end result was that, two and a half years later, Michael Eisner would no longer be the blue-eyed boy of Hollywood and Wall Street. The Disney stock price would be in full retreat, and the business press would be openly debating whether Eisner should step down at Disney. Here again, besides the natural rise and fall of business cycles, and the woes that a character like Eisner can bring on himself when he is out of form, if there was one person who could be said to have brought Eisner down, it was Rupert Murdoch. The question is, back in early 1997, what started Eisner's slide? What should Eisner have done to beat off Murdoch's relentless war on the Mouse? It is easier to locate the point where Eisner's slide became irreversible. It was that moment twelve months later that he committed to a $9.2 billion blunder and bought NFL rights. Why did Eisner do it? What made him so desperate? What was it in 1997 that left Eisner with nowhere to go, except to pull out the cheque book, swallow hard and sign off on a deal that he knew would cripple Disney's earnings?

Eisner's prospects in January 1997 didn't look too bad. In films, Disney remained the most profitable studio under Joe Roth, who had left Murdoch's Twentieth Century Fox to replace Katzenberg as Disney's studio head. Fox in turn hired Bill Mechanic from Disney to work under Peter Chernin at Fox – chiefly for his overseas marketing savvy. After the success of *Independence Day*, Mechanic and Peter Chernin appeared to have stumbled badly with a lavish film directed by James Cameron. Production of *Titanic* was running late, and Hollywood gossip had costs blowing out from $100 million to beyond $250 million.

Meanwhile, Jeffrey Katzenberg at DreamWorks had been hiring animators from the Disney studios for million-dollar salaries. In the process he had doubled the cost to Disney of making animated feature films, which were the company's lifeblood. *The Lion King* had grossed $761 million at the box office for Disney, another $500 million in video sales, and $225 million from consumer products. Eisner could blame Murdoch for this new threat. In March 1994, Bill Mechanic at Twentieth Century Fox had hired two former Disney animators, Don Bluth and Gary Goldman, to build a $100 million animation studio in Phoenix Arizona. Fox's move had sparked a new interest in animated films by the major studios. By the end of the decade animated films would account for a quarter of Hollywood film production. Warner Brothers built a new studio and beefed up its animation staff from 140 to 400. DreamWorks built a $150 million studio with 400 employees. Fox's first film, *Anastasia*, was due out in September 1997. Eisner planned to bury *Anastasia* in a Disney sandwich, releasing Disney's latest children's film, *Flubber*, and re-releasing *The Little Mermaid* back-to-back to coincide with the *Anastasia* launch, to lock up the children's audience. *Anastasia* cost $50 million to make. Disney's strategy would ensure that the Fox film grossed only $63 million at the US box office. Three years later Fox would close its animation studio in Phoenix. In Hollywood, you don't mess with the Mouse.

In television, the ABC network's ratings were slumping. Eisner was depending in part on a couple of new Fox-produced hits, *The Practice* and *Dharma and Greg*, to put the network back on track. Here again, it looked like Eisner was a couple of steps behind the pace. Peter Chernin had convinced Murdoch to go after the top ten television comedy writers. Chernin offered these writers twice or three times their existing salaries, with contracts worth between $10 million and $15 million to come up with new ideas for shows. Fox ended up with half a dozen of the people it was targeting. In 1995 Fox spent $17 million on writers. By 1997 that had blown out to $60 million – probably more than News Corporation's total payroll for journalists. In the process Fox also blew away the production budgets of its rivals, who had to match offers to hold on to their writers. 'We knew we were going to screw up the business a little,' Chernin conceded to *Fortune*.

Chernin's strategy had paid off with shows like *Ally McBeal* and *The Practice* by Michelle Pfeiffer's husband David E. Kelley, and writer Chuck Lorre's *Dharma and Greg*. With other hits like *Buffy* and *King of the Hill*, by 1999 Fox had 29 prime-time television series in production. Like film-making, producing television series is a huge gamble. Most series bomb and are not renewed the next year. For the first three years the shows that survive are produced at a loss. But once a show reaches that magic three-year point, it can by syndicated – and then a show can be very profitable indeed. *King of the Hill*, for example, sold for $4 million an episode. That translates into $104 million for a season of 26 programs, almost all of it profit. Murdoch had gambled hundreds of millions of dollars making television programs. With any luck, in five years time he stood to make billions. Logically this was an area where Disney and ABC should have been expected to excel, now that Congress had lifted the decades-long ban on Hollywood studios producing television programs. But Murdoch already had the ground staked out.

'This has nothing to do with attacking Disney,' a News spokesperson said when asked about the growing rivalry. 'We are entering businesses we find attractive.'

The real clash was over sport.

In late September 1996, David Hill, the garrulous head of Fox Sports, pulled off a minor coup. Even before the LA Dodgers came on the market, he bought the Dodgers' local pay-television rights. Hill was an Australian who had been called in to run Murdoch's new American sports division in 1994 after his success as sports chief at BSkyB. For $6 million, Hill picked up broadcast rights for 45 Dodgers games a season from a failing wireless pay-television service in California called Tele-TV. The Dodgers' rights gave Fox Sports West cable in southern California an embarrassment of riches. The network already broadcast the LA Lakers, the Clippers in basketball, the Mighty Ducks in hockey and the Anaheim Angels in baseball. In order to fit the Dodgers into the crowded line-up, Fox Sports West announced it was launching a second cable sports channel.

Fox Sports West 2 launched on 27 January 1997. Besides the Dodgers, it carried the Clippers, the Mighty Ducks, USC and UCLA basketball and football, horse racing and high school sports. Apart from the Dodgers, these were games for which Fox Sports already held the rights. The economics were simple. Fox West Sports had 4.2 million subscribers paying $1 a month for the channel, a total of $50 million a year. The only extra programming cost to run Fox Sports West 2 would be the $6 million a season for the Dodgers. Against that, Fox Sports West 2 would charge 70 cents per subscriber per month – that is, extra annual revenue of up to $35 million. This looked like money for jam.

It was unfortunate that the Dodgers' season didn't start until April. Fox Sports West 2 launched in January in the middle of the hockey season. The timing meant that in the early weeks the channel's major drawcard was the Mighty Ducks, which was owned by Disney. The Ducks were indignant that to watch them you had to buy FSW2. For Disney, this was no ordinary team to be messed with. The Ducks had gone way beyond sport. They were a branding exercise. Fox Sports was messing with Disney's sporting mascot. Disney was counting on the Ducks and the Anaheim Angels as the cornerstone for the regional sports channel it was planning, ESPN West. So Fox Sports West 2 was bad news for Disney. Rupert Murdoch had got there ahead of Michael Eisner, to launch his own California sports channel. Just to rub salt in the wound, he was launching the channel with Disney's pride and joy, the Mighty Ducks. Disney executives began calling their lawyers.

In February 1997, with Pat Robertson blowing hot and cold on the Fox Kids deal, tempers rising in the London High Court over Michael Clinger's wiretapping allegations, and Rupert Murdoch lining up to meet Charlie Ergen, the Mighty Ducks sued Fox Sports West 2 on 4 February to force them to put the team back on Fox Sports West. Three weeks later on 24 February, as Murdoch and Ergen were announcing their Sky merger on the Fox studio sound stage, Fox Sports returned fire with an antitrust suit against Disney for inciting cable companies not to carry Fox Sports West 2.

The affair played out with all the moral outrage that typifies a media turf war. In the Orange County Superior Court the Mighty Ducks claimed they had contracted for games to be shown on Fox Sports West (FSW) with 4.2 million subscribers, and that moving them to FSW2 which had less than 300,000 subscribers voided the contract. The Duck's greatest concern was for the fans. In the US District Court nearby the Fox federal antitrust suit claimed a conspiracy by Disney and ESPN who wanted to use the Ducks and the Angels to start their own new network.

Disney had made false and disparaging comments about Fox Sports' rights to telecast the Angels and Mighty Ducks and deceived cable operators into believing that FSW2 would not be able to deliver its scheduled programming, Fox Sports claimed. 'Disney has enormous leverage over cable operators,' the writ said. Because of its extensive programming interests, 'Disney is in a position to pressure, punish and reward cable operators.'

Behind the colourful claims, the problem for Fox Sports West was that the cable companies were refusing to pay for another sports channel that they didn't want, even when Fox Sports West offered the first year for free. This opposition intensified after the threat of Murdoch and Ergen's Sky rose above the horizon on 24 February. Disney and Fox continued manoeuvring for position through the spring. Disney was reported to be bidding to buy the Los Angeles Clippers to give them three California sports teams on which to base their planned sports channel, while Murdoch was in talks with the Lakers and the Kings, but nothing eventuated. Fox Sports offered $100 million for rights to Angels and Ducks games for the next ten years, but Disney wasn't interested.

'It's not a personality war per se, not like Ted and Rupert,' a media chief executive said. 'It's that every ball field they show up in, the other guy's there. Inevitably a rivalry builds up.'

Everyone agreed that this was so very not-personal. It was not conflict so much as healthy competition. With the judges still out on FSW2, attention switched to the next stage of this competition: the pursuit leg. This involved a race to find a man in New York called Charles Dolan, wrestle him to the ground, then offer him $850 million. The winning side – and this was the tricky part – had to convince Dolan to take their money.

Dolan ran America's sixth largest cable company, Cablevision. John Malone had been feuding with him forever. Malone and Dolan had both built up remarkably similar regional sports networks. While Malone's Prime Ticket networks, which became the heart of Fox Sports, were based in California and the American South, Dolan's Rainbow Media sports nets were based in New York, Chicago and Boston. In 1994, Dolan beat Malone in a furious bidding war to buy Madison Square Garden from Sumner Redstone at Viacom for $1.075 billion. The Garden, its sports teams and its sport networks gave Dolan an unassailable position in New York, with broadcast rights locked up for all the city's major teams. Dolan's partner, the ITT hotel group, had funded most of the Garden deal. When ITT put its half share in the Garden up for sale in February 1997, Dolan insisted he had pre-emptive rights to buy ITT out for $765 million. Dolan was to settle the deal on 19 June, when he needed a bank credit line of $850 million. Cablevision was already hopelessly over-leveraged, with $3.9 billion of debt, so Dolan needed to find someone else to come up with the money.

The Fox Sports and Rainbow Media networks were 'two halves of a $100 bill' that Malone and Dolan couldn't put together, according to Cablevision executive Marc Lustgarden. Malone's hope in 1995 when he proposed the Fox Sports merger had been that Rupert Murdoch would be the 'rubber joint' between himself and Dolan, but so far it had not worked. If a deal could be done, though, the result would be a merged network of regional sports channels that had national coverage. It would be finally a solid threat to Disney's ESPN.

Not that Disney was worried. In 1998 ABC/ESPN president Steve Bornstein told HBO: 'I kind of look at Fox as a big mosquito.' Under the disdain, however, winning Rainbow Media had become as important to Michael Eisner as it was to Rupert Murdoch. In one stroke, a Rainbow deal would stop Fox Sports' expansion plans in its tracks, and give ESPN a solid platform of regional sports networks. Chuck Dolan, however, would prove an elusive quarry.

Back in Los Angeles, Murdoch's concern to secure the future of Fox Sports West 2 had prompted his dinner invitation to Peter O'Malley. O'Malley in turn invited Murdoch to watch a game at Dodger Stadium and eat a Dodger Dog when the season kicked off on 1 April. The sale of the Dodgers was finally hammered out over three hectic days of negotiations from Thursday 8 May to Saturday 10 May, for $311 million. Life had become impossibly complicated for Murdoch. In the first days of May, he had wrestled with the death throes of his merger with Echostar . . . and also with Pat Robertson's extraordinary call on 2 May for Murdoch to give him less money in the bid for IFE and the Family Channel. On Tuesday 6 May Ergen had been left on the tarmac at Denver International Airport, waiting in vain for Chase Carey to call. On Wednesday 7 May the legal battles with Echostar had begun. News Corp execs were deeply enmeshed in the

Dodgers negotiations on Friday evening when Ergen was lodging his $5 billion lawsuit. As if all of this was not enough, 28 April had been Rupert and Anna's thirtieth wedding anniversary. 'We had five days in Bermuda,' Anna said unhappily several week later. 'It rained.'

Peter O'Malley's announcement on Monday 12 May that he was seeking permission from Major League Baseball to begin sale procedures with Murdoch triggered fresh outpourings of public grief. LA's ball team was to be run by a multinational company. Would the Dodger ethos be forever lost? Was Rupert Murdoch colourful enough, was he enough of a character for this sacred trust, columnists pondered. The wilder reports even suggested he didn't like baseball. The general consensus was that Murdoch was too much a faceless businessman to run the city's pride and joy. The ball team needed someone who was more of a pirate.

Throughout May, Rupert Murdoch kept moving the troops forward, making the deals, but he was desperately vulnerable. He had lost MCI's financial support. He had blown away the Echostar merger with Charlie Ergen. This left Murdoch with a satellite licence and operation with no partner to pay for it. And his programming was blocked on all sides. The media was full of stories of Murdoch's humiliation. The only people who could save him were the cable operators who owned the Primestar satellite operation . . . and they hated him. They weren't buying Fox News, they weren't buying Fox Sports, and unless he could resolve his problems with Pat Robertson they wouldn't be buying Fox Kids. Murdoch had realised by April that he was in trouble with his Echostar plan and had made the leap to join his enemies. But no one at Primestar seemed ready to catch him.

Primestar's medium power DBS operation was the second largest satellite service in America, with 1.8 million subscribers. It was a partnership owned by the country's five largest cable companies: John Malone's TCI, Gerry Levin's Time Warner, Comcast Corporation, Cox Communications, and MediaOne Group. In seven years of squabbling, the Primestar partners had almost never been able to agree on anything – even the simple process of turning the partnership into a company. Their distrust of Murdoch was matched only by their distrust of each other. The basic problem they faced was that, no matter how much they disliked Murdoch, they needed the satellite slot at 110WL that he had wrestled off them two years before. To get it back, they would have to agree to merge Sky into Primestar.

Leo Hindery at TCI lobbied the Primestar partners to drop their resentments and do a deal with Murdoch for his satellite licence that would solve all the problems. Hindery was 'a peacemaker . . . He kept trying to convince everybody that there was more profit in peace than war', Malone testified later. Most of the resistance came from Time Warner. Malone himself was wheeled in for the tougher meetings, where he said he was 'a proponent of, at least, exploring whether or not we could make peace (with Murdoch)'.

Murdoch was insisting that before he did a deal with Primestar, the cable partners had to contract to run his cable channels. The cable operators wouldn't do this, but by mid-May there was talk of an informal agreement about the channels. Murdoch wasn't going to get any money for the licence either; instead he would have to take a complicated package of quasi equity that would leave him with a 33 per cent share of Primestar, but no voting rights. It was almost ludicrous, the terms the cable partners were insisting upon, to ensure that some way, somehow, Murdoch did not pull another Houdini act on them, whip off the handcuffs and waltz off with control of their company. What was definitely ludicrous was that, despite all these precautions, within a year it looked like Murdoch and Malone had set up a structure that, if not for the intervention of the Justice Department, could have allowed them to do precisely this.

Malone argued Murdoch's position to his partners: 'It just really says, "Hey guys, I'm not Darth Vader any more. If you carry my programming, you won't be subsidising the enemy and, therefore, feel free to treat me as a friend, not as an enemy".'

By Monday 19 May, Hindery was hopeful enough that a deal could be reached that he told Goldman Sachs analysts that 'he expected news soon that would calm competitive concerns about satellite versus cable'. At the Time Warner annual meeting the same day, Gerry Levin was saying the reverse: 'Time Warner is not standing in the way of any agreement (over Murdoch and Primestar),' he said. 'There is no agreement. There's nothing to be stood in the way of.' It didn't help that the previous Friday, Judge Weinstein in the New York District Court had thrown out most of the Fox News case against Time Warner, that dated back to the previous October.

Murdoch's future now hung on a knife's edge. For months he had kept any number of balls up in the air. There was ASkyB and the satellite licence, there was Fox News, there was the Family Channel, there was Haim Saban at Fox Kids, and Fox Sports, the fracas over Fox Sports West 2, the pursuit of Chuck Dolan, and the Dodgers. It had been a great show, but the curtain was going down. Murdoch had about two weeks to finish the juggling act, to bring all of these balls safely to earth. And now Michael Eisner was on his case.

The Dodgers had been the big wake-up call for Eisner. Now that Murdoch had the Dodgers, no matter which way the Mighty Duck court cases went, the future of Fox Sports West 2 was assured. Would Eisner and Murdoch face off directly, now that both owned a baseball team? 'Well, he and I won't unless he improves his batting average,' Eisner told the *New York Times*. 'But I hope the Angels end up in the National League – then we'll kick Rupert's butt, right here in Chavez Ravine.'

'We generally can't compete with Rupert on costs,' Eisner told *Fortune*. 'He's a much bigger gambler than we are – and by the way, it's paid off for him. I'm more a sleep-at-night kind of executive.'

Eisner was never going to be as acquiescent as he sounded. At Team Disney, the corporate culture was that Disney execs didn't talk about their competitors: they talked about their 'enemies'. In New York, Fox Sports was offering Chuck Dolan an $850 million investment in Rainbow Media. Eisner put another $100 million on the table to trump Murdoch's bid. In the week of 19 May, Eisner also contacted Pat Robertson to do due diligence on IFE's accounts. The IFE board had said it would enter into exclusive negotiations with the first bidder to offer $35 a share – which happened to be Fox Kids. Eisner threw another $100 million in the pot and said he was ready to offer $37 a share. It was never quite clear why Eisner suddenly wanted the Family Channel. The major reason seemed to be that Rupert Murdoch wanted it.

Are media battles personal? It's 'completely personal', Eisner told *Fortune*. 'I mean, it's not really personal, but – I always felt from the time I was trying to fix Tuesday nights at ABC in the 1970s that it was personal. I gotta win. I gotta get the best programs on the air. My problem is, I like [rival media executives] and I've known them forever . . . Rupert is totally charming.'

'More intelligently, it's about business,' one cable executive said as the Disney-Fox competition intensified. 'But it's looking like a fight.'

It was unfortunate timing for Eisner to be making overtures to Pat Robertson. On 1 May, ABC had screened the controversial episode of the *Ellen* sit-come when Ellen DeGeneres' lead character comes out as a lesbian. Robertson was supporting a campaign by Christian fundamentalists to punish Disney's moral laxity by boycotting its products.

'God has little obligation at the present time to spare America, because we are polluting the world with our television programs, our movies and so forth, our books,' Robertson had said on the *700 Club* 18 months before. 'We are polluting the whole world. We've made the world drunk, if you will, with the wine of our fornication.'

Admittedly, Robertson had also had harsh things to say in the past about Fox shows and had called for an advertisers' boycott on *Married . . . With Children*. Gary David Goldberg, the producer-writer of *Family Ties*, once put the cynical industry view: 'Left to their own devices, the three networks would televise live executions. Except Fox – they'd televise live naked executions.' Thankfully this had never seemed to affect Robertson's relationship with Murdoch.

While Eisner was making forays against News Corp, Rupert Murdoch was on *Morning Glory*. To make amends for their rained out anniversary in Bermuda, the Murdochs had flown to board the yacht at Hamilton Island on Australia's Great Barrier Reef and spent the week of 20 May cruising the Whitsunday Passage, the idyllic spot that was used for the movie *Dead Calm*. Running a media war from a boat moored somewhere off the coast of Paradise can be hell. But that was why Murdoch had put so much communications gear into their yacht.

Murdoch's telephone negotiations inched forward. By Friday 23 May, Chase Carey and Hindery were reported to have hammered out a rough agreement to sell ASkyB to the Primestar partners. The following Monday, UBS Securities analyst Rick Westerman was calling it 'a done deal'. Primestar itself confirmed that merger talks were under way the next day. The most promising sign was that one of the Primestar partners, Cox Communications, agreed on the Tuesday to carry Fox Sports West 2. Days later another Primestar partner, MediaOne, also signed a ten-year deal to carry the channel.

If Murdoch was facing his Waterloo, it still wasn't clear whether he had been cast as Wellington or Napoleon. So it was that Thursday evening 29 May found Murdoch back in New York, putting on his best togs before heading for the Waldorf Astoria. On the eve of the final clashes that would determine Murdoch's future in America, the great night had finally arrived when the United Jewish Appeal inducted him as Humanitarian of the Year. More than a thousand people had braved the crowd of protesters outside – five separate groups were waving placards – to gather in the Waldorf Astoria's grand ballroom for a dinner dance. There to greet them was the master of ceremonies, the Duchess of Richmond herself, Liz Smith, gossip writer extraordinaire for the *New York Post*.

'I like Rupert Murdoch,' Smith told the assembled dignitaries. 'He's not just the best game, he's the only game in town. Hell, he is the game.'

'I will undoubtedly be described as kissing Mr Murdoch's ring,' she conceded, but continued undaunted. 'The future will lead us to the continued rise of the Murdoch news empire, where creativity with reign, energy and enterprise will dominate, and loyalty will bear its ancient Old Testament meaning.'

There was 'not a single person in the world who is more deserving of this honour (than) . . . my friend, Rupert Murdoch,' the evening's chairman, Viacom chief Sumner Redstone, assured the $1,000-a-plate crowd.

'If you don't know Rupert as well as I do, believe me, it's better to have him as a friend than as an enemy. Ask Gerry or Ted. They're not here tonight.'

Privately Redstone was less averse to a little rivalry: 'I do share (a similar) sort of background with Rupert,' Redstone said at the time. 'But people say I want to emulate him. I don't want to emulate him. I'd like to beat him!' Redstone was actually still vying against Murdoch as a late bidder for IFE. Whatever was said over dinner, by the next day Viacom had pulled out of the race. Pat Robertson himself had shown up at the UJA dinner. With a neat display of ideological suppleness, he had managed to put aside for the night his views on worldwide Jewish conspiracies.

Israeli Prime Minister Benjamin Netanyahu in a video-tape segment saluted Murdoch's newspapers and television interests for the 'commitment to the battle for truth', and their support for Israel. The crowd ended the night on the ballroom floor, while Natalie Cole sang 'Midnight Sun'. The UJA raised $2.3 million.

For Murdoch the next morning it was back to the war zone.

Murdoch had until Monday evening to commit to an unconditional bid for International Family Entertainment. Over the weekend a new snag emerged. The IFE board met at 6.30 on Monday evening to be told that Fox Kids had not met the deadline. Talks would continue, but Murdoch's exclusive rights to negotiate with IFE were over. The board was now free to accept a higher bid from Disney. Michael Eisner wanted his own exclusive negotiating period starting with a bid of $37 a share. To help clarify their thoughts, the IFE board approved themselves a special $100,000 payment for each of the directors.

Relations between News Corp and Disney worsened. 'It got pretty ugly,' said one executive involved in the negotiations. All that stood between Michael Eisner and victory here were Pat Robertson and John Malone, who still had veto-rights over any stock sale by the Robertsons. The sticking point was again the *700 Club*. Robertson had agreed to move the program out of prime time, to 11 p.m. For $37 a share and $1.9 billion, Eisner felt entitled to dump the *700 Club* altogether. Robertson refused. On Disney's side, the sleep-at-night kind of executive wavered. With no concession from Robertson, the price was too high.

The fight to do a deal with Cablevision was going no better for Eisner. Chase Carey had put together a complex deal where Fox Sports paid $850 million for a 40 per cent stake in Dolan's Rainbow Media and Madison Square Garden. Chuck Dolan was ready to take it, despite a higher bid from Disney that reportedly went as high as $1 billion.

'Eisner is pulling his hair out,' an ESPN executive told the *LA Times*. 'A network of regional channels would have been the perfect complement to ESPN. It would have given us local footage and saved enormously on production costs.'

Why would Dolan turn down Eisner's higher bid and go with Murdoch and Malone at Fox Sports? Various reasons were advanced, but the most convincing was that Chuck Dolan had discovered he had a new best friend. It all came together for Murdoch in a remarkable 48-hour period. On Monday 9 June, Malone sold Dolan some of TCI's best cable systems, in the New York metropolitan area. It was a cash and stock deal worth $1.1 billion, which left Malone holding a third of the shares in Dolan's Cablevision Corporation. It was the beginning of a beautiful relationship. Cablevision stock doubled overnight. It would take another two weeks to finalise the Fox Sports deal with Rainbow Media, but there was no more talk of doing a deal with Disney.

'At this point, the regional war is lost,' a Disney executive conceded.

On 11 June, two days after Malone's deal with Dolan, Primestar finalised the $1.1 billion deal to buy Sky from Murdoch. At noon that day the IFE board was told there was now no further hold-up for Fox Kids to buy IFE, and the takeover agreement was announced forthwith. Cox Communications signed up a long-term deal to take Murdoch's FSW2 sports channel in California. A string of other cable deals to carry Fox News followed.

Suddenly Rupert Murdoch was in the clear. He had done it. Through his daring alliance with Charlie Ergen he had taken on not just the cable operators, but most of the American media industry as well. And he had been beaten. Yet he had forced the cable guys to swallow their resentment and to take him back. He had recovered more than he had lost. He had no voting rights in Primestar, but he still owned a one-third stake in the second largest satellite DBS operation in North America. He had finally achieved financial viability for Fox News. He had ensured that Fox Kids would roll out on the Family Channel as 'a great international children's network' on one of the widest distribution channels in the world. And with Fox Sports, he had broken through to build a national network out of a bunch of regional nets based on loyalties for local teams, that could eventually threaten ESPN. 'We are extremely confident it will be very profitable,' he said.

After Shocks: The Winners and Losers

With the end of the 1997 Murdoch Wars, the American media industry had remade itself – out of its own fears. On the whole it was a positive outcome, which just goes to show the widespread social benefits that can flow from a media-business culture that runs on angst, corporate anguish, and high levels of personal animosity. No one really understood the consequences of this obsession with defeating one man. Even after Rupert Murdoch and the cable industry had signed their corporate peace agreement in June, none of the participants had any idea of the chain reactions they would trigger, or of the flood of capital they would release on Wall Street. For many media investors in the second half of 1997, the first warning that the earth had moved was when they looked up and saw an advancing wall of money.

In July at the Sun Valley conference Murdoch sat down with Gerry Levin and Richard Parsons and worked out a deal under which Time Warner would run Fox News in New York. The agreement was announced on 23 July. Ted Turner hadn't liked the Primestar deal with Murdoch. Keeping the Hitler comparison alive, he said the deal was 'just like Munich'. Now Turner decided he could live with Fox News: 'What Martin Luther King is to brotherhood, I am to the cable business.' Turner's commitment to brotherhood and universal suffrage was given a little assistance when Fox lifted its objections to Turner's TBS, which had just changed from a super station into a playing cable channel, continuing to carry games of Turner's Atlanta Braves baseball team.

Wider moves were afoot in the media world. On 9 June, the same day that John Malone unveiled his new alliance with Charles Dolan at Cablevision, Bill Gates at Microsoft pulled off another surprise. He announced a deal to invest $1 billion into the Roberts family's Comcast Corporation. Malone later came to believe that it was part of a wider strategy by Gates to covertly bid for the TCI stock owned by Bob Magness' estate, to snatch control of Malone's company. It didn't really matter if this was true; for Wall Street the critical thing was that Sky, the Murdoch-Ergen threat, was no longer hanging over cable companies. Also, Bill Gates was now so confident that the future of the information revolution lay with cable networks that he was putting out serious money to get involved.

Sky proved to be the unmaking and remaking of Rupert Murdoch. There was more at stake in the titanic struggle that spring than just another corporate deal. This would be one of the turning points for communications at the turn of the century. Sky was the nightmare that cable operators had been dreading for a decade. Whether it worked or not, Sky offered a very different future for America and for the information revolution. If it had succeeded, Sky would have decimated the cable industry and turned cable executives into dinosaurs. If Murdoch had won the legislative changes he was seeking from Congress, he could have spread the cable industry on toast. While Sky would cost $3 billion in start-up funds to cover all of North America, cable companies would spend $3 billion to put fibre-optic cable into just three million homes. The *Economist* magazine likened the cable networks to the canal systems of the nineteenth century – expensive constructions that were out of date as soon as they had been constructed.

Even if Sky failed, it would still have pulled enough revenue from the cable operators to force radical cutbacks in their grand plans to roll out fibre-optic networks. Fibre-optic cable had been one of the two constants of the information revolution, along with faster microchips. It was an industry law: while the processing speed of computer chips doubled every 18 months, the amount of data that fibre-optic cable could carry doubled every 12 months. But cable was expensive. With Sky creaming off the cable companies' profit margin, they would not have been able to afford a wide rollout of upgraded cable. There would be no rewiring of America.

This carried profound consequences, because the future that Murdoch was offering America was not fully interactive. Geostationary satellites could not carry full two-way Internet broadband access, telephony, and eventually video telephones. In 1997, it seemed that all of these things would require either fibre-optic cable, or wireless telephone technology which was still years away, or the high speed DSL telephone lines that the Baby Bell telephone companies seemed to be backing away from. With his Echostar deal in February 1997, Rupert Murdoch was offering America a very different future, an immediate alternative that would push the future of communications in a new direction. The information highway had come to a fork.

The thing to note here is that satellite services were always going to be a threat to the cable industry, with or without Murdoch's Sky. The critical thing that Murdoch did was to trigger a knee-jerk response in the cable industry that overwhelmed the DBS threat and locked up the key DBS satellite slots for the next two years. What changed the future of media was not what Murdoch attempted, but the response he provoked. Murdoch's contribution to history was to be defeated.

Eleven months later, the US Justice Department would step in to try to reverse this tide, with an antitrust suit to reverse the deal that Murdoch and

Malone had so painfully negotiated. The suit claimed, quite understtably, that the only reason the cable operators who owned Primestar wanto buy Murdoch's satellite slot was to stop anyone else using it. But the government intervention would be too late. The changes brought in by this summer of 1997, by the American media industry's overwhelming obsession with beating Rupert Murdoch, would be irreversible. The earth had moved.

The ripples spread wider. In the cable companies and the telephone industry, two huge blocks of capital had been rushing at each other for more than a decade. Inevitably they would become competitors. If the threat of satellite scared the cable guys, this was nothing to the anxiety that a cashed-up cable industry could inspire among the Baby Bell telephone companies. What would the telephone companies do when cable customers started to use their cable connection to make telephone calls? The future that this conflict promised was alive with possibilities.

Once Sky was history, what followed was like watching a landslide in slow motion. With satellite no longer a threat, Bill Gates' investment in cable signalled that he believed this was where the future of communication lay. In effect, Murdoch had closed the back door for cable, while Gates opened the front door. It forced Wall Street to reappraise the way it understood media. The result was huge rises in stock prices for cable companies. It was a win for everyone involved in the Sky fight – even for News Corp. In April 1997, with hostilities at their peak, the seven biggest cable investors – TCI, Time Warner, Comcast, US West, Cox, Cablevision and MediaOne – together with News Corp, had a total market value of $74 billion. A year later, their stock prices had more than doubled, and the group was valued at $159 billion.

That was just for openers. In June 1998 the biggest telephone company in the US, AT&T, saw the growth in the cable companies, and began a new wave of telephone/cable mergers by bidding for TCI. That set off another round of rises for cable company stock. By July 1999, stock in the original group of seven cable companies (including those now merged into AT&T) together with News Corp was worth $338 billion. In two years, stockholders had grown $265 billion richer. Microsoft's market valuation meanwhile jumped from $117 billion in April 1997 to touch $514 billion in July 1999.

This all happened as Internet revenues were taking off, and as the huge growth in Internet business captured Wall Street's imagination. It was no coincidence that the AT&T merger with TCI coincided with the start of the Internet stock craze. AT&T was going to use the cable networks for local telephony – and to give its customers access to the Internet at blinding speeds. The cable-telco mergers had convinced Wall Street that America would have the new fibre-optic networks that it needed to underwrite the e-commerce of the next decade – and even if the new cable guys didn't do this, it was now clear that someone else would. America would be rewired, the future dominance of the Internet seemed assured, and Internet stocks jumped $570 billion in the six months from October 1998 to April 1999.

Investors call this a virtuous circle. The more that the various arms of the communications revolution converged – the television, the telephone and the computer – the higher the prospective profits were for everyone concerned, as one sector fed off the other. The tidal wave of money swept along computer and chip makers, software groups and telephone companies. It even made Charlie Ergen at Echostar richer than he had ever hoped. By April 1999, the total flow-on effect from this chain of events had topped $2 trillion – a sum equal to 25 per cent of America's Gross Domestic Product, arguably the largest transfer of private wealth in history.

The wealth came in the form of higher stock prices rather than cash payments. It seemed particularly apposite that the technological revolution that began by promising the paperless office ended by delivering paper profits. However, it wasn't all paper. About $10 billion in new cash was pumped into Internet companies for working capital in the first half of 1999 alone. What was arguably just as significant was the change in thinking that this new wealth triggered, a radical shift in the way the corporate world viewed its future. For most executives in 1997, on-line commerce was an exotic option with no great relevance beyond e-mail. The six-month Internet boom that began in October 1998 changed that assessment, buried it under a mountain of new money. By mid-1999, the on-line future had become a dominant obsession for business. The world would never be the same.

Neither Murdoch nor Murdoch's defeat was the direct cause of this remarkable confluence of events. At the end of the twentieth century, huge new forces were coming together in the American economy. Yet in a strange way the Murdoch wars became a catalyst for the process. Beating Murdoch broke the technological and financial logjam in multimedia. It changed financial perceptions. Did Rupert Murdoch intend any of the consequences? He wasn't looking to change the world when he flew in to Denver to meet Charlie Ergen. He was just mad at Ted Turner for shutting him out of New York, and he needed a trophy deal to show the analysts.

In any case, the game in 1997 had moved on. Wherever Murdoch moved that year – in baseball, football, or basketball, in film, in children's programming, in books, even in the coupon inserts you get at the supermarket – he triggered a landslide. If Murdoch's satellite gamble determined where the information superhighway would go, his content deals would determine what ran on it.

Michael Eisner was the major loser in all this. Skirmishes between Disney and News Corp continued through the year, until January 1998, when Eisner, the sleep-at-night kind of executive, committed to the biggest sports deal in history, with a $9.2 billion rights contract with the National Football League. Eisner had beaten off Murdoch's ambitions to extend his grasp on the NFL, but the huge price made it a Pyrrhic victory. When Murdoch first snatched the NFL rights from CBS in 1993, Larry Tisch had leaned how painful it was to emerge from a battle with Murdoch as the loser. As the Disney stock price began its spiral down in 1998, Eisner would learn how much more painful it could be to come out of the battle as the winner.

PART THREE

MURDOCH'S ARCHIPELAGO

CHAPTER FIFTEEN

THE TROUBLE WITH TONY

London, 1998

Almost a year after he became Prime Minister of the United Kingdom, Tony Blair learned, as Rupert Murdoch had before him, the perils of accepting long-distance telephone calls. The Italian Prime Minister, Romano Prodi, had called to clarify some details about schedules for European Union meetings that Blair would chair. The date was Wednesday 18 March 1998, a detail which gave a curious historical twist to the conversation that followed. The two men never revealed exactly what was said and nothing more would have come of the call. But five days later, on Monday, 23 March a Turin newspaper, *La Stampa*, reported the conversation and claimed that in the middle of an otherwise mundane discussion of European Union business, Blair had raised the subject of Rupert Murdoch. Murdoch had just offered Silvio Berlusconi, the Italian Opposition Leader, £4 billion to take over Berlusconi's Italian television network, Mediaset. *La Stampa* claimed Blair had asked Prodi if the Italian government would block the deal.

The next day, Tuesday, the *Financial Times* also reported that Blair had intervened on Murdoch's behalf when speaking with Prodi. Blair was in Paris when the story broke. Murdoch was in Los Angeles, where he and Anna had attended the Academy Awards on Monday night. It was one of the last public appearances of the Murdochs' marriage. *Titanic*, despite early pessimism, had become a huge box office success on the way to grossing more than $2 billion. It also won nine Oscars, including three for director James Cameron.

It took some time to get a coherent account of the telephone conversation with Prodi from Blair's office. Blair's press secretary, Alastair Campbell, briefed British journalists that the story that Blair had intervened on Murdoch's behalf was 'a complete joke' and 'C–R–A–P, balls'. He later said that he had been misreported, and denied reports in the *Financial Times* that he had said Murdoch had not been mentioned. He declined to say what had been discussed by Blair, but said, 'This was not a conversation about Rupert Murdoch'. When Campbell was questioned later about his comments by a parliamentary subcommittee, he said:

> I described [the *FT*] story as a joke and I happen to think it was a joke.
> I think it is the oddest form of intervention to sit in your office waiting
> for a phone call from the Italian Prime Minister.

The private secretary who sat in on the phone call was unavailable in Paris early in the week the story broke, and later was said to be in the Middle East. Blair's office backtracked steadily as further details of the call came to light. His cause was not helped when the British embassy in Rome confirmed the conversation. Blair told reporters he had certainly not been doing Murdoch any favours: 'There is no question of offering assistance to anybody. I treat Mr Murdoch no differently from anybody else in respect of any business with British interests.'

On Friday 27 March *The Times* confirmed that Blair had intervened on Murdoch's behalf. The *Guardian* reported that Murdoch had been boasting to his peers about the incredible level of access he had with Blair. When Murdoch asked Blair for his help, even the pressures of Blair's government presenting its first Budget on 17 March had not distracted the British Prime Minister. Blair had called Murdoch back two days later, with news that the Italian government would not view the deal favourably.

The *Financial Times* quoted a News International exec who had been suitable impressed: 'Rupert's access to the Prime Minister is pretty amazing. We were all a bit bowled over.'

News Corp issued a huffy disclaimer from New York: 'It is perfectly common for major businesses to enlist the heads of government and heads of state on issues of this sort.'

Blair's position was to stress that as British PM he was prepared to go in to bat for the interests of *any* British concern. 'I have made it clear that BSkyB will be treated no differently from any other company,' he added.

It gave Tony Blair's government its worst week in the House of Commons since it had come to office eleven months before. The criticism came from all sides. The Labour Chair of the Public Administration

Committee referred to 'the rather unedifying spectacle of half truths and non-denial denials' in the government's handling of the issue. Back-benchers like Norman Banker, the member for Lewes, ventured a little heavy humour: 'It seems that the Prime Minister is very much in bed with Mr Murdoch, and I do not envy the Prime Minister in that respect.'

It wasn't just Blair feeling the heat. The Prodi affair came just as a month of torrid press coverage of Murdoch's empire had been about to subside. While Murdoch had always shown himself to be impervious to whatever was thrown at him in the press, this time he had been forced to go on the defensive, to make more public statements than he had in a decade. The raw emotion in some of his outbursts that month indicated something of the personal stress he was under, what a year of constant crisis had cost him.

Three separate disasters had come together to produce this horror month for Murdoch. The common feature in each of them was the strength of the link that Murdoch had forged with Blair. It was a complex relationship which had been evolving for three years. The key to understanding it is a more complicated set of relationships between Tony Blair, Rupert Murdoch, and the American who had become so influential to both of them, Irwin Stelzer.

Stelzer, who grew up in a poor Jewish neighbourhood in New York, founded a highly successful international consulting firm, National Economic Research Associates, in 1961. NERA specialised in antitrust, electricity and telecommunications issues. In 1983 he sold the firm to March & McLennan and took a sabbatical in Aspen, the Colorado ski resort. Stelzer found himself living in the exclusive Starwood Community next door to one of his best friends, Rupert Murdoch. Stelzer was one of Murdoch's most trusted advisers, not merely on economic matters but in Murdoch's broader view of the world. Stelzer's views on society reflected and shaped Murdoch's own views. He had arguably done more to colour Rupert Murdoch's internal landscape than anyone else in Murdoch's life. It was said the two men got on so well together that they once talked about building a tunnel to join their two houses, though their wives were not as enthusiastic.

Stelzer's consultancy arrangement with Murdoch and News Corporation was reported to be worth more than £1 million a year. In addition, Stelzer wrote columns for the *Sunday Times* in London, the *Post* in New York, the *Weekly Standard* in Washington and even a column in Australia for the Queensland Press flagship, the *Courier Mail*, which gave him a voice and public profile any economist would die for. Writing for such different audiences required a degree of rhetorical flexibility. In

Britain, Stelzer argued unceasingly that embracing European Monetary Union (EMU) and adopting the euro as currency would take away British jobs and be bad news for Britain. On the other side of the Atlantic he took the view that EMU could threaten New York's position as the world's financial capital, and would be bad news for America. After his Aspen sabbatical Stelzer went on to to lecture at Oxford and run an energy program at Harvard University. At some point he was also a managing director at the Rothschild Investment Bank. After Harvard he joined the world of right-wing think-tanks with a stint as a director of regulation at the American Enterprise Institute. In 1998 he moved to the Hudson Institute of Indianapolis.

Friends describe Stelzer as highly likeable with a formidable intelligence. Stelzer is a phenomenal networker. He has a gift for spotting bright young (or not so young) men and becoming their patron. One effective way to further their careers was to introduce them to his friend Rupert Murdoch. Stelzer became close to Andrew Neil of the *Economist* in the 1970s. In 1983 he arranged for Neil to meet Murdoch and recommended Murdoch make him editor of the *Sunday Times*. Stelzer, who often wrote or co-wrote Murdoch's speeches, was also an admirer of Peter Huber of the Manhattan Institute, whose views on the need to deregulate the telecommunications industry (and the shortfalls of George Orwell), meshed neatly with Stelzer's own. It is likely that Stelzer wrote both Murdoch's speech in the Banqueting Hall in London in September 1993, and the speech on Orwell in Melbourne the following year.

Stelzer was also a strong supporter of Charles Murray, whose book attacking the American welfare system, *Losing Ground*, triggered a decade and a half of legislation to reduce welfare payments. Stelzer, who had introduced Murray's ideas to Murdoch, arranged for the *Sunday Times* to pay for Murray and his family to spend a month in Britain to write a series of articles about a crime-ridden British underclass that he called the 'New Rabble', and the need to cut welfare support for unmarried mothers. Stelzer also arranged, after Murray had been paid for this work, for the *Sunday Times* to slip Murray another $10,000 cheque on top. An appreciative Murray described Stelzer as 'the godfather'. Murray addressed News Corporation executives at a management conference in Aspen. On one occasion when Murray visited Stelzer in Aspen, Murdoch sent his Gulfstream to pick Murray up. In 1993, Murray's warnings of a developing white underclass led to a flurry of political moves to deny welfare to unwed mothers.

In 1994, Murray was stirring up controversy again with *The Bell Curve:*

Intelligence and Class Structure in American Life, a new book written with the late Richard Herrnstein of Harvard. It tackled the ticklish topic of connections between race, class, genes and intelligence. Its central thesis was that the technology-fuelled economic boom of the late twentieth century had created a meritocracy, a new upper middle class whose advancement was due entirely to their own skills and abilities. In the technological society, the stairway upward was open to anyone with intelligence. Some people were smarter than others, and they became rich because of it. Others stayed poor because they were less intelligent, a cognitive underclass. It followed, Murray said, that the reason that the majority of blacks in America were poor was because they were less intelligent. This reflected differences in intelligence between different races. The Bell Curve suggested that some people would always be at the top. Murray believed that affirmative action programs penalised smart white people and produced a distorted and unfair society. Attempts to redress the genetic balance, such as education programs in the ghettos, in Murray's view were a waste of money.

Murray was resurrecting in modern form a bleak social outlook which has surfaced whenever wide economic moves trigger social changes. It is the rhetoric of the new winners. History suggests that when a new group climbs the class staircase, their first move is to lock the stairwell door behind them. The Murdochs have always believed in the superiority of their genes. In December 1999 Rupert Murdoch made a speech in Oxford where he emphasised the importance of IQ and genetic inheritance. The *New York Post* has a history of criticism for inflammatory coverage of blacks. However, by late 1994, when *The Bell Curve* appeared, Murdoch had a black son-in-law. Elisabeth Murdoch married Elkin Pianim, whose father was a prominent Ghanaian dissident, in September 1993.

Of all Irwin Stelzer's bright middle-aged men, his greatest discovery was Tony Blair. When Stelzer reviewed John Kenneth Galbraith's *The Good Society* for *The Times* in 1996, Stelzer argued that while the book had 'a few kernels of wisdom', he had not shown:

> so much as a nod in the direction of studies of social scientist Charles Murray and others that show that the poor are no different from the middle-class worker in responding to incentives: pay them to have babies and they will; pay them not to work, and they won't. In this area of public policy the good professor appears less well read than Tony Blair.

As a young backbencher in the British Labour Party, Blair had stayed aloof from the fervent anti-Murdoch rhetoric during the Wapping dispute in 1986. He told Andrew Neil at the *Sunday Times*: 'I hate the print unions even more than you.' In the later 1980s he caught Stelzer's attention because of his opposition to the Conservative government's moves towards nuclear energy, away from the country's traditional reliance on coal. Blair saw the issue in terms of employment, while Stelzer by conviction and from his long-term association as a consultant with the US power groups acquiring Britain's coal power stations, saw coal as more efficient. Stelzer wrote several columns praising Blair as an up-and-coming star of the future. The casual links deepened after Blair became Labour leader in 1994. Eventually the two began regular meetings to discuss Labour policy. They became so close that the *Guardian* speculated that Stelzer had become a paid consultant to the Labour Party. Stelzer did not comment.

According to Andrew Neil, Murdoch met Blair for the first time on 15 September 1994 over dinner at a private room at Mosimann's restaurant in Belgravia. The dinner was arranged by Gus Fischer, but it is difficult to believe that Stelzer did not play a part. Stelzer reportedly arranged for Blair to address the American Enterprise Institute in Washington. In July 1995, Blair flew to Australia to address a News Corporation management conference at Hamilton Island on the Great Barrier Reef. There he made it clear he had dumped Labour's longstanding policy to force News International to reduce its media holdings. Murdoch observed in his opening remarks before Blair spoke:

> If the British press is to be believed, today is all part of a Blair/Murdoch flirtation. If that flirtation is ever consummated, Tony, I suspect we will end up making love like two porcupines. Very carefully.

Through 1995 and into 1996, Stelzer produced a series of columns written with the tone of a disinterested spectator, which grew ever warmer towards Blair. Stelzer considered gravely the charge that Blair was another Clinton clone, or even that he was Clinton Lite. He then went on to argue the contrary, that Blair should be seen as Margaret Thatcher's natural heir: 'I know Tony Blair . . . Blair is one of Thatcher's children. And I think he knows it.'

In the summer of 1996, Stelzer wrote a remarkable tribute to Blair for *Public Interest*, a conservative journal edited by Irving Kristol. The article was based on an interview that Blair had given at Easter, in which he said he was an ecumenical Christian. Stelzer went on to argue that Blair had led a revolution in the British left: 'Christ in, Marx out.' Stelzer took Blair's somewhat diffident comments and his decision to send his children to a Catholic school, and discovered Blair as a man who 'has room for Christ in his Christianity'. Blair was a modern reformer who had put the Methodist chapel back at the centre stage of the Labour Party, Stelzer proclaimed. He had put 'sin' – a concept that Stelzer linked with 'the undeserving poor', back into political discourse. He would 'leave it to the theologians and philosophers' to debate what Blair actually believed:

> One thing is clear, however: the leader of Britain's left-wing party finds it acceptable, politically, to profess his Christianity and to look to the New and Old Testaments for a central core around which to develop his political program. Of necessity, that requires a cultural stance not very different from that of America's Christian Coalition . . .

Stelzer had already concluded that Blair was Margaret Thatcher's ideological heir. Now in this highly crafted essay he set up a parallel between the ecumenical faith propounded by the leader of the British Labour Party, and the fundamentalism of America's religious Right. It was a juxtaposition that less agile minds than Stelzer's might have missed. Stelzer had produced a dazzling piece of rhetoric with the apparent aim of convincing the American right wing that Blair was almost one of them. The question is why the ideological gymnastics were necessary. What made the American view of Blair so important? As the article kept returning to the Christian Coalition, the most obvious answer was that Stelzer's real target was the Christian Coalition founder, Pat Robertson. At that period there was a suggestion Stelzer was anxious to obtain Robertson's good opinion of Blair, which could in turn influence Murdoch's support for the Labour leader. This may be so. Then again, in many ways the juxtaposition Stelzer proposed was eerily similar to Rupert Murdoch's own description of himself as a product of Catholic leanings and his Methodist roots.

By early 1997, Blair had convinced Murdoch that he would not move against News Corp's interest once he was in power, and that he would hold off from joining the European Monetary Union. On Monday 18 March 1997, the first day of the election campaign, Blair and Major woke up to the realisation that the earth had moved. Murdoch's *Sun* newspaper, after nearly two decades of backing the Conservative Party, had changed horses.

On 14 April, Labour's media spokesman, Dr Lewis Moonie, announced that a Labour government would relax rules on cross-media ownership, allowing large newspaper groups like News International more opportunities to own broadcasting groups. Labour also would support widening the tax net for commercial television to include BSkyB. Blair probably would have won the election with or without the backing of Murdoch's papers, but their support arguably turned a probable victory into the largest majority in history for the Labour Party in the House of Commons. Murdoch's support continued after the election on 1 May. Blair reportedly dined privately with Rupert and Anna Murdoch twice before the election, and hosted them at the Prime Minister's residence at Chequers on several occasions in the following year. However, by early 1998 the price for this special relationship was beginning to become apparent.

Three separate strands came together for them in February and March of 1998. The first was Murdoch's ongoing quest to swing a deal with Silvio Berlusconi. Italian politicians had been agitating to pass a law to ban politicians from owning television stations. It would either force Berlusconi to retire from politics, or would turn him into a forced seller of his half share in Mediaset. Murdoch had already tried and failed to extend his empire into France, he was still battling and getting nowhere in Germany. Italy would prove no easier. In December 1999, Murdoch would sell his yacht, *Morning Glory*, to Berlusconi for £4.5 million, apparently in a bid to cement a friendship. Whatever his sentimental attachment to the boat, business was business.

The second strand was the price war that Murdoch's News International newspapers had been waging in Britain since 1993. In stage one of the price war, Murdoch had slashed the cover price of the *Sun*, in a successful bid to restore its flagging circulation to 4 million. However, the move turned into a disaster when the price of newsprint doubled. Just when News International was poised to capitalise on the higher sales, it found its newsprint supplies were restricted. It was losing money from the price discounts and the higher paper price, and without extra supplies of newsprint the *Sun* could not print enough copies to capitalise on its gains. Murdoch's strategies often have two parts. First there is the great gamble, the big outlay that risks the empire or the division, like the decision to launch Sky Television, or Fox News, or buying the NFL rights. The second part – the critical part – is the payback, the period when the huge returns are secured that justify the gamble. The newsprint crisis meant the *Sun*'s price war had no payback.

Murdoch's British executives protested that the newsprint problem was not their fault: newsprint for the group was ordered from New York. But for whatever reason, Murdoch staged one of his periodic management culls in Britain. News Corporation's chief executive officer Gus Fischer went in early 1995, News International managing director John Dux went in March. By the end of 1995, only two of the 13 executive directors of News International remained. These were Murdoch himself, and company secretary Peter Stehrenberger.

Stage two of the price war involved cutting the cover price of *The Times* to 10p on Mondays, and 40p on Saturdays. It was an aggressive move to steal market share from Tony O'Reilly's *Independent* and Conrad Black's *Daily Telegraph*. According to Dan Colson, deputy chairman and chief exec of Telegraph Group plc, in 1993 Murdoch had told Sir David English, of Associated Newspapers: 'Don't worry about the Telegraph. Leave them to me. I'll put them out of business for you.' Colson estimated *The Times* price cutting alone cost News International £30 million a year, a total £150 million over five years to 1998. Hit by the newsprint rise and the discounting it had taken to counter *The Times* price cuts, the Telegraph Group's earnings dropped from £60 million in 1993, to £1 million in 1996.

By late 1997, backbenchers in the new Labour government were concerned enough about the threat that Murdoch's price policy posed to the future of newspapers like the *Independent* to agitate for legal bans on anti-competitive pricing. Murdoch's supporters argued that he was merely doing what any good businessman would do. On 12 November, with talk in the air of parliament passing an amendment to trade practices legislation to outlaw predatory pricing in the newspaper industry, Murdoch was unrepentant. He told reporters at the BSkyB annual meeting, 'No way will I call a truce. No one else wants to call a truce. They insult me everyday, so they can go to hell. People do not much seem to like competition in this country.' But just to be sure, Murdoch made an appointment to see Tony Blair at Downing Street the next day.

In February 1998, Blair drew criticism from Labour ranks by opposing the amendment on predatory pricing, which was passed in the House of Lords. On 9 February, rebel Labour members of the House of Lords combined with other parties to amend the government's new Competition Bill, bringing it into line with legislation in the US and Australia. The amendment banned any 'abuse of dominant position . . . if it may reduce the diversity of the national newspaper press in the United Kingdom by reducing, retarding, injuring or eliminating competition'.

The Times, in an editorial headlined, 'The Enemies of Success', complained: 'We have initiated a pricing policy that has increased the market for broadsheet newspapers by 14 per cent, brings more buyers and readers to ourselves and many of our competitors, countering an international trend of decline.' *The Times* did not wish to destroy the *Independent*, as had been claimed, the paper argued. 'We would only say that those who wish to keep this title alive have chosen a market-distorting route that will guarantee the continuation of its current state of death-in-life. If that is press freedom, it is the freedom of the specimen jar for the insect.'

Tony Blair announced his government would not support the amendment, and it would not be passed in the House of Commons. However, the debate had rekindled many of the old passions about Rupert Murdoch that the Labour Party had held for two decades.

The third strand in the controversy that engulfed Murdoch in Britain early in 1998 began with a secret meeting on 3 July the year before. A week after stitching up Fox Sports' $850 million deal over Madison Square Garden in New York, Murdoch headed for Hong Kong for the handover ceremonies of the former British colony on 30 June. After the formalities he had been granted a meeting in Beijing with Zhu Rongji, one of the Chinese Vice Premiers and the man tipped as the next Prime Minister. It was a moment that Murdoch had been working towards for nearly four years, ever since the Chinese government abruptly banned his Star TV satellite broadcasts in China, in the wake of Murdoch's indiscreet comments in London that technology 'was an unambiguous threat to authoritarian regimes everywhere'. Westerners had found two approaches possible in dealings with China. When Disney released Martin Scorsese's film *Kundun* about Tibet, Beijing had public chastised Disney and threatened to pull Disney's plan for a theme park in China. In response, a group of Hollywood's creative elite held a widely covered press conference at which they released a public letter of protest to Chinese Ambassador Li Daoyu. The Chinese backed down.

The alternative strategy was appeasement. In April 1994 Murdoch dropped the BBC World Service in the face of Chinese criticism of its coverage. 'The BBC was driving them nuts,' Murdoch said later. 'We're not proud of that decision. It was the only way . . . The truth is – and we Americans don't like to admit it – that authoritarian countries can work . . . The best thing you can do in China is engage the Chinese and wait.' This was a long way from his position in the 1980s, when Murdoch told *Sunday Times* editor Andrew Neil he believed Britain should lob a 'warning nuke' into a Chinese desert as a wake-up call over Hong Kong.

In 1995 HarperCollins published the biography of Deng Xiaoping's daughter, Deng Rong, and Murdoch personally escorted her to the promotional press conferences in the US. The difficulty with appeasement was that in Chinese eyes it created a loss of face. When Murdoch was shown in to see Zhu Rongji on 3 July 1998, it appeared to have been a second-best option. Initially the editor of *The Times*, Peter Stothard, had been promised an interview with President Jiang Zemin, in return for hosting the board of the *People's Daily* on a tour of Britain, first-class air travel and arranging interviews with senior British politicians. This was downgraded into an interview with Vice Premier Zhu, which had not gone happily. Stothard never filed a story about it. Murdoch's interview with Zhu appears to have been tied into this process. When Zhu saw the head of News Corporation, he felt sure enough of himself to pull Murdoch's chain a little. Zhu broke through the usual exchange of pleasantries via an interpreter to address Murdoch in English. He had heard, Zhu said, that Murdoch had taken out US citizenship when he wanted to operate a television network in America. Would he consider taking out Chinese citizenship to further his interests in China?

Murdoch was clearly taken aback. Zhu watched his reaction for a moment before turning to his entourage behind him and repeating the question in Chinese . . . to general mirth. Murdoch hung in there slugging. He told Zhu that broadcasting via digital satellite 'would be a powerful means to provide information, education and medical services to the population, which is scattered across this vast country'. The year before, Murdoch had launched the Phoenix Channel, a Mandarin channel beamed from Star TV's satellite owned 55 per cent by Singapore Chinese and business interests in China close to the Red Army. While ostensibly it was still illegal to receive satellite broadcasts, Star was claiming to have 36.5 million viewers. Murdoch wanted to turn that into officially approved distribution across China's cable systems. Zhu gave Murdoch an attentive audience, but after Murdoch headed back to the US for the Sun Valley conference six days later, nothing was immediately forthcoming. In August the Chinese government released 55 new regulations banning foreigners from holding television interests.

The breakthrough came in September. Phoenix was granted formal sanction to be carried on two cable channels in Guandong and Guangzhou provinces, reaching 2.5 million people. This was still only the tiniest of toeholds in the door, but it was the first official approval for Murdoch. 'I don't think the Chinese in any way will expect us to be agents of propaganda,' Murdoch said that summer. 'They certainly don't want us to be agents of subversion, and we have no intention of being that.'

'There is a great deal of change happening in China and on present indications we are getting a much warmer welcome,' Murdoch told shareholders at the News Corp annual meeting in Adelaide on 7 October.

A week later the *People's Daily* reported that the Chinese Ministry of Foreign Affairs had granted approval for Sky News to open a Beijing office. When the Chinese President Jiang Zemin made a brief visit to the US at the end of the month, Murdoch was reported as one of the business leaders that would fete him. Murdoch was in the audience at the Waldorf Astoria in New York on 31 October to hear Jiang speak. Two days later Murdoch bobbed up at another Jiang address in Los Angeles at the Beverly Hilton.

Murdoch's growing interests included an information technology joint venture with the *People's Daily*, with an Internet home page called ChinaByte. When Jiang visited Australia in 1999, Murdoch's *Australian* newspaper published an entire section of the paper in Chinese for a week. In 1998 there was even talk of Murdoch buying a soccer team, Dalian Wanda, the top team in the Chinese National Football League. Back in December 1997, the Hong Kong papers were full of Murdoch's most daring gambit yet. He had been speaking to executives from China Central Television and Communist Party officials about broadcasting CCTV's Channel 4 via satellite to Europe and North America. Murdoch had offered nine of News Corp's satellite transponders to broadcast the propaganda channel for three years, free of charge. The strength of the gesture was that it was a straight gift, with nothing requested in return. CCTV officials did not answer press queries on the deal. In January 1998, at this critical moment when events in China finally appeared to be turning his way, Murdoch focused on a new problem.

In the early hours of 1 July, as Hong Kong was still celebrating the handover ceremony the previous night, and the last Governor of Hong Kong, Chris Patten, relaxed on the royal yacht *Britannia* in Kowloon Harbour, HarperCollins secured a deal with agent Michael Sissons to publish a forthcoming book by Patten, *East and West*, for a £125,000 advance. Eddie Bell, the portly, cigar-smoking executive chairman of HarperCollins UK, the head of trade publications, Adrian Bourne, and the trade publisher, Stuart Profitt, had won the book with a bid that fell just under the level that required approval from HarperCollins in New York.

Even at the time it was a brave decision. A chill wind was blowing through the publishing house. Earlier that month, Anthea Disney, the chief executive of HarperCollins' parent, News America Publishing in New York, had dumped 106 book contracts. Seventy of the authors involved had not made their completion deadline, while another 36 were deemed non-commercial. 'Let's clean house,' Disney said, on the way to writing off $270 million from the HarperCollins balance sheet. While the contracts were paid out, authors and agents saw the move as a breach of trust.

It was a mark of the internal power balance at HarperCollins that when Disney ruthlessly pruned the publishing lists in the US, Eddie Bell showed no sign of following suit in London. Bell was 48 years old, a gruff Glaswegian who had survived for eight years as head of HarperCollins.

Whatever befell the Patten book later, there was no shortage of courage at the outset. Bell committed to the book although it was common knowledge that Murdoch detested Patten. Later that month, after returning from his meeting with Zhu Rongji, Murdoch took Bell to task over the Patten deal, to express 'extreme displeasure', as Profitt later described it. Patten was badly on the nose in China. The government-controlled press referred to him variously as a 'criminal of a thousand antiquities', a 'serpent', a 'drooling idiot', or a 'perfidious whore'. When the editorial writers were really cross, they called him a 'tango dancer'.

Bell risked his boss's ire and remained committed to the book. Later that year Murdoch again complained to Bell about the book. Bell remained resolute. In January, however, Bell's position became untenable. According to Andrew Neil, former editor of the *Sunday Times*, Murdoch was furious that despite raising the matter with Bell twice already, the book contract had not been cancelled. 'Kill the book!' he ordered Disney in New York. 'Kill the fucking book!' Murdoch strongly denied this version of events.

Bell continued a rearguard action, resisting something he saw as folly. Bell wrote to Disney on Tuesday 20 January:

> Following your instructions to relinquish rights, I have given considerable thought to the potential ramifications of such action. The more I have thought about this, the more concerned I have become. I felt therefore that I must write to ensure that you are fully aware of the ramifications of not publishing which are potentially serious for News Corp and HarperCollins. KRM (Keith Rupert Murdoch) has outlined to me the negative aspects of publication . . .

Bell had included a report by Stuart Profitt, the publisher of the trade division who would be editing the Patten book, that described the first six chapters that he had just received as 'probably the best written and most compelling book I have read by a politician since I came into publishing'. Bell quoted advice from HarperCollins' public relations agency that dropping the book would be a disaster, then went on to discuss PR strategies to contain the damage. He concluded by asking Disney to confirm that she had passed the memo to Murdoch.

Anthea Disney flew to London to discuss the matter on Monday 26

January. Profitt, who was aware of the axe hanging over the book, heard nothing further that week. On Thursday 29 January, he proceeded as planned with a dinner for 55 booksellers and HarperCollins staff at the Savoy Hotel to introduce them to Chris Patten, who had flown across from France. Profitt introduced Patten and described *East and West* as 'the most intelligently written book I've read by a politician in 15 years of publishing'.

On the following Tuesday, Profitt had still heard nothing of the Disney meeting of the week before, and went to his immediate superior, Adrian Bourne, to ask about it. Bourne said he also had heard nothing. However, on Wednesday, Bourne asked Profitt to come to see him the following day. At that Thursday meeting, Bourne said he and Bell had decided to drop the Patten book, not because of the meeting with Anthea Disney, but because they both judged the book did not conform to the outline, 'or indeed inspire us from a commercial standpoint'. He said that 'the text was disappointing and that it was not worth what we had paid for it'. Bourne asked if he had Profitt's support in the decision. When Profitt said he would have to think about it, Bourne handed him a gagging letter drawn up by HarperCollins' lawyers.

> It is imperative that you make no communication with any individual employed by HarperCollins about this decision, and of equal importance is that you make no approach to any outside body or individual . . . that this decision has been made.

On the Friday, Profitt asked for written reasons for the decision to cancel the book contract. The following Monday he asked again in writing, and was promptly suspended from his position. A week later, HarperCollins leaked a story to the *Mail on Sunday* that the Patten book had been 'dumped for being too boring'. At this point the story was playing out as planned. HarperCollins' public relations advice in New York had been that the whole affair would blow over, in the same way the Disney decision to axe 106 book contracts the previous June had. It was a storm in a teacup. What the New York spin doctors had overlooked, however, was that the decision to suspend Profitt over the problems he was making about the Patten book was made on the day that the House of Lords was passing its amendment aimed at reining in predatory commercial practices in the News empire.

On Friday 27 February the *Daily Telegraph* ran details of the saga, the writ that Patten had lodged against HarperCollins for breach of contract, as well as a writ that Profitt had just lodged for constructive dismissal. It even reproduced Eddie Bell's letter to Disney of 20 January. In a statutory declaration prepared for the legal action, Profitt had said that the reason given for dumping the Patten book was:

> clearly not a true or sustainable position and it is not one which I can support, as I have been asked to . . . to do so would have meant . . . both lying and doing enormous damage to my own reputation. Though I have some sympathy for Eddie Bell, he has tried to make me the scapegoat. He has chosen the wrong man.

The furore that followed awakened all of the anti-Murdoch phobias of the past. Here it seemed was a decision taken to impose draconian censorship in one of the world's largest publishing houses in order to pursue Murdoch's commercial interests elsewhere in the world. It came just as the House of Lords was debating a predatory pricing policy pursued by News International which sought to make *The Times* Britain's bestselling quality newspaper. And at this critical time, *The Times* declined to run with the Patten book story. On the Saturday it carried a small story giving News Corporation's response to the claims, denying any attempt to make changes in the book.

'As is well known, the editors of News Corporation publications are free to express their opinions and often have been critical of the Chinese, as well as other governments,' News Corporation said.

The Times media editor, Raymond Snoddy, said later that the lack of coverage was an 'unacceptable error', but his attempts to interview Patten, Bell or Murdoch had failed. The paper's editor, Peter Stothard, by Tuesday 3 March was saying that he had thought the Patten book was 'a pretty minor story' but he might have 'underplayed it'. The hapless Stothard was then hit by reports in the *Daily Telegraph* of claims made two months before by *The Times* former East Asia editor, Jonathan Mishky, that *The Times* had gone soft on reporting China. 'From four days after the handover (in June) until the end of September, the readers of *The Times* would have thought that Hong Kong had been lifted up to Pluto . . . *The Times* has simply decided, because of Murdoch's interests, not to cover China in a serious way.'

'Contrary to (Mishky's) statement the China coverage of *The Times* is wholly and solely in the hands of the Editor,' Stothard responded. 'I have never taken an editorial decision to suit Mr Murdoch's interests, nor have I ever been asked to.'

Labour backbenchers were muttering about referring the original *Times* takeover in 1981 to the Mergers and Monopolies Commission, on the grounds that Murdoch had not honoured the pledge of independence for the paper that he had given when he bought it. 'It's worrying this man has such immense power,' Thurrock MP Andrew Mackinley said. 'There's an overwhelming case for his UK media empire to be broken up by legislation.'

'I'm concerned about the concentration of media ownership and the way owners interfered in editorial policy,' the chairman of the Parliamentary Labour Party, Clive Soley, said.

To some extent this was just the usual list of suspects sounding off about their favourite demon. A more pragmatic response came from Murdoch's one-time tormentor at Oxford, Gerald Kaufman. Kaufman, now chairman of the Culture Select Committee, dismissed any talk of an inquiry: 'This does not seem to be an issue about public policy. It is an issue of public controversy.'

On Tuesday 3 March, Rupert Murdoch responded to the barrage of criticism. After a brief stopover in London, he gave an interview to Snoddy in a car on his way to Luton airport. Murdoch described the Patten book deal as a 'cock-up', and put the blame on the senior executives at HarperCollins for not being more forthright in handling the issue.

Murdoch told Snoddy:

I did not tell people to try and censor the book or invent excuses not to do it. I said, 'Why don't you go and say we would rather have someone else publish this and if there is any chance of losing money we will make it good?' They chickened out and got themselves into the position where they were inventing reasons why they just didn't want to publish it which were nonsense, leaving me in a completely inexcusable position.

Murdoch said the HarperCollins execs had 'screwed it up'. As a result Mr Profitt, who was a very good editor, was able to take up the 'position of a martyr' and Mr Patten's agent, Michael Sissons, was able to 'work it for a lot of publicity to sell a lot more books'. Murdoch believed that no one had been hurt by the row 'except us in a PR sense because our people cocked it up at the end. I just regret that our people weren't more forthright about it at the very beginning when I was with them.'

It never looked like this would be an adequate response to the moral outrage that was being hurled at Murdoch. As reports came in of other books on China that HarperCollins had put on hold, some of the publishing house's leading authors began talking about jumping ship. Three days later, on Friday 6 March HarperCollins settled its lawsuit with Patten and expressed grovelling contrition. In an agreed statement, HarperCollins 'unreservedly apologised' for any suggestion that *East and West* was rejected for not being up to proper professional standards or being too 'boring'. HarperCollins said it accepted 'that these allegations are untrue and ought never to have been made'.

Rupert Murdoch weighed in to say that there had been no winners or losers in the controversy. 'Mistakes have been made and we all share responsibility,' he said.

> I have total confidence in the proven talents and abilities of Eddie Bell and the entire publishing team . . . Eddie, Adrian Bourne (managing director) and Adrian Laing (general counsel) have had a difficult few days but I know that their professionalism, experience and above all their determination will take the company successfully forward.

Patten's agent, Michael Sissons, remained unimpressed. 'Mr Murdoch's comments of Tuesday and yesterday offer an insight into his mind,' Sissons responded.

> Clearly the notion of a graceful apology does not come easy to him. He acknowledges a 'cock-up' and adds that 'mistakes have been made and we all share the responsibility'. That, I suppose, is one way to describe a malicious falsehood concocted with the sole purpose of protecting, mistakenly as it turned out, the wider interests of the empire. Moreover he cannot resist a sneer at all of us who have raised the matter.

By and large, the HarperCollins admission took the sting out the debate. However, Murdoch was concerned enough about the collateral damage that his interests had taken to meet Tony Blair. According to a News International executive the meeting took place at the end of February. Quentin Davies, the Conservative Member for Grantham and Stamford, later told the House of Commons that Blair hosted Murdoch at the Prime Minister's country house, Chequers, in the first week of March. Other reports identify this as Sunday 8 March. Whatever was said during that visit, clearly the personal chemistry between them was still strong. Murdoch was reassured about his high standing with the Prime Minister.

On Monday 16 March, Murdoch met with Silvio Berlusconi, the Italian Opposition Leader, and offered £4 billion for Mediaset. Murdoch gave

Berlusconi 72 hours to think the offer over, then retired to a villa in Milan to wait for the response. Murdoch is not a man who takes forced delays well. He fidgets. As he waited, his concern grew that even if Berlusconi agreed to the deal, the Italian government might intervene to stop its leading television network from falling into foreign hands. Murdoch badly needed to know if it was worth proceeding with this bid. But who was he going to call? By Tuesday 17 March, Murdoch's thoughts had turned to Tony Blair. It was exactly a year since John Major had called the British election, and Murdoch had made the ground-breaking decision to back Blair. On the anniversary of this decision, Murdoch decided to call in a marker.

Two weeks later, as criticism of the Prodi incident burned hot, Blair told the House of Commons, 'As for newspaper proprietors, I meet all of them regularly, I know all of them. I regard that as a sensible part of being the leader of a major political party. As a matter of fact, I have no illusions about any of them. They are all highly able, highly ruthless and dedicated to the success of their businesses, as I am dedicated to the success of mine.'

It was a statement that seemed to be as much about describing Blair's view of himself as of any newspaper proprietor. Learning to live with Murdoch was a piece of Realpolitik, to which the architects of New Labour had committed at least three years before. On 12 May, when the amended Competition Bill went back to Commons for the second reading, the government announced it would vote down the amendment on predatory pricing.

The most damaging issue to arise from the weeks of controversy was not that Murdoch, like many newspaper proprietors before him, dictated the editorial policy and news coverage of the publications that he owned, nor that he was prepared to intervene to ensure his publishing house did not print books on certain subjects. The underlying conflict was rather that Murdoch's media empire, News Corporation, was a multinational con-glomerate whose corporate objectives did not necessarily correspond with Britain's national interest. The threat that price wars posed to Britain's quality newspapers was in part directed at undermining Conrad Black and winning control of an Australian newspaper chain. Murdoch's international media operations had an agenda to present to the world the Chinese government's view of itself.

In 1999 when NATO aircraft mistakenly bombed the Chinese embassy in Belgrade, the coverage on Murdoch's Phoenix Channel was so stridently anti-British that the British Embassy in Beijing lodged a complaint. In the United States, News Corporation was still struggling against larger rivals. In the rest of the world, the picture was quite different. The issue was whether multinational media groups like News Corp were now too big and too powerful for politicians in medium-sized economies like Britain's to control. This was not to impute particular malice or ill intent on the part of Rupert Murdoch or his companies. It was rather to acknowledge that, in the rising threat to national sovereignty that large multinational corporations had come to pose at the turn of the century, Murdoch was on the very edge of the wave. Just how little control national governments had over Murdoch was shown most markedly in News Corporation's money trail. It was concern over this money trail that had triggered a secret meeting in Sydney three months before.

Just before Christmas in 1997, a secret task force of tax officers met in Sydney to devise a strategy to monitor News Corp's international money movements. As well as Australian tax officials the group that assembled in the Australian Tax Office building included senior officers from the US Internal Revenue Service, the British Inland Revenue and the Canadian tax authority. The Australian Tax Commissioner, Michael Carmody, had called the meeting under the umbrella of tax agreements that linked the four countries to discuss a way to investigate News Corporation's tax structures. He believed that the finances of modern multinational companies had become too complex and crossed too many borders for one national tax authority to be able to regulate.

The Australian Tax Office had been investigating the News group for at least two years as part of its Large Audit program. According to an internal memo dated May 1996, an Australian Tax Office team had examined Australian companies that were 'thought to represent significant FSI [Foreign Sourced Income] risks . . . The analysis that was done resulted in News Limited being classified as high-risk.'

News Corporation dismissed reports of the international tax inquiry. 'News is subject to the normal rotational audits that all large corporations face and the company pays its taxes according to the laws around the world.'

The tax officers meeting in Sydney operated in a world that is bewildering to most taxpayers. Even the terminology to describe what they were looking for sounded like another language. The May 1996 memo concluded:

The risk assessment in respect of News Limited shows substantial funds movements from unlisted CFCs (Controlled Foreign

Companies) to listed CFCs and the audit team is presently identifying the transactions and structures responsible for these movements. The other CFC areas to be examined include the control rule, the active income test, and the attribution percentages escalation.

Other issues studied by the ATO included,

implications of offshore structures, residency and PERs (Permanent Establishment Requirements). Royalties (transfer pricing), FIF (Foreign Investment Funds), cross-border finance, losses on redemption of shares (and) increase in share premium account.

To outsiders, it was the next best thing to magic. By a strange alchemy, each year hundreds of millions of dollars of News Corporation earnings bounced around some of the most exotic parts of the world, touring the archipelagos of offshore tax havens. Huge money streams flowed through more than 75 News Corporation companies in the British Virgin Islands, the Cayman Islands, the Netherlands, the Netherland Antilles, Hong Kong and Bermuda. By the time News Corp's profits made it to the balance sheet to be reported to shareholders, they had accumulated more frequent flyer points than most accountants could dream of. In the course of this alchemy, most of News Corp's tax bill disappeared. At the heart of the News Corporation accounts, the group's accountants had produced a wonderful piece of virtual reality.

It was 1986 when News Corporation stopped paying tax in any meaningful way. In 1984 it had paid a respectable 30 cents in the dollar of its reported earnings in tax. A year later this had dipped to 23 cents in the dollar. In 1986 the tax rate fell to 9 cents in the dollar. It is important to remember that, while the effect could appear almost magical, the end result was the product of more prosaic – and perfectly legal – tax planning. The move coincided with Murdoch's big expansion into the US with his purchase of Twentieth Century Fox and the Metromedia television stations. Murdoch had structured his US operations through holding companies in the Cayman Islands. The structure also allowed him to claim interest payments on the debt that he had raised against News International in Britain, which was producing most of his profits. The tax rate blipped up to 15 per cent in 1989, then stayed below 10 per cent for the next decade. Australian corporate tax rates during this period moved between 36 per cent and 38 per cent. By 1997, the tax savings that the News Corp accountants had produced in the previous decade were worth a total $A2.4 billion in extra profits for News.

The architect of the first tax structures was an accountant called Richard Sarazen, who had advised Murdoch on one of his first US deals in 1983. He joined News America as vice president of finance, took a two-year sabbatical in 1980 to run a failing manufacturer called Xcor International, before rejoining News to serve as finance director until being moved sideways just as the group's 1990 debt crisis took hold. His successor, David DeVoe, was a retiring figure. His News Corp company biog in the 1990s was seven lines long. Besides giving his present titles, the biog said only two things about DeVoe: that from 1985 to 1990 he was deputy finance director of News Corp, and that prior to 1985 he was CEO of Xcor, a company controlled by Louis J. Nicastro. Press reports in the early 1990s described DeVoe as joining News Corp as an auditor after an acquisition.

Sarazen was always more comfortable with numbers than with people. 'I can remember a number for years,' Sarazen would say, waving a cigarette in the air. 'A name, I'll never get straight.' And what amazing figures Sarazen produced. Apart from his tax skill he notched up several hundred million dollars of both profits and losses from foreign exchange trading. But perhaps his most amazing achievement was a line item in the News Corporation annual accounts each year. Sarazen could make Magic Numbers.

It began in 1987. The profit after tax on News Corporation's operating earnings (a figure described in Australia as profit before extraordinary items), came in at $A364.364 million. It was a cute little entry. The first three digits were the same as the last three digits. There was nothing terribly unusual about this. Australian accounting protocols offered four key profit figures that showed how a company was travelling. The odds that one of them should repeat the first three numbers after the decimal place were about one in 250.

But it happened again the next year: same profit line, this time the result was $A464.464 million. The 1989 result was $A496.496. In 1990 the figure was $A282.282 million (an Australian accounting change meant the line was now described as profit before abnormal items). At this stage, the chance that one profit figure would repeat itself like that four times in a row was one in one trillion (1,000,000,000,000). There were two ways to interpret this. One was that it truly was a remarkable coincidence. The alternative view was that it was a piece of pure machismo. It was Sarazen's signature on the accounts. It was discreet, of course. It only worked in Australian dollars. As soon as US and British investors looked at the result in US dollars or pounds sterling, the effect disappeared.

Company accounts are a snapshot of a company at one moment in time, which is midnight on 30 June in News Corp's case. For multinational companies that snapshot is based not just on the company's earnings, but on where exchange rates are at that same moment. Once 30 June is past, the numbers are sacrosanct. Companies may have an idea of what their results will be, but they do not know what the exchange rates to convert their foreign earnings will be. So if Sarazen was producing these Magic Numbers, he had to be doing it after the balance date. Any large corporation has arguments back and forth with its auditors about what is and is not profit.

The 1991 accounts were critical to the future of News Corp. After surviving the debt crisis by the barest of margins, DeVoe as the new finance director had to produce a solid result which would rally the group's stock price for a stock offering. DeVoe also needed to show that whatever financial hubris that News had suffered from in the past, now the News accountants were on the straight and narrow path.

David DeVoe celebrated News Corp's escape from the debt crisis with the accounting equivalent of a barrel roll. Sarazen had produced his party trick once in the News Corp accounts each year. DeVoe did it three times in the same set of accounts. Profit before abnormal items came in at $A391.391 million. Minority interests of $A70.070 million were subtracted, to give a profit of $A321.321. The odds against three numbers repeating themselves like this were more than 100 million to one. The Magic Numbers appeared to have become an obsession with the News bean counters. They did it again in more restrained style in 1992 (profit before abnormal items $530.530 million), then News abruptly began reporting its profits only in millions of dollars, dropping the decimal places.

There is nothing actually wrong with such results. Auditors take the view that when a result comes to hundreds of millions of dollars, the minor numbers in the result are not significant. But the results suggest a unique accounting culture at News. The uneasy question which this cheap party trick leaves is: if this accounting team is so confident that they can make the minor numbers in a profit report say anything they want, then what does this say about the big numbers News was reporting? Why should the number technicians stop there?

DeVoe was running a virtual reality machine in the News Corp accounts. In effect there were three separate News Corporations, each of which was quite real. Or rather, it was as if News Corporation existed in three parallel universes. The simplest way of seeing this was to ask the most basic question about News Corp, which was, how much did it earn? In the shareholders' universe, the answer to this question appeared in the News

Corp annual report each year. In the six years from fiscal 1992 to fiscal 1997, for example, excluding tax News Corp reported profits totalling $A5.8 billion. The accounts broke up the profits by division and by country, and showed strong earnings flowing from the group's operations in America, Britain and to a lesser extent Australia. That was version one. Several months later, News Corp filed an alternative reality with the Securities and Exchange Commission in Washington, and these results were not so rosy. The earnings News Corp announced to its shareholders were based on Australian accounting standards. The results News filed with the Securities and Exchange Commission were based on US accounting rules. As News invested heavily in satellite and cable channel start-ups, the American and the Australian views of News Corporation began to diverge. Under US rules, almost half of News Corp's reported earnings disappeared, and its net profits totalled a more modest $A3 billion. This was version two. By 1997, there was a $A1 billion gap between what News Corp reported that it earned each year, and the result it reported to the Securities and Exchange Commission. The gap was produced largely by huge losses in the start-up businesses. In Australia, News treated the losses as an asset and capitalised them. In America they wrote them off as a cost.

The US earnings were still a fabulous result compared with the third version of News Corporation, which is what the tax officers meeting in Sydney in December 1997 were focusing on. In the same six years, News Corp companies paid $A351 million tax, which was the equivalent of six cents in every dollar of profit it reported to shareholders. The tax authorities of the world were not giving News Corp a special break here. News paid the same rate of tax on its taxable income as every other company. What made the difference was the ingenuity with which the News accountant were able to reduce the amount of the group's income that was actually taxable. Working backwards from the tax paid in those six years of $351 million, and assuming an average tax rate levied of 35 per cent, what this means is that in the eyes of tax authorities, News Corp's taxable income during the six years from 1992 to 1997 was only $A1 billion. In those six years alone, the News Corp accountants had moved $A4.8 billion of income beyond the reach of the tax authorities in Britain, the United States and Australia. For many ordinary taxpayers this seems an outrageous result. What seems just as outrageous is that governments around the world did not move to block the loopholes which allowed News Corp to cut its tax payments so drastically.

There was no suggestion that News had acted illegally, that the result was anything other than smart tax planning. The only suggestion to the contrary had come from the Israeli tax office. On 3 April 1998, even that suggestion was lifted. As debate continued in the House of Commons over how much help Tony Blair had offered Rupert Murdoch with the Italian Prime Minister, News Corp announced a $3 million settlement with the Israel Income Tax Commission. The News companies did not make any admission of wrongdoing, but agreed to a change in the method for calculating tax payable since 1992. The full extent of the settlement was not clear. For example, the prospectus for the NDS float in 1999 referred to commitments, made to Israeli tax authorities during the investigation period, to invest unstated amounts of money in its Israeli operations.

A News Corp spokesman said the company welcomed the settlement.

NDS has agreed to settle this matter in order to terminate the uncertainties and the exaggerated rumours that have been affecting the company for over a year, as well as to avoid incurring further legal costs.

The investigation had begun in 1995. The Jerusalem tax raid took place in October 1996. Israeli newspapers had reported that a settlement was near almost a year before. In November 1997 Arthur Siskind said a settlment was expected within weeks. The mystery in the settlement announcement on 3 April 1998 was why it had taken so long . . . and what had finally broken the deadlock. With the Blair-Prodi debate still continuing in London, the settlement announcement raised wider questions. The key issue in the News Datacom tax case was which country was entitled to levy tax upon Israeli-developed technology owned ultimately by NDS Group, which was a British company. NDS was about to start earning substantial revenues. According to Quentin Davies' account, Rupert Murdoch visited Tony Blair at Chequers in early March, most likely Sunday 8 March, after resolving the HarperCollins fiasco. Whatever happened at that meeting, Murdoch emerged confident enough of his relationship with Blair to be sure a week and a half later that when he lifted the phone to ask for help with the Italian Prime Minister, Tony Blair would rally around. On the face of it, News Datacom had a greater justification for the Prime Minister's intervention than BSkyB had. In the Prodi affair, the question was merely whether a British company invested in Italy. The News Datacom case was about whether NDS would pay tax to Israel or Britain.

The Israeli Prime Minister, Benjamin Netanyahu, met with Blair at Downing Street on 9 March, the day after Murdoch's reported meeting with Blair. The NDS case settled in Israel three and a half weeks later. Did

Blair raise the NDS investigation with Netanyahu? If Rupert Murdoch didn't ask Blair to raise the matter with Netanyahu he missed a golden opportunity. The second conclusion is that, on the basis of what Labour politicians called 'the rather unedifying spectacle of half truths and non-denial denials' that unfolded over the Prodi affair, there may be no way of ever being sure.

Again the issue was to which country Murdoch was responsible. It is not just tax men that Murdoch could threaten on the other side of the world. News Corp as the ultimate trans-national corporation moves markets and routinely transforms industries in one country to provide a benefit in another. Beyond America, the Murdoch effect has rippled from country to country around the globe. He calls Tony Blair in London so that Blair can phone the Italian Prime Minister about a Murdoch deal in Rome. Murdoch causes a sensation in Britain by having his HarperCollins London company drop the Chris Patten book about Hong Kong in order to win favour in Beijing. News Corporation as an entity had long since outgrown its Australian roots; its British past; its American heart. It had taken up permanent offshore residence. It existed stateless somewhere beyond the archipelagos.

CHAPTER SIXTEEN

RUPERT'S ROCKET

London, 1998

On Sunday 9 April 1998, just as the controversy over Tony Blair's telephone conversation with the Italian Prime Minister Romano Prodi was dying down, Rupert Murdoch faced a more personal crisis. Anna moved out of the Murdochs' house on Angelo Drive. It was a week before the Murdochs' 31st wedding anniversary and six weeks after Murdoch's 67th birthday. Anna flew to London to stay with Elisabeth, whose marriage to Elkin Pianim had broken down several months before. The split took members of Rupert Murdoch's family by surprise. Even in telephone calls on the Saturday there was no hint of what would follow.

In October 1999, Murdoch described for *Vanity Fair* the process where he and Anna 'drifted apart to the point where things became unhappy'. It is the only time he has ever talked about the personal toll that his battles in 1997 exacted: 'So I was travelling a lot and was very obsessed with the business and perhaps more than normally inconsiderate, at a time when our children were grown up and home was suddenly an empty nest.'

The Murdochs' marriage had been one of the few stable points in News Corporation. Its stability had provided Rupert Murdoch not just with a personal centre, but also the moral vantage point from which his empire could pour scorn on the emotional foibles and infidelities of others. There had been the odd report of friction between Rupert and Anna, particularly over where they lived. Andrew Neil, in his biography *Full Disclosure*, described disagreement over Rupert's desire to move back to New York. 'You're a perpetual motion machine,' Anna snapped. 'I've had enough of keeping pace with you. I'm staying in LA.' Otherwise, however, they remained the model couple. When parliamentarian turned journalist Woodrow Wyatt died, the Murdochs attended the funeral in early April 1998 and Rupert read the lesson, again with no obvious sign of tension between them.

At the time of the split, Anna was at the height of her social power in Los Angeles. In 1996 she had been appointed chairwoman of the board of the Regents of Children's Hospital of Los Angeles. The Regents were a high-powered group founded in 1993 for a $25 million fundraising drive. She had become a major donor and advocate, regularly lobbying with politicians in Sacramento and Washington for government assistance of at-risk children. Anna was also an influential member of The Colleagues, a group that had supported the Children's Institute International in Los Angeles since the 1950s. Its members included Nancy Reagan and socialite Betsy Bloomingdale. On 19 July 1997, as Murdoch was tying up the details of his Fox Sports deal with Charles Dolan in New York, Anna was named president of the board of trustees for the Children's Institute International in Los Angeles. Five days later she was honoured 'for her many efforts on behalf of vulnerable youngsters', at the opening of the Anna M. Murdoch Education and Training Centre at the institute. She had been honoured by the B'nai B'rith Anti-Defamation League, a home for babies addicted to drugs called Hale House, and others. The positions carried extensive commitments to social engagements. She had even gone on Fox News to talk about Rupert Murdoch's lobbying on behalf of children.

In early 1998 Anna had clearly been concerned about Rupert's health. With her insistence he stuck to white meat, white wine and carrot snacks. As he approached 67, the age at which his father died, Anna Murdoch was creating a potent series of symbols, all of which said closure to Rupert's frenetic schedule at the helm of News Corp. They were to do with recognition for what Rupert Murdoch had achieved in nearly half a century of empire building. Her clear hope was that such recognition would allow Murdoch an opportunity to walk away, his place in history secure; to retire gracefully, or more likely just to slow down a little.

First there was the fingerprint. In late 1997, Anna arranged for a Californian artist to make an 11-metre, ten-panel tin and wood mural for the lobby of a new building at Twentieth Century Fox, based on a massive enlargement of the whorls on Murdoch's right index finger. It was undoubtedly a unique tribute, a none too subtle statement that Murdoch had left his fingerprints across the world. By happy timing there was also the Humanitarian of the Year award in May 1997. And the papal knighthood. On 11 January 1998 at St Francis de Sales church in Los

Angeles, Cardinal Roger M. Mahony invested Rupert and Anna as knight commander and dame in the Pontifical order of St Gregory the Great. The Murdochs were no strangers to Mahony. They had contributed $10 million to the building fund for a new cathedral. The spokesman for the LA Catholic diocese, the Reverend Gregory Coiro, told reporters that the Pope bestowed the titles on people of 'unblemished character', including non-Catholics, who had 'promoted the interests of society, the Catholic Church and the Holy See Vatican'.

In April 1998, after a lifetime of striving, after a year of honours and achievement for Rupert, Anna appeared to have made an ultimatum: her husband had to slow down and make room for her in his life. When Murdoch refused, Anna packed her bags.

The next day, Monday 20 April 1998, Murdoch briefed Liz Smith at the *New York Post* about the split. Smith announced the separation in her gossip column on Tuesday 21 April:

> It is with some personal sadness that I announce the amicable separation of Rupert Murdoch and his beautiful wife Anna after thirty-one years of marriage and three children. The Murdochs say their situation is very painful and leaves them torn but they are attempting to work out their differences. Mrs Murdoch, a novelist and philanthropist, will remain on the board and continue in the Murdoch businesses.

There would be no reconciliation. Murdoch had spent a lifetime leaving people behind. It wasn't just that he never mended relationships. He had built his life around a driving ambition to build a worldwide media empire. Former executives claimed that he had no friends. He had the business and his family, in that order. In demanding that he throttle back, Anna was asking him to give up the greater part of his life. As Murdoch would put it a year later, stepping down as head of News Corporation was a pretty dismal prospect. What would he do? 'Die pretty quickly,' he told a British documentary-maker. He and Anna continued to talk. According to court papers, the final break came on Friday 26 June. 'I don't feel I belong anywhere any more,' Anna told friends.

Some close to the family have suggested that the break-up was sparked by Anna's concern over the rivalry her husband was fostering among their children. The empire's future now depended upon the succession struggle shaping up between Lachlan, aged 26, Elisabeth, 29, and James, 25: the dutiful son, the ambitious daughter, and the scruffy young man. There was also Prudence MacLeod, 38, the child of Rupert's first marriage to Patricia Booker, whose importance was often underestimated. Part of what gives News Corporation its ferociously competitive culture is Rupert Murdoch's habit of putting two people in the same job, and leaving them to battle it out. With the best of intentions, Murdoch's even-handed insistence that any of his children might succeed him at the helm of News Corp inevitably gave family relations a competitive edge. The pressure was stoked by continual media speculation.

The Murdoch succession arguably represented the largest transfer of wealth and global power of the late twentieth century. For four years the four heirs to this fortune had been feted across the world, revered like Indian moonstones, objects of fabulous wealth and power in whose tracks lay the professional corpses of those who fought to control them. Murdoch had lost senior executives wherever his children worked in the News empire. Just after Christmas 1996, Murdoch's long-time Australian lieutenant, Ken Cowley, had sent his deputy, Lachlan Murdoch, home to get a more conservative haircut after he appeared at work with a radical Mohawk. Cowley would be shuffled into retirement by April, sparking some wry lines about ruffling the hair apparent.

When asked in 1993 whether his children would succeed him at News Rupert Murdoch said, 'The board will have to make their judgment in time . . . I will certainly engage in sufficient nepotism to see that my kids get a good opportunity.'

Ostensibly there seemed little doubt about whom Rupert Murdoch was grooming to succeed him. This was a close family that nevertheless had always maintained a pecking order, a routine that extended to which family members were served first at the dinner table. With Lachlan the elder son, Murdoch set out to replicate his own history, to create another version of himself. The clearest sign of the intense pressures that this produced on Lachlan was his intense sensitivity to media criticism.

At Geelong Grammar, Murdoch had produced a school magazine called *Isis Revived*. Lachlan at 16 at his Trinity School in New York helped to found the Trinity Conservative Society. It was open to all who have a 'clear conservative conscience' he wrote in his 1987 high-school yearbook. His holiday jobs ranged from working as a reporter on the *San Antonio Express-News* in Texas, to the press room for the News Limited papers in Sydney. Like Rupert, Lachlan left home for a distant university. At Princeton his thesis on Kant and Hegel suggested he studied a little harder than his father had. From there Lachlan spent several months on the sub-editors' desk at the *Sun* in London – the equivalent of his father's 1953 stint with the *Daily*

Express. At 22, Rupert Murdoch was publisher of the Adelaide *News*. Lachlan at the same age in August 1994 became general manager of Queensland Press Limited, the family inheritance sold by Sir Keith's executors. John Cowley – Ken Cowley's brother, who was manager at Wapping during the riots – was entrusted with Lachlan's early education in Brisbane. The *New York Times* described Australia as Murdoch's 'social laboratory' where his son could learn his trade away from serious scrutiny.

By late 1996 Lachlan was back in Sydney, buying a sailing boat with right-wing News columnist Piers Ackerman and leaning to sail. He was appointed managing director of News in Australia in September 1996, and executive chairman seven months later, aged 25. He drove a silver BMW to work, and kept a Ducati Monster and Harley Davidson in the garage. In August 1997 he and his father spent a week at Hamilton Island on the Great Barrier Reef where Lachlan competed with his luxurious Swan 51 cruising yacht *Karakoram* in Racing Week. Back in Britain Murdoch told writer Mathew Horsman that his children had agreed that Lachlan was the 'first among equals' in the succession. That Christmas Lachlan sailed *Karakoram* (named for Lachlan's love for mountain climbing) in the Sydney to Hobart. His father flew to Hobart and at 4 a.m. accompanied *Karakoram* in a rubber dinghy on the last stretch of the race up the Derwent River. Murdoch, who had finally been on a winner in the Sydney to Hobart in 1995 when he crewed on Larry Ellison's *Sayonara*, wanted Lachlan to buy a faster boat. Instead Lachlan joined the crew on *Sayonara* which battled through huge seas to win the following year.

From the start, Lachlan gave the impression of being a nicer man than his position allowed him to be. He was unusually kind and attentive to the people who worked for him. While he could be highly aggressive in business dealings, he did not always give the impression that his heart was in it. Nevertheless he notched up a high body count of sacked executives, particularly senior executives who were older than he was. He wore his youth like a badge, rolling up his sleeves on formal occasions to show his two tattoos. On the upper arm he had a gecko lizard. The second tattoo, a band around his wrist, was done in 1997 the day after his father flew back to the US after a visit. In the same period he shaved his head and bought a Rhodesian ridgeback called Grace. To head up the News Limited digital strategy he brought a school friend across from the US. Zeb Rice, the son of a former head of Fox, Gordon Van Sauter, would be best man at Lachlan's wedding. He stayed with Lachlan in his waterfront home on Sydney Harbour. 'One morning Zeb and Lachlan came to work with exactly the same crew cuts, and you realised just how young the generals at

News really were,' former News IT editor Tony Sarno said.

Lachlan gave few interviews and on occasion appeared distraught at adverse press stories about himself. In Brisbane he had confided his belief that he should get married, though his engagement to American merchant banker Kate Harbin foundered. He was throughout the dutiful son. When he was asked on the Hobart docks if there was anything as challenging as the Sydney to Hobart race, he said, 'Yes. Getting up each morning, going to work and running News Limited.'

Lachlan was loyal to his small circle of friends. The month he was appointed chief executive of News Limited in Sydney, a new column in the *Sunday Telegraph* announced that Dr Moose, 'a renowned book lover, cultural critic, gourmet and committed sports fan' would be making reading suggestions each week. The recommended books could be bought by ringing the Mooseline, a 24-hour telephone hotline which was run by The Moose Corporation, a play on The News Corporation. Dr Moose appears to have been Lachlan himself. Moose Corp was a private company owned by Lachlan and his friends Zeb Rice and a lawyer, Jeremy Philips. In the four months the Moose column appeared, one of the most frequent recommendations was a book co-written by Philips. When questioned, a News Corp spokesman in New York said arrangements between News Corp and Moose Corp were conducted on an arm's-length basis.

In March 1997, the month Lachlan was appointed executive chairman of News Limited, the National Rugby League, now controlled by News, dumped Young & Rubicam from its $10 million advertising account. In its place the NRL appointed boutique Sydney agency VCD, founded and run by Lachlan's close friend, artistic director George Betsis. In the messy politics of advertising, it wasn't clear what caused the switch. Betsis said the appointment had nothing to do with his links to Lachlan. In March 1999, the month Lachlan married model Sarah O'Hare, Queensland Press (where Lachlan was now chairman) invested $10 million for control of a futures trading operation run by Joe Cross, 33, who was one of Lachlan's ushers. A News Corp spokesman said the deal was conducted on an arm's-length basis.

Before Ken Cowley resigned, he surrounded Lachlan with a kitchen cabinet of advisers which would essentially run News in Australia. Lachlan's track record was blighted by the $A550 million Super League disaster. However it would be unfair to blame Lachlan for Super League. He was 23 at the time, with just seven months of executive experience. The mistakes were made by older heads. At the same time, this lack of experience did not stop him being appointed chief executive of News in Australia 18 months later. He and James Packer had some success negotiating peace treaties between their warring fathers. Lachlan notched up a $A62 million profit from an investment in a racing satellite channel with the Packer family, but News lost more than it gained selling the Packers half of News Corp's holding in the Foxtel cable company. Lachlan played the Australian political scene clumsily. And by January 2001 a $A582 million investment in telephone company One.Tel was showing a $A370 million paper loss. Overall, the results on his watch were poor to indifferent. Given his level of experience, it would be hard to expect otherwise. He was working in a mature market where the growth areas were controlled by the Packer family, with better political connections, and a government that saw him as an American doing an apprenticeship. He faced huge pressure from within News Corporation and a stream of daily advice from his father. In February 1999 Lachlan was made a senior vice president at News Corp, with responsibility for newspapers and the inserts business in America. He was bound for New York. Significantly, his father did not feel the need to replicate his own experience of living in London.

Elisabeth Murdoch, three years Lachlan's senior, attended the Brearley School in Manhattan, then went on to Vassar. In October 1990 she began work at Kerry Packer's Channel Nine studio in Sydney. Sam Chisholm had left Nine for Sky in London five weeks before. She went on to work in Salt Lake City, then in programming for Fox television in Los Angeles. In 1992 she had been agonising over her relationship with Elkin Pianim, the son of a well-known Ghanaian political prisoner, whom she met at Vassar. She gave him until Christmas to propose. 'He proposed on Christmas Eve,' she said later.

They were married in September 1993 and settled in Los Angeles. In February 1995, they borrowed $35 million with a bank loan guaranteed by Elisabeth's father to buy two television stations in California, near the Murdochs' Carmel Valley ranch. Their first child, Cornelia, was born two weeks after the purchase. Elisabeth was back at work two weeks later. After a torrid and sometimes brutal year reorganising the stations, the Pianims sold them for a $12 million profit. They moved shortly afterwards to London, where Elisabeth joined BSkyB as a general manager (broadcasting) and later director of programming. Meanwhile Pianim launched *New Nation*, a newspaper aimed at London's Afro-Caribbean community, and a venture capital company called Idaho Partners. Soon after their second child, Anna, was born, their marriage was reported to be on the rocks. They had separated by the end of 1997.

Elisabeth made it clear that she continued to strive for the top job.

Lachlan's promotions in Australia were a reminder to her that she had to 'get a hurry on', she said. In 1999 she told Channel Four, 'I have always and will always strive to be qualified and considered for that position.'

Elisabeth had a thorny relationship with Sam Chisholm at BSkyB, but Chisholm denies that it was the reason for his departure in June 1997. Rupert Murdoch complained that Elisabeth had expected Chisholm would 'teach her everything, but he didn't. He tried to cut her out.'

'She has some things to work out,' Murdoch said. 'She has to decide how many kids she is going to have, where she wants to live.'

Of the Murdoch children, Elisabeth was the one in 1998 who could most clearly be said to have had a real job. This is to say, she worked in a high-profile position as head of programming for BSkyB where her success or failure really mattered to the future of the News empire. Lachlan and James were in executive positions where, surrounded by advisers and with a constant stream of advice from the daily telephone conversations with their father, it could be difficult to judge their individual performance. The huge investment decisions they initiated were peripheral to the daily running of the empire, and could take years to show up as profit or loss. While Elisabeth had no shortage of advisers, BSkyB programming required creative decisions from her, and their success or failure could be measured in weekly viewer numbers. Her critics claimed that while she was clearly ambitious, and had the technical experience in television for the job, she did not have the creative flair that programming required. BSkyB's digital launch, which she headed, was initially unimpressive. On the other hand, several of the programs she commissioned went on to become much more successful when copied elsewhere. *Castaway* became the huge ratings winner *Survivor* in America.

James arguably cuts the most appealing figure among the Murdoch children, with his black glasses, laid-back appearance and manic energy. Even in a suit, James Murdoch gives the impression that unless he has done something magical with velcro, it is only a matter of time before his shirt comes out. As a child he was regarded as the brightest of the Murdoch brood. In 1999, when Michael Eisner was asked who he could see as his successor running Disney he said either his son or James Murdoch.

When James married his agent, Kathryn Hufschmid, in June 2000, the best man's speech by his long-time friend Jesse Angelo shed some light on his and James' shared history: 'A best friend would stop you from getting a tattoo,' said Angelo. 'A best friend would stop you from starting a hip-hop label. A best friend would stop you from getting a second tattoo. A best friend would stop you from getting kicked out of Harvard.'

James interjected to deny strenuously that he was ever at risk of being kicked out of Harvard. Angelo responded: 'You don't have to live that lie tonight.'

At Harvard, James helped edit the *Harvard Lampoon*, a post which his father suggested had 'more to do with drinking', but dropped out in 1994 to start Rawkus Records, a hip-hop label with friends in New York. In November 1996 his father brought him back into News by buying his company. He headed the small music division at News and was named vice president for new media. Periodically, News was said to be considering a bid for EMI, but Mushroom Records in Australia was his only music purchase. In early 1997 James was a key figure in his father's $450 million offer to buy Pointcast, a hot Internet company promoting 'push' technology. In a lucky escape, Pointcast management turned the deal down. Two years later the company was sold for $7 million. In November 1997, James was named president of News America Digital Publishing, a new division which encompassed News Corp's American on-line business, reporting to Anthea Disney. Its biggest asset was Kesmai, the most popular gaming site on the Web. Within weeks of James' appointment, Steve Case's America Online dumped Kesmai from its home page, replacing it with its own gaming site. Overnight, 90 per cent of Kesmai's business disappeared.

It was the perfect time to move into what at the time was a nothing job. The Internet boom, and James' investments in TheStreet.com, Juno.com, PlanetTx, sixdegrees and Jim Clark's Healtheon put him suddenly on News Corp's star track. In November 1999 he would become executive vice president for News Digital Media. In June 2000 he was named executive chairman for Star TV. He met Kathryn Hufschmid when she was handling public relations for Bob Guccione Junior's *Gear* magazine. Among other things, James describes himself as a professional cartoonist. At Harvard he began a politically incorrect cartoon strip called Albrecht the Hun. Hufschmid arranged for his cartoon strips to run in *Gear*.

Prudence is the only child to stay outside of the family business, looking after her three children in a house in Notting Hill near Elisabeth. She said she was horrified when she learned her second husband, Alasdair MacLeod, was joining News.

In 1997, in an attempt to settle media speculation about who would succeed him at the head of the empire, Murdoch told journalist Mathew Horsman that the shares in Cruden had already been divided between the children. News Corp spokesman Howard Rubinstein was reported to have said the major stakes went to Lachlan, Elisabeth and James. Accounts differ whether this is accurate, but the whole thrust of the family's succession planning – who would guide News after Rupert – has been based around Anna's *uterini*. At the October 1997 News Corp annual meeting, Murdoch was asked a question about the succession. He later said he had been misquoted when he referred to his three children, when he actually referred to his three children in the company.

Prudence was furious at being overlooked, at least in the press reports of the conversation. She said later:

> I didn't speak to him. It was the biggest row I've ever had with my father. I rang up, I screamed at him, I hung up. He was very upset. He then sent the biggest bunch of flowers – it was bigger than that sofa – and two clementine trees. The flowers kept coming, and he felt awful.

After two weeks she made peace again with her father. In an interview, she said it still 'caused a huge amount of hurt' and indicated she would like to take a non-executive position on the News Corp board when her three children are older. She said she had grown used to the way that the media overlooked her in the constant speculation about Murdoch's successor. 'I used to get very upset by it, but there's no point,' she said. 'Dad has always made it very plain that there are four of us and that's the way it goes.'

Prudence's carefully planned remarks – she made it clear in the interview that she expected her father to read the resulting article – were a reminder that, no matter how well advanced the professional careers of the young Murdochs might have been in 1998, there was a personal price they paid for being who they were. How does anyone cope with the pressure of growing up as the child of one of the most powerful media barons in the world?

In the 1980s when Anna Murdoch took her children to live in Aspen after reports of behaviour problems at school, they spent their summer vacations working in various arms of the News empire around the world. When he was fifteen, James spent a summer working at the old *Mirror* in Sydney. It was the afternoon tabloid where Murdoch had learned his craft. James' best known exploit was at a momentous press conference when the Fairfax newspaper group announced it was selling its Seven television network to a young entrepreneur called Christopher Skase. It was a deal that only a few years before, Rupert Murdoch would have killed for. Halfway through the press conference James was found and duly photographed at the back of the room, curled up asleep on a couch. The Fairfax *Sydney Morning Herald* ran James' picture alongside its story. James refused to work any more summers in the family business. 'Everybody knew who I was,' he said later. 'I wouldn't do it again.' He would never again work under what he called 'the long shadow of my father'.

This isn't a family that values introspection. 'We are a family that doesn't look back, always ahead,' Lachlan told the *New York Times* in August 1998. His sister Elisabeth expressed similar views that same month, when she offered British broadcasters at the Edinburgh International Television Festival 'a little self-help, Murdoch style – no couches, no Freud'. She appeared in jeans and boots for the address. The British press tried hard not to like her. The worst thing that *The Economist* could say was that she had Californian hair. Her comment about self-help Murdoch style, as well as being the Murdoch family credo, was a little in-joke. It was a tacit reference to her blossoming romance with Matthew Freud, the great grandson of the great psychoanalyst.

It must be one of history's great encounters – Sigmund meets Rupert; the father of psychoanalysis runs up against the Sun King. Sigmund's grandson works in public relations. Rupert's daughter was in television programming. It was a particularly interesting pairing because of what Freud wrote about the difficulties faced by children with over-achieving fathers. One of his case studies was based on a man who dreamed of shouting at the sun – which Freud interpreted as the symbol for a father figure. The dream, Freud said, was about a son faced with an overwhelmingly powerful father, struggling to meet him on his own terms, a healthy attempt to cast his own shadow.

Five generations of Murdochs have struggled with the problem of living up to their fathers. The question for Rupert's children would be, how would they assert their own autonomy in the court of the Sun King? It became quickly clear that the flirtation with the left that their father had enjoyed at Oxford was not an option for his children. Their political views have been closely allied with their father's. The children's statements of autonomy have been more subtle affairs.

Any left-wing views that Rupert Murdoch espoused at Oxford were burnt away in the two decades of torrid struggle that followed his father's death. For a brief period in the late 1960s, News Limited's unofficial employment policy in Australia had become an informal mantra: 'No blacks, no poofters (gays), no suede shoes.' At least this was the popularly held view on the News Limited papers, though it never spilled overseas to Fleet Street. Rupert Murdoch's children grew up with these and other entrenched maxims. They had challenged most of them.

From his daughter Elisabeth, Rupert has two black grandchildren,

Cornelia and Anna. When Elisabeth left BSkyB and News Corporation in 2000, it was to have a child with Freud, a relationship of which her father reportedly did not approve. Freud holidayed with Elisabeth and the family in Australia over Christmas 1998, but was conspicuous by his absence at subsequent family occasions. James dropped out of Harvard to start a fringe record group whose first album was called 'Whoregasm'. Lachlan's relations with his father have seemed less conflicted. He has great personal regard for his father and shares his social views, ideologies and business style. If there has been another side to Lachlan's public filial adherence, it is expressed covertly in his private life.

Their parents' divorce would prove as painful for the Murdoch children as it is for most families. By July 1998 Anna had hired a high-profile LA divorce lawyer, Daniel J. Jaffe. She signed a divorce petition on 5 July. Jaffe signed a certificate of assessment three days later, then filed the petition in Los Angeles Superior Court on 21 July. Anna's petition asked for 'spousal support' while the divorce was finalised. Anna said she did not know what her husband's assets were. Rupert's lawyer, Robert Kaufman, responded two days after receiving the summons. Rupert said he didn't know what his assets were either.

The divorce petition froze Murdoch's assets. So it was as well that, four days after the final break with Anna on 26 June but before she signed the divorce petition on 5 July, the National Australia Bank took security over a parcel of the News Corp shares held by the family holding company, Cruden Investments. A Murdoch lawyer said at the time that this move on 30 June, Anna's birthday, reflected a change in the security held on an already existing loan facility, rather than any pre-divorce money-shuffling. Part of this loan would be the $A373 million borrowed in February 1996 for the family buyout. Murdoch was due to pay another $A314 million to his sisters' families in March 1999. The divorce proceedings cast some uncertainty on that. Any payout might be subject to Anna's approval. Rupert Murdoch's position was that although he was a director of Cruden, the company was ultimately owned and controlled by the A. E. Harris trust, and other interlocking trusts throughout the corporate structure of the Cruden group, which had been set up to avoid paying death duties. Murdoch had the power to appoint trustees to the trust but not to direct the trustees. Therefore the huge wealth locked up in Cruden didn't belong to him.

Under California's community property laws, however, divorce courts do not always accept trust structures set up to shelter assets. At this point, it still looked like a low-key and relatively amicable divorce. According to News executives, Anna was prepared to accept $100 million and the Murdoch homes in Los Angeles and London as a property settlement. She was also insisting on a guarantee about the future of their three children within News Corporation. Murdoch's advisers urged him to settle the divorce quickly.

The early court filings referred to a five-day hearing, but the case seemed unlikely to come to trial. That would change ten weeks later.

On Sunday 4 October 1998, the *New York Times* published a brief by Geraldine Fabrikant that stated what had become an open secret in Manhattan media circles: Rupert Murdoch had moved into the Mercer Hotel in Soho with a young Chinese executive from Star TV, Wendi Deng. The four sentences in Fabrikant's story were picked up and speculated upon in newspapers around the world. Within days the paparazzi had struck.

'The *Mirror* had a picture on a boat taken with a very long lens,' Murdoch later told *Vanity Fair*. 'I was testing a new sailboat which Lachlan was thinking of buying.' The picture, which was reprinted widely, showed Murdoch, Lachlan, Sylvio Berlusconi, and a tall slim woman identified as Wendi Deng, otherwise known as Deng Wen Di.

Deng Wen Di was born in the eastern Chinese city of Xuzhou. Her family later moved to Guangzhou, capital of the prosperous southern province of Guangdong, where her father ended up as the director of a machinery factory. Reportedly he was also well connected politically. Bruce Dover, the News executive in Beijing who introduced Deng to Murdoch, believed she was married briefly to a young American businessman in Beijing, David Wolf. She had come to America in 1991 to study at California State University, before completing an MBA at Yale.

'She was a fun person to talk to, always happy and eager about her work,' said her economics lecturer, Professor Ken Chapman. 'But it was always kind of hard to figure her out.'

Another lecturer, Professor Dan Blake, rated Deng as one of the best students he had taught: 'I've been teaching here for about 30 years and I haven't seen many students who were that brilliant. She was really sharp. She didn't speak much English when she got here but she picked it up really quickly.'

In November 2000 the *Wall Street Journal* gave a slightly different history for Deng. It quoted divorce records with the Los Angeles County Superior Court which showed that she was married for two years and seven months to an American called Jake Cherry who was in Guangzhou in 1987 working on the construction of a manufacturing plant. Deng, who was 18, received English lessons from Cherry's then wife, Joyce, who later assisted Deng to enrol at California State University.

Joyce and Jake separated in 1988 over Jake Cherry's infatuation with Deng, who stayed briefly in the couple's home in Los Angeles. After their divorce, Jake Cherry married Deng in February 1990. He was 53. According to the *Wall Street Journal*, the marriage broke down after four months over Deng's relationship with a man in his twenties, David Wolf. A later reconciliation with Cherry failed, and Deng spent several years living with Wolf.

The two-year Master of Business Administration course at Yale requires students to work as an intern during the summer. In 1996 Deng booked herself a first-class ticket to Hong Kong. On the flight over she reportedly made such an impression on the businessman sitting next to her that he offered her the internship she needed. The businessman was Bruce Churchill, a long-time executive with Star TV. During her stint at the Star offices at One Harbourfront, in Hunghom, and in Beijing, Deng impressed executives with her intelligence, tremendous drive and remarkable ability to network. In conversation she was street smart, focused and surprisingly un-American.

Deng met Rupert Murdoch in autumn 1996 at a cocktail party at tycoon Li Ka Shing's harbourfront Plaza hotel, which stands next to the Star offices. The then chief executive of Star, Gary Davey, had flown the team working on the Phoenix Television project down from Beijing to meet Murdoch. Star executives later spoke with some awe of the purpose and speed with which Deng approached News Corporation's chief executive.

'We need more people like that in the office,' Murdoch later told Star executives.

Among those present who recalled the meeting, the most memorable aspect was the number of times that Deng said, 'Oh Lupert.'

Murdoch himself says the story that he met Deng in 1996 is 'complete nonsense. I never met Wendi then.'

Deng returned to Star in a full-time capacity in the autumn of 1997, armed with her Yale MBA. She moved into a three-bedroom, thousand-square-foot flat in Crescent Heights, Tung Shan Terrace, in Hong Kong's Happy Valley, valued at about $HK5 million. She reportedly acted as interpreter for Murdoch on several trips he made to Beijing that year. According to *Punch* drivers in the Star car pool began talking about Murdoch and Deng holding hands. *Asiaweek* quoted a friend of Deng's saying that the two had been romantically involved since the northern spring of 1998. Murdoch denies both of these accounts. He says he began seeing Deng in June 1998, about seven weeks after he and Anna separated. He told *Vanity Fair*:

I met her casually once or twice at meetings of Star TV in Hong Kong. But I first took her out in June (1998) in London when she came over with a group from Star in Hong Kong and Beijing. I was a recently separated, lonely man, and I said, 'Let's go out to dinner one night,' and I talked her into staying in London a couple of extra days – and that was the start of it.

By June 1998, Anna had re-established a base in rental accommodation in Beverly Hills. The 26 June separation date cited in the divorce papers suggests that the final act in the breakdown of the Murdochs' marriage took place after the London tryst with Deng – though presumably by this point it must have been clear that the marriage was indeed over. After the final break with Anna, Murdoch flew to Beijing, where President Clinton was making a historic state visit. There Murdoch and Deng attended a cocktail party for News Corp executives at the home of James Pringle, *The Times* correspondent. Deng, who came dressed in tight, cream coloured jeans and a close-fitting top, described herself as Murdoch's translator for the Beijing visit but gave little detail of the role when queried and left early.

The breakdown of his parents' marriage had been 'a blow to everyone', Lachlan told the *Financial Times*. 'For a long time, people in this company looked up to them because here was a couple who obviously sacrificed a lot yet had a wonderful marriage. So when it breaks up, they are obviously disillusioned.'

Of the Murdoch children, Prudence has been the one most accustomed to living at a distance from her father. Prudence described her relationship with Anna Murdoch as civilised and warm, though they had contrasting personal styles. 'I completely wear my heart on my sleeve, I'm over-sensitive and just different,' she said.

When Rupert and Anna separated, she was the most obviously accepting of her father's new romance, saying:

Who knows what goes on in a marriage. It's very sad. I think it's very sad for anyone to put that much time into a marriage then wake up and think, 'Oh, maybe it's not so great any more.' But I also think it is important that if you are unhappy you've got to get on and if there's a chance for happiness somewhere else, you have to go for it.

Sources close to the family said that Anna was furious about the reports of Rupert's new companion, and court filings showed a dramatic change in legal strategies. Initially Anna's lawyer Daniel Jaffe had been seeking a five-day hearing. By late 1998 this had become a nine-week hearing. Anna's demands from the settlement grew far higher.

Rupert Murdoch, in return, seemed to be playing hardball. When the News Corp annual report was released in mid-September, it said Anna was resigning from the board. On 17 September 1998, Liz Smith announced that Misty Mountain, the house on Angelo Drive so cherished by Anna, was for sale for $19.5 million. Murdoch's position was that, although he controlled one of the world's major fortunes, the huge wealth in Cruden did not belong to him. To satisfy Anna's demand for spouse support, the couple needed to sell some of the few assets held in their names, beginning with Angelo Drive, a house which had been the base for Anna's social power in Los Angeles. The price of Angelo Drive was pitched high, however, and attracted no satisfactory offers. In October the Murdochs sold part of their Carmel ranch to a neighbour instead.

Rupert Murdoch's lawyer, Robert Kaufman, put enormous pressure on Anna's lawyers. Two days before the Christmas break, Kaufman applied for the court to set a date for the hearing. By insisting on a tight schedule, Anna's lawyers would have limited time to wade through the mountain of paperwork detailing one of the world's most convoluted fortunes, which had been served on them as part of discovery procedures. In January, Anna's lawyers applied to have the trial-setting conference on 11 March, Rupert Murdoch's birthday. The date was later postponed, but News Corp insiders were comparing the bitter Murdoch family relations with the warring Ewing dynasty on the long-running evening soap *Dallas*.

Running concurrently with the private passions of the Murdoch divorce were the much more public battles over Murdoch's bid to buy Britain's best known football club, Manchester United. On 1 July 1998, the Manchester United chairman, Martin Edwards, had what he expected to be a routine lunch appointment with the chief executive of BSkyB, Mark Booth. Instead Booth dropped the small talk and asked him what he would think about BSkyB making a bid to buy the club. For BSkyB, owning the most high-profile football club in the world would ensure it could retain broadcast rights to the Premier League, or even, if need be, form its own football competition, as it had in Australia. The deal faced some major hurdles. The largest would be convincing the government not to refer the deal to the Mergers and Monopolies Commission. Margaret Beckett, the secretary for the Department of Trade and Industry (DTI), seemed likely to oppose the deal.

Four weeks later, prospects brightened considerably when Beckett was replaced by New Labour's spin doctor, Peter Mandelson. Elisabeth Murdoch, who was one of the major advocates for the deal, was a close friend of Mandelson's. Rupert Murdoch's links with Tony Blair continued to be tight. In April, BSkyB had hired a senior aide of the prime minister's as a lobbyist. On 12 May Blair announced his government would vote down the anti-Murdoch amendments that the House of Lords had tacked on to the Competition bill in February. In August 1998, with Mandelson now heading the DTI and a sunny outlook on the political front, BSkyB began talking money to the Manchester United board. On 7 September, BSkyB and Manchester United both issued statements to confirm that they were having takeover talks. A day later the bid was announced at £623 million.

The news unleashed a storm of protest. 'Red Devils' was the *Mirror* headline, as the non-Murdoch press set out to do justice to a mood of national indignation. It was not just Manchester United fans who felt threatened. Owning the club would give BSkyB the most influential seat at the Premiership League table when it came to re-negotiating television rights. What would prove decisive here was the ability of groups like the Manchester United Supporters' Association to mobilise community outrage. The Super League war in Australia had shown that the courts offer traditional supporters of sport little comfort when facing big business: the future of sport would be decided by politicians. Ominously, the protests did not die down. As with Wapping a decade before, the longer the dispute lasted, the more community opposition grew. By 27 October, however, BSkyB had acquired 47 per cent of Manchester United shares, and appeared to be days away from wrapping up the takeover.

On Monday evening 26 October 1998, the Secretary for Wales, Ron Davies, took a walk on Clapham Common. He was mugged in circumstances that led him to tender his resignation as a Minister to Tony Blair at Downing Street the next day. He denied it was a gay liaison. The incident led to widespread media comment, and late on Tuesday night Matthew Parris, a former Tory politician and columnist for the *Sun* and *The Times*, prompted a storm of controversy on a BBC discussion program by outing two members of Cabinet, including the Trade Minister, Peter Mandelson. Parris, who is gay himself, described Mandelson as 'certainly gay'. The comment prompted a furious response from Mandelson, which resulted in a BBC directive to make no further reference to the incident. On the

Wednesday morning, however, the editor of the *Sun*, David Yelland, planned to run the story on page one. After frantic telephone calls from Mandelson and from Tony Blair's chief press officer, Alastair Campbell, Yelland reluctantly agreed not to run with the story. However, he ran an editorial urging Mandelson to come out. The next day, Mandelson as Trade Minister announced that the government had decided to refer the Manchester United takeover to the Mergers and Monopolies Commission.

It is tempting to think the two sets of events were connected. But Manchester United was not a spur-of-the-moment decision. The rising swell of protest over the bid had alarmed the government. The week before, a large body of Labour backbenchers had protested over the deal. Opposition seemed as strong in the City as anywhere, and the protest groups were receiving high-powered advice. The Prodi controversy had served notice on Blair that he was no longer untouchable. If the government waved the Manchester United deal through, it would face a substantial backlash both from United fans and from those who saw Blair as tied to Murdoch's strings. Reluctantly the government came to the view that it would have to refer the deal. From that point, BSkyB's bid would be doomed.

The hardest part would be breaking the news to Rupert Murdoch. Clearly he had to be told in advance of the public announcement on Thursday. That meant that Mandelson had to tell Murdoch the bad news just as the *Sun* was gunning for him. It was a bizarre sub-text. Murdoch wasn't happy about the Manchester United decision, as he made it clear at the BSkyB annual meeting on the Friday, when he said: 'It's regrettable that BSkyB shareholders should be penalised for supporting the government in the last election,' he said.

A week later, the *Sun* used its front page to ask whether Britain was being run by a gay mafia. It urged all gay politicians and public servants to reveal themselves and offered a telephone hotline to assist them. And then, abruptly, the *Sun* changed tack again, promising that it would no longer out gays, unless it was in the public interest. Was this Rupert Murdoch's way of getting even with the government? It seems unlikely. Most of the British press seemed to be going through an episode of homophobia. And it wasn't as if gay-bashing was a new discovery by the *Sun*. What was new was that this time it throttled back. The reputation of the *Sun* was such that it could influence politicians as much by what it did not say as by what it did.

One bright spot for News Corp that autumn was that Justice Lindsay handed down his judgment in the News Datacom fraud case on 17 November. Michael Clinger was duly crunched. Clinger had promised that

Rupert Murdoch and other senior News Corp figures would be called to testify. However, when the case began in the Old Bailey in June 1998, Murdoch was out of the country and unavailable. The legal expression was 'over the seas'. Siskind was also over the seas, as was News Corp's star witness, Leo Krieger. The hearing received no media coverage.

Michael Clinger testified via video link from a television studio in Israel. He said enough to convince Justice Lindsay that he was a 'highly intelligent man, astute and experienced . . . and well equipped to make a fortune in business'. Unhappily though, Lindsay went on to comment, 'Mr Clinger has not been content to receive only that reward to which his undoubted experience, ability and intelligence might properly have entitled him'. He was also 'a skilful liar on whose evidence no reliance can be put'. Lindsay found that Clinger had defrauded News Datacom and News International, and awarded damages of £30 million. He rejected Clinger's counterclaim that News had underpaid him for his 20 per cent stake in the News Datacom companies (now NDS Group). Lindsay considered $5 million an excellent return on a $2000 investment. In one of the many ironies of the case, Lindsay handed down his judgement on what was a fair return just as American investors kicked off an Internet stock boom that 15 months later would value NDS Group at $5 billion. Extracting the damages News had won out of Clinger would be another story. But Lindsay's judgment finally gave News clear title to the technology on which its future depended.

Cavan, March 1999

The day was cold and wet. A small fortune had been spent on flowers, a freshly landscaped rose garden, a marquee draped with red and green and hand-painted dance floor, a white-frame outdoors chapel built on the river-bank for the occasion, an army of security guards and an air exclusion zone to keep out the pesky media helicopters. And still it rained. The Murdochs had been gathering over the last week. A fortnight before, Rupert Murdoch had paid $A314 million to complete the buyout of his sisters' families from the holding companies that held the Murdochs' News Corp shares. Now, on Saturday 27 March 1999, the Murdochs had gathered at their Cavan property near Canberra to celebrate Lachlan Murdoch's marriage to Australian Wonderbra model Sarah O'Hare. His friend Zeb Rice was best man. Wendi Deng was staying with Rupert in the hotel nearby, but at Anna's request she did not appear at the wedding. Feelings between the groom's parents were still running high. The 11 March trial setting date in the Los Angeles Superior Court had been put back to early June to give the two sides time to negotiate a settlement. Now it was the turn of Lachlan's mother to make a speech. She rose to her feet and began dryly, 'Now I have the microphone, and one man in the room must be rather nervous.'

'My wife will not do anything that hurts the children,' Rupert Murdoch had told the *Los Angeles Times* two months before, as reports of the divorce infighting spread. What he meant was that any attempt to break up the Cruden trusts or to launch a messy and expensive court case would only hurt the Murdoch heirs. In addition, the more he had to pay Anna, the less money there would be to buy more News Corp voting stock to ensure his children stayed at the helm of News.

According to a source close to the family, in 1998 Murdoch changed arrangements to ensure Prudence received an equal share as a natural heir. If true, this would have changed the dynamics of family decision-making. It also appeared to open the door for other natural heirs, if he and Wendi had children. Media reports had been saying since October 1998 that Murdoch planned to marry Deng. Chinese newspapers had been quoting friends of Deng saying that she was planning to start a family as soon as possible. This was a claim that Murdoch himself denied, but the succession became a major issue in the divorce talks. On Tuesday 1 June, Murdoch made Anna an offer she didn't refuse. The next day Cruden raised $A214 million selling some of its News Corp stock. Under the settlement regime at Australian stock exchanges, Cruden would have received the sale proceeds on Monday 7 June. The Murdochs' divorce was finalised by mutual consent the next day. In addition, Anna was reported to have received two of the houses, for a total payout of around $200 million. By then she had moved to New York, and in October would marry William Mann, a New York businessman five years senior to Rupert. Anna's ex-husband described him as 'a nice old guy'.

What clinched the divorce settlement appears to have been a commitment Anna extracted that the four children would be the exclusive heirs to the bulk of the shares in Cruden. According to sources close to the family, the only remaining block of Cruden shares is the 10 per cent stake still held by Dame Elisabeth which will pass to Rupert on her death, and which he is free to settle upon Wendi. As part of the new arrangement, in the following six weeks the four children each appointed a representative to the boards of Cruden, Kayarem and other companies in the group. Prudence appointed British merchant banker Richard Oldfield, the oldest at 44; Elisabeth selected television producer Henrietta Conrad, 36;

Lachlan's appointee was Sydney ad man George Betsis, 40; and James called in his long-time friend Jesse Angelo, 26, a reporter at the *New York Post*.

Late in the afternoon of Friday 25 June, 17 days after the Murdochs' marriage was dissolved, a 50-metre yacht slipped away from Chelsea Pier in New York. Through the evening it plied back and forth across the Hudson River, past Ellis Island and the Statue of Liberty. Somewhere near the old immigration processing halls on Ellis Island, Rupert Murdoch married Wendi Deng. The 81 guests on board included his four children and their partners, and Michael Milken and Boris Berezovsky. Any tactless question about pre-nuptial agreements appeared to have been resolved by the choice of celebrant. The twilight wedding ceremony which began as Murdoch's yacht cruised past the Statue of Liberty was conducted by New York's senior divorce judge, Jacqueline Silberman, who heads the matrimonial division of the New York Supreme Court. The photographs of the event reflect some of the awkwardness among the Murdoch children. All four of them – Elisabeth, 30, Lachlan, 27, James, 26, and Prudence, 40 – were there on the huge yacht. In the festive scenes caught by photographers on the dock, in picture after picture it is Prudence, the one most used to living with her father at a distance, who is at her father's elbow. Even with the spectacular backdrop of fireworks on New York harbour, it was difficult for the occasion not to be overshadowed by the figure who did not appear: Anna Murdoch, the smooth social face of what had been one of the most solid partnerships in the media business.

Murdoch settled the inevitable rash of questions about who would be his successor by announcing that if he fell under a bus tomorrow, News Corp's Chief Operating Officer, Peter Chernin, would run News Corp, perhaps with Lachlan as chairman. Chernin took the comment without flinching. He was merely the latest in a long line of News Corp executives who had been designated Murdoch's successor. In the court of King Rupert, such an honour generally meant that the executive in question was nearing the end of his shelf life. A year later Murdoch was saying that Chernin 'my very good friend' might share the top job with one of his sons.

Cape Canaveral, August 1999

As the east coast of America braced itself for Hurricane Floyd, insurance underwriters were already reaching for their ulcer tablets in anticipation of the damage toll. In the first week of August 1999, weather forecasters were describing Floyd as one of the worst storms ever to hit the US coastline. As it bore down on Florida, three rockets sat exposed on the launch pad at Cape Canaveral, too massive to be moved under cover. The rockets' gantries were strong enough to handle winds up to 110 miles per hour. At Floyd's centre, the winds were touching 140 miles per hour. The rockets' survival would depend upon how close the centre of the hurricane came to them. Perched on top of one of the launch vehicles was a $250 million communications satellite due to be fired into the 110 west longitude orbital slot above North America – the satellite television slot that had caused Rupert Murdoch and Charlie Ergen at Echostar so much grief. Satellites are covered by insurance policies during their construction, their storage and ground transportation. Separate insurance policies covered the launch and any loss of the satellite in orbit. What wasn't clear was who bore the cost if a satellite was damaged while it was still on the launch pad. Was it still covered? Media executives held anguished conversations as Hurricane Floyd headed towards Rupert's rocket.

Floyd never lived up to the pre-publicity. It swerved away from the coast and petered out. Murdoch's predicament – exposed on the pointy end of a Titan booster – was the product of 15 months of disastrous reverses in America. In the same period that his marriage had collapsed and he had been wrongfooted in his bid to buy Manchester United, Murdoch's American satellite dreams had come crashing down again.

On 12 May 1998, the US Justice Department filed a suit in the Federal Court to block Murdoch's sale of the ASkyB satellites and orbital licence to Primestar. The writ argued that allowing cable operators to gain the key 110WL orbital licence 'would be like hiring the wolf to guard the sheep'. After some huffing and puffing, it became clear that the Justice Department would not allow the deal through in its existing form. The peace agreement that Murdoch and Malone had worked so hard to forge the year before would be thrown out. From June through August, the two men kicked over compromises that would satisfy the concerns of the Justice Department. One alternative was to bring new investors into Primestar that would buy the cable operators out. It would incidentally leave Murdoch in control, once again using someone else's money. That would satisfy the government, but Time Warner and the other cable operators were never going to allow this.

There was more bad news for Murdoch on the corporate front. Murdoch had spun his US television assets off in a $3 billion Initial Public Offering for Fox Entertainment in October 1998, but it failed to set Wall Street on fire. On 14 October News Corp released a one-paragraph statement which said ASkyB had terminated its relationship with Primestar. Five months of trying to find a compromise that would satisfy both the US Justice Department and the cable partners in Primestar had failed. Now News had its satellite slot and two satellites back on its hands, and the only option was to go back to do a deal with an angry Charlie Ergen at Echostar.

Back on 11 June 1997, when the cable operators announced their Primestar deal with Murdoch, Ergen had been on stage in Denver at the Global DBS Summit. Reporters noticed that Ergen was speaking a little strangely. On closer inspection it became apparent he had braces on his teeth. Stephen Keating in his book *Cutthroat* tells the story that one of Ergen's daughters had been advised to get braces. When she said she was frightened, her father told her he would get braces put on as well. When the day came, he had second thoughts about going through with it. His daughter played hardball. 'Daddy, that's just like what Mr Murdoch did,' she said.

When Murdoch came calling again in 1998, Ergen was taking no prisoners. He knew Murdoch had no other buyer for his satellite assets. He knew he could take his time and do the deal on his own terms. 'Rupert had no choice but to come back and deal with Charlie . . . and he held his hands to the hotplate,' one analyst said. Ergen insisted that in exchange for the ASkyB assets, News and MCI would end up with 37 percent of Echostar stock, but only 9 per cent of the votes. The terms were such that whether Echostar's share price went up or down by settlement date, the deal could only get better for Ergen and worse for Murdoch. Ergen would pick up ASkyB's satellite uplink station in Phoenix, but News would have to rip out all the electronics and the News Datacom technology. As well, Ergen would be given lucrative contracts to manufacture News Datacom set-top bosses for News clients. News would also have to pay for the two satellites it was providing and insure them for the first year in orbit. If Murdoch agreed to all this, Ergen would take Murdoch's satellite assets and call off his $5 billion lawsuit from the previous year. News Corp wrote off a $A616 million loss on the deal. Rupert Murdoch left no doubt whom he blamed for this disastrous outcome. It was the fault of the Clinton administration. Murdoch had always been a virulent critic of Bill Clinton. Five days before Murdoch signed the deal with Ergen on 30 November, the *New York Post* broke the unofficial media bar on writing about the President's family, with a front-page story about Chelsea Clinton's distraught visit to a university clinic after a failed romance.

The original Sky deal in February 1997 had been for News and MCI to get 45 per cent of Echostar's stock and voting rights – equal to Ergen's holding. When Ergen agreed to a new deal with Murdoch on 30 November 1999, he was in no mood to be generous. This time News and MCI would receive 240 million Echostar shares valued at just under $1.2 billion. They would end up with 37 per cent of Echostar stock, but have only 8.5 per cent of the voting rights and no board representation. That was bad enough. But the final deal would be based upon the price of Echostar stock on the settlement date. In his 1996 deal with Ron Perelman, Murdoch had used this device to win an advantage. With Echostar, Ergen would win and Murdoch would lose whether the stock price went up or down. If it went down, then News Corp and MCI would receive stock that was worth less than the sale price, and that was just their bad luck. If Echostar stock went up, then it was bad luck for News Corp and MCI again, because they would receive less Echostar stock, so that they would never get more than their $1.2 billion sale price.

The only way that Murdoch would have agreed to this condition was if he didn't believe Echostar had much of a future. Unfortunately, the market loved the news that Charlie Ergen had swung this deal with Murdoch, and Echostar stock went through the roof. The stock was at $4.85 when the sale contract was signed in November 1998. By the time the deal closed on 24 June 1999, Echostar stock had hit $17.13. Nine months later it hit $81. Instead of getting 240 million shares the day before Murdoch's wedding, News and MCI received just 68.8 million shares and 1.7 per cent of the voting rights. Put another way, doing the deal with Murdoch transformed Ergen's company. But Ergen cleverly structured it so that Murdoch could not benefit from this. If News and MCI had picked up 240 million Echostar stock as the November 1998 contract stipulated, at the peak in March 2000 that $1.2 billion investment would have been worth $19.5 billion. Because of the way the contract was written, News and MCI ended up with less than a quarter of the 240 million shares originally contracted – and within months they had sold nearly half of the stock they did pick up. Charles Ergen's revenge on Rupert Murdoch was a mountain of lost opportunity. The opportunity cost to News Corporation and MCI at the peak of the market was more than $8.5 billion. And Murdoch still had to sweat it out through Hurricane Floyd.

CHAPTER SEVENTEEN

THE MANHATTAN WINDOW

After half a century working in the industry, the media business still had the ability to take Rupert Murdoch by surprise. Never more so than in New York. When his marriage collapsed, like an old crocodile Murdoch headed for the place in the world that he loved most and understood best. New York was still his lucky city, where politicians were still for the moment Republican, the *New York Post* was outrageous, and fortune smiled on the brave. After a stint at the Mercer Hotel in Soho, in 1999 Murdoch and Wendi Deng bought a three-story loft apartment on Prince Street. It was a lifestyle change that provided the media with endless delight. Media Mogul in Soho Love Nest was the line taken by the non-Murdoch British press. The headline writers did their best, but you knew that the more ingenious minds at the *Sun* would have found some way to slip something a little more colourful into the second deck. British columnists were obliged to take matters into their own hands to demonstrate their wonderful sense of irony.

The Murdochs had moved into Soho in force. Lachlan and Sarah O'Hare bought half the penthouse floor in an apartment building in nearby Lafayette Street. James and Kathryn Hufschmid had a four-storey terrace in the West Village. At 69, surrounded by his sons, Rupert Murdoch was looking pretty chipper. He was off the Pritikin diet that his ex-wife Anna had kept him on for years, and had bulked up a little. 'There's no doubt she's put a spring in the old man's step,' one of his executives said of Wendi.

At the turn of the millennium great things were afoot. A rolling series of technological and financial crises and advances loosely called the

Information Revolution were sweeping through the world's capital markets, transforming national economies, making whole swathes of industry obsolete, changing the way the world did business. In two years it had also created more individual wealth than anyone had ever seen. It was changing how we communicate, how we interact with other people, how and what we watch, what entertains us, how we read books, what we value, who we believe ourselves to be.

So it was hard to figure out what Rupert Murdoch was doing at the end of 1999, hunkered down in New York. His life was the same hectic schedule of dealmaking: a billion dollars here, a few hundred million there. All he needed to run his empire was a telephone. The quiet voice would still reach out over thousands of miles of telephone line to whichever part of the group needed his attention. It was a voice that haunted News Corp executives. Some of them dreamed about it. The voice was alternately seductive, endlessly persuasive, or frigidly dismissive. Murdoch was the master of the little politeness, the long silence, the questioning pause, the icy rage. He could inspire remarkable loyalty as well as enormous bitterness. Like the British Empire before it, at the end of the twentieth century News Corporation was an undertaking on which the sun never set. What that really meant was quite the reverse. Somewhere around the world there was always a News Corp executive that he could get out of bed.

There was no shortage of action for Murdoch in 1999. Yet oddly for someone who lived at such breakneck speed, for the first time in his life Murdoch gave the strange impression that he was a spectator. After a lifetime of striving, and despite the huge potential influence that this global empire offered him, he was reduced to peering through his Manhattan window at the big moves on Wall Street, watching the madness of the Internet stock boom transform share markets around the world. He was condemned to wait until the bubble had finished its course, run out of puff and slid back to earth . . . to observe with resignation someone else's spectacular good fortune.

Even in hindsight it is difficult to say when the Information Revolution stopped being a load of hocus pocus and became a part of everyday life. Through the 1980s and most of the 1990s, the most memorable feature of the revolution was its miserable record of broken promises. In the 1980s there was the paperless office. Then there were the 500 cable channels that Americans were promised in 1992. There were the fortunes lost on wild schemes for interactive television and on-line services – the multi-media programming, the video telephones – that never met their product description. It never quite got there. By early 1997 the information superhighway that Bill Gates liked to talk about had more the aspect of a parking lot. For all the hype, the tidal wave of digital data that the information revolution promised was going to transform the world's living rooms hadn't found a way to arrive. The revolution, it turned out, was all about getting there. It was about distribution.

Appearance is everything. What changed the appearance of the superhighway was money. In September 1998, Wall Street embarked on as wild a ride as capital markets had seen. Within six months a small group of Internet companies that had modest revenues, no profits and limited cash reserves were worth $600 billion. Those months changed the whole perception of the Information Revolution. Suddenly the information superhighway was the place where everyone wanted to be. This was the shape of the future, and the future would make us rich. The superhighway was still a parking lot, full of people who weren't making any money, whose revenues were still only a tiny fraction of the old-media companies that they were ready to replace. But now it was a parking lot with a chequebook.

In *Cinema Paradiso*, Giuseppe Tornatore's moving film about a child's love affair with a small-town movie theatre in Sicily in the 1940s, there is a poignant scene where the building catches fire. The projector keeps turning, faithfully projecting the image of the film as it bubbles, curls, and goes up in smoke. I have spoken to media executives and bankers who find this scene too painful to watch, evoking as it does so many unhappy memories of their own experiences in film and television investment. It's the nature of the industry. Half a century after Tornatore's childhood cinema closed, the media business remained highly flammable, the metaphorical aroma of singed celluloid all too pervasive. The medium might have changed, but the risks of total annihilation were higher than ever.

The quality that distinguished the leaders of the new media was their total indifference to the risks of conflagration. They burned through money like there was no tomorrow. Indeed, the market expected them to burn through the funds that investors were throwing at them. These were dizzy days. The wealth created by rising stock prices had triggered in investors a global suspension of disbelief. All the old yardsticks used to measure the value of a stock or a start-up company – profits, cash reserves, previous history – were discarded. All that anyone wanted was a piece of the future. On the wild edge of the wave, investors would believe anything.

But they wouldn't believe Rupert Murdoch. He was on record as an Internet sceptic. He had invested in on-line businesses like Delphi before anyone else had, and he didn't like the business model. The Internet, he said in February 1999, would destroy more value than it created. Five months later he interrupted his honeymoon to clarify that what he had meant to say was that the Internet was 'the most important development in business since the invention of the telephone'.

'Whenever a major change of this order takes place, traditional business models are challenged and sometimes destroyed,' he said. 'That is what is happening now.'

The suspicion remained that he was not a true believer. So his empire sat heavy on the beach as this wild tide came in. Even visionaries have their moments of self-doubt. In December 1999, Rupert Murdoch's biggest problem was that he didn't believe in himself quite enough. His senior executives – most notably News Corp finance director David DeVoe – had been selling down their News Corp stock. Murdoch had been selling call options on his News Corp shares to raise money. At least for the moment, Murdoch and his lieutenants clearly believed the company was becalmed. And then, incongruously in this dark moment, opportunity beckoned.

In the first weeks of the new millennium, two events changed the future. The first began on Monday 10 January 2000 with a press conference in New York, at the Time Warner offices at the Equitable Centre on 52nd Street. Gerry Levin was there, the head of Time Warner, the largest media company in the world. It was immediately apparent that he had news of great import, because he had elaborately removed his tie and misplaced his moustache. The new look was the marker for a twenty-first-century kind of guy. Next to him was Steve Case, chairman and CEO of America Online, the world's largest Internet company. Steve Case is to Hawaiian shirts what Rudolph Nureyev is to ballet tights: a true artist for whom expense is no object. Sometimes it looks like Case has paid as much as $20 for some of his brighter combinations. But not that day. You could tell someone was really working on corporate symbolism here because they had crammed Steve Case into a business suit. Case and Levin were there to announce the end of the world as we knew it.

The AOL-Time Warner liaison they proceeded to announce was the biggest corporate merger or takeover – however you want to put it – in history. It would leave Levin as CEO, but with Steve Case as chairman and his cyber cowboys from America On Line in the box seat running Time Warner. The *New York Times* valued the deal at $165 billion, the *Financial Times* put it at $230 billion, but in the confused hours following the announcement you could stick any number you liked on it. After Levin's media briefing Levin and Case went into a full body clinch. It was quite a moment: the heads of the largest and toughest media organisations in the world hugging as if their lives depended on it. During the media briefing Ted Turner, Time Warner's deputy chairman and biggest individual stockholder, was there on the stage beside Levin and Case. Turner, who had separated from his wife Jane Fonda a fortnight before, assured all and sundry that he'd signed his stock over for the merger the night before with all the excitement of the first time he made love. On his appearance that morning that would have been, oh, say 400 years before.

In 1996 Rupert Murdoch had been on the point of buying AOL when he made the mistake of asking advice from Bill Gates, who told him AOL wouldn't be around long enough to be worth the trouble. Murdoch said later that Gates:

> Didn't believe in it at all. He thought there wasn't a real business model there, and you know, none of us quite know yet . . . the jury is still out on AOL. But naturally, we had an opportunity to come in when it was worth $4 billion or $5 billion and it went up to being worth $150 billion. So it was a pretty serious opportunity that we missed there.

The AOL-Gates episode makes a funny story at Rupert Murdoch's expense, and sitting there on the stage at the 10 January press conference you could almost sense how much Ted Turner was dying to re-tell it. Murdoch had been chasing Time Warner and before that Time Inc and Warner Brothers in one shape or another for almost three decades. The new entity that would emerge from the AOL-Time Warner merger was a super-heavyweight ludicrously beyond the reach of any of its competitors. Quite apart from everything else, on a personal note it was Ted Turner's final victory over the ancient enemy.

The US media tackled the story with a full court press. The *New York Times* spelt out the numbers on the deal, told the background story of how Steve Case had wooed Gerry Levin, and agonised over the way media outlets were consolidating into fewer and fewer hands. The *Wall Street Journal* spelt out different numbers on the deal, speculated on the synergies of the alliance and began identifying suspects for the next mega-merger. Michael Wolff at *New York* magazine suggested that as both Time Warner and AOL were richer and more powerful than most medium-size countries, newspapers should assign the story to the corporate-state desk. *Vanity Fair* immediately picked up on the hugging thing and asked what this meant for the future of social intercourse. Everyone agreed that this was the most significant deal in the history of media. It was a little harder to say what in particular it signified.

The AOL-Time Warner deal's status as the biggest merger in history lasted for all of one week. Then British mobile phone group Vodafone-AirTouch won a hostile takeover battle for German telco Mannesmann for 181 billion euro, with a little help from Jean-Marie Messier, the little-known head of French media group Vivendi. This was the second event that would change the future. The significance went largely unnoticed at the time, but it was a warning signal to the US communications industry that the Europeans were coming.

Wall Street thought about the Time Warner-AOL deal for a bit then after an initial burst of enthusiam decided it didn't like it. When the news first broke, Time Warner's stock price jumped from $64.75 to $90, but by 6 March it had crashed back to $57. At that level, Ted Turner's Time Warner stock was worth $885 million less than it had been before the deal was announced. This was all the more painful because everyone else with media stock was taking in money with a bucket. The tech boom on Wall Street had established a cycle whereby the market took off in September or October and ran like a mad thing until March or April, then the Federal Reserve clamped down on money supply, the mutual funds lost their nerve, the day traders knocked off for the summer, and the market slid down. In October 1999 a fourth wave of investment in Internet and tech stocks had swept in. The world's central brankers were worried about the millennium bug – the fear that when clocks ticked over into the new century, computer chaos would break out – so they had deliberately pumped liquidity into the world's banking system. The millennium bug turned out to be a dud, but the extra money in the system had put the Nasdaq index of tech stocks into turbo-drive.

All of these technical issues were working together to ensure that in the middle of January, the telco-media-technology stock wave finally picked up News Corporation and carried it along. In seven weeks the News Corp stock price doubled. Rupert Murdoch's personal fortune jumped $6.7 billion. Murdoch had made almost as much money in those seven weeks as he had in the previous 48 years. He owed it all to Ted, of course. His old adversary's support for the AOL deal had changed once again the way media stocks were valued. Was Murdoch thinking of merging with an Internet stock too, the market wanted to know? 'Hell no,' he told one of his journalists insensitive enough to ask.

It took a little time to work out what had happened here. First, everyone agreed that the AOL-Time Warner deal was a turning point. It validated the new economy, it was proof that the huge surge in Internet stocks was not a fly-by-night pehenomenon. Rather, it was a change in value that was here to stay. Gerry Levin had been making bets on technology all his life. His track record showed he had been right about half the time. But even if he had got it wrong this time and the AOL-Time Warner combination was a fizzer, it had still changed the world. The next point was that if Levin's rivals in conventional old media companies wanted to keep up, they would have to make some sort of alliance of their own with the new media operators. They had to get bigger. What came after that was a little harder to say.

It's important to keep in mind just what the information revolution was all about. The sharp edge of the revolution had lain not with the digital technolgy and interactive services that it offered, but rather with finding a way of getting it into people's homes and then convincing them to use it. Technology was not an end in itself. The fax machine was developed in the 1970s, but it was decades before it suddenly became indispensable to the modern office. Steve Case was not pursuing Time Warner for its cable channels, its Warner Brothers studio and film library, its music division or its magazines, or indeed for any of its content. AOL wanted to get hold of Time Warner's network of hybrid coaxial-fibre-optic cable, a delivery system for data into 12 million American households. This was a great fat pipe into people's homes that Steve Case wanted to use to pump data, information, interactive television, and everything else that the information revolution had been promising, right to the customer.

The high-speed Internet access provided by Time Warner's cable changed the whole picture of what the Internet could deliver. Broadband had been around for several years, but the telephone and cable companies that operated it had been dismally unsuccessful at convincing people to use it. But in the whole world of media, no one had ever been as successful about convincing customers to take a new product as AOL. In new media, they were the master salesmen. AOL's whole future was based around its belief that it could persuade its 19 million customers to take up broadband. It was a given. Its $157 billion stock valuation was based around that belief. If anyone could make this work, it was Steve Case.

That didn't mean that the merger would be a success. What the AOL-Time Warner deal did was to establish that, one way or another, we were now in a broadband universe. Click. It was another change in perception. In five years time everyone would have broadband. The question now was what was the best way for broadband to get there. Would it be through Time Warner's cable? Would it be Wireless Application Protocol over mobile phones? Would it be the telephone companies' ADSL lines? Or by satellite? It all came down to the distribution question. Overnight, anything that could deliver broadband was worth a lot of money. This is where Rupert Murdoch saw his big chance.

It took Murdoch five weeks to go from a standing start to announcing a $50 billion deal. He owned the best distribution system on the planet. The BSkyB satellite pay-TV service in Britain was a model he had copied around the world. He had brought in partners, but he retained management rights. In Asia there was Star TV, which had a footprint that reached from Israel across India and China to the Eastern Pacific. In Japan Murdoch owned 10 per cent of Sky PerfecTV! In Latin America he had 36 per cent of Sky Brazil; 30 per cent of Sky Mexico; and 30 per cent of Sky Multi-Country Partners, which broadcast into Colombia, Chile and was moving into Argentina. In Australia, Murdoch had 25 per cent of the leading cable operation Foxtel. In Europe he was moving to 50 per cent of Stream SpA, an Italian pay-TV service, and BSkyB owned 24 per cent of Germany's digital pay-TV platform Premiere World.

North America was the only significant gap in Murdoch's world-wide satellite reach. There his conventional media interest in the Fox television network, television program production, Twentieth Century Fox and cable channels for Fox News, Fox Sports and Fox Kids made him one of the biggest content producers in the US. It was content that he could re-use in his satellite systems around the world. This mix of content and distribution made News Corporation unique. Holding the system together he had *TV Guide*, which he was folding into US company Gemstar to produce an electronic television guide for Internet users and pay-TV subscribers; he had just floated the NDS Group, which provided the technology for more than half the world's digital television users; and the Open system for interactive television that Murdoch was using for BSkyB. Only weeks before, no one had been valuing this combination. Time Warner-AOL had changed all that.

America's most high-profile media analyst, Merrill Lynch's Jessica Reif-Cohen, was enthusiastic about News Corp's place in this Brave New World, saying:

> The combination of News Corp's satellite investments into one seamless distribution platform, in our opinion, will launch News Corp into an unparalleled global position as the only company truly capable of providing a video and data infrastructure to the rest of the world.

When News floated 20 per cent of NDS in October 1999, the company was worth $900 million. By March the stock market valued NDS at $5 billion. News Corporation's own stock price doubled. But BSkyB was the bellwether of Murdoch's fortunes. On 24 September 1999 its shares were selling at £5.20. On 7 March, five months later, they hit £22.64. News Corporations' 37.6 per cent holding in BSkyB jumped from £3.5 billion to £15.5 billion. This had a leveraging effect. If BSkyB's value had gone up that much, so had the value of the eight other major pay-tv operations that Murdoch operated round the globe.

On 14 February News Corporation announced it was examining proposals to floats its international delivery platforms, a project that was code-named Plaformco, or Platco. Lachlan Murdoch told analysts that the new company would be a vehicle for strategic alliances with companies like Yahoo!, Microsoft and Vivendi in France. News Corp would remain the controlling shareholder. Jessica Reif-Cohen described the Platco project as the 'dream beam' and valued the company at $30-$50 billion and upwards. On Wall Street, merchant bankers were floating around plans to raise $18 billion in cash by spinning off 20 to 30 per cent of Platco. With the initial public offering cash and the investments from the new partners, this meant Platco could be worth as much as $90 billion.

To recap here. On Friday 7 January Rupert Murdoch's worldwide empire was worth $35 billion and Murdoch himself looked like he was spinning his wheels. Five weeks later the Platco initial public offering together with Fox Entertainment in the US and his newspapers plus the various ventures around the world that Murdoch managed with minority stakes meant that he controlled an empire that would be valued at more than $120 billion. His Millennium Gamble had been to reinvent himself.

By late March 2000, the first sign of how long Murdoch's arm had grown came when reports swept Wall Street that he was about to buy General Motors. Twenty years before, Murdoch had bought an airline to get hold of a television station. The same principle seemed to be involved here. Murdoch would buy GM and immediately recover all of the purchase price by selling on all those old-economy car plants. He would hold on to General Motor's subsidiary Hughes Electronics, which owned America's largest satellite television operator, DirecTV. The reality that the stock market had not factored into the General Motors stock price was that DirecTV was now worth more than General Motors itself. Murdoch would have filled the North American gap in Platco in effect for nothing. Murdoch's negotiations with General Motors to buy DirecTV would stretch into 2001.

However, in mid–March 2000, the world's love affair with telecom-media-technology stocks faltered. The Nasdaq index dived from 5000 to touch 3300. Overnight many of the valuations on which the Platco plan had been built were overturned. Platco, which would be renamed Sky Global, was still viable, but now its value – and the value of the partners that Murdoch was trying to bring on board – was uncertain. The would-be partners wanted to see what sort of an animal Sky Global would be, how the market would value it, before they committed to an equity stake. To make it work, Murdoch needed to get the Sky Global initial public offering away that summer before the Nasdaq fell over completely. That depended on keeping the BSkyB share price up. In turn, that depended upon winning the Premier League rights. That meant getting past the two powerful men standing in Murdoch's way.

In the summer of 1999, even as he was resolving his messy matrimonial problems. Murdoch's threat-detection system began pinging as he realised he was being stalked by two very different adversaries: Bill Gates at Microsoft, and a little-known French executive called Jean-Marie Messier. Gates had just invested £2.5 billion in Murdoch's cable rivals in Britain and encouraged them to merge so that they could challenge BSkyB. He'd also tried to poach BSkyB managing director Mark Booth, and was then reported to be offering £1 billion to Barclay Knapp at NTL to win the Premier League rights, to snatch BSkyB's core programming.

'I think Bill's going at everybody. Bill wants to take over the world,' Murdoch told *Vanity Fair* in October 1999. 'I don't say it nastily about Bill . . .'

Gates responded to the jibe in a BBC interview later that month. How could a software company possibly exert power, he asked expansively. It was Murdoch, he said, who wanted to take over the world: 'He's hiding behind me, he's your man.'

Gates had declared war on BSkyB because when Murdoch launched BSkyB's interactive television service in October 1998, he made the conscious decision to exclude Microsoft's Windows CEW from the digital set-top box.

'We don't want Bill Gates to get control of our pictures,' Murdoch told the *Financial Times* in July 1997. 'That's the real thing.'

Instead BSkyB's system used software from OpenTV, developed in part by Microsoft's rival, Sun Microsystems. BSkyB was the dominant pay-TV delivery system in Britain, and Gates was locked out of it. The danger was that, just as Murdoch had used BSkyB as the model to build his satellite empire around the world, he would use this non-Microsoft operating system for South America, for Germany, for Italy, for India, China and Australia.

Rupert Murdoch is a dangerous man to try to outspend. He learned three decades before Bill Gates how to use money like a club. Murdoch retained Booth with a special remuneration package, and put him in charge of a new $300 million Internet investment fund called e-partners. Eight days later on 5 May 1999 BSkyB announced that it would provide its digital boxes to customers free of charge, along with free Internet access and a 40 per cent reduction in their telephone bill. BSkyB would make a straight-off £450 million charge against its earnings to cover this. And it would keep shelling out whatever it cost to protect its position of market dominance. Pay-TV operators around the world had offered subsidised prices to customers before, but the sheer scale of this handout was like nothing yet seen. Overnight it turned BSkyB into the world's leading operator of interactive digital television. Murdoch blew the cable operators away – just when it looked like they were getting on a roll. He also had a few tricks up his sleeve when it came to football rights.

Jean-Marie Messier, the man the French press called Jean 2M, was a different kind of headache. He was a former French public servant who had turned France's oldest water treatment group, Générale des Eaux, into one of Europe's biggest media groups, renamed Vivendi. Among his other accomplishments, Messier had a remarkable ability to press Rupert Murdoch's button. In February 1999, Murdoch had met with Messier and Pierre Lescure, the chief executive of Canal Plus, Europe's largest pay-TV operator, which Messier controlled. They had talked about merging Canal Plus with BSkyB, but fell out over who would end up with control.

'We will have the leadership or there will be no agreement,' Lescure told French newspaper *Liberation*.

Once the merger was scuttled the real point of the meeting – at least as Italian politicians came to believe – was that Messier and Lescure wanted Murdoch to stay out of Italy. His investment in the Italian pay-TV operator Stream SpA and moves to buy up broadcast rights for Italian soccer would hurt Telepiu, the leading Italian pay-TV operator controlled by Canal Plus. If Murdoch backed off, Messier undertook not to buy any more shares in BSkyB, in which he had picked up an indirect 16.6 per cent interest the month before. In the spirit of the meeting, Lescure and Messier agreed to let Murdoch have Germany. They would not oppose his plans to link up with Bertelsmann or Kirsch Group there. (Murdoch had bought the rights for the European football championship, which he planned to broadcast on what up until then had been a tiny women's cable channel.) It may be that this part of the negotiations never happened. It doesn't really matter. The reality was that senior Italian politicians believed that Murdoch and Messier had genially carved up Europe between them. They were hugely indignant. While the prospect that Rupert Murdoch would take over Italy's media and its national sport terrified them, it was outrageous for Murdoch to back away from doing this just because of what someone in Paris told him.

If there was an agreement between Messier and Murdoch, it didn't last. In July Messier bought British media groups Granada and Pearson out of a joint holding in BSkyB stock. Messier now owned 24.5 per cent of BSkyB. Whether by accident or design, he discovered that the most annoying way to inform Rupert Murdoch of this was to telephone him in New York in the middle of the night and get him out of bed. It wasn't a happy conversation. Murdoch told his new shareholder, 'I don't like waking up in the morning thinking I have to look over my shoulder,' Messier recalled later. The two men did not speak for months after.

In November 1999, the British Trade and Industry Minister, Stephen Byers, referred both Messier's purchase of BSkyB shares and Barclay Knapp's £8.3 billion deal for NTL and France Telecom to buy Britain's third largest cable group, Optus & Wireless Communications, to the Mergers and Monopolies Commission. Rupert Murdoch has always had a curious affinity with the political process. It is not that Murdoch tells politicians what to do – merely that he has a happy knack for realising what is the best thing for whatever country he is in at the moment, a little before the country's elected officials come to the same conclusion. On 12 November, it turned out that the best thing for Britain was to put on ice both of the big media deals which threatened Rupert Murdoch's position in BSkyB.

Murdoch had wanted the government to get Messier 'off my back'. The Trade and Industry Minister Stephen Byers overruled the advice of the Director General of Fair Trading, John Bridgman, on at least one of the deals. His rivals called the referral a 'bizarre decision' and an 'act of appeasement towards Murdoch'. The NTL referral bought Murdoch time. After the Cable & Wireless merger, analysts expected NTL to merge with Telewest and provide a united front at the Premier League auction. Byers' referral stopped the merger plans. In fact NTL and France Telecom received final approval for the deal only on 10 May 2000, the day that the first round of bids for the Premier League were due. Without Telewest to share his costs, Knapp was bidding with one hand tied behind his back.

In the New Year, as Murdoch set off on his Sky Global quest in the aftermath of the AOL-Time Warner deal in January, Jean-Marie Messier had plans for his future every bit as expansive as Murdoch's. As the price for delivering victory to Vodafone-AirTouch in its battle for Mannesmann that month, he had negotiated a wireless Internet joint venture with Vodafone called Vizzaviz (pronounced vis-à-vis). The aim was to make it Europe's leading broadband Internet portal with the next generation of 3G-mobile phones. He was also about to begin sporadic talks with Edgar Bronfman Junior about buying the distilling/media group Seagrams, which owned Columbia Pictures. Messier remained as keen as ever about doing a merger with BSkyB. He wasn't very subtle about it. He kept communicating with Murdoch via press statements. At the end of January he publicly called on Murdoch to reopen talks about joining forces in light of the AOL-Time Warner deal: 'Mr Murdoch found our entrance into BSkyB a little too quick but this man of character shows a great sense of realism.'

Several days later, with Murdoch talking to Europe's largest company, mobile telephone group Nokia, Messier broke cover again: 'It's not impossible to think that the AOL-Time Warner/Air Touch-Vodafone deals could give an opportunity (for News and Vivendi) to talk.'

In early April, when Messier and Murdoch finally did start talking, Messier said: 'I consider Rupert Murdoch be a wise and pragmatic businessman. When the world has changed, your relationships can change.'

By April, when Messier began talks to join Sky Global, Murdoch no longer wanted the British government to force Vivendi to sell its BSkyB shares. A forced sale by Vivendi would devastate the BSkyB share price which could be lethal for the Sky Global initial public offering. Byers cleared the Vivendi acquisition of BSkyB shares deal on 18 April, just as Messier and Murdoch appeared to have reached some sort of understanding. From there the preparations for Sky Global went quiet. The only sign of movement came like a line of bubbles, a trail of carefully managed leaks around the world.

On 16 May News Corporation held a 'New Media Workshop' in New York led by Peter Chernin, to spread the virtues of the businesses that would be going into Sky Global. The analysts were disappointed by the failure to nail down partners for Sky Global. Through the last week of May, BSkyB and News Corp execs briefed the *Financial Times* in London extensively on BSkyB and the progress of the initial public offering. BSkyB's stock price rose strongly. With the change in sentiment that this coverage produced, BSkyB shares clawed their way back from £9.80 on 22

May to £14.53 on 2 June. A week later the focus switched back to the US where News briefed the *Wall Street Journal*. Then it was show-time for the Premier League auction.

London, 14 June 2000

There are two critical sports deals in the world. In America there is the broadcast rights for the National Football League. In Britain there is Premier League. The two deals set the currency, the monetary value of sport that washes through the culture. The bidding is dominated by intrigue, manipulation and blinding amounts of money. Olympic broadcast deals may be bigger, but they're a crap shoot. You pay your billion dollars and you pray that for a two-week period in eight years' time it doesn't rain, your satellite doesn't die, and no one boycotts. Football rights, on the other hand, are your passport into the country's living room every week. They make you part of the furniture. If you're a serious broadcaster you have to have them. Price is no object. Almost.

On 9 June 2000, Richard Scudamore, the managing director of the UK's Premier League, convinced the chairmen of the 20 clubs that make up the Premier League that they should entrust their future to him. Deciding who would win the broadcast rights of Premier League games for three years – and how much they paid for them – was the biggest issue that British football had ever faced. It had been the major discussion item when the chairmen met the week before the Premier League's summer conference. It might as well have been the only item.

Some of the bidders had already complained to the Office of Fair Trading and to the European Union about the selection process since first offers were submitted on 10 May. The threat of European Union intervention had convinced the prickly chairmen to whom Scudamore answered that they should keep their fingers out of the negotiations. In a locked room at the Chancery Lane offices of the Premier League's solicitors, Denton Wilde Sapte, on 14 June 2000 it would be entirely Richard Scudamore's call where this auction ended up.

The rules that Scudamore announced on Friday 9 June were simple. The Premier League was breaking its broadcast rights for the next three years into different packages. There was the major package of rights to broadcast 66 games live each season that would attract the most serious bidding. There was a less valuable package of rights for pay-per-view broadcast of another 40 games per season; and there was a package of match highlights for free-to-air television. Bidders could win only one package, and their offer document had to be in by 2 p.m. Wednesday 14 June. Each winning bid had to be at least 10 per cent higher than the next offer, or a new round of bidding would be conducted by fax. In practice the final selection would be quick and brutal, but for the media executives huddled in offices in London and New York waiting on Scudamore, the judging would take an eternity.

'It has been a pressure-cooker 48 hours,' the BBC's acting director of sport Richard Sambrook told the *Sunday Telegraph*. 'It was like a game of poker. You (were) sitting by a fax and phone waiting for call, a bundle of nerves trying to second-guess what the competition has done.'

The competition between the BBC and ITV for the match highlights would turn remarkably bitter. But the feature bout at this auction was an all-American grudge match – between Rupert Murdoch, whose media empire News Corporation controlled BSkyB, and Barclay Knapp, the aggressive New York wheeler dealer who in five years had built NTL into the biggest cable company in Britain. When the first bids were made five weeks before, Knapp had offered more than £1 billion for all of the broadcasting rights. In the weeks that followed, newspaper reports had him raising the offer to about £1.25 billion – some reports put it as high as £1.7 billion. NTL was looking like a runaway train.

A sudden-death auction offers two lines of approach. The first is a conventional auction strategy, where you convince your competition that you are crazy enough or have a big enough bank balance to blow them out of the water. The second is where your competitor wins the prize, but only after you have forced them to bid a price that will ruin them. In May 2000 BSkyB was losing both ways. It could either lose the football rights, which would be disastrous for its new digital strategy; or it could win the rights at an extortionate price, which would be just as lethal. Between 4 May and 22 May, as news of NTL's bids filtered out, BSkyB's share price dropped from £17.50 to £9.80. Just like that, £14 billion had been wiped off BSkyB's market value. Almost half the company had disappeared in two and a half weeks. This was an auction that BSkyB absolutely could not afford to lose – but it was just as important not to win by paying too much. If Bill Gates was bankrolling NTL, as Murdoch believed, how long was Knapp's line of credit? It became a game of bluff and double bluff as the BSkyB team led by chief executive Mark Ball and Sky Sports consultant Ian Frykberg agonised over what they had to do to haul themselves back into the fight.

The good news for BSkyB was the Premier League's decision to break the broadcast rights down in separate packages. The rights were worth more as a single commodity that would give the winning bidder clear control of football. A share of football, even a dominant share, would be less attractive. If NTL was prepared to bid more than £1.5 billion for the whole shooting match, how high would it go just for the top package of live games? Under the auction rules, if the highest bid was not more than 10 per cent clear of the next bidder, Scudamore would conduct another round of bidding over the telephone. Each new bid would have to jump by 10 per cent – or more than £100 million. A series of inconclusive bidding rounds could see a disastrous blow out in the price.

At BSkyB Ball and Frykberg believed NTL was bluffing with the reports of a £1.7 billion bid. The most that NTL would offer for the top package was £1 billion. Ball added 10 per cent to that, then added another £10 million for safety, and that was the number: £1.11 billion. If NTL bid more than £1 billion, then BSkyB still had a chance to make another bid. On the other hand, if Barclay Knapp offered more than £1.22 billion, BSkyB would be knocked out and NTL would walk away with the prize. Ball's bid was considerably less than analysts were expecting, but still kept BSkyB's hopes alive if it had guessed wrong . . . unless Barclay Knapp was a wild man. Would it be enough?

New York

In June 2000 Rupert Murdoch was staring at the drop-dead date on a $40 billion deal. He had 16 days to file a prospectus with the US Securities and Exchange Commission for Sky Global Networks Inc, the initial public offering that Murdoch had been working on since February. After 30 June Murdoch would be into a new reporting period. New Sky Global accounts would have to be audited. In the meantime the momentum for the initial public offering would disappear.

In April after a routine health check-up in Los Angeles Murdoch was diagnosed with prostate cancer. His cancer was described as low grade, but his family history offered little comfort. Doctors had operated on Murdoch's father three times for prostate cancer. If Sir Keith had not died of a heart attack, it seemed only a matter of time before he was hit by a further wave of secondary cancers. This was not a condition to trifle with. However the diagnosis came at a critical period for Murdoch in the negotiations for Sky Global. 'He has no intention of changing his work schedule,' a News Corporation spokesman announced quickly. Murdoch put the radiation therapy on hold for a month.

His family was showing signs of the stress. On 2 May his daughter Elisabeth resigned from her position as head of programming at BSkyB. She said at first that she was resigning to start up her own production company. A day later she revealed that she was having a baby with her companion, Matthew Freud, a public relations consultant whom Rupert reportedly detested. They parted later that year. Later it would emerge that her decision to leave the family business coincided with their father's decision to include his two sons, Lachlan and James, on the board of Sky Global. Elisabeth, who at BSkyB was program manager for Sky Global's core operation, appeared to have been overlooked. The struggle to determine which of Rupert's children would succeed him seemed to have claimed another casualty.

By June it had come down to this: the Nasdaq composite index was still wobbling along. It looked shaky, but was holding just below 4000. Murdoch had not yet been able to secure the strategic partnerships needed for his Sky Global strategy. Sources close to Murdoch said that after finally beginning nine weeks of radiotherapy, the treatment had left him for the moment too weak to begin another frenzied round of dealmaking. The biggest asset that Murdoch was putting into the Sky Global IPO was his 37.5 per cent stake in BSkyB. If Nasdaq stayed buoyant, then the critical issue for getting the Sky Global flotation away was keeping BSkyB's share price up. In turn, BSkyB's share price depended on winning the rights for Premier League games at a price that wasn't ruinous. So Murdoch's entire future was riding upon Richard Scudamore's deliberations behind a locked door in London.

Within an hour of the bid deadline on 14 June, Scudamore had sorted through the offer documents and was on the phone to BSkyB. Barclay Knapp at NTL had blinked. His bid for the top package of rights was under £1.01 billion. Under the bidding rules this meant that BSkyB had won outright with its offer of £1.11 billion. There would be no further bidding. NTL ended up with the pay-TV package for £328 million. In all, the Premier League would receive £1.643 billion for three years' broadcasting rights – though NTL would later walk away from the pay-TV package. BSkyB's bid of £1.11 billion would kick the share price up again because it was £100 million less than analysts had expected. Ball called Murdoch with the news then took his team for beer, burgers and champagne at Soho House, a popular media haunt in West London.

Sky Global had its green light. On Thursday 15 June, Peter Chernin briefed the *New York Times*, which reported on Friday that the Sky Global initial public offering prospectus could be filed with the Securities and Exchange Commission as early as that afternoon. Last-minute hitches held the prospectus up over the weekend. Not the least of these was James Murdoch's wedding. On the Saturday the Murdochs gathered on a riverbank in Connecticut to watch James marry Kathryn Hufschmid. Two weeks before, James had been appointed executive chairman of Star TV. As the younger brother he had little to lose. But if he could turn Star TV into a money-spinner, he would have far stronger claims on the succession than Lachlan. The Sky Global initial public offering went to the Securities and Exchange Commission on Tuesday. It helped upstage Jean-Marie Messier's announcement that Vivendi and Canal Plus were coming to Hollywood, with a $34 billion bid for Seagrams. It was 22 June, the first summer solstice of the century. Murdoch's great gamble had begun. Sky Global was about to make an appearance. And appearance is everything.

POSTSCRIPT

London/New York/Beijing/Sydney, 1999–2000

In the fifth century BC, two Greek philosophers living in a refugee city in Italy concluded for different reasons that reality is just a state of mind. Parmenides took the early Greek notion that it is impossible for the human mind to consider something that does not exist, and declared that the universe could not cope with the state of non-being. Empty space – that part of the world where nothing exists – must be an impossibility. Nature might abhor a vacuum; Parmenides had rather stronger views. Of course that meant that all motion was impossible because there was no space to move *into*. The cosmos is in a state of perpetual gridlock where nothing really changes, although our senses deceive us into believing the reverse. Parmenides' disciple Zeno took another tack by expounding a serious of paradoxes. His most famous involves shooting an arrow. At any moment the distance to the arrow's target, however close you set it, may be divided into an infinte number of points along the way that the arrow has to pass. An infinite number by definition can never be reached. Thus the arrow will never arrive at the target. In fact, nothing ever gets anywhere. We only think that it does.

Parmenides and Zeno posed complex philosophical arguments. At a more personal level, it is easier for us to share a moment of recognition with them as people living in a world of chaos, trying to derive some coherence out of a society overwhelmed by a tidal wave of change. Twenty-five centuries ago, in a world where everything was under challenge, Parmenides and Zeno were able to construct a philosophical standpoint from which they could look down to survey the carnage all around them and say: 'This can't be happening.' And yet of course they knew that it was.

At the start of the twenty-first century the world's great media organisations fight their own battles with doubt and disbelief. Undeterred, they sail resolutely on into an uncertain future, buffeted but still buoyant as the waves of change continue to crash in. The frail craft in which they travel, the traditional media mindset that has served them well for so long, now seems quaint and outdated.

The prospectus for Murdoch's Sky Global Networks initial public offering (IPO) was filed with the Securities and Exchange Commission on 24 June 2000. In hindsight, Murdoch should have kept running. The Nasdaq composite index of high-tech stocks, which was the surest guide to the state of the tech economy, in the first three weeks of April had dropped 34 per cent down to 3200. But by mid-July it had clawed its way back above 4100. That is when Murdoch *should* have floated Sky Global, and if he had not been on daily radiation therapy for nine weeks through June and July he probably would have done. Instead Murdoch decided to wait until the market jumped again in October. In the meantime he did a quick deal at the start of August, snatching the Chris-Craft group (the television station chain that had blocked Murdoch's run at Warner Brothers 17 years before) for $5.3 billion from under the nose of Sumner Redstone, who had been negotiating to buy Chris-Craft for months. Murdoch's move set off a new scramble among US broadcasters to keep up with him. A week later Murdoch was at the News Corporation annual profit announcement to assure analysts that he was back in charge. The cancer treatments were over, he said, and the whole experience had only 'convinced me of my own immortality.' But the chance to float Sky Global in a still buoyant market had slipped away.

The hoped-for October 2000 rally on Wall Street, on which so much of Murdoch's plan depended, never eventuated. By the start of 2001 it was clear that the unthinkable had happened. The wave of technological euphoria that had dominated the last years of the twentieth century was for the moment in full retreat. Propelled by the new mood of disenchantment, the price of technology stocks fell like a stone. Among scenes of devastation that unfolded on stock markets across the globe, the biggest losses were in New York, where the Nasdaq composite index of technology stocks dropped 46 per cent in the three months to 2 January 2001. In nine months, American technology investors lost more than $3 trillion. The pain was felt across the board. In early 2001, a good technology investment was one that had fallen less than 90 per cent from its 2000 high.

The shock waves that this disaster set off reflected more than just a mountain of missing money. After all, there would be other stock rallies – and the chairman of the US Federal Reserve, Alan Greenspan, was cutting US interest rates doggedly to achieve this. In any case, the process of technological change would go on. The real casualty had been a belief system, a credo fostered by a decade of huge tech stock rises, that information technology had ushered in a new economic order. The premise for the tech stock boom was that the path of the Information Revolution led ever upward, somehow invulnerable to economic cycles. This belief had not survived the first signs in late 2000 that the American economy was turning down.

It is difficult to describe how damaging this disenchantment proved. In many ways, belief in technology had become the dominant social paradigm after the end of the Cold War. Technology's fall from grace threw the world into paradigm crises. If, contrary to appearances, technology turned out to be mortal after all, what did the future hold? As media companies slashed back their ambitious plans for the Internet, the information highway was once more characterised by a rush back to the parking lot.

At the News Corp annual meeting on 18 October 2000 in Adelaide, Murdoch was still upbeat. The Sky Global Networks IPO, now valued at $40 billion, had 'a lot of moving parts', he told shareholders. These included talks to buy DirecTV for a price reported between $40 billion and $60 billion; and to buy Vivendi's 21.3 per cent holding in BSkyB, after the European Union ordered Messier to sell the stake as a condition of its Seagrams takeover. To buy out Vivendi, Murdoch would need to mount a full-scale bid for all of BSkyB. 'If everything went like lightning it would be three weeks' before Sky Global went to market, Murdoch said.

On 3 November Murdoch told BSkyB shareholders in London that the Sky Global IPO could get off by Christmas. Five days later when he announced disappointing results for News Corp's first quarter, Murdoch put Sky Global's launch date back to March 2001. A week after that, Peter Chernin told the *Guardian* that the Sky Global plans were being reconsidered, with a possible float by June.

An $8 billion deal in September 2000 saw John Malone emerge as both a founding shareholder in Sky Global, and an 18 per cent shareholder in News Corporation. While Malone's Liberty Media group took non-voting shares, the stake was only marginally smaller than Murdoch's. If one disregards the portion of Murdoch's holding in News which is actually owned by News Corp itself (through its holding in Queensland Press), Malone was now the biggest stakeholder in Murdoch's company. A week later, as speculation grew about Malone's growing role, Lachlan Murdoch was appointed deputy chief operating officer for News Corporation. Regardless of this, if anyone could threaten the family succession – Murdoch's determination that one of his sons should succeed him at the helm of News – it was still Malone. The fact that Murdoch was prepared to accept that risk, to allow his closest and most dangerous friend into the News tent, underlined how important the Sky Global deal was to him, and how close Murdoch believed he was to success. He had pinned all his hopes upon acquiring DirecTV. When joined to the satellite businesses already in Sky Global, it would make Murdoch master of the skies. The 15 million-plus digital subscribers that he would end up with would give him a huge head start over everyone else in developing interactive television. Anyone developing interactive technology would need to come to him. It promised a very Murdoch future.

Elsewhere, the scorecard was mixed. In June 2000 after the animated movie *Titan A.E.* flopped, Fox closed the studio in Phoenix that had triggered the animation boom of the 1990s. After a falling out with Murdoch, Haim Saban pushed the escape button on Fox Kids, exercising his right in the ownership agreement to insist that Murdoch buy him out in January 2001. With analysts speculating that Murdoch would need to pay Saban $1.6 billion cash, the credit agencies put News Corp back on credit watch. Results at Fox Sports were up, and Fox News finally broke even. In May 2000, the NDS group won approval to help China set up a high-speed digital cable network. With 80 million subscribers by 2001 it would be the biggest cable network in the world – larger than all the other cable networks put together. It was Murdoch's speech in 1993 about technology as the great threat to totalitarian regimes that had prompted the Chinese government to pull the plug on satellite television. Fear of Murdoch persuaded the Chinese that their future lay with cable rather than satellite. 'They feel comfortable that at the end of the day someone with a pair of wire-cutters can always cut a cable,' a News Corp executive said. The decision to let NDS provide encryption, set-top boxes, software and restricted access to Internet sites suggested that Murdoch was in line to become gatekeeper to the market after he himself had locked the door. The media industry's need for secrecy – or at least to restrict information, sounds and images to the paying customers – continued unabated. The furore over copyright, and programs like Napster which allowed Internet users to swap bootleg copies of music and films, loomed as the biggest roadblock that the Internet had faced.

In the US, as a result of Murdoch's 1997 battles, the future of communication was dominated by cable. For the rest of the world,

Murdoch was offering a very different kind of future. The heart of the AOL-Time Warner merger that had made the Sky Global float possible was the move to broadband. In the early 1980s, computers talked to each other over telephone lines at 300 bits per second. By the late 1990s, cable modems were pumping out 2 Megabits of data per second – which worked out at more than 6,000 times faster than the modems of a decade and a half before. It takes about 3 Megabits of data per second to carry a television picture. The advent of broadband suddenly made television on the Internet seem terrifyingly close, even with the crash of technology stocks. There were still huge technical and legal problems – not least copyright – which would take some years to resolve. But one way or another they would be resolved, either with cable, or the 3G generation of mobile phone, or the next generation of low-orbit two-way satellite.

The casualty toll would be enormous. In North American winters, why would consumers venture out in the snow to be mugged on the way to the corner video store, when they could download a wider selection of videos online? That meant conventional video chains were living on borrowed time. Why would pay-TV viewers subscribe to a cable company which gave them a bundle of channels, most of which they didn't want, when they could order Discovery Channel directly online? That would be the end of cable companies. If today there were 3,000 radio stations on the Net, what would life be like with 3,000 televisions stations? What would that do to local free-to-air televisions? 'At some point the concept of prime-time scheduling ceases to exist,' said one Internet consultant.

Up to the Time Warner-AOL merger, the information revolution had been about finding a way to pump the tidal wave of digital data into the home. Now there was a new race: to get from the home computer that was hooked up to cable in the study, five metres down the hallway to the living room. They called this process convergence, by which they meant the home computer terminal would morph into a television set. Rupert Murdoch had a different vision of the future. When the Internet technologists solved the technical problems and found a way to cross that final five metres into the living room, they would find they were not alone. Rupert Murdoch would already be there, perched on the sofa with his feet up. Actually he didn't really believe they would ever arrive.

At BSkyB Murdoch had pioneered the most successful interactive television service in the world. It had 5 million digital subscribers. It offered multiple camera views for covering sport. It moved seamlessly to Open, its retail interface that allowed viewers to buy products on-line in seconds. It offered a small selection of Internet sites at blinding speed as well as email, cheaper telephone calls, and soon video on demand. In short it offered nearly everything that the Internet offered. But it wasn't the Internet. It was built on the belief that television and the Internet would never really converge. When people sat down to watch TV, they didn't want the frustrations of a computer experience. They wanted television, and maybe a bit of shopping. Murdoch wanted to replace e-commerce with t-commerce.

I'm sorry to break the bad news, but there's been a divorce,' Elisabeth Murdoch announced at the Edinburgh Television Festival in August 1998, two months before BSkyB launched its digital service. It was a little inside joke about the family's marriage problems as well as a comment on convergence. But it underlined that at the heart of Murdoch's strategy was a profound scepticism about where the information superhighway was going. Sky Global was an attempt to change the road map. Murdoch was also furiously investing in Internet ventures, covering his bets with a strategy to move into the next generation of wireless Internet and two-way satellite systems. 'We are platform-netual,' James Murdoch said at News Corp's New Media Workshop in May 2000 in New York. But at heart BSkyB's interactive system was a direct challenge to the new-media view of the future. The advance of the World Wide Web through the last half of the 1990s had come to seem so inevitable that the Sky Global strategy sounded like heresy. It would have seemed ludicrous if it had been anyone other than Rupert Murdoch propounding it.

For Murdoch, Sky Global offered some sort of final redemption. It represented a chance to redefine himself, to stamp his own version of reality across the world: his legacy determined by one throw of the dice. Murdoch has never had an infallible gift for seeing into the future. For much of his life he has got it wrong with the crystal ball as often as not. He is more businessman than wild-eyed visionary. He has made his empire betting against technology rather than for it. When he moved his British newspapers to Wapping in 1986, the move was so focused on secrecy and overturning the power of the print unions that Murdoch installed antiquated presses that had to be replaced within a couple of years. With Sky Television in Britain, Murdoch bet the company that existing, off-the-shelf PAL television would out-sell the latest technology. By defeating the government-approved BSB satellite service, Murdoch put high-definition television in Britain – and arguably Europe – on hold for a decade. His great Sky gamble in 1997 was about detailing the move towards a technological future based upon fibre-optic cable. Murdoch's Sky Global platforms in 2000 were based upon putting limits on the Internet, replacing e-commerce with a simpler t-commerce. What Murdoch lacks in crystal-ball abilities or in commitment to technology he makes up for with his remarkable capacity to spot a commercial opportunity and seize upon it. More than that, his genius lies in the survival skills he shows when his latest venture goes wrong. His ability to change the rules, to produce his own versions of reality, to produce the grand illusions that dreamers need, is unparalleled.

There is another feature to this drama. In London, in New York, in Los Angeles, in Jerusalem, in Sydney – on each stage Murdoch is the compelling player when he appears, the figure around whom so much else turns. Yet he is also the least substantial figure, the most elusive and inexplicable player to track through a dozen costume changes. His appearance varies depending upon whom he is standing next to. Where are the hard edges to define this character? Murdoch is arguably the most secretive figure in world media. Where in his privileged childhood, in a business career conducted over three continents and half a century, and in the frenzy of deals he initiated at the turn of the millennium, do we find the keys to understanding this opaque figure? In half a century, the only constant in Rupert Murdoch's life has been the dazed expression on the faces of those he leaves behind. Faced with the succession of images thrown up by this master reality shaper, which is the real one?

The same question may be asked of the empire that Rupert Murdoch has built. He has always maintained that News Corporation reflects 'my values, my character'. But which News Corporation are we talking about? Is it the successful world media empire that reports substantial profits each year? Or the more modest earner that US accounting standards record? Is it the offshore entity that pays minimal tax, or the one that hires private investigators to mount an international manhunt through the tax havens of the world? Or the one that told the Federal Communication Commission year after year that Americans controlled the Fox television stations, while at the same time it told the Securities and Exchange Commission that control of the stations lay with News Corp? When lawyers for the Australian Rugby League, the football code that Murdoch overran, referred in court to an ethical void in News Corporation's corporate culture, it was an emotional judgment. It is easier to say that the heart of News Corporation's corporate culture is a mystery. It is a place that creates magic. It is hard to say what will happen to News when the master magician departs.

Appearance is everything. At the heart of the post-modern view of the world is the notion that we continue. We survive. Impermanent life goes on, no matter how exhilarated, bleak or mundane is the mood of the day. The gossamer thread that weaves our world from a thousand unresolved moments continues to unravel unmindful ahead of us. If there is no final bright morning or dark sunset, if reality is instead a succession of jerky frames that stretch before and behind us, like a silent film played upon an ancient, flickering projector . . . then what are we to make of Rupert Murdoch? This figure who endlessly reinvents himself, who can only be known as a disconnected sequence of strobe photographs, remains at the end of the day as Medusa-like, as fickle and unknowable as the realities he creates. He is, in the full sense of the phrase, the man of the moment.

NOTES ON SOURCES

INTRODUCTION

page

x   'It's a dream' . . .' James Harding, 'Murdoch pushes for DirecTV', *Financial Times*, 10 November 2000.

xii   'Lachlan is in a very . . .' Conservation with author, 6 March 2001.

xiii   'It's what keeps us young . . .' Rupert Murdoch, 'The Century of Networking', Speech for the Centre for Independent Studies, Melbourne, October 1994.

xv   More than $600 billion: Unless otherwise indicated, all $ figures quoted are in US currency.

CHAPTER 1

page

4   'It's amazing looking around this: Driving Dame Elisabeth', *Australian Story*, Australian Broadcasting Corporation, 25 March 1999. A request by the author for an interview submitted via Rupert Murdoch was declined. In any case the focus of this section is how Dame Elisabeth is portrayed by the media. Unless otherwise indicated, quotes from Dame Elisabeth are from the ABC documents, though she has been quoted extensively with similar comments elsewhere.

5   'Her son is . . .': Caroline Jones, 'Driving Dame Elisabeth', *Australian Story*.

5   'Now look darling . . .': John Monks, *Elisabeth Murdoch: Two Lives* (Sydney: Macmillan, 1994), p. 113.

6   'It's not that we *mind* . . .': Unpublished interview with Australian journalist Ali Cromie, April 1997.

6   'The sisters are slavishly devoted . . .': Matt Handbury in interview with the author, April 1993.

7   'I suppose a fairly average person . . .': 'Rupert Murdoch', *Six Australians: Profiles of Power*, Australian Broadcasting Corporation, 1 January 1966.

11   'Toughen him up a bit . . .' and 'I used the slipper . . .': From 'Driving Dame Elisabeth', *Australian Story*, Australian Broadcasting Corporation, 25 March 1999.

11   'My mother is a strong character . . .': Rupert Murdoch, 'KRM Proposal/September 1990'. Proposal prepared by Rupert Murdoch for an autobiography.

11   'I clearly recall . . .': John Monks, *Elisabeth Murdoch: Two Lives*, p. 311; 'I suppose I wanted . . .', p.305.

12   'Wild, sullen boy . . .': A quote of Sir Keith related in correspondence by a family friend, who asked not to be named.

12   'I don't think Rupert . . .': Thomas Kiernan, *Citizen Murdoch* (New York: Dodd Mead & Co, 1986), p. 18.

12   'Never do anything . . .' and 'Making money by betting . . .' from Patrick Murdoch, *Sidelights to the Shorter Catechism*, issued by the Sunday School Committee of the Presbyterian Church of Victoria (Melbourne: Harcliffe, Waddell and Falconer, 1908), pp. 74, 76.

13   'As a boy he was rough as guts . . .': Interview with Australian journalist Dimity Torbett, 1981.

13   'I was quite overwhelmed . . .': John Monks, *Elisabeth Murdoch: Two Lives*, p. 174.

14   'Necessary crockery . . .'; 'Rupert, give a few half hours . . .'; 'I do hope dear boy . . .': Letter from Sir Keith Murdoch to Rupert Murdoch, 12 September 1950.

14–15   Quotes by Michael Weigall, James Mitchell, Patrick Seale, a 'former contemporary', 'another fellow undergraduate', Frank Cioffi, Robert Shackleton, from Australian journalist Dimity Torbett's record of interviews, 1983–84.

16–21   Quotes by J. R. Sargent and Michael Weigall from Dimity Torbett interviews, 1983–84.

19   'Cataclysmic chauffeur': *Cherwell*, 11 June 1952, 28 May 1952.

20   Politician's Paradox: Farquharson began by looking at a vote
engineered two millennia ago in the Roman Senate by Pliny the
Younger. The consul Alfranius Dexter had been found murdered
and, in the absence of any evidence as to who was responsible,
the Senate was split between those who, like Pliny, wished to
acquit the consul's freedmen, those who wanted to banish them,
and those who wanted them put to death. In effect what
Farquharson's maths shows is that the end result in any vote
depends on the order that you put the various issues. You need
to get the voting protocol right so that other parties, as their own
preferred options are eliminated, decide to support your cause in
preference to a less desirable alternative. Pliny's trial bears an
uncanny similarity to the drama that unfolded in 1998 in the US
Senate, which split three ways on whether it should acquit,
censure or impeach President Clinton. Robin Farquharson,
Theory of Voting (New Haven: Yale University Press, 1969).

21   'I was the victim . . .': Robin Farquharson, *Drop Out!* (London:
Blond, 1968), pp. 74, 79, Introduction.

21   'I'm worried about my son . . .': George Munster, *A Paper Prince*
(Melbourne: Penguin, 1987), p. 36.

22   'The Queen? Nice little woman . . .': Philip Townsend,
'Murdoch by his butler', *Punch*, Issue 58, 4–17 July 1998, p. 17.
Townsend was later jailed for fraud and theft after he left the
Murdochs' employ.

23   'I can't die yet . . .': Aside by Sir Keith in 1952, recorded in
correspondence by Murdoch family friend.

24   The jackhammer story was related by Herald and Weekly Times
journalist Peter Thompson, later deputy editor of the *Daily
Mirror* and editor of the *Sunday Mirror* in London. He told
Dimity Torbett: 'Whether the jackhammer story is fanciful or
not, Williams is credited with getting inside that safe and
establishing the truth about the organisation. The story went that
he then got on the phone doing deals interstate to establish a *fait
accompli*, to join hands with other arms of the empire and freeze
out the Murdoch family – that is, steal it, wrest control,
whichever is applicable.'

26   'I felt very bitter . . .': Written comment, but made with request
for anonymity, after the publication of Simon Regan's *Rupert
Murdoch: A Business Biography* (London: Angus & Robertson,
1976).

'Murdoch was a fascinating study . . .': John Hetherington, 'The Man in the Paper Mask', *Australians: Nine Profiles* (Melbourne: F. W. Cheshire, 1960).

26   'Williams said that Murdoch . . .': Interview with Dimity Torbett, 5 September 1983. Torbett, 'The King of Fleet Street', *Times on Sunday*, Sydney, 7 June 1987, p. 26. King was not unbiased. He said his uncle, Lord Northcliffe, at first lent, then gave Sir Keith Murdoch £5,000 in 1922 for a failed takeover of a Sydney newspaper – which was 10 times more than Northcliffe left King. While he had nothing but praise for Dame Elisabeth, he said Rupert was 'not a good man . . . an ill-mannered little nobody with nothing to match the personality of his father . . . all sound and fury signifying nothing very much'.

Sale of Queensland Newspapers: Various accounts of Sir Keith's newspaper holdings are given by Desmond Zwar (*In Search of Sir Keith Murdoch*), C. E. Sayers (whose biography of Sir Keith, commissioned by the Murdochs, was never published), Cecil Edwards (*The Editor Regrets*) and historian Michael Cannon (Age, 21 November 1979). The company articles of Queensland Newspapers Pty Ltd also described a change of control which would be triggered by Sir Keith's death, though there is no reference to the Herald and Weekly Times.

28   'It could be . . .': John Monks, *Elisabeth Murdoch: Two Lives*, p. 177.

28   Exchange of cables: Thomas Kiernan, *Citizen Murdoch* (New York: Dodd Mead & Co, 1986), p. 41.

CHAPTER 2

page

31   Australian accounts of Turner press conference: Philip Cornford, 'Mouth of South is drunk as skunk', *Daily Telegraph*, 20 September 1977, 'Skipper Ted's cup runneth over . . . and over', *Australian*, 20 September 1977. Both are Murdoch papers.

32   'A new newspaper is very exciting . . .': Maxwell Newton, in 'Rupert Murdoch', *Six Australians: Profiles of Power*, Australian Broadcasting Corporation, 1 January 1966.

33   Divorce from Patricia Booker: In the years after the divorce Patricia Booker had a series of unhappy relationships. Rupert

Murdoch is believed to have provided support for her until her death in 1998, significantly beyond the requirements of the divorce settlement.

35   'No, no one can help him . . .': Anthony Blond account given in interview with Dimity Torbett, 1982.

37   Turner's Jamaica race: David Miller, 'Turner's Goodwill crusade rolls on', *The Times*, 2 August 1994.

37   'The Sydney to Hobart is a little like childbirth . . .': Bryan Burrough, 'Storm Warning', *Vanity Fair*, May 1999, No. 465, p. 97. Article pp. 94–101, 139–46.

38   'I ordered the crew . . .': Simon Kent, *Sun-Herald*, 24 December 1995, p. 36.

40   'He wiped out our antenna . . .': 'Nirvana crosses line first, but double protest clouds result', unattributed report, *Sydney Morning Herald*, 30 December 1983.

'We're good sports . . .': Rob Mundle, 'Condor wins on protest and Turner sheds a tear over the race that never was', 31 December 1983.

'Go home, foul-mouthed drunken bum yachties.': 'Crews set for rumpus rum round', unattributed report, *Daily Telegraph*, Sydney, 31 December 1983. Bruce Montgomery, 'xxx the sadness', *Australian*, 7 January 1984.

41   Turner's speech: This at least is the Turner camp's version of how the Turner-Murdoch feud began, as related by Turner's biographer, Porter Bibb, to the *Washington Post*: 'There was this big drunken dinner after the race, and Turner got up and made mincemeat of Rupert. He went on and on and on. (Murdoch) was absolutely humiliated. I don't think he ever forgot it.' Paul Farhi, 'Mogul Wrestling; In the war between Murdoch and Turner, similarity breeds contempt', *Washington Post*, 18 November 1996, p.C1. Bibb's account incorrectly dates the incident in 1979, and appears to assume Murdoch was present.

41   'They are the monolithic companies . . .': Transcript of testimony by Rupert Murdoch at public hearing of the Australian Broad-casting Tribunal, 26 July 1979, pp. 222–3.

42   Corporate form of feudal warfare: Judge Wright, Warner Communications Inc v. Murdoch, et al No. 84–13 CMW. Delaware District Court, 16 March 1984.

43   'For a limited period of time': A 17 November 1983 memo from Squadron Ellenoff Plesent & Lehrer associates Philip Altman and

Howard Topez addressed to Siskind tabled in court said that Siskind told Altman that Mariotta's ownership of Wedtech stock was for a limited duration. The Squadron Ellenoff lawyers said the memo was an outline of possibilities that were never put into practice.

43   'Mr Guariglia asked me . . .': 'On the Record', *Manhattan Lawyer*, 19–25 July 1998, p. 16. See also Howard W. French, 'Lawyer admits default scheme was discussed', *New York Times*, 13 July 1988, Section B, p. 3: Howard W. French, 'Prosecutors suggest Wedtech lawyers violated ethics code', *New York Times*, 9 July 1988, Section 1, p. 31; Paul Moses, 'Squadron accused in Wedtech trial; Ex-Exec: Lawyer knew contract was a fraud', *Newsday*, 24 March 1988, City edition, p. 4; Michele Galen, 'Too close for comfort', *National Law Journal*, 6 July 1987, Section: Counsel for Wedtech, p. 1: Ira Lee Sorkin, 'Squadron Ellenoff replies on Wedtech role', *National Law Journal*, 13 July 1987, Section: Letters, p. 12.

43   'Tactical move . . .': Telephone interview with the author, 12 November 1996.

43   'At no time did anybody indicate . . .': Testimony by Arthur Siskind 12–13 July 1988 in the trial of Wedtech executives. Reported in Edward Frost and Rifka Rosenwein, 'Wedtech defense witness says he helped prosecutors', *Manhattan Lawyer*, 19–25 July 1988, p. 6.

45   'He sat in that very chair . . .': Glenda Korporaal, 'The king of cable television', *Australian Financial Review*, 27 January 1984.

48   'I had three choices . . .': Ted Turner, National Press Club Luncheon, 27 September 1994. Transcript from Federal News Service.

49   Commitment to Wapping: The legal actions that grew out of Wapping would devote considerable time to arguing whether Murdoch always proposed to move all of his newspapers there. In hindsight one can say he was driven by a financial imperative to do so, whether or not it was a conscious decision. The close interweaving of developments in the US and the UK suggests Murdoch always saw Fox and Wapping as interconnected.

51   Murdoch's view of Michael Heseltine: From interview with former News International director, 1996.

52   Murdoch and the Australian Tax Office: Richard McGregor, 'Tax office queries Murdoch's returns', *Sydney Morning Herald*, 21 September 1985.

54 Gearing limit: The debt restriction was 110 per cent of equity.

55 'Under Australian accounting principles . . .': D. M. Osborne, 'Murdoch's Secret Weapon', *American Lawyer*, December 1993, p. 45.

CHAPTER 3

page

57 Telephone call to Anna: Related in book proposal prepared by Rupert Murdoch for an autobiography, September 1990.

60 'A smokescreen . . .': Stuart-Smith J, *News Group Newspapers Ltd and Others v SOGAT '82 and Others* [1987] ICR 181, [1986] IRLR 337. Queen's Bench Division, 31 July 1986.

60 'The *Post* was a ruse . . .': Andrew Neil, *Full Disclosure* (London: Macmillan, 1996), p. 97; Freelancing for MI5, p. 102; Murdoch railing at Adams, p. 125.

61 'Since the very first day . . .': Letter from Geoffrey Richards to Bruce Matthews, 20 December 1985, cited in Richard Belfield, Christopher Hird, Sharon Kelly, *Murdoch: The Decline of an Empire* (London: Macdonald, 1991), pp. 93–4.

62 For ease of comparison, in describing the issue of junk preferred stock, which was in US dollars, Australian share prices have also been converted into US currency at the then prevailing rate. News Corp stock actually traded in the US as American Depositary Receipts (ADRs), each of which included four News Corp shares. Initially, when the payback provision kicked in after three years (in March 1989), it would apply only to one sixteenth of the debt – that is, one sixteenth of the debt would increase by whatever proportion that the News Corp stock price had risen, while the rest of the debt would be unchanged. But each quarter after that, the proportion of debt affected by the new provision would ratchet up until by December 1992 it applied to the entire package of junk prefs.

NOTES ON SOURCES

CHAPTER 4

page

69   'Those next to him . . .': William Shawcross, *Murdoch: The Making of a Media Empire* (New York: Touchstone, 1993) 1997 edit.. p.363.

72   Geraldine Brooks, 'Murdoch', *The New York Times*, July 19 1998, Section 6, p. 20.

74   'I couldn't . . .': Interview with the author, February 2000.

74   Time zones: William Shawcross, *Murdoch*, actually alternates between the two dates, p. 15.

75   'An account manager . . .': Interview by Karen Maley, March 2000.

75   The author attended the ASC briefing at the request of Robin Chapman, who sought further details of the 1987 Queensland Press transaction. In July 1990 he had consulted Chapman, who was then a partner in a Brisbane legal firm, about the Queensland Press deal, in the course of researching a magazine article about a looming debt problem in the Murdoch family's private companies for *Australian Business*. While the article was never published, as a courtesy gesture the author later supplied a copy of the article to Chapman. This prompted her to launch the ASC inquiry. Adams' question at the ASC briefing about the effects of reversing the Queensland Press transaction was directed at the author.

78   'Best-heeled revealed by *Forbes*', *Advertising Age*, October 19 1987, p.104.

79   'I hope . . .': Nadine Brozan, 'The Evening Hours', *The New York Times*, October 16 1987. Section A p.26.

80   Cruden's correspondence: 'P G Chegwyn to Mr R J Wyatt dated 28 September 1987 with attached duplicate copy terms sheet', referred to in Australian Securities Commission, 'Report about an investigation into the affairs of Queensland Press Limited & Ors pursuant to section 17 of ASC Law," second draft, January 1993, paragraph 3.04. The ASC report, while never released, is quoted at length in the official response and comment to the report from Allen, Allen & Hemsley, representing Queensland Press Ltd, News Ltd, Cruden Investments and Queensland Press directors, addressed to Greg Tanzer, Queensland Regional General Counsel, Australian Securities Commission, 3 March 1993, p.8. John Atanaskovic is believed to have been the principal author of the Allen, Allen & Hemsley document.

63 ss3S3

81 Penthouse docket: Record of security in favour of Commonwealth Bank of Australia given by Rupert and Anna Murdoch, New York City UCC Filings, 21 October 1987. Discharged 24 December 1990. Filing number: 87PN61099, Lexis.

81 'In late 1987 . . .': Correspondence from Rupert Murdoch reproduced in Richard Belfield, Christopher Hird, Sharon Kelly, *Murdoch: The Decline of an Empire*, Macdonald & Co (London), 1991. p. 302.

81-2 Details of the deal are contained in the Allen, Allen & Hemsley response of 3 March 1993 to the ASC report (detailed above). Further details appear in *Commissioner of Stamps v Telegraph Investment Company & Anor*. FC 95/050, High Court of Australia, 21 December 1995. The case arose after officers of the South Australian Stamp Duties Office raided News Corporation's offices in Adelaide, and the Commissioner sought to impose $4 million in stamp duties on the Queensland Press transaction.

82 'Later that day . . .': Record of security in favour of Commonwealth Bank of Australia given by Rupert and Anna Murdoch, New York Department of State, UCC Record, 23 October 1987, Filing number 318155, discharged 25 January 1991.

82 New $A1 billion loan facility: Of the other $500 million, News Corp promptly on-loaned another $A170 million to Queensland Press for the stock purchase (using another loophole in the restriction on a company financing its own shares) and later loaned a further $A222 million to Dexenne Pty Ltd, a company half owned by Queensland Press, to buy the News Corp convertible notes held by Advertiser Newspapers.

82 'I dropped . . .': Deborah Light, *Sydney Morning Herald*, November 1987.

82 'The deal . . .': Conversation with the author, March 1996.

82 'It appears . . .': ASC, 'Report about an investigation into the affairs of Queensland Press Limited & Ors pursuant to section 17 of ASC Law', second draft, January 1993, paragraph 3.12. Quoted in Allen, Allen & Hemsley response to the ASC report, 3 March 1993, p.15; 'Doubly insulated': Summary of notes made by Keith McDonald of telephone conversation with John Atanaskovic, 17 November 1987, quoted in ASC, 'Report about an investigation', paragraph 3.10. Quoted in Allen, Allen & Hemsley, p.13; 'The books also indicate . . . ': ASC, 'Report about an investigation', paragraph 3.10, quoted in Allen, Allen & Hemsley, p. 6; 'Such conduct by a company

director . . .': ASC, 'Report about an investigation', paragraph 3.15, quoted in Allen, Allen & Hemsley, p.20.

83   Bank's termsheet: 'P G Chegwyn to Mr R J Wyatt dated 28 September 1987 with attached duplicate copy terms sheet', referred to in Australian Securities Commission, 'Report about an investigation into the affairs of Queensland Press Limited & Ors pursuant to section 17 of ASC Law', second draft, January 1993, paragraph 3.04. Quoted in Allen, Allen & Hemsley, p.8.

83   'Probably the most . . .': Allen, Allen & Hemsley, p. 11.

84   'Section 129(1)(A) . . .': Correspondence with the author, July 1990.

84   Allen, Allen & Hemsley, p.2; 'Although the investment was a large one', pp. 11, 16

84-5   Atanaskovic's comments are drawn from correspondence with the author, 10 April 2001.

87   US and Australian corporate filings show News Corp had $A633 million on its books as the holding value of its 44 per cent of Queensland Press. It had loaned Queensland Press $170 million directly, and of the joint $A1 billion debt facility with the Commonwealth bank, $A500 million went to Queensland Press. In addition News had loaned $A230 million to Dexenne, a total of $A1.53 billion.

87   Cost of Roland MAN presses: DM 800million.

88   Date of settlement: *Commissioner of Stamps v Telegraph Investment Company & Anor.* FC 95/050, High Court of Australia, 21 December 1995.

88   Only half of the $A1 billion loan was for Queensland Press. News used the other half to takeover Advertiser Newspapers, but both loan facilities shared the same lenders: Ida Picker, 'Bummer Dude! Inside the Murdoch workout', *Institutional Investor*, p.36. Advertiser's News Corp notes were sold into Dexenne Pty Ltd.

88   Skase comparison by ASC staffer was made in conversation with the author. 'Routine matter': ASC spokesperson Janet O'Connor in conversation with the author.

CHAPTER 5

page

92   'You're interested in fucking smart cards . . .': Recounted by Hundertmark to the author, October 1996. Early history of News

Datacom in Neil Chenoweth, 'Secret Empire', *Australian Financial Review*, 15 November 1996, Weekend Review, p. 1; Neil Chenoweth, 'Outsmarted', *Australian Financial Review*, 28 June 1996, Weekend Review, p. 1.

93   International Development Group; Bruce Hundertmark began legal action against Clinger in Israel in 1995, claiming that he and Clinger were to have equal shares in IDG, but that Clinger had defrauded him. News Corp subsequently claimed that Hundertmark had abused his position as an adviser to take a secret shareholding in NDSP through the IDG holding, so that any money retrieved from IDG should be paid to News Corporation. Hundertmark produced detailed diary notes that recorded a conversation in which he cleared his IDG holding with Rupert Murdoch. Hundertmark settled his dispute with News Corp on undisclosed grounds, but continued to press his action against Clinger in Israel.

94   'We are seeing the dawn . . .': *The Times*, 9 June 1998.

96   'Without his drive . . .': 'News Datacom sues former employees', *Cable & Satellite Express*, February 1996, p. 4.

97   'Mr Clinger left the country . . .': Telephone conversation with the author, 19 June 1996. Details of Clinger's SEC settlement in SEC Litigation Release No. 11503/27 July 1987, Accounting and Auditing Enforcement Release No. 142, *Securities and Exchange Commission v Michael Clinger and others* (US District Court for the District of Columbia, Civil Action No. 87–2070).

Clinger's claim of discussion with lawyer: Letter to the author from Michael Clinger, March 1997. Hundertmark's claim was made in conversation with the author, November 1996. The lawyer to whom Hundertmark says he sent his letter detailing Clinger's history declined to comment upon the allegation.

97   Topless girls and Disney logo: Michael Eisner, *Work in Progress* (London: Penguin, 1998), p. 347.

98   Murdoch's approach to Davis: Peter Chippindale & Suzanne Franks, *Dished!* (London: Simon & Schuster, 1991), p. 276.

'No cash has changed hands . . .': Neil Chenoweth, 'Mr Television: How Sam Chisholm saved Rupert Murdoch's bacon', *Australian Financial Review*, Weekend Review, p. 1.

98   False names, Melloward: Peter Chippindale & Suzanne Franks, *Dished!*, p. 279.

98 'BSB would not be dead . . .': Arden J, *Re BSB Holdings Ltd (No 2)* [1996] 1 BCLC 155, 28 July 1995.

99 BSB board meeting invalid: Arden J, *Re BSB Holdings Ltd (No 2)* [1996] 1 BCLC 155, Chancery Division, High Court, London, 28 July 1995.

100 'Clinger never paid the money . . .': Telephone conversation with the author, 19 June 1996.

101 'It's Rupert's technique . . .', 'Arthur really couldn't stand Frank . . .', 'Look, my heart can stand it . . .': Matthew Horsman, *Sky High* (London: Orion, 1997), p. 130.

102 'I have no evidence . . .': Lindsay J, News International & Others v Michael Clinger & Others, CH 1996 N4257 & 5450, No. 104, High Court, London, 17 November 1998. The account in this chapter is drawn from Justice Lindsay's detailed chronology of the development of the News Datacom business.

102 'Merely occasional, uninformed . . .': Justice Lindsay, 17 November 1998.

'You know, it is, how you say . . .'; 'Yeah, but you know . . .': transcript of tape provided by Leo Kreiger, cited in affidavit by Arthur Siskind, signed 16 February 1996, *News International & Others v Michael Clinger & Others*, 1996 N No. 104, High Court, London.

104 Date News management learned of Clinger's history: Telephone interviews with the author, June and November 1996. Of Hundertmark's claim that he informed a British lawyer about Clinger's history in 1989, Arthur Siskind told the author in a telephone conversation on 12 November 1996: 'It's not a matter that made its way to the top of News management.'

105 Vatistas young and inexperienced: Justice Lindsay, 17 November 1998.

CHAPTER 6

page

107 'I'm a great believer . . .': Interview of Hundertmark by the author, November 1996.

107 Account of Handbury and Murdoch conversation: Neil Chenoweth, 'New kid on the media block', *Bulletin*, 11 May 1993, p. 79.

109   'In those early days . . .': John Monks, *Elisabeth Murdoch: Two Lives* (Sydney: Macmillan, 1994), p. 308. Monks also details the round-robin of £50,000 in cheques in Giddy's office, p. 170. The details of Cruden shareholdings have been derived by the author from analysis of public filings by the Murdoch companies over the last 50 years. Cruden's annual revenues since 1970 were calculated from dividend and shareholding information in News Limited and News Corporation annual reports.

110   Cruden's issue of partly paid shares: In 1978 Kayarem was issued 392,000 B shares and 108,000 A shares in Cruden. The $2 shares were at an $8 premium, giving a total issue price of $5 million. Corporate filings show only $500,000 of this had been paid when they were absorbed in a share reconstruction. There is no record in the Corporate Affairs Commission filing that the final $4.5 million was paid up on these shares, though the record may be incomplete.

111   'We are reading . . .': Anna Maria Murdoch, 'Motherhood & Mythology: Summer Thoughts on Sex and Creativity', *Commonweal*: 31 August 1979, pp. 466–9. Niobe's seven sons and seven daughters were killed by Apollo and Artemis after she boasted that her children's beauty rivalled theirs.

113   'Part-person. Parturition . . .': Anna Murdoch, 'Motherhood & Mythology', p. 467; 'Is that all there is?', p. 469.

113   The Murdoch household: Philip Townsend, *Just Rupert*, serialised in 'Murdoch by his butler', *Punch*, Issues 58–59, 4–17 July 1998, 18–31 July 1998.

113   It was Anna . . . : Quoted in Louise McElvogue, '. . . And the other front-runners in the family', *Guardian*, 22 April 1996, p. T17.

114   'He is a very good . . .': *Washington Post*, 23 October 1985.

114   Anna 'had buried herself . . .': Thomas Kiernan, *Citizen Murdoch* (New York: Dodd Mead & Co, 1986), p. 284.

115   'You'd be wrong to say . . .': Conversation with the author, October 1993. Neil Chenoweth, 'The story behind News' super shares', *Australian Financial Review*, 3 November 1993, p. 1.

115   'No one was banging . . .': Conversation with the author, October 1993. Neil Chenoweth, 'The story behind News' super shares', *Australian Financial Review*, 3 November 1993, p. 1.

116   'There's been a bit of money . . .': Conversation with the author, May 1993.

116   'Some will piss it . . .': Philip Townsend, *Just Rupert*, serialised in *Punch*, Issues 58–59, 4–17 July 1998.

CHAPTER 7

page

119   Murdoch does not really exist: Peter Bart, 'The Back Lot; 'Rupe Group' theory explains multiple Murdochs', *Daily Variety*, 29 July 1996.

121   'The country creates a tidal wave . . .': Elise O'Shaughnessy, 'The New Establishment', *Vanity Fair*, October 1994, p. 222.

121   'Where smart people go to talk . . .': Alan Citron, 'When Herb Allen talks, star makers listen', *Los Angeles Times*, 2 July 1993, Part D, p. 4.

121   'Circus animals . . .': David Lieberman, Tom Lowry, 'Media titans meet again, Allen & Co conference draws big players; What will they cook up this time?', *USA Today*, 9 July 1996, p. 1B.

121   'It's a bazaar . . .': Jane Martinson, 'Cyber stars corralled at the ranch', *Guardian*, 10 July 1999, p. 27.

123   'That's not the question . . .': Howard Anderson, 'The Man Who Would Be Media King', *Upside*, Vol. 9, No. 8, pp. 110–16.

124   'Trying to catch Rupert . . .', 'John's just saying that . . .': Diane Mermigas, 'What's Murdoch want? Programming', *Electronic Media*, 7 October 1996, p. 8.

124   'It's no different . . .': Elise O'Shaughnessy, 'The New Establishment', *Vanity Fair*, October 1994, p. 227.

125   'Herbie and the boys . . .': David Lieberman, Tom Lowry, 'Media titans meet again, Allen & Co conference draws big players; What will they cook up this time?' *USA Today*, 9 July 1996, p. 1B.

125   'They're all short . . .': Mark Warbis, 'Playground of the Rich Unphased by Gathering of Media, Computer Moguls', Associated Press, 9 July 1999. Sourced on Lexis.

125   'I think I hate the little midget . . .': Julian Borger, 'Disney admits defeat in $580m suit; Settlement ends long-running dispute with "little midget"', *Guardian*, 8 July 1999, p. 23.

125   'Stand him on the desk . . .': Porter Bibb, *It Aint As Easy As It Looks* (Boulder: Johnson Books, 1993).

126   'It's funny . . .': Interview on *Larry King Live*, CNN, 12 September 1994.

126   Arrangements are made: Tom Lowry, 'Chats, rafts – but no word on deals', *USA Today*, 11 July 1996, p. 10B.

126   Murdoch's raft trip: Ian Vevvender, 'CBD', *Sydney Morning Herald*, 23 May 1991, p. 31. An alternative version of this story puts this incident in Alaska.

126 Katzenberg's Supersoaker: Michael Eisner with Jack Schwartz, *Work in Progress* (London: Penguin, 1998), p. 361.

126 Schneider's awards: Elise O'Shaugnessy, 'The New Establishment', *Vanity Fair*, October 1994, p. 222.

126 'The biggest prick in Hollywood': 'Letter from Camp Allen', *Vanity Fair*, October 1996, p. 109. Founding Dream Works SKG: Kevin Maney, 'Paul Allen's eclectic empire', *USA Today*, 21 March 1005, p. 1B.

127 Disney/ABC deal: Michael Eisner with Tony Schwartz, *Work in Progress*, pp. 363–5. Warren Buffet's letter to Berkshire Hathaway shareholders, reproduced in 'This year, Buffet's letter highlights Geico; Letter quotes JFK, Woody Allen, Gilbert & Sullivan', *USA Today*, 18 March 1996, p. 4B.

127 'The pioneers that have made America . . .': Interview on *Larry King Live*, CNN, 12 September 1994.

128 Bill Gates and Internet: 'Bill Gates: Interview', *Playboy*, July 1994, Vol. 41, No. 7, p. 55.

128 'Andy Grove set me down . . .': Charles Dubow, 'Getting On Line with Herb Allen', *Forbes*, 30 April 1999.

129 Ovitz search for Katzenberg: Claudia Eller and Sallie Hofmeister, 'Ovitz smoothing feathers around town', *Los Angeles Times*, 20 September 1996, Part D, p. 4.

129 Diller's claim of brokering meeting: 'Letter from Camp Allen', *Vanity Fair*, October 1996, p. 109.

129 Murdoch and Perelman meet on the porch: Geraldine Fabrikant, 'Murdoch Bets Heavily on a Global Vision', *New York Times*, 29 July 1996, Section D, p. 1.

129 Court-appointed psychiatrist: William Neuman, Bill Sanderson, 'Mind games in Revlon divorce', *New York Post*, 7 December 1998.

130 'Which market?': *Electronic Media*, 2 January 1995, p. 12.

130 'Rupert is driving . . .': Ted Turner, National Press Club address, 27 September 1994. Transcript from Federal News Service.

132 'This has caused . . .': Address to shareholders, News Corp annual general meeting, 18 October 1994.

139 'He had me over a barrel . . .': Geraldine Fabrikant, 'Murdoch Bets Heavily on a Global Vision', *New York Times*, 29 July 1996, Section D, p. 1.

000 'Murdoch's view . . .': Geraldine Fabrikant, 'Murdoch Bets Heavily on a Global Vision', p. 1.

CHAPTER 8

page

142   'Actually, Rupert took it very well': Kim Masters, Bryan Burrough, 'Cable Guys', *Vanity Fair*, January 1997, pp. 64, 125.

143   Morgenthau's comments: Associated Press, 29 June 1992.

144   'What the hell . . .': David Henry, Scott Ladd, '*Post*'s Fiscal Physical', *Newsday*, 24 February 1993, City edition, p. 28.

144   'I am assuming . . .': Martin Peers, 'Three cheers for Murdoch,' 31 March 1993, *Australian Financial Review*, p. 19.

146   'He's ten years older . . .': 'Poised for the home run – Ted Turner founder of Cable Network News', *Financial Times*, 20 September 1993.

146   'I can't hate him . . .': Matt Roush, 'Ratings, Rivals and Ted Turner', *USA Today*, 12 July 1994, p. 3D.

146   Murdoch's speech honouring Turner: *Newsday*, 10 April 1994.

146   'Ted Turner has been . . .': Rupert Murdoch, Transcript of news conference, Federal Document Clearing House Political Transcripts, 26 February 1996, Sourced on Lexis.

147   'Money is something . . .': Richard Karlz, 'Ailes Talks Tough on Fox Launch', *Multichannel News*, 23 September 1996, p. 3.

148   At $11 each: the deals are too labyrinthine to uncover. This was the same month that TCI and News Corp closed the deal to set up the Fox Sports venture, and TCI ended up with a small stake in Murdoch's Star TV in Hong Kong. TCI reported that it received $100 million more in the deal than News Corp reported that it had paid.

149   'They were within . . .': Diane Mermigas, 'Murdoch Vows Action Against Time Warner', *Electronic Media*, 23 September 1996, p. 1.

150   Fox News budget: David Lieberman, 'Ailes Tackles Toughest Assignment', *USA Today*, 23 September 1996, p. 9B.

150   'What the hell happened?': Kim Masters, Bryan Burrough, 'Cable Guys', *Vanity Fair*, January 1997, p. 125.

150   'an enormous breach of faith . . .': David Lieberman, 'Time Warner Picks MSNBC over Fox News', *USA Today*, 20 September 1996, p. 1B.

150   'We were dealt with . . .': David Lieberman, 'Fox TV Chief Says Time "Lied"', *USA Today*, 23 September 1996, p. 9B. Bill Carter, 'Fox Reacts Angrily to Move by Time Warner on Cable', *New York Times*, 21 September 1996, Sec. 1, p. 32.

150   'We have a contract . . .': Diane Mermigas, 'Murdoch Vows Action Against Time Warner', *Electronic Media*, 23 September 1996, p. 1.

151   'These were not Adam- and Eve-like innocents . . .': Judge Jack B. Weinstein, *Fox News Network LLC v. Time Warner Inc et al*, 96-CV-4963 US District Court for the Eastern District of New York, 1997 US Dist. Lexis 6940, 16 May 1997.

151   'It is quite possible . . .': Diane Mermigas, 'Murdoch Vows Action Against Time Warner', *Electronic Media*, 23 September 1996, p. 1.

151   Details of events drawn from Judge Denise Cote, *Warner Cable of New York City and others v. City of New York, Bloomberg LP*, 96 CIV. 7736 (DLC), District Court for the Southern District of New York, 943 F. Supp. 1357; 1996 US Dist. Lexis 16479, 6 November 1996.

152   'This kind of venal rhetoric . . .': Martin Peers et al, 'Will Clash of Titans Leave Bruises Across the Biz?', *Variety*, 30 September 1996, p. 11. Arthur Spielgelman, 'Ted Turner and Rupert Murdoch are at War', Reuters, 27 September 1996.

153   'Paper over the deal': Details of Fran Reiter's meeting and comments made drawn from Judge Dennis Cote, *Warner Cable of New York City and others v. City of New York, Bloomberg LP*; also described in Kim Masters, Bryan Burrough, 'Cable Guys', *Vanity Fair*, January 1997.

153   'You don't have to lecture us . . .': Quoted in Judge Denise Cote, *Warner Cable of New York City and others v. City of New York, Bloomberg LP*.

154   'Very unpleasant and unnecessary . . .': Quoted in Judge Denise Cote, *Warner Cable of New York City and others v. City of New York, Bloomberg LP*.

154   'By fair means or foul': Judge Denise Cote, *Warner Cable of New York City and others v. City of New York, Bloomberg LP*.

154   'To beat Time Warner': Judge Jack B. Weinstein, *Fox News v. Time Warner Inc et al*, 10 April 1997.

155   'A frivolous piece of junk . . .': Gary Levin, 'Fox Sues TW over NY Cable', *Daily Variety*, 10 October 1996, p. 3.

155   'Very fundamental issues . . .': Kent Gibbons, 'See You in Court, Rudy', *Multichannel News*, 14 October 1996, p. 1.

CHAPTER 9

page

158 The 31 March 1995 meeting and its aftermath is described in an affidavit by Arthur Siskind, 16 February 1996, filed in the High Court action against Clinger, paragraph 59, p. 18; and an accompanying affidavit by Greg Clark of February 1996.

158 Nantel's claim: An extensive description of the fraud is contained in Justice Lindsay's 17 November 1998 judgment in *News International & Others v Michael Clinger & Others*, CH 1996 N4257 & 5450, No. 104, High Court, London, paragraphs 26–139.

158 'Peter is aware . . .': Greg Clark affidavit, February 1996, filed in the High Court action against Clinger.

159 Details of Fischer's meeting: Robert Lindsay, 'A&O fails to get injunction after faxed evidence blunder', *The Lawyer*, London, 2 June 1998, p. 48.

159 'To enable him . . .': Affidavit by Arthur Siskind, 16 February 1996, filed in the High Court action against Clinger, paragraph 73.

160 'We know everything . . .': Johnnie L. Roberts with Mark Dennis, 'Villain or victim?', *Newsweek*, 4 November 1996, p. 40.

160 'There is a message to be sent . . .': Neil Chenoweth, 'Secret Empire', *Australian Financial Review*, 15 November 1996. Weekend Review, p. 1. Based on telephone interview with the author, 12 November 1996.

160 Clay Harris comments: Telephone interview with the author, 27 June 1996. Neil Chenoweth, 'Secret Empire', *Australian Financial Review*, 15 November 1996. Weekend Review, p. 1. In a telephone conversation with the author on 25 June 1996, Siskind said: 'During the course of the investigation it came to our attention that Mr Clinger had made many phone calls to Mr Lewis, including calls to his home.'

160 'We have not engaged . . .': Telephone interview with the author, 12 November 1996. Reported in Neil Chenoweth, 'Secret Empire', *Australian Financial Review*, 15 November 1996. Weekend Review, p. 1.

160 Hundertmark attack: Interview with the author, November 1996.

161 Standard practice for research companies: Interview with author, 12 November 1996.

161   Clinger's tax agreement: Justice Lindsay, *News International v. Michael Clinger et al*, CH1996 N4257 & 545, interim judgment 11 November 1996.

162   'Mr Clinger has the tiger . . .': Interview with the author, 12 November 1996.

163   High Court case: *News International v. Michael Clinger et al*, CH1996 N4257 & 545.

164   Call to Evans-Lombe: Details of this call and Sheppard's allegations are drawn from a judgment by Justice Lindsay on 10 February 1997. *News International v. Michael Clinger et al*, CH1996 N4257 & 545.

165   'If any tape recordings exist . . .': Facsimile letter to the author, 4 March 1997. Clinger described the News Datacom building as a high-security installation, with continuous video monitoring and with access controlled by keys, smart cards and a code, with guards on call, with Peled's office situated in a section of the office with even more security. By facsimile to the author on 11 March 1997. Gavenchak denied that access to the News Datacom building was via keys, smartcards and a code, and said that Peled's office was used as a conference room. She declined to give more details. Clinger repeated his claim and said that Peled's office had not been used as a conference room since the early 1990s, while only three people knew the combination for Peled's office safe. He said the security precautions were necessary because the very nature of News Datacom business was encryption and the need for secrecy.

166   Testimony by Sheppard, Kirsch and Jerusalem District Attorney: Conversation between the author and Audley Sheppard, March 1997.

166   A week after Sheppard's call to Evans-Lombe, Clifford Chance stopped acting for Clinger. News Corporation drew an adverse inference from this. In correspondence with the author, Clinger said Clifford Chance was too expensive for him in what was becoming a very costly court case. Certainly it was not clear that Clinger showed any more enthusiasm for paying his lawyers than he showed for paying anybody to whom he owed money. Sheppard did not comment upon the reason for the switch, but said Clifford Chance continued to be concerned about the possibility that some telephone conversations had been recorded.

CHAPTER 10

page

168   'They were so outraged . . .': William Shawcross, 'Murdoch's New Life', *Vanity Fair*, October 1999, No. 470, p. 186.

170   'That's Charlie . . .': Rebecca Cantwell and John Accola, 'Echostar's Charles Ergen's gambling savvy serves him well in the satellite TV game', *Denver Rocky Mountain News*, 29 December 1996, p. 2B.

170   'We honestly believed . . .': Jim Carrier, 'Dish was doorway to dream; Satellite TV pioneer sets industry agenda', *Denver Post*, 22 September 1996, p. 1–01.

170   'A gust of wind . . .': Rebecca Cantwell and John Accola, 'Echostar's Charles Ergen's gambling savvy serves him well in the satellite TV game', *Denver Rocky Mountain News*, 29 December 1996, p. 2B.

172   'I'm not worried about . . .': Details of Malone's appearance from Australian journalist Mark Furness of the *Australian Financial Review*, who spoke to Malone shortly after the announcement. Malone's comment was widely reported by Furness and others.

173   'Both of us felt . . .': Rebecca Cantwell and John Accola, *Denver Rocky Mountain News*, 29 December 1996, p. 2B.

173   Details of bidding drawn from FCC filings.

173   'We weren't going to bid . . .': Stephen Keating, 'TCI quits satellite TV bidding; EchoStar, MCI in hot competition', *Denver Post*, 25 January 1997, p. C-01. Bidding details from FCC filings.

174   '[Ergen] is a smart guy . . .': *Communications Today*, 25 January 1996.

174   'DeFranco and I . . .': Rebecca Cantwell and John Accola, 'Echostar's Charles Ergen's gambling savvy serves him well in the satellite TV game', *Denver Rocky Mountain News*, 29 December 1996, p. 2B.

175   'There is no business model . . .': *Denver Post*, 25 January 1997, p. C-01.

175   MCI pulling out: Ostensibly MCI had committed to invest only $2 billion in News convertible stock, but if News used this to fund its half share of ASkyB, MCI would have to outlay another $2 billion to match it, on top of the $672 million licence fee, which as a foreign company News could not hold or pay for.

176   '[Murdoch] extracts so much blood . . .': Martin Peers, 'News Corp satellite TV plan stumbles', *Business Review Weekly*, Australia, 2 December 1996, p. 26.

177   'The fever has broken': Martin Peers, 'Murdoch Gets the Cold Shoulder from MCI', *Business Review Weekly*, 2 December 1996, p. 26; *Business Review Weekly*, 16 December 1996, p. 48. *Broadcasting & Cable*, 9 December 1996, No. 51, Vol. 126, p. 64.

177   'Treat the plaintiffs' answer . . . as conclusive . . .': Justice Lindsay, *News International & Others v. Michael Clinger & Others*, CH 1996 N4257 & 5450, No. 104, High Court, London, 10 February 1997.

177   Lindsay ruling: Things were looking up in Israel as well. Two weeks after Murdoch's UJA dinner with the tribute from Prime Minister Netanyahu, the Israeli Finance Minister resigned in a party power struggle. He was replaced by former Justice Minister Ja'kov Ne'eman (newly vindicated after charges of witness tampering). Outside of politics Ne'eman headed the corporate division of Herzog, Fuchs and Ne'eman, which were the News Datacom lawyers raided eight months before. This did not affect the impartiality of the Israeli taxman, but for News shareholders the prospect that its former lawyer now headed the department which was investigating the company for tax fraud was strangely warming.

179   News Corp accounting: Neil Chenoweth, 'Murdoch and the $1bn Gap', *Australian Financial Review*, 21 March 1998, p. 1.

179   'Charlie, you remind me . . . ': Stephen Keating, *Cutthroat* (Boulder: Johnson Brooks, 1999), p. 24.

179   'The personal chemistry . . .' and 'one little bank away . . .': Interview of Ergen by *Australian Financial Review* journalist Eric Ellis, March 1997.

180   'Our competition isn't . . .': Jack Egan, 'For Satellite Television, the Limit is the Sky', *US News & World Report*, 3 March 1997, p. 54.

180   'News Corp made sense': Interview of Ergen by *Australian Financial Review* journalist Eric Ellis, March 1997.

181   Ergen overruled his advisers: 'First amended complaint', *Echostar Communications Corporation v. The News Corporation Limited*, 96–960, Colorado District Court, paragraphs 27–8. News Corporation's defence contested both these paragraphs in the Echostar complaint.

182   Peled interview: Eugenie Gavenchak, deputy general counsel of News America publishing, stated in correspondence with the author in March 1997: 'Mr Peled had scheduled appointments one month and two weeks in advance of his meetings with the Tax Authority and the National Serious Crime Unit for the purpose of assisting in their investigations and presenting News's evidence as to the facts. He was not met at the airport, escorted anywhere or detained by any government authority.'

182   'Our goal is not to be complementary . . .': Tom Skotnicki, 'News Corp reaches for the Sky', *Advertiser*, Adelaide, 26 February 1997, p. 42.

182   'Four years ago . . .': *Rocky Mountain News*, 25 February 1997, p. 1B.

182   'We never want to be beholden . . .': 'Why Investors in News Are Smiling', *Sydney Morning Herald*, 28 May 1997, p. 30.

182   'Rupert may have known . . .': Terry McCrann, 'Murdoch's American appetites', *Australian*, 1 March 1997, p. 25.

182   'The presentation of the deal . . .': Stephen Keating, *Cutthroat*, p. 30.

183   'We're aiming for the big cable market . . .': Stephen Keating, *Cutthroat*, p. 26.

183   'Plan A: Hope Murdoch's plans . . .': *Cutthroat*, p. 206.

184   'Rupert, we're trying to sell . . .': Stephen Keating, *Cutthroat*, p. 207.

184   'Rupert Murdoch is an old friend . . .': 'Cable sees clouds in Sky', *Broadcasting & Cable*, 24 March 1997, p. 53.

184   'internal rhetoric': 'Heard at last week's National Cable Television Assn. Convention', *The Hollywood Reporter*, 25 March 1997.

184   Sky business plan: *United States of America v. Primestar Inc., et al*, 1:98CV01193, US District Court, District of Columbia, 12 May 1998.

CHAPTER 11

page

185   'Rupert Murdoch at his best . . .': 'Who's afraid of Rupert Murdoch', *Frontline*, PBS, 1 January 1995.

185   'Historically, copyright legislation . . .': Matt Pottinger, 'Murdoch Calls on Congress to Remove Legislative Hurdles', State News Service, 10 April 1997. Sourced on Lexis.

186   'I don't know . . .': Ariana Huffington, 'Newt returns a changed man', *Chicago Sun-Times*, 13 April 1997, p. 35.

187   'In two years we've come . . .': Maureen Dowd, 'Genghis Newt', *New York Times*, 9 April 1997, Section A, p. 21.

187   'A bit of a hobby . . .': Edmund L. Andrews, 'Mr Murdoch Goes To Washington', *New York Times*, 23 July 1995, Section 3, p. 1.

187   'It was like he'd seen . . .': Ken Silverstein, 'His biggest takeover: How Murdoch bought Washington', *The Nation*, 8 June 1998, p. 18.

189   'I am particularly fond . . .': Michael Gill, 'Satellite celebration of brave news world', *Australian Financial Review*, 3 September 1993, p. 5.

190   'Those of us who make our living . . .': Rupert Murdoch, 'The Century of Networking', Eleventh Annual John Bonython Lecture, Centre for Independent Studies, Melbourne, 20 October 1994.

191   Details of royalties payment, and *Nineteen Eighty-Four* is still the most important book . . .': 'Huber's Orwellian Act', *Information Law Alert: A Voorhees Report*, 30 November 1994, No. 19, Vol. 2.

191   'We are all becoming broadcasters . . .' and following quotes: '*The Progress Report with Newt Gingrich*' 15 August 1995. Transcript accessed by Lexis, June 1996.

192   'The current view of the World Wide Web . . .': David Bicknell. 'Only in America', *Computer Weekly*, 19 October 1995, p. 42.

193   'We should do everything possible . . .': Benjamin Wittes, 'Telecom Bill Empowers Agency', *Legal Times*, 5 June 1995, p. 1.

193   Book on FCC: Peter Huber, *Law and Disorder in Cyberspace: Abolish the FCC and Let Common Law Rule the Telecosm*, (Oxford: Oxford University Press, 1997).

194   'Jabbed his finger . . .': 'Press Clips', *Village Voice*, 13 December 1994, p. 8.

194   Gingrich-Murdoch meeting: Karen Tumulty, 'When Rupert Met Newt', *Time*, 23 January 1995, p. 34.

195   'bizarre', 'sick', 'cheat' . . .: Jill Lawrence, Jessica Lee, 'Gingrich's triumph and debacle: GOPAC', *USA Today*, 16 January 1997, p. 8A.

195   'Described what we need to do . . .': Donna Kelley, 'Text of Gingrich Press Conference on His Book Deal', 30 December 1994, CNN Transcript, Sourced on Lexis.

196   'The most insignificant meeting . . .': Karen Tumulty, 'When Rupert Met Newt', *Time*, 23 January 1995, p. 34.

196   'It was a ten-minute meeting . . .': Ken Auletta, *The Highwaymen* (New York: Random House, 1997), p. 283.

196   'Right at the end . . .': Karen Tumulty, 'When Rupert Met Newt', *Time*, 23 January 1995, p. 34.

196   'They said something about . . .': *Communications Daily*, 18 January 1995, p. 9.

196   'And that's when I immediately began . . .': Katharine Q. Seelye, 'Murdoch, Joined by Lobbyist, Talked of Regulatory Problem at Meeting with Gingrich', *New York Times*, 15 January 1997, Section 1, p. 18.

197   'I was telephoned in Beijing . . .': Auletta, *The Highwaymen*, p. 287.

197   'I'm so sorry that I'm late . . .': Transcript, 'News conference with House Majority Whip David Bonior (D-MI)', Federal News Service, 22 December 1994. Accessed by Lexis. Bonior's reference to $4 million was apparently a reference to the Penguin USA bid.

198   Gingrich royalty payments: Timothy J. Burger and Jennifer Bradley, 'It's D-Day on Hill (As in Disclosure): Gingrich Book Nets Less Than $500K', *Roll Call*, 17 June 1996; David Eisenstadt, 'Newt opens books on literary front', *Daily News*, New York, 15 June 1996, p. 9.

200   'If anyone ever says . . .': Christopher Stern, 'Piqued pols left holding phone', *Variety*, 17 March 1997.

201   'It's a silly premise . . .': Matt Pottinger, 'Murdoch Calls on Congress to Remove Legislative Hurdles', State News Service, 10 April 1997. Sourced on Lexis.

201   'More specific information . . .': Matt Pottinger, 'Murdoch Calls on Congress to Remove Legislative Hurdles', State News Service, 10 April 1997. Sourced on Lexis.

201   'It's too much, too soon . . .': Matt Pottinger, 'Murdoch Calls on Congress to Remove Legislative Hurdles', State News Service, 10 April 1997. Sourced on Lexis.

201   'Copyright issues are complex . . .' and 'All the hearings in the world . . .': David Leiberman, 'Murdoch No Longer Reaching for Sky? Media Giant may shift focus to Primestar', *USA Today*, 11 April 1997.

202   'Nothing that (Murdoch) does . . .', 'You don't have a deal . . .', 'Uh, not this wife': Edited transcript of interview with Larry

King, 'NCTA 1997 wrap-up: Turner speaks up (as usual)', *Electronic Media*, 24 March 1997, p. 36.

203 'It's never going to get off the ground . . .': Michael Burgi, Richard Katz, 'What Business are We in Anyway?' *Mediaweek*, 24 March 1997.

203 'Every meeting we've had . . .': Fred Dawson, John M. Higgins, 'Cable Puts on Brave Face Amid Worries', *Multichannel News*, 24 March 1997, p. 1.

203 'If Rupert Murdoch gets malaria': Michael Burgi, Richard Katz, 'What Business are We in Anyway?' *Mediaweek*, 24 March 1997.

203 Marcus-News Corp meeting: Sally Hofmeister, 'Murdoch Outfoxing Himself with New Satellite Venture?' *Los Angeles Times*, 12 March 1997, Part D, p. 1.

203 'A slow no . . .': Justice Department statement of claim, *US v. Primestar Inc and others*, Civil No.: 98CV01193 (JLG), District Court, District of Columbia, 12 May 1998, paragraph 54.

203 'I don't think, generally . . .': Fred Dawson, John M. Higgins, 'Cable Puts on Brave Face Amid Worries', *Multichannel News*, 24 March 1997, p. 1.

204 '(ASkyB) will be a formidable competitor . . .': Malone's memo and O'Brien's comment in statement of claim, *US v. Primestar Inc and others*, Civil No.: 1: 98CV01193 (JLG), District Court, District of Columbia, 12 May 1998, paragraphs 53, 101.

204 'Let's not whale . . .', '. . . lunacy . . .' and 'What is Plan B? . . .': statement of claim, *US v. Primestar Inc and others*, paragraphs 54, 58.

204 'I wouldn't be surprised . . .', 'You don't take Rupert lightly . . .': Justice Department, *US v. Primestar Inc and others*, paragraph 53.

204 Murdoch-Malone meeting: David Leiberman, 'Murdoch No Longer Reaching for Sky? Media Giant may shift focus to Primestar', *USA Today*, 11 April 1997.

205 'He called to say . . .': Stephen Keating, *Cutthroat*, p. 211.

205 'I haven't heard anything . . .': Kent Gibbons and John M. Higgins, 'Murdoch Notion Dashed; Primestar rolls-up rolls along', *Multichannel News*, 21 April 1997.

206 Hindery 'a peacemaker . . .': *US v. Primestar Inc and others*, paragraph 56.

206 Clashes over linoleum: Padden's plan for the glass-lit lobby of the Phoenix uplink facility had been a '150-foot-long granite wall of water . . . with finishes of cherrywood, marble stainless steel and

terrazzo': Ken Western, 'Rupert Murdoch hastens building of Arizona TV broadcast facility', *Arizona Republic*, 20 February 1997.

206   '(News Corporation) cannot agree . . .': 'First amended complaint', *Echostar Communications Corporation v. The News Corporation Limited*, 96–960, Colorado District Court, paragraph 51.

207   'It's dead . . .': Stephen Keating, p. 213.

207   'The reality that I did not have a job . . .': *Electronic Media*, 5 May 1997, p. 1A.

207   'From what I understand . . .': 'Digital Jam', CNN, 2 May 1997. Transcript accessed through Lexis.

207   Meeting at Denver airport: 'First amended complaint', *Echostar Communications Corporation v. The News Corporation Limited*, 96–960, Colorado District Court, paragraphs 60–1.

207   Writ on the kitchen table: Stephen Keating, *Cutthroat*, p. 214.

207   Onerous terms: The $3.5 billion figure represents opportunity cost, due to the unusual terms that Ergen built into the settlement agreement (see Chapter 16). News Corp wrote off only $375 million, much of which it would have recovered when it sold its rising Echostar stock. Neil Chenoweth, 'The Man Who Outfoxed Rupert Murdoch', *Australian Financial Review*, 24 June 1999, p. 1.

CHAPTER 12

page

209   'You can say what you like . . .': Andrew Neil, *Full Disclosure* (London: Macmillan, 1996), p. 166.

210   Televangelists 'have greater unrestricted access to media . . .': Richard N. Ostling, 'Power, Glory – And Politics', *Time*, 17 February 1986, p. 62.

211   'socialist anti-family political movement . . .': Fidelma Cook, 'I love gays and lesbians but I hate their sins and wicked ways', *Mail on Sunday*, 2 May 1999, pp. 18–19.

211   'You're supposed to be nice . . .': Gregory Palast, 'Inside Corporate America', *Observer*, 23 May 1999, Business section, p. 4.

211   'I have been on TV . . .': Fidelma Cook, 'I love gays and lesbians but I hate their sins and wicked ways', *Mail on Sunday*, p. 18.

212   'Pat's not going to live forever . . .' and 'It was an eye-opener . . .':
       Mark O'Keefe, 'Pat Robertson's ever-growing business king-
       dom', *Virginian-Pilot*, 19 June 1994, p. D1.

212   'I make no bones about it . . .': Mark A. Perigard, 'Family
       matters', *Boston Herald*, 27 April 1997, p. 6.

213   'We buy it . . .' and 'We buy where . . .': Jim Forkan, 'Family
       bumps "700 Club" for crime time', *Multichannel News*, 12 May
       1997, p. 19.

213   'I personally funded . . .': Letter to the author, 10 November 2000.

214   Description of attack on Naghiu: Judge Murray M. Schwartz,
       Leslie Naghiu and Laverne Naghiu v. Intercontinental Hotels Group,
       Delaware District Court, 94–437. 165 F R D 413; 1996 US Dist.
       Lexis 2263, 23 February 1996 judgment.

214   'Today I am still at a loss . . .': Letter to the author, 10 November
       2000.

215   'You can look at it one way . . .': Fidelma Cook, 'I love gays and
       lesbians but I hate their sins and wicked ways', *Mail on Sunday*, p.
       19.

217   'They basically thought . . .': Lynne Heffley, 'Low-Tech Equals
       High Ratings', *Los Angeles Times*, 25 November 1993.

217   'You're right – you're too old . . .': Tim Carvell and Joe
       McGowan, 'Showdown in Toontown', *Fortune*, 28 October
       1996, p.100.

218   Details of Fox-Saban deal: Preliminary prospectus for Fox Kids
       Worldwide Inc, Securities & Exchange Commission, 27
       September 1996.

219   Saban's links with Clinton: Michael Weisskopf, Charles R.
       Babcock, 'Donors Pay and Stay at White House', *Washington
       Post*, 15 December 1996, p. A1. David Finnigan, *Hollywood
       Reporter*, 8 September 1999.

219   Progress of IFE deal: Details of Robertson's negotiations in this
       chapter are drawn from International Family Entertainment Inc's
       Proxy Statement, Securities & Exchange Commission, filed 25
       June 1997, pp. 5–14.

220   Pat Robertson's cold feet.: Michael Burgi, 'Murdoch and Malone
       Pursue Joint Bid for IFE', *Media Week*, 10 February 1997, p. 8.

220   'I think it's firmly on the rocks . . .': Andrew Collier, 'Robertson
       Snag in sale of IFE,' *Hollywood Reporter*, 18 February 1997.

221   'We were really neutral in it . . .': *Advertising Age*, 29 September
       1997.

221   'We want to remain partners . . .': 'News Corp Family talks "on track"', *Broadcasting & Cable*, 14 April 1997, p. 10.

221   'Let's not whale . . .' and 'What is Plan B?' from statement of claim, *US v. Primestar Inc and others*, paragraphs 54, 58.

222   8 April meeting: International Family Entertainment Inc's Proxy Statement, Securities & Exchange Commission, filed 25 June 1997, pp. 5–14.

223   'I was offered a substantial premium . . .': Letter to author, 10 November 2000.

224   'There's the medical strike force . . .': Bill Sizemore, 'Operation Blessing planes were used mostly for diamond mining, 2 pilots say; Pat Robertson's spokesman says planes were used, but as a benevolent gesture and Robertson reimbursed the relief group', *Virginian-Pilot* (Norfolk, Va.) 27 April 1997, p. A1.

224   Reimbursement for planes: Bill Sizemore, 'Inquiry faults Operation Blessing; But diamond-mine questions won't lead to action against charity', *Virginian-Pilot*, 18 June 1999, p. A1.

225   'I've turned my cheek . . .': Liz Szabo, 'Robertson: Pilot's report on inquiry is 'wrong'; Operation Blessing solicitations were focus of investigation', *Virginian-Pilot*, 22 July 1999, p. A1.

225   'My relief efforts in Zaire . . .' and 'We gave up about $150 million . . .': Letter to author, 10 November 2000.

226   'When hell freezes over . . .': *Daily Variety*, 28 January 1997, p. 1; 17 January 1997, p. 1; 5 February 1997.

CHAPTER 13

page

229   'Coca Cola plumbing . . .': Robert A. Jones, 'Hearts of the City: H2 O'Malley, with regret', *Los Angeles Times*, 8 January 1997, Part B, p. 2.

229   'I think family ownership . . .': Robert A. Jones, 'Hearts of the city', Part B, p. 2.

230   'But I'm not saying that absolutely . . .': Eric Ellis, 'Murdoch 'hesitating' about buying the Dodgers', *Australian Financial Review*, 20 January 1997, p. 10.

231   'He wanted to know . . .': James Bates, 'Watch the money; Like it or not, Rupert Murdoch is touching the lives of everyone in

southern California. How can anyone predict where he'll strike next?' *Los Angeles Times Magazine*, 31 January 1999, p. 10.

232 'I was astonished . . .': Connie Bruck, 'The Big Hitter', *New Yorker*, 8 December 1997, p. 82.

232 'He's not dancing on the roof . . .': James Bates, 'Watch the money', p. 10.

232 'The first time we met . . .': Connie Bruck, 'The Big Hitter', p. 82.

233 'The previous holders . . .': Michael Kinsley, 'Rupertvision', *Sporting News*, 2 January 1995.

234 'Rupert was a crazy man.': Connie Bruck, 'The Big Hitter', p. 86.

238 'I love the game . . .'; 'Whatever happens . . .': Justice Burchett, *News Limited v. Australian Rugby Football League and others*, NG 197 of 1995, Fed No. 72/96 Federal Court of Australia, 23 February 1996.

238 'Accepting the honesty . . .': Justice Burchett, *News Limited v Australian Rugby Football League and others*, 23 February 1996.

239 Ribot and McCracken: Jerrard McCracken, *A Family Betrayal* (Sydney: Ironbark Pan Macmillan, 1996), pp. 19–21.

240 'I had nothing to do with that': Interview with Ali Cromie, November 1999.

240 Justice Hill's findings: Jennie Curtin, 'Players word preferred over Anderson, Ribot', *Sydney Morning Herald*, 22 December 1995, p. 34; Jennie Curtin, 'Players were 'preyed upon': Four Bulldogs released from contracts', *Sydney Morning Herald*, 22 December 1995, p. 34; AAP, 'Super slipshod, claims judge: Ribot, Anderson charged with 'unconscionable dealing' as contracts declared void', *Australian*, 22 December 1995, p. 18; AAP, 'Super League Canterbury contracts declared void', *Australian Financial Review*, 22 December 1995, p. 4. Justice Burchett, *News Limited v. Australian Rugby Football League and others*, 23 February 1996.

241 'Some of them can't even . . .': Roy Masters and Steve Mascord, 'Super Under-19s to tackle the rest', *Sydney Morning Herald*, 15 March 1996, p. 38.

242 'Entirely wrong . . .': Neil Chenoweth, 'High Wire Act', *Australian Financial Review*, 10 May 1996, Weekend Review, p. 1.

242 'This battle split': Connie Bruck, 'The Big Hitter', p. 87.

242 'Mr Moore had not less than . . .': Justice Burchett, *News Limited v. Australian Rugby Football League and others*, 23 February 1996.

243   'The divine right of supernationals . . .': Kathryn Bice, 'Attack on judge shows News has ethical void: QC', *Australian Financial Review*, 31 May 1996, p. 14.

244   'Perhaps the criticism was too harsh . . .': *News Limited v. Australian Rugby Football League and others*, 96000870, Federal Court of Appeal, Australia, 4 October 1996.

244   'They were hard-bitten executives . . .': Judge Jack B. Weinstein, *Fox News Network LLC v. Time Warner Inc et al*, 96–CV–4963 US District Court for the Eastern District of New York, 1997 US Dist. Lexis 6940, 16 May 1997.

246   'Out of the last negotiations . . .': Michael Freeman, 'TV Sports – Fox readies Super Bid II', *Media Week*, 21 January 1997.

CHAPTER 14

page

248   'Larger than even the expert . . .': Judge William B. Chandler III, *Re The Walt Disney Company Derivative Litigation Consolidated* C.A. No. 15452 Court of Chancery of Delaware, New Castle 731 A.2d 342; 1998 Del. Ch. Lexis 186 7 October 1998, William B. Chandler III, Vice Chancellor.

248   'Not good. A mistake . . .': Mike Bygrave, 'Daggers drawn in the magic kingdom', *Sunday Telegraph Magazine*, London, 18 May 1997, p. 40.

250   'Something has happened to me . . .': Michael Eisner with Tony Schwartz, *Work in Progress* (London: Penguin, 1998), p. 350.

250   'He hates us . . .': Ian Hyland, 'Superstar Wars', *Sunday Mirror*, 19 January 1997, p. 27.

250   'The more we go it alone . . .': Frank Rose, 'There's no business like show business', *Fortune*, 22 June 1998, p. 86.

252   Disney's box office figures: Jennifer Oldham, 'Diminishing returns', *Los Angeles Times*, 23 July 1996, Part D, p. 1.

253      $60 million on writers: Merrill Lynch report on News Corp analysts' briefing, 19 March 1997.

253   'We knew we were going . . .': Marc Gunther, 'The rules according to Rupert', *Fortune*, 26 October 1998, p. 92.

253   'This has nothing to do . . .': John M. Higgins and Stephen McClellan, 'When media moguls collide', *Broadcasting & Cable*, Vol. 127, No. 28, 7 July 1997.

255   Fox $100 million offer for rights: Sallie Hofmeister, 'Fox–ESPN fight over sports rights raising cable rates', *Los Angeles Times*, 29 August 1997, Part D, p. 1.

255   'It's not a personality war . . .': John M. Higgins and Stephen McClellan, 'When media moguls collide', *Broadcasting & Cable*, Vol. 127, No. 28, 7 July 1997.

255   Dolan's $850 million credit line: This included refinancing some existing debt, Dolan paid $168.75 million to ITT on 18 February 1997 to bring his holding to 50 per cent, $500 million on 19 June for a further 38.5 per cent, and options to buy the remaining 11.15 per cent in two years for $150 million.

256   'I kind of look at Fox . . .': Leonard Shapiro, 'Spots giants battle for air-traffic control', *Washington Post*, 15 August 1999.

258   Murdoch–Malone Houdini act: Murdoch was to be issued non-voting stock in Primestar which became ordinary voting stock the moment that he sold it to a company not controlled by him. In June 1998, Murdoch sold *TV Guide* into a company called United Satellite Technology, which also held convertible stock in Primestar. Malone and Murdoch ended up each holding 49 per cent of the voting rights of United Satellite, which was renamed TV Guide Inc. As neither man controlled TV Guide Inc, it appears that it would have been the perfect vehicle for Murdoch and Malone to hold their Primestar stock (now with full voting rights), which eventually would give them close to half of Primestar's voting shares.

258   'It just really says . . .': Justice Department statement of claim, *US v. Primestar Inc and others*, Civil No.: 1:98CV01193 (JLG), District Court, District of Columbia, 12 May 1998.

259   'We generally can't compete . . .': Frank Rose, 'There's no business like show business', *Fortune*, 22 June 1998, p. 86.

259   'Completely personal . . .': Frank Rose, 'There's no business like show business', *Fortune*, 22 June 1998, p. 86.

259   'More intelligently . . .': John M. Higgins and Stephen McClellan, 'When media moguls collide', *Broadcasting & Cable*, Vol. 127, No. 28, 7 July 1997.

261   'It got pretty ugly . . .': John M. Higgins and Stephen McClellan, 'When media moguls collide'.

262   'Eisner is pulling his hair out . . .': Sallie Hofmeister, 'Fox–ESPN fight over sports rights raising cable rates', *Los Angeles Times*, 29 August 1997, Part D, p. 1.

262   'At this point . . .': Sallie Hofmeister, 'Fox-ESPN fight over sports rights raising cable rates', *Los Angeles Times*, 29 August 1997, Part D, p. 1.

262   'We are extremely confident . . .': Comments by Rupert Murdoch at News Corporation annual meeting, 7 April 1997.

266     $2 trillion flow-on: From extensive analysis of stock prices by the author, Neil Chenoweth, 'The mighty have fallen: The future of internet stock', *Australian Financial Review*, 14 August 1999, p.22.

CHAPTER 15

page

272   'I described [the *FT*] story as a joke . . .': Robert Preston, 'Blair's press chief faces Murdoch probe', *Financial Times*, 28 March 1998, p. 4; Select Committee on Public Administration Minutes of Evidence, Examination of witnesses, 23 June 1998.

272   'There is no question . . .': Robert Preston and Liam Halligan, 'Government pressed on newspaper market', *Financial Times*, 25 March 1998; p. 12; George Jones, Robert Shrimsley and Bruce Johnston, '"No special help" for Murdoch', *Daily Telegraph*, 25 March 1998.

272   'Rupert's access to the Prime Minister . . .': Michael White and Ewen Macaskill, 'Murdoch boast amazed staff', *Guardian*, 26 March 1998, p. 11. Philip Webster, 'Blair: No BSkyB favours', *The Times*, 26 March 1998.

273   'It seems that the Prime Minister . . .': *Hansard*, 24 April 1988, Column 1155.

273   Stelzer's background: Llewellyn King, *White Horse Weekly*, 28 September 1998.

273   Report of consultancy arrangement: Matthew Norman, *Guardian*, 16 July 1998, p. 20.

274   Stelzer on EMU: Irwin M. Stelzer, 'Creating the City of the Future', *New York Post*, 6 May 1998.

274   Stelzer and Neil: Andrew Neil, *Full Disclosure* (London: Macmillan, 1996), p. 25.

274   'The godfather': Jason Deparle, 'Are Poor People Just More Stupid Than Rich People', *Sydney Morning Herald*, 29 October 1994, Spectrum, p. 6.

275 'A few kernels . . .', 'so much as a nod . . .': Irwin Stelzer, 'Just an Illusion', *Sunday Times*, 1 September 1996.

276 'I hate the print unions . . .': Andrew Neil, *Full Disclosure*, p. 131. *Guardian* on Stelzer: Matthew Norman, *Guardian*, 16 July 1998, p. 20.

276 'If the British press . . .': Olga Craig, 'How Labour rewards its friends: When business and Number 10 get too close', *Sunday Telegraph*, 29 March 1998, p. 24.

276 'I know Tony Blair . . .': Francis Wheen, *Guardian*, 28 May 1997, p. 28.

277 Blair's Christianity: Irwin M Stelzer, 'Christian Socialism in Britain', *Public Interest*, Summer 1996, No. 124, pp. 3–11.

279 'Don't worry about the *Telegraph*': Daniel Colson, 'The Cost of the Newspaper Price War', *Daily Telegraph*, 11 May 1998.

280 'We would only say . . .': 'Enemies of Success', *The Times*, 10 February 1998.

280 'The BBC was driving them nuts . . .': Ken Auletta, *The Highwaymen* (New York: Random House, 1997), p. 268.

280 'Warning nuke': Andrew Neil, *Full Disclosure*, p. 169.

281 Murdoch and Chinese citizenship: Author's interview with a News executive, June 2000.

281 'Would be a powerful means to provide information . . .': Masahiko Sajima, 'Murdoch eyes Chinese broadcasting market', *Daily Yomiuri*, 31 July 1997, p. 3.

281 'I don't think the Chinese . . .': Masahiko Sasjima, 'Murdoch eyes Chinese broadcasting market', *Daily Yomiuri*, 31 July 1997, p. 3.

283 'Kill the fucking book!': Andrew Neil, 'Murdoch diminished by bowing to China', *Manchester Guardian Weekly*, 8 March 1998, p. 12.

283 'Following your instructions . . .': 'Position paper' by Eddie Bell, quoted in statutory declaration by Stuart Profitt, published in edited form as: 'They have tried to make me a scapegoat but they have chosen the wrong man', *Guardian*, 28 February 1998, p. 2.

284 'The most intelligently written . . .'; 'It is imperative'; 'clearly not a true or sustainable position': Stuart Profitt, 'They have tried to make me a scapegoat but they have chosen the wrong man', *Guardian*, 28 February 1998, p. 2.

285 'From four days after the handover . . .': Barbie Dutter, 'We blundered, says *Times* media editor', *Daily Telegraph*, 2 March

1998, p. 7; 'pretty minor story . . .': 'Murdoch's Chinese walls', *Daily Telegraph*, 3 March 1998; '*The Times* has simply decided . . .', Stothard's response: Philip Johnston, '*Times* man hits at censor Murdoch: "Cut in China coverage to protect business"', *Daily Telegraph*, 4 March 1998, p. 1.

286   'There's an overwhelming case . . .', 'I'm concerned about the concentration . . .': Nigel Morris, 'PM faces revolt over his ties with Murdoch', *Mirror*, London, 3 March 1998, p. 14.

286   'This does not seem to be . . .': George Jones, 'Labour MPs are uneasy over Chris Patten book row', *Daily Telegraph*, 2 March 1998, p. 7.

286   'I did not tell people . . .': Raymond Snoddy, 'Our people screwed up in Patten row, says Murdoch', *The Times*, 4 March 1998.

287   'That these allegations are untrue . . .', 'Mistakes have been made . . .': Raymond Snoddy, 'Patten wins apology from HarperCollins over book', *The Times*, 7 March 1998.

287   'Mr Murdoch's comments . . .': Michael Sissons, 'The Patten saga – chapter and verse', *Guardian*, 7 March 1998, p. 5.

288   'As for newspaper proprietors . . .': Tony Blair, *Hansard*, 1 April 1998, column 1253.

289   'The risk assessment . . .': Australian Tax Office internal memo, May 1996, cited in Neil Chenoweth and Fiona Buffini, 'News Corp tax inquiry goes global', *Australian Financial Review*, 5 February 1998, p. 1.

'One of the most controversial wheeler dealers . . .': Patrick Reilly and JoEllen Goodman, *Crain's New York Business*, 15 December 1986, p. 3.

291   'I can remember a number . . .': Nancy A. Nichols, 'The Man Who Stirs the Pot', *Boston Business Journal*, 25 May 1987, p. 1.

293   USGAAP accounts: Neil Chenoweth, 'The $1 billion gap', *Australian Financial Review*, 5 February 1998, p. 1. The differences in accounting were actually wider than reported, because of a curious twist in which News had written off $180 million more on its NFL contract under US accounting than it had in Australia. This bigger write-off disguised some of the divergence between the profit results under US and Australia accounting in subsequent years.

CHAPTER 16

page

296 'Drifted apart to the point . . .': William Shawcross, 'Murdoch's New Life', *Vanity Fair*, October 1999.

296 'You're a perpetual motion machine . . .': Andrew Neil, *Full Disclosure* (London: Macmillan, 1996).

297 Murdoch's fingerprint:, 'Talk of the Town', *New Yorker, February* 1998.

298 'Promoted the interests of society . . .': 'Pope cites Bob Hope, Murdoch and Disney', *New York Post*, 3 January 1998, p. 13.

298 'It is with some personal sadness . . .': Liz Smith, *New York Post*, 21 April 1998, p. 6.

298 'I don't feel I belong . . .': Neil Chenoweth, 'Three weddings and a magnate', 3 July 1999, p. 26.

299 Lachlan's haircut: Paul Kelly, then the editor-in-chief of the *Australian*, had been with staff at an exotic Sydney restaurant in early 1997 when he saw Lachlan sporting the new haircut. He swore all staff to secrecy.

299 'The board will have to make . . .': Ali Cromie, 'Just who is the chosen one?', *Business Review Weekly*, 26 November 1999, p. 84.

300 'One morning Zeb and Lachlan . . .': Paul Sheahan, 'Inside the new lair', *Sydney Morning Herald*, 19 April 1997, p. 35.

301 'Yes. Getting up each morning . . .': Amanda Lulham, 'Lachland flies the family flag', *Daily Telegraph*, Sydney, 1 January 1998, p. 57.

301 Moose Corporation: Neil Chenoweth, 'Lachlan the heir apparent', *Australian Financial Review*, 10 February 1999, p. 1; Ali Cromie, 'Dr Moose on the loose at News', *Business Review Weekly*, 26 November 1999, p. 86.

302 'He proposed on Christmas Eve': Richard Kelly Heft, additional reporting by Emilya Mychasuk, 'Child's play', *Sydney Morning Herald*, 30 December 1995, p. 3.

303 'Get a hurry on . . .': Richard Kelly Heft, 'Dynasty daughter', *Scotsman*, 28 February 1996, p. 17.

303 Murdoch on Chisholm and Elisabeth: Mathew Horsman, *Sky High* (London: Orion, 1997).

303 Eisner on James Murdoch: Geraldine Brooks, 'The unlikely Murdoch', *GQ*, October 1999, p. 137.

303   'A best friend would stop . . .': Annette Sharpe, 'Diary', *Sun-Herald*, 25 June 2000, p. 24.

'I didn't speak to him . . .': Penelope Debelle, 'First Among Equals', *Sunday Age*, 21 March 1999, Agenda p. 15.

306   'Everybody knew who I was . . .': Philip Delver Broughton, 'Murdoch's children ruled out as he names successor', *Daily Telegraph*, London, 7 July 1999, p. 4.

306   'We are a family that doesn't look back, always ahead': Geraldine Brooks, 'Murdoch', *New York Times*, 19 July 1998, Section 6, p. 20.

307   Murdoch's assets: Response filed by Robert S. Kaufman, 23 July 1998, *Anna Murdoch v. Keith Rupert Murdoch*, California Superior Court, BD2823955.

308   Murdoch at Mercer: Geraldine Fabrikant, 'Go east, not so young man', *New York Times*, 4 October 1998, Section 3, p. 2.

308   'The *Mirror* had a picture . . .': William Shawcross, 'Murdoch's New Life', *Vanity Fair*, October 1999, p. 183.

308   'She was a fun person . . .': David Lague, Mark Riley, Penelope Debelle, 'The mistress and her mogul', *Sydney Morning Herald*, 30 April 1999, p. 11.

308   Wendi Deng's marriage to Jake Cherry: John Lippman, Leslie Chang, Robert Frank, 'Wife wields Influence at News Corp', *Wall Street Journal*, 1 November 2000.

309   'Oh Lupert . . .': Interview with News Corp executive.

309   'Complete nonsense . . .': William Shawcross, 'Murdoch's New Life', *Vanity Fair*, October 1999.

309   Talk in car pool: 'Rupert's Dragon Lady', *Punch*, 27 February – 6 March 1999.

309   Friend of Deng: Alexandra A. Seno, 'People', *Asiaweek*, 23 October 1998 and 25 December 1998.

310   'I met her casually . . .': William Shawcross, 'Murdoch's New Life', *Vanity Fair*, October 1999, p. 135.

310   Pringle's cocktail party: David Lague, Mark Riley, Penelope Debelle, 'The mistress and her mogul', *Sydney Morning Herald*, 30 April 1999, p. 11.

310   'Blow to everyone', 'For a long time . . .': John Gapper, 'A chip off the old block', *Financial Times*, 4 October 1998.

310   'Who knows what goes on . . .': Penelope Debelle, 'The day I screamed at my dad Rupert', *Sun-Herald*, Sydney, 21 March 1999, p. 58.

311   Booth-Edwards lunch: Emily Bell, Denis Campbell, Mark Honigsbaum, 'How Murdoch was caught offside in United takeover', *Sunday Telegraph*, 11 April 1999.

314   'Highly intelligent man . . .': Justice Lindsay, *News International & Others v. Michael Clinger & Others*, CH 1996 N4257 & 5450, No. 104, High Court, London, 17 November 1998.

315   'Now I have the microphone . . .': 'Observer', *Financial Times*, 1 April 1999, p. 27.

315   'A nice old guy . . .': Comment by Rupert Murdoch at press conference after News Corp annual meeting, October 1999.

317   'Like hiring the wolf . . .': Justice Department statement of claim, *US v. Primestar Inc and others*, Civil No.: 1:98CV01193 (JLG), District Court, District of Columbia, 12 May 1998.

318   'Daddy, that's just like . . .': Stephen Keating, *Cutthroat* (Johnson: Boulder, 1999), p. 222.

318   'Rupert had no choice . . .': Brian Hale, 'Echostar snares News's US satellite assets for $A1.8bn', *Sydney Morning Herald*, 2 December 1998, p. 28.

319   News and MCI's 240 million Echostar shares: This figure is after allowing for 8:1 stock splits. The allocation at the time was to be 30 million A shares. Details of the deal from SEC filings.

319   Echostar stock at $4.85: This price is after allowing for stock splits. The actual price was $38.81.

319   Cost of Echostar deal: When Echostar hit $81 in March 2000, its total market value was $38 billion. News and MCI picked up 14.6 per cent of Echostar rather than 37 per cent. The 22.4 per cent difference in March 2000 was worth $8.5 billion in opportunity cost. News Corp wrote off only $375 million in realised losses, much of which it would have recovered when it sold its rising Echostar stock.

CHAPTER 17

page
320   'There's no doubt . . .': Mark Honigsbaum, 'Astrologer adds to fears sweeping media empire as Rupert and Wendy wed', *Observer*, 27 June 1999.

323   'Whenever a major change . . .': 'Media mogul ties the knot with the Internet', *Nation*, 9 July 1999.

324   'Didn't believe in it at all . . .': Willow Bay interview with Rupert Murdoch, *CNN Moneyline News Hour*, 20 September 1999, Transcript No. 99092003V19. Accessed by Lexis.

327   'The combination of News Corp's . . .': Jessica Reif-Cohen, Merrill Lynch research report on News Corporation, 10 April 2000.

329   'I think Bill's going . . .': William Shawcross, 'Murdoch's New Life', *Vanity Fair*, October 1999, p. 183.

330   'We will have the leadership . . .': Cited in Shane Danielson, 'Soccer Wars', *Australian*, 24 June 2000, p. 24.

331   'I don't like waking up . . .': 'Wake up call', *Financial Times*, Observer Column, 7 April 2000.

331   'bizarre decision . . .', 'act of appeasement towards Murdoch . . .': Andy McSmith, 'Secret DTI report to help Murdoch keep grip on Sky', *Daily Telegraph*, 9 April 2000.

332   'Mr Murdoch found . . .': Interview with *Le Monde*, quoted in 'Vivendi knocks on News Corp's door', *Guardian*, 1 February 2000.

332   'It's not impossible . . .': Sheryle Bagwell, 'Vodafone buy tipped to spark merger frenzy', *Australian Financial Review*, 7 February 2000.

332   'I consider Rupert Murdoch . . .': Amy Barrett, Dow Jones Newswires, published as 'The European powerhouse making Murdoch nervous,' *Australian*, 14 April 2000.

334   'It has been a pressure-cooker . . .': Grant Ringshaw, *Sunday Telegraph*, 18 June 2000, p. 7.

POSTSCRIPT

page

339   Lost more than $3 trillion: This was the total fall in value of just 51 high-tech stocks from their 2000 highs. Eleven stocks accounted for $2 trillion of the total. Neil Chenoweth, 'Technology's mortal limitations', *Australian Financial Review*, 20 January 2001, p. 25.

BIBLIOGRAPHY

Auletta, Ken. *The Highwaymen: Warriors of the Information Superhighway.* New York: Random House, 1997

Barry, Paul. *The Rise and Rise of Kerry Packer.* Sydney: Bantam, 1993

Belfield, Richard, Christopher Hird and Sharon Kelly. *Murdoch: The Decline of an Empire.* London: Macdonald, 1991

Bibb, Porter. *Ted Turner: It Ain't As Easy As It Looks.* Boulder: Johnson Books, 1993

Block, Alex Ben. *Outfoxed: Marvin Davis, Barry Diller, Rupert Murdoch, Joan Rivers, and the Inside Story of America's Fourth Television Network.* New York: St Martin's Press, 1990

Bruck, Connie. *Master of the Game: Steve Ross and the Creation of Time Warner.* New York: Penguin, 1994

Bruck, Connie. *The Predators' Ball: The Junk-Bond Raiders and the Man Who Staked Them.* New York: American Lawyer, 1988

Cashmore, Ellis. *Making Sense of Sports.* London: Routledge. 3rd edition 2000

Chippindale, Peter, Suzanne Franks. *Dished! The Rise and Fall of British Satellite Broadcasting.* London: Simon & Schuster, 1991

Chippindale, Peter, and Chris Horrie. *Stick It Up Your Punter.* London: Heinemann, 1990

Coleridge, Nicholas. *Paper Tigers: The Latest, Greatest Newspaper Tycoons and How They Won the World.* London: Mandarin, 1993. 1994 edition

Crainer, *Business the Rupert Murdoch Way: 10 Secrets of the World's Greatest Deal-Maker.* New York: Amacom, 1999

Davis, L. J. *The Billionaire Shell Game: How Cable Baron John Malone and Assorted Corporate Titans Invented a Future Nobody Wanted.* New York: Doubleday, 1998

Eisner, Michael D., with Tony Schwartz. *Work in Progress*. London: Penguin, 1999

Ellul, Jacques. *The Technological Bluff*. Translated by Geoffrey W. Bromiley. Grand Rapids, Michigan: William B. Eerdmans Publishing Company, 1990

Evans, Harold. *Good Times, Bad Times*. London: Coronet Books, 1984

Farquharson, Robin. *Theory of Voting*. New Haven: Yale University Press, 1969

Farquharson, Robin. *Drop Out!* London: Blond, 1968

Frow, John. *What Was Post-Modernism*. Sydney: Local Consumption Publications, 1991

Greenwall, Harry J. *Northcliffe: Napoleon of Fleet Street*. London: Allan Wingate, 1957

Horsman, Mathew. *Sky High*. London: Orion, 1997

Inglis, K. S. *The Stuart Case*. Melbourne: Melbourne University Press, 1961

Jackson, Tim. *Inside Intel*. London: HarperCollins, 1997

Keating, Stephen. *Cutthroat: High Stakes and Killer Moves on the Electronic Frontier*. Boulder: Johnson Books, 1999

Kiernan, Thomas. *Citizen Murdoch*. New York: Dodd Mead & Co. 1986

Kornbluth, Jesse. *Highly Confident: The Crime and Punishment of Michael Milken*. Melbourne: Bookman, 1992 edition

Leapman, Michael. *Barefaced Cheek: The Apotheosis of Rupert Murdoch*. London: Hodder & Stoughton, 1983

Lewis, Michael. *The New New Thing: How Some Man You've Never Heard of Just Changed Your Life*. London: Hodder & Stoughton, 1999

McCracken, Jarrod, with Daniel Lane. *A Family Betrayal*. Sydney: Ironbark Pan Macmillan Australia, 1996

Mair, George. *The Barry Diller Story: The Life and Times of America's Greatest Entertainment Mogul*. New York: John Wiley & Sons, 1997

Marjoribanks, Timothy. *News Corporation, Technology and the Workplace: Global Strategies, Local Change*. Cambridge: Cambridge University Press, 2000

Monks, John. *Elisabeth Murdoch: Two Lives*. Sydney: Macmillan, 1994

Munster, George. *Rupert Murdoch: A Paper Prince*. Melbourne: Penguin, 1987

Murdoch, Patrick. *Sidelights to the Shorter Catechism*. Melbourne: Harcliffe, Waddell and Falconer, 1908

Neil, Andrew. *Full Disclosure*. London: Macmillan, 1996

Ramsay, Douglas K. *The Corporate Warriors: The Battle of the Boardrooms*. London: Grafton, 1987

Regan, Simon. *Rupert Murdoch: A Business Biography*. London: Angus & Robertson, 1976

Shawcross, William. *Rupert Murdoch: Ringmaster of the Information Circus*. London: Pan, 1993. First published 1992, Chatto & Windus Ltd. Also as *Murdoch: The Making of a Media Empire*. New York: Touchstone, 1992, 1997 revision

Stewart, James B. *Den of Thieves*. New York: Simon & Schuster, 1991

Sykes, Trevor. *Operation Dynasty: How Warwick Took John Fairfax Ltd.* Melbourne: Greenhouse, 1989

Thompson, Marilyn W. *Feeding the Beast: How Wedtech Became the Most Corrupt Little Company in America*. New York: Charles Scribner's Son, 1990

Traub, James. *Too Good To Be True: The Outlandish Story of Wedtech*. New York: Doubleday, 1990

Tucille, Jerome. *Murdoch: A Biography*. London: Piatkus, 1990

Wasserstein, Bruce. *Big Deal: The Battle For America's Leading Corporations*. New York: Warner Books, 1998

Wolff, Michael. *Burn Rate: How I Survived the Gold Rush Years on the Internet*. London: Orion, 1998. 1999 edition

Zwar, Desmond. *In Search of Keith Murdoch*. Melbourne: Macmillan, 1980

INDEX